A Stranger to My Time

Essays by and about

Frederick Philip Grove

Edited by Paul Hjartarson

NeWest Press
Edmonton

First edition

Canadian Cataloguing in Publication Data

Grove, Frederick Philip, 1879-1948.
   A stranger to my time

(Western Canadian literary documents; 5)
ISBN 0-920316-71-9 (bound). — ISBN 0-920316-69-7 (pbk.)

1. Grove, Frederick Philip, 1879-1948 — Criticism and interpretation. I. Hjartarson, Paul Ivar. II. Title. III. Series.
PS8513.R83A6 1987   C814'.54   C87-091021-3
PR9199.3.G76A6 1987

Credits

Cover design: Susan Colberg
Typesetting: June Charter
Book production: Katheryn Charchuk
Printing and binding: Hignell Printing Limited, Manitoba
Financial Assistance: Alberta Culture, The Alberta Foundation for the Literary Arts, and The Canada Council

NeWest Publishers Limited
Suite 204, 8631 - 109 Street
Edmonton, Alberta
Canada   T6G 1E8

for Becky, Aune and Kaley

and for
the Baroness

Contents

IV   The Figure of Posterity

Acknowledgements

NeWest Press gratefully acknowledges permission from **A Leonard Grove** to translate and publish 'Flauberts Theorien über das Künstlertum' and to publish 'Rebels All: Of the Interpretation of Individual Life'; from the **Department of Archives and Special Collections, University of Manitoba** to publish 'Of Nishivara, the Saint,' *Thoughts and Reflections*, and photographs from the Grove Collection; from A. Leonard Grove and **The Canadian Forum** to reprint 'Apologia Pro Vita et Opere Suo'; from A. Leonard Grove and **The Dalhousie Review** to reprint 'The Flat Prairie'; from A. Leonard Grove and **Maclean's** to reprint 'Assimilation' and 'Canadians Old and New'; from A. Leonard Grove and **The University of Toronto Press** to reprint 'The Plight of Canadian Fiction? A Reply' and 'A Writer's Classification of Writers and Their Works'; and from A. Leonard Grove and **Queen's Quarterly** to reprint 'Postscript to *A Search for America.*'

Grateful acknowledgement is also made to the following for permission to reprint their work: **E.D. Blodgett** for 'Ersatz Feminism in F.P. Grove's German Novels' (retitled, from *Configuration: Essays on the Canadian Literatures*); **CAUTG** for Walter Pache, 'Frederick Philip Grove: Comparative Perspectives' (retitled, from *Annals/Annalens 4: German-Canadian Studies in the 1980s*); **The Dalhousie Review** and **Margaret R. Stobie** for 'Grove and the Ants'; **The Journal of Canadian Studies** for Kenneth C. Dewar, 'Technology and the Pastoral Ideal in Frederick Philip Grove's Writing'; **The Literary Half-Yearly** for W.J. Keith, 'Grove's *Over Prairie Trails:* A Re-Examination'; **The University of Toronto Press** for Camille La Bossiere, 'Of Words and Understanding in Grove's *Settlers of the Marsh* and Henry Makow, 'Letters from Eden: Grove's Creative Rebirth'; **MOSAIC: A Journal for the Comparative Study of Literature and Ideas** for R.D. MacDonald, 'The Power of F.P. Grove's *The Master of the Mill*'; **Studies in Canadian Literature** for J.J. Healy, 'Grove and the Matter of Germany: The Warkentin Letters and the Art of Liminal Disengagement'; and **Twayne Publishers**, a division of G.K. Hall & Co., Boston, for Margaret R. Stobie, 'An Innocent Abroad: Grove's *A Search for America*' (retitled, from *Frederick Philip Grove*).

Preface

> From a humanist's point of view it is less damaging to be determined
> not to misunderstand than it is to be determined to understand; and a
> person does well to take care of his ignorance because it is the matrix
> of his knowing.
>
> —*George Whalley*[1]

Fifteen years ago, in a brief notice published in *Queen's Quarterly*,
Douglas Spettigue announced his discovery that prior to 1909
Frederick Philip Grove was the German translator and author, Felix
Paul Greve.[2] With that announcement, Grove became this country's
most talked about but least understood author—least understood
because Spettigue's biographical discovery was, paradoxically, that
we did not in fact know the man who called himself 'Grove.'
Although Spettigue titled his announcement 'The Grove Enigma
Resolved,' the effect of that article, and of his subsequent book, *FPG:
The European Years* (1973), was not to make the unknown known,
the unfamiliar familiar; on the contrary, the effect of 'The Grove
Enigma Resolved' was to make the familiar, the Grove we had come
to know, *unfamiliar*, the known, *unknown*. Spettigue's announcement was, in short, an act of estrangement. It removed Grove from the
context in which we had begun to understand him; it called into
question his place in the narrative of this country's literature and
made him, once again, a stranger to us.

'He was a stranger,' Ronald Sutherland quipped at the University
of Ottawa's Grove Symposium in 1973, 'and he took us in.' The
purpose of this volume is to reintroduce that stranger to us. It does
not pretend to make the unknown known—there is still much we do
not know about the man who called himself Grove. It does, however,
attempt to make the unknown a little better known, to put us on a
more familiar footing with the writer and his texts. It does this in a
number of ways.

First, in the essay 'Of Greve, Grove, and Other Strangers: The
Autobiography of the Baroness Elsa von Freytag-Loringhoven,' it
examines a startling new discovery—that Elsa Greve was a party to
her husband's 'suicide,' that she followed him to the United States,
that Greve abandoned her in Kentucky, and that she made her way to
New York where she subsequently became a literary figure in her
own right, publishing poetry in such magazines as *The Little
Review*, *The Transatlantic Review*, *transition*, and *Broom*. This
remarkable information is contained in an unpublished and untitled

autobiography which Elsa Greve, who in 1913 became the Baroness
Elsa von Freytag-Loringhoven, wrote in the last years of her life. She
addressed that autobiography to her good friend Djuna Barnes, the
author of *Nightwood,* among whose literary papers it was recently
discovered. That autobiography gives us an intimate look at the
enigmatic 'FPG.'

Second, this volume makes the stranger better known by letting
him speak for himself. Over half of *A Stranger to My Time* is devoted
to essays by Grove. Some of the essays, including 'Rebels All: Of the
Interpretation of Individual Life' and 'Nishivara, the Saint,' have
never previously appeared in print; others, such as 'Canadians Old
and New' and 'Assimilation' are not readily accessible to Grove's
readers; and one, 'Flauberts Theorien über das Künstlertum' has
been translated from the German specially for this volume. Since
Grove's best known and most frequently quoted essays are those
gathered in *It Needs to be Said,* and since that collection was
reprinted by Tecumseh Press in 1982, I have felt free to choose for *A
Stranger to My Time* lesser known but no less important essays,
including 'Apologia Pro Vita et Opere Suo,' 'Assimilation,'
'Canadians Old and New,' 'The Flat Prairie,' 'The Plight of
Canadian Fiction? A Reply,' 'A Writer's Classification of Writers and
Their Works,' and the fascinating 'Postscript to *A Search for
America.*' The essays represent every period in Grove's career, from
his earliest pronouncements as an aspiring writer and translator in
Germany to his final statements in the closing decade of his life. Also
published for the first time is *Thoughts and Reflections,* a diary
Grove kept from 1933 to 1940, the years during which he wrote many
of his most important books, including *Fruits of the Earth*—begun
years earlier in Manitoba—*Consider Her Ways, Two Generations,
The Master of the Mill,* and *In Search of Myself.*

Finally, this volume makes the stranger better known by collecting
essays on Grove by his most perceptive critics. The volume is divided
into four parts. The first, titled **The Figure of the Other,** focuses on
Grove's German writing and features essays by the German scholar,
Walter Pache, by E.D. Blodgett, and by D.O. Spettigue. Spettigue's
'Fanny and the Master,' on Grove's first novel, *Fanny Essler,* was
commissioned specially for this volume. Part II, **The Figure of the
Immigrant,** focuses on Grove's best known works, those he wrote in
Manitoba during his first two decades in this country. In addition to
the five essays *by* Grove, Part II includes the intriguing Eden letters,
edited by Henry Makow—intriguing, in part, because in one of them
Grove reveals that he began *Settlers of the Marsh* in German—and
important essays by J.J. Healy, Camille R. La Bossière, and Margaret

Stobie. Part III, **The Figure of Estrangement**, focuses on the texts Grove wrote after he moved from Manitoba to Ontario in 1929; it collects, in addition to four essays by Grove himself, articles by Kenneth C. Dewar, R.D. MacDonald and Margaret Stobie. Part IV, **The Figure of Posterity** features Grove's diary, *Thoughts and Reflections.*

In *Clearing the Ground: English-Canadian Literature After Survival* (1984), Paul Stuewe argues that Canadian literature has suffered greatly from a critical preoccupation with themes and cites Grove as one writer whose significance has been greatly exaggerated by thematic criticism.[3] As the title of Stuewe's book suggests, he wants to 'clear the ground.' There can be no denying that Grove's writing has sometimes been praised uncritically; however, the fault for that, as Stuewe's own study suggests, lies not with the writer but with his critics. Rejecting theme-hunting, Stuewe calls for clear-sighted, rigourous criticism. His assumption seems to be that Grove, for one, has not been subject to such clear-eyed scrutiny. I very much doubt, however, that critics of this country's literature have read a more uncompromising and rigourously evaluative study of a Canadian writer in recent years than Margaret R. Stobie's *Frederick Philip Grove* (1973). And while in her study Stobie finds much to criticize, she is not prepared, as Stuewe apparently is, to dismiss Grove's writing out of hand. She recognizes the historical significance of Grove's work—'Grove commands attention,' she affirms, 'as a literary phenomenon of the twenties'—but what she celebrates in his best work is the *quality* of the writing.[4] (See, for example, her essay 'An Innocent Abroad: Grove's *Search for America* in Part II of this volume.)

Most of us, I suspect, find ourselves closer to Stobie's position than to Stuewe's; that is, while we may feel that this or that Grove novel has been overvalued, we are not prepared to dismiss his work altogether. I undertook the editing of *A Stranger to My Time* because I believe that current critical views of Grove's writing are based on a very limited number of texts and on a very narrow conception of the novelist as a 'prairie' realist or naturalist. My hope is that in coming to know more of Grove's writing we can arrive at a more accurate conception of the novelist and a more balanced view of his work.

In the closing pages of his study, in a chapter significantly titled 'Rediscovering Our Literary History,' Stuewe cites approvingly Desmond Pacey's call for 'hard scholarship.' Although Stuewe himself echoes that call, he does not in his own study of Canadian criticism cite a single critical text prior to Northrop Frye's *Anatomy of Criticism* (1957); most date from the last decade and many of the texts he cites are occasional magazine articles. 'Clearing the ground,' like razing historical buildings, is relatively easy. What we need are readers willing to do the time-consuming, painstaking work needed to locate, preserve, and restore. Such work invariably finds the best of us wanting. To undertake it is to return to earlier scholarship with a renewed sense of wonder.

The critical essays collected in *A Stranger to My Time* approach Grove's writing from different points of view and with very different interests; but each critic is engaged, I believe, in the task of locating, preserving and restoring. Such work is always a community effort. I should like to thank the contributors for their cooperation in the preparation of this volume. *A Stranger to My Time* would not have been possible, however, without the encouragement and support of A. Leonard Grove, who not only granted NeWest Press permission to print his father's essays but who very kindly responded to my many queries. To him, our many thanks. I should also like to thank Shirley Neuman, the general editor of the Western Canadian Literary Documents Series, for her advice and support; D.O. Spettigue, for his continued kindness and for his many insights; E.D. Blodgett and Axel Knoenagel for their assistance in the translation of 'Flauberts Theorien über das Künstlertum'; Richard E. Bennett and his staff in the Department of Archives and Special Collections at the University of Manitoba's Elizabeth Dafoe Library for assisting me in my study of the Grove Collection; Joene MacArthur, my research assistant, for her tireless and diligent work; and the staff at NeWest Press for their support and their patience. I should also like to acknowledge a research award from the University of Alberta's Central Research Fund for the translation of the Greve article, and a Research Travel Award from the Canadian Plains Research Centre in support of my editorial work.

Edmonton, Alberta

---

¹' "Research" and the Humanities,' *Studies in Literature and the Humanities: Innocent of Intent*, ed. and introd. Brian Crick and John Ferns (Kingston and Montreal: McGill-Queen's Univ. Press, 1985), 109.

²'The Grove Enigma Resolved,' *Queen's Quarterly*, 79 (1972), 1-2.

³'The Case of Frederick Philip Grove,' *Clearing the Ground: English-Canadian Literature After **Survival*** (Toronto: Proper Tales Press, 1984), 37-41.

⁴*Frederick Philip Grove* (New York: Twayne, 1973), 17.

I
The Figure of the Other

Published in the Rheinisch-Westfälische Zeitung, No. 1065 (1904), 'Flauberts Theorien über das Künstlertum,' which appears here under the title 'Flaubert's Theories of Artistic Existence,' developed out of Frederick Philip Grove's work as a translator of Gustave Flaubert's letters. Grove translated three volumes of Flaubert's letters: Briefe über seine Werke [1907]—the preface is dated September 1904—Reiseblätter (Briefe aus dem Orient, über Feld und Strand) [1907?]—the preface is dated October 1905—and Brief an Zeit-und Zunftgenossen [1907]. The three volumes of letters, and Grove's translation of La Tentation de Saint Antoine, published as Die Versuchung des heiligen Antonius [1907], were reprinted as part of the collected works, Gustave Flauberts Gesammelte Werke [1906-07], edited by E.W. Fischer and published by J.C.C. Bruns.

Frederick Philip Grove

Flaubert's Theories of Artistic Existence
Translated by Ann Henderson-Nichol

We are emerging from an era in which it was believed that the best and only way to understand the works of an artist was to research his life. An artist's life was considered a commentary on his works. The result of this belief is the modern concept of 'artistic existence.' Today, those who say we are living at a time when art is ridiculously overrated are met by fierce opposition. Undoubtedly it would be truer to say that we are living at a time when the artist is ridiculously overrated. This overvaluation derives from a totally inexplicable ignorance about the nature of the artist—and likewise, of art. A clear perception of oneself is nowadays the rarest thing in the world; personal integrity the second rarest. Both attributes are to be found to an amazing degree in one of the best artists of the century which has just passed: Gustave Flaubert.

The artist has been called a symptom of the diseased in mankind. From the standpoint of science there is no such thing as disease, for entailed in the word 'disease' is judgement and science never judges, it dissects. From this point of view, it is hostile to life, for all life involves judgement and selection. Only applied science judges; it wants change; the physician in particular wants change. And today, when the psychologist vivisects the artist, he also wants change, but his goal justifies himself in his own eyes: to dethrone gods who are not gods at all.

The present investigation wishes to provide documentary evidence in support of the statement that there is no bridge between life and creativity. Whoever experiences the artist's calling has a choice: he must renounce life if he wants to create, otherwise he can never be more than half-successful. Whoever experiences as an artist a longing for life is inconsistent and contemptible. And every artist who wishes to engage life has to pay the penalty: in most cases, he is utterly crushed. If people today require an artist to be a guide for their lives, they are demanding beans from a rose-tree. 'Philosophies of life' are not the produce of art; they are the fruit of life. An artist can depict them but never create them. The 'philosophies of life' of an artist as a human being, whose milieu is necessarily limited, are always narrow and to the man of practical experience, usually laughable. The 'opinions' of an artist are irrelevant.

But let us listen to our artist himself. Of all who have talked about themselves, he is the most consistent, although even he made mistakes. He had a clear picture of himself and was possessed of the most daring honesty, and it is on account of this that the psychologist can attempt to use him as a mouthpiece. One thing immediately distinguishes Flaubert from the mass of modern artists: his works are documents neither of his life nor of his human psyche. Whoever writes the history of his literary output will write the history of his work, not a biography. None of Flaubert's views can be derived from his works; none of his theories can be inferred from them. 'Art is not there,' he once wrote to George Sand, 'to paint only the exceptions; and besides, I have an indomitable aversion to putting down on paper something that is in my heart. Furthermore, I do not think a novelist has the right to express his opinion about anything. Did Almighty God ever express His opinion?' There is, however, a source for Flaubert's views on being an artist, a source which is easier to use because in it he speaks to us directly, namely, his letters, which we shall soon possess in a German edition.*

At the age of twenty-nine, when he is in the Orient, surrounded by everything which can stimulate consciousness, he writes for the first time and expresses his viewpoint clearly: 'As far as life is concerned, there is only one position for the artist, that of spectator.' Basically, this statement expresses everything: the artist may never become involved with life. It is an error without parallel to think that the artist, more than anyone else, is there to relish life. The opposite is

---

*E. Brun Publishing Company. The same publishing house is publishing Gustave Flaubert's *Die Schule der Empfindsamkeit*.

true. Whoever starts taking pleasure in things ceases to be an artist. More than four years earlier Flaubert had already personally said the same thing about himself, at that time still with a note of regret, of mild lament; for he was just in the midst of young love and did not yet have the courage to sever himself from the rest of the world (Letters, August 9, 1846): 'I was not made to taste of pleasure.' And at the age of fifty-five, when he had long known the truth about himself, he confesses that dark sentiment to George Sand in the following words: 'I was a coward in my youth: I was afraid of life.' That means, I felt myself called to become an artist and was afraid that as an artist I would be destroyed by life.

What does it mean, this demand that the artist renounce life? The twenty-nine-year-old Flaubert answers: 'You depict wine, women and fame, on the condition, my dear chap, that you are neither a drinker, nor a lover, nor a husband, nor an infantryman. Caught up in life, one's view becomes distorted, one suffers from it or one derives too much pleasure from it.' A typical artist who knew this truth in theory and forgot it in practice, thereby bringing about his destruction, was Oscar Wilde, who expressed the same thought in the following manner: 'All bad art comes from true emotion.' Whoever construes this as a frivolous paradox is mistaken. About a year after the statement which I have just quoted, Flaubert says (Letter to Mme. X—): 'The less one feels something, the more one is in a position to express it as it really is. . . .' Every feeling is suffering, it costs strength, it costs the strength with the aid of which one could have given that feeling expression. The artist is the man who is eternally sterile as far as life is concerned. Carefully protecting all his powers of sensitivity from any exposure, that is his secret. If he has exposed any, he has thereby gained in experience, he knows the symptoms and can depict the external details of this exposure, that is to say, this is something which teaches him to observe; but the inner spirit is missing, the glow is missing. 'The artist,' says Flaubert in a letter dated December 15, 1850, 'is in my opinion a monstrosity, something which exists outside of Nature; all the misfortune which Nature heaps upon him derives from the obstinacy with which he denies this axiom; he suffers from it and makes others suffer.' Think of artists' marriages. The woman who is not artistically or sexually corrupted (artistically or androgynously inclined) but marries an artist even so, demonstrates confusion of the instincts. 'Ask those women about it,' Flaubert continues in that same letter, 'who have loved poets and the men who have loved actresses.' Mrs. Carlyle once responded to such a question in this way (see Lady Blemerhaffer's excellent character study): 'Do anything you want to in life,' she says, 'but don't marry a genius.' And the other side, the artist's admonition to the artist who is his pupil: 'You associate with women too much,' Flaubert writes to the young Guy de Maupassant (July 15, 1878), 'you row too much, you take too much exercise.' And in the same letter, 'For an artist there is only one thing: to sacrifice everything to art. He may view life only as a means and the first person on whom he sh. . . is himself.'

But the artist is a craftsman, nothing more. His craft is creating form, the clay which he shapes is life, in all its manifestations: in colour and shape, in thought and passion. What differentiates him from every other craftsman is solely his material, never the nature of his work, at most the degree of its difficulty. And it is precisely on account of this that the true artist is indifferent as a man. 'I would certainly welcome the chance,' Flaubert writes to George Sand (December 1, 1875), 'to say what I think and so through words bring relief to Mr. Gustave Flaubert. But what is the significance of the said gentleman?' 'Every Mr. X,' he says in another place, 'is more interesting than Mr. Gustave Flaubert. Mr. X is more universal.' And in that same letter, 'The man is nothing, the work of art is everything.' One can see that here an honest artist is saying the opposite of current general opinion and yet one needs to have lived among great artists for only a short time to be convinced of their human insignificance. One has in Flaubert, the consistent artist, the remarkable spectacle of a lifelong struggle with his medium of expression, language. A craftsman without peer, he files and files away at a single sentence often for days on end. I call language his medium of expression—his marble is life, language his chisel and he is consumed by this struggle. All his inner struggles are struggles with language. All his despondency and pain derive from his feeling of impotence to wield the word so that it creates the form that hovers in his mind, that is to say, to conjure up in the reader the desired, imagined impression. He reserves his greatest joy for a successful sentence. The loss of the woman whom he has loved for a week and who has loved him does not elicit from him one word and does not cost him as much pain as an unsuccessful page. 'I have always lived from day to day,' he writes at the age of fifty-four, 'without plans for the future and in pursuit of my goal (only one, literature), without looking right or left. Everything which surrounded me has disappeared and I now see myself in the desert.' —The artist is a craftsman. He is no more dependent on something outside himself than anyone else is. His material does not come to him in any particular way or for any particular reason. 'I believe,' Flaubert writes at the end of 1853, 'that one can make art out of anything, anywhere.' Work, work, that is the eternal refrain of all his advice. During sleepless nights don't wait for something to come to you. You go out to whatever it is you are searching for and then it will come to you. 'One must mistrust everything (letter of December 14, 1846) which looks like inspiration and is often only a desire and an artificial excitement which one stirs up arbitrarily, which did not come of its own accord. By the way, one does not live by inspiration; Pegasus walks far more often than he gallops. Keep in mind that with patience and enduring energy one succeeds in making beautiful things; moderate your impetuous spirit, which has already caused you so much suffering; fever drains the mind; anger has no fire, it is a Colossus, whose knees tremble and who harms himself more than others.' Never work when you are in a mood. 'I turn phrases the way a worker turns napkin rings.' So to repeat it once more, the work of an artist is a craft and nothing but a craft. The tool of the language artist is language. But language exists in its own right, it is something which has its own laws, in exactly the same way that marble cracks according to its own laws and the woodcarver's wood splits according to its laws. Often, when the language artist wrestles with language, it is the language which guides him, rather than he who guides the language. What superficial artists understand as inspiration is rarely anything other than this guidance by language. This was known to the ancients, who taught language technique. Every art which links up with the ancients, is linked at this very point if it does not want to become pseudo-classical [*Klassizismus*]. What Flaubert is teaching here is basically something quite obvious, and yet we in Germany remain without techniques of prose and verse. Seen from this angle, the German language remains unexplored territory. But the one thing that distinguishes the artist from every other craftsman—and it does not matter whether his medium is language, colour or form—is the kind of material with which he works. His material is life. And more so with the artist of language than with any other. The artificial in art is the form. Doubtless there are artists who are nothing but artists of form. This form can be learned. Therefore, everything about art which is art can be learned. But to give to a work of art its own life-force, a life which continues to exist when the life-forms among which it was conceived have long since disappeared, now that is something different, that requires something other than just this craftsmanlike labour. The artist nourishes his work of art with all the strength of his own life. Art is the receptacle, the drain into which all his powers flow. Let us not misunderstand this. An artist who wants to live what he creates is no artist. That explains why such an ardent priest of beauty like Flaubert could bear to live in an environment which was by no means beautiful, in rooms which mock every kind of taste. An artist, who is an artist with all the strength of his passion, has no strength left for life. If blood is to circulate in the work of art, it has to be the artist's blood, but it is precisely for this reason that the work may not be written with a "bleeding heart." The artist is not allowed to pour his own passion into his work of art, but he must fill it with the strength of his passion. 'I have always been at pains,' writes Flaubert, 'never to degrade art to satisfy an individual. —I have written very tender pages without love and ardent pages without fire in my blood.' The thing that lends stupendous vitality to Flaubert's works is actually suppressed passion, the reserved strength of passions ('des passions rentrées'). No 'great free life'—this is the very thing that is the doom of the artist, it costs too much. The life which is the most hidden, the simplest, the most sober, the most ascetic, is always the best. 'Yes, I maintain,' writes Flaubert, 'one must divide one's existence: live as a citizen and think as a demi-god. . . . Let us keep in reserve the life-force of our hearts, in order to expend it in tirades; likewise the secret juice of the passions, in order to put it into bottles. Let us save the last remains of our whole self to nourish posterity. Who knows what gets lost every day as feelings disintegrate?' And all his contempt is aimed at those who allow their daily passions and feelings to flow over into art instead of nourishing their characters with that squandered energy. That amounts to the same thing as an artist wanting to live! 'Bad art,' he shouts, 'bad art!' And in another place, 'I'd rather be flayed alive than exploit something like that in style. I am not willing to view art as a drain for passion, as a barely cleaned chamber-pot, or chit-chat, or an intimate message. No! No! Poetry is not permitted to be bubbles of the heart, that is neither serious nor good!' 'The sentimental personality will cause a good part of contemporary literature to be called, in the future, childish and rather foolish. What sentiment, what sentiment, what tenderness, what tears!' Sentences need blood in them, not water! and blood means heart—heart, the power of undisclosed passion! 'If Lafontaine,' he says, 'had expended his strength of love in the portrayal of his personal sentiments, would there have been enough left for him to depict the friendship of two birds?' And the closing exclamation in this letter states decisively: 'Let us be on our guard against giving out our gold in small change!'

With that we come to our point of departure. The artist is a guardian of life; art is the greatest record of history. That is precisely why I personally consider 'historical' literature hybrid. Great art which captures present-day life is already historical for that very reason. The artist collects the life of his times and bottles it up, to borrow an image from Flaubert. But he himself may not drink from these bottles. He is either an ascetic or only half an artist—inevitably. But nothing is proved by words alone. I should like to mention two more points, in order to prove the case, one small matter and one of greater significance in Flaubert's life.

First the small detail. At the time of his most intimate friendship with George Sand, she asked him time after time to visit her in Nohant. Time after time he declined the invitation. He would have loved to have gone. He is almost fifty years old and his loneliness is weighing heavily upon him. But he is consistent. His novel *L'Éducation sentimentale* is of greater consequence to him than any private gratification. 'You have no idea,' he writes to his friend, 'how much pain you are causing me! Despite my desire, I am answering "No." And yet the desire to answer "Yes" is tearing me apart. This just creates the picture of a gentleman who does not allow himself to be disturbed, and that's quite ridiculous. But I know myself: if I came to you, to Nohant, I would dream about my journey for a month afterwards. Real images would supplant in my brain those images which were so painstakingly devised. My whole house of cards would collapse.'

And then the other case: it concerns his relationship with Mme. X—. Scarcely has he allowed himself to be caught unawares by his blazing love (to the extent that there is a momentary union), then he flees. For four years there are infrequent meetings, complaints on the one side, rejections and justifications on the other. He knows, he feels: I may not yield, otherwise farewell literature, farewell art! His journey to the Orient intervenes, an absence of a year and a half: during that time he comes to a clear understanding of himself. Soon after his return he responds to renewed accusation with final trenchancy: 'Yes, I wish that you didn't love me and that you had never got to know me, and having said that I think that I am expressing regrets which have a bearing on your happiness. How I wished that my mother didn't love me, how I wished I didn't love her or anyone else in the world: I didn't want anything to pass from my heart to the hearts of others, or from their hearts to mine!' And when, four years later, the relationship reaches a crisis, when everything becomes public, when Mme. X's position is utterly compromised, when there would be only one course left to every other man, to every man, namely, to marry her, Flaubert remains consistent; he says not a word, he takes not a step, he drops his lover. What would have been dishonourable behaviour in any other man is in the artist the most admirable penance for a great mistake, the great mistake of his life: for having once, in love, ventured into the world of reality.

But be on your guard against one thing: against pity. The artist is no martyr! Flaubert never needed to work for his bread. He could have lived, if he had not preferred the renunciation of life and artistic creativity in an ascetic existence. A compromise would have been contemptible. The artist does not win himself any honour through his renunciation and his ascetic life. He does what he has to do. He is a tiny coral creature, which is forced by nature to construct its coral-tree. The artist is as unable to live in life as is the coral creature unable to live on land.

Walter Pache

Frederick Philip Grove: Comparative Perspectives

Grove's isolation

Frederick Philip Grove's isolation is one of the greatest obstacles confronting any critical attempt to assess him as a writer and as a man. It is also a theme that recurs in his work. In his diary Grove notes in February 1935 (while finishing *The Master of the Mill*): 'I have, of late, read a great deal of antarctic exploration, and for some time I have felt pretty much as Scott—whom I dislike—must have felt in 1911/12 when he pulled south to reach the pole. It's a race against everything—the weather, the surface, the food supply, the oil, etc.'[1] Grove later changed his mind about Scott, but insisted on his view of the writer as antarctic explorer, who turns his back on the familiar social and cultural context and sets out alone into unknown territory. Grove camouflaged his origin, severed all ties with his native Germany and, to a certain extent, the literary scene that shaped him. Even as a writer in Canada, Grove remains a lonely figure— surrounded by an isolation partly forced upon him by ignorant or envious contemporaries, partly self-imposed, it would seem, in an arrogant refusal to accept reality.

Grove's isolation has of course not gone unchallenged. Even during his own lifetime, there were various attempts to penetrate his intriguing isolation—not just by finding out who he was, but by fitting the author and his work into available and convenient critical categories. Primarily, Grove has been claimed as one of the father figures of realism in Canada, or, more specifically, as one of the chief exponents of what is sometimes called the 'Canadian experience.' 'A *Canadian writer*,' Malcolm Ross called him in 1957, 'wholly absorbed by the Canadian scene and by the pioneer drama of a diverse yet single people.'[2] On the strength of his decision to emigrate to Canada, to live there, to adopt a new language and to give voice to the new country, Grove qualified as a 'modern classic.'

Undoubtedly, this emblematic view of Grove as the archetypal *New Canadian* has been modified of late, chiefly in the wake of Douglas O. Spettigue's investigations, establishing with reasonable certainty the identity of Frederick Philip Grove and the German writer Felix Paul Greve. Grove's biography had to be revised as a first step towards a more adequate appreciation of the subtle interplay of truth and fiction in the autobiographical writings, and of the roots of Grove's descriptive realism. However, readers and critics alike—unless they frankly confess to utter boredom—continue to think of Grove as quintessentially Canadian, shaped by the country and dedicated to its tradition. (It might be mentioned in passing that the recent revival of interest in Grove has not extended to Germany. Greve remains in eclipse, a nondescript *'Verschollener der frühen Insel.'*)[3]

Grove's image today is largely the result of certain prevailing tendencies in Canadian criticism—an image projected by a new national literature in search of a literary tradition. Such an approach may yield persuasive results but frequently at the expense of simplifying the complexities of a writer whose works are international in more ways than one, and do not readily fit into national patterns.

Frederick Philip Grove's case thus calls for a comparative approach, posing methodological problems that I must briefly mention. The usual conception of comparative literature either as a comparison of national literatures mirroring national individualities or as a canon of authoritative masterworks is based on the system of national literatures in nineteenth-century Europe. It cannot be applied without modifications to a changed situation where these formerly clear-cut distinctions have become blurred, due to the emergence of 'new' literatures claiming 'national' status but no longer meeting the established definition.

During the formative phase of a nation, literature is frequently assigned the task of expressing or even anticipating a collective national consciousness. In such a situation, critics are quite often dissatisfied with traditional formalistic standards. Instead, they tend to interpret literature in terms of archetypal patterns of collective behaviour and experience. A comparative criticism based on such patterns tends to undercut verifiable literary relations and to derive its conclusions from contrastive—and reductive—formulae which aim at giving literature a recognizable profile: frontier vs. garrison, aggressive individualism vs. passive survival, the Western vs. the 'Northern'[4] are examples of contrastive terms used for the American/Canadian relationship.

Another difficulty for comparative literature arises from what has been called the 'internationalization' of English language and literature.[5] (The term is George Steiner's.) In Canada, this means conflicting values, an intricate pattern of dependence on and emancipation from European (i.e. largely British) models, and an increased mobility of writers and literary movements—requiring comparative methods *within* one language of communication and one literary context.

It is with these difficulties in mind that I have singled out three areas where Grove's position between established linguistic, literary and, perhaps, ethnic contexts seems to manifest itself.

Grove and the fin de siècle

Grove's *fin de siècle* background had a lasting influence on his 'Canadian' period. Far from marking a complete break with his earlier aestheticism, Grove's 'escape' to Canada introduces a new phase that in a modified form and under different conditions is essential to an understanding of his Canadian writing.

Whatever his personal involvement with his own generation of writers, Greve knew their work: Aubrey Beardsley and André Gide, Algernon Swinburne and Gabriele d'Annunzio, Edward Burne-Jones and Stefan George are referred to, amongst others, in his essay on Oscar Wilde, published in 1903—one of several publications on Wilde. If we also consider Greve's translations of Wilde's plays, he might be called one of the leading exponents of the critical reception of Wilde in Germany between the mid-nineties (*Salomé* was written in 1893/94, and translated in 1903) and the year 1905 when Strauss' opera celebrated a *succès de scandale* in Dresden.

It was not only as dandy and connoisseur that Wilde must have impressed young Greve. The fact that he translated Wilde's poetic dialogue *Intentions* (1891; *Fingerzeige*, 1903) testifies to Greve's affinity for the concept of the dilettante and his view that life has to follow art. If Wilde's influence was strong it was also ambiguous, and Greve's reaction clearly wavered between identification and critical distance. In *Oscar Wilde* (1903), Greve emphasizes Wilde's split personality proclaiming the victory of art over real life and its moral code, but being himself unable to put it into practice. We may debate the wisdom of Greve's judgement as far as Wilde is concerned, but it is very revealing for the young writer himself (Greve was only twenty-four when he wrote the essay) who repeatedly stresses the importance of life—*Leben*—as the universal yardstick against which success and failure are to be measured. An active life, somewhat surprisingly, emerges as the supreme form of self-realization; a purely aesthetic attitude is condemned as dangerously deceptive and conflict-bound.

Greve's comments on Wilde—in his characteristically con-
descending and magisterial tone—may seem incongruous at first
sight, but they elucidate a dilemma fundamental to an understanding not only of Greve's subsequent career but also of his generation:
the dilemma of the refined aesthete hopelessly infatuated with the
crudity of real life. This concept of *Leben* as a way of overcoming the
anaemic decadence of the dilettante has found its most prominent
expression in Thomas Mann's *Tonio Kröger* (1903). Here Tonio—
poet and *verirrter Bürger*—talks to Lisaweta about his desire to share
a normal, bourgeois life. No one is a true artist, he argues, 'der die
Sehnsucht nicht kennt nach dem Harmlosen, Einfachen und
Lebendigen, nach ein wenig Freundschaft, Hingebung,
Vertraulichkeit und menschlichem Glück . . . nach den Wonnen der
Gewöhnlichkeit.'[6] I do not wish to suggest that Felix Paul Greve was
another Tonio Kröger. But the underlying pattern, the dialectic of
aesthetic refinement and practical life, is common to both. While
Thomas Mann's protagonist remains undecided, Greve decides to
confront life—first by adopting the themes and narrative strategies of
literary naturalism (*Fanny Essler*, 1905; *Maurermeister Ihles Haus*,
1906), and later by beginning a new life in North America, where
practical skills were indeed called for.

Grove stages his return to life as an escape from life—a paradoxical
aspect reminding us that his realism and his theory of realism must
not be misunderstood as naive and straightforward. On the contrary,
Grove's Canadian *oeuvre* has its roots in *fin de siècle* European
literature. Its 'realism' is the result of a highly complex and artificial
mental and emotional process—a process which, by the way, Grove
shares with a number of his contemporaries. A characteristic feature
of this generation is its wavering between aesthetic isolation and
commitment to social or religious causes, between symbolism and
naturalistic or realistic modes of writing. Like Oscar Wilde himself,
Joris-Karl Huysmans, the French decadent writer, originally a
disciple of Zola, became a Catholic not long after writing *À rebours*
(1884), one of the *chef d'oeuvres* of symbolism. Thomas and Heinrich
Mann, in their different ways, also follow the same pattern shortly
after 1900.

Canadian literature as world literature

A modified view of Grove, the European, is bound to change our
image of Grove, the Canadian. I have already pointed out that

Grove's move from Europe to North America may be called a move from 'Life for art's sake' to 'Art for life's sake' in a very qualified sense only. Even when Grove started to write in English—some time between 1909 and 1912—he was certainly far from looking for a new literary tradition he might join. His savage attacks on the Canadian literary scene in his early letters, and in entries he later made in his diary 'Thoughts and Reflections,' offer plenty of evidence that his sympathy for existing authors and existing literary movements in Canada was limited indeed, and that he despised most of them for their provincialism and lack of scope.

Grove set out to become a writer in Canada rather than a Canadian writer. His sense of distance emerges very sharply when he insists on a new literature no longer based on commercial considerations but on an analysis of life from a more universal vantage point. Even in his prairie novels, which seem to come closest to being 'Canadian' literature, it is obvious that they are not really 'novels of the soil' but use their Canadian themes as paradigms of universal problems. 'No, I said, it wasn't the soil, it's cultivation,' Grove replied when a neighbour commented on his excellent corn crop.[7] Time and again, Grove insists that he does not see himself as contributing to a national literature but uses local material to express his views on life and civilization, on nature and on the conflict between spiritual and material values. 'I have remained in Canada,' he remarked for instance in a paper read in 1940, 'because there was in me one urge more powerful than any other, the urge to express certain things. In other words, to write.' As an afterthought he scribbled into the typescript: 'And what I wanted to write about had offered itself in this country.'[8]

Grove's emphasis on a world literature by no means diminishes his importance for Canadian letters. If he rejects the literature produced during his own lifetime and refuses to subscribe to the current environmentalism, he does not reject the concept of a Canadian literature. Rather, he redefines it as a part of world literature.

Grove compares whenever he writes about literary problems, ignoring the national framework as well as the targets of literary criticism in a specialized sense: literature to him appears as one manifestation of a universal process of evolution. To confront Canadian literature with this process, thus providing an authoritative standard for it, is the obvious intention of many of his essays on the 'great European tradition,'[9] as he occasionally calls it. Balzac, Dostoevsky, Flaubert, Thomas Hardy, Thomas Mann, Stendhal,

Tolstoy, Zola—these names stand for a literature conscious of its humanistic and universal implications, possessing at the same time what Grove calls *Schwungweite* (drive and momentum),[10] the ability to fit all seemingly trivial details into the general picture. Thus it is largely the tradition of nineteenth-century realism that Grove prescribes as an antidote not only to his own latent aestheticism but also to what he saw as the provincialism and sterility of Canadian literature.

Grove's intention to bring new cultural standards to Canada clashed sharply with Canadian tendencies to establish an indigenous culture. Though misunderstood in his own time, Grove sought to overcome the dual standards in Canadian literature: British tradition vs. colonial literature. In envisaging the literature of the future, Grove rejected any compromise with the provincial past: 'What we need in Canada, and today, is not a pretty poem nor a handsome building here or there; what we need is a frontal attack of the artistic spirit along the whole line.'[11] This utopian vision—utopian in the sense of a radical alternative rather than a gradual change—is apparent even where Grove seems to advocate a national literature as an expression of a collective identity: 'A nation is a section of mankind but has a distinctive voice, and its voice is merely the outward and audible sign of a distinctive spirituality.'[12]

Clearly, it was Grove alone who knew the secrets of this 'spirituality.' The re-birth of Canadian literature as world literature is closely linked with the person of the mediator himself claiming to be the new literature personified. A recurrent theme in Grove's diaries is his bitterness about the Canadian public refusing his leadership and forcing him to react to the situation as it existed, rather than allowing him to follow his own directions and accepting his role as another Prometheus.

But we must not be taken in by Grove's negative tone. Like other moderns, he sees alienation as an essential part of the writer's existence. Grove is not the only one to find himself in a vacuum where extended monologues have to replace real communication. But, again, Grove's attitude is thoroughly ambiguous. Isolation, while at times oppressive, also provides imaginative freedom. Commenting on his own lack of an audience, Grove writes in *In Search of Myself:* 'The lack of an audience? But even the lack of an audience is not the important thing. The important thing is that *you* have such an audience *in mind* when you speak. Whether it is really there does not matter. In case of need you can imagine it.'[13] It is through this loneliness that the expatriate writer is able to mediate between self and the world outside, to analyse man's reaction to reality rather than to reconstruct reality itself.

Grove and Germany

Is Frederick Philip Grove a German-Canadian writer? After what we have said about his international standards, it seems dangerous and misleading either to draw conclusions from his ethnic background or to assess his work in terms of 'ethnic literature.' It seems questionable whether 'ethnicity' in Grove's case is a relevant critical category. At the biographical level, the answer is obvious: Grove renounces his German past, de-personalizing it and transforming it into an archetypal *Bildungserlebnis,* into the story of initiation into European civilization. During his Canadian period, Grove's image of Germany remains static and general, reflecting his desire to vindicate his decision to emigrate rather than any real political or cultural awareness. 'Conclusion: there is no genius growing up in Germany,' he laconically writes to Watson Kirkconnell in 1927 after looking through a recently published anthology.[14]

After Hitler's rise to power, Grove's occasional comments show that he is increasingly out of touch with German politics. His letters and diary entries, however, reveal that his reaction to Nazi Germany is not entirely negative but ambivalent, a mixture of admiration and disgust.[15] He sees Hitler and Mussolini as personalities of historical rank, stressing at the same time their limitations because their success depends on favourable circumstances. 'He is a great man,' he writes in 1936, 'whom the event aligns with itself,'[16] a politically dubious statement which does, however, reflect his deterministic philosophy.

Grove always insisted on interpreting reality in philosophical categories. He saw political constellations—in Germany and elsewhere—as transitory manifestations of the universal laws governing the world. But below the carefully polished surface, Grove's suppressed past was demanding its rights. Memories of his youth in Europe, of early impressions, are sometimes only thinly disguised as fictional motifs. In an unpublished short story ('Radio Broadcast'), a German immigrant fails as a farmer on the prairies.[17] He buys a radio set and listens to classical music which allows him to escape into a dream world of nostalgic illusion. Eventually he dies during a broadcast of Beethoven's Ninth Symphony. As a story, this does not come off. But the central motif recurs both in Grove's fictional account of his youth and in his 'Thoughts and Reflections': 'I have treated myself yesterday, on the gramophone, to the Ninth Symphony (Beethoven's—is it necessary to name him?); and it made me homesick for Europe—the landscape of lower Austria, Upper Bavaria—and for my youth.'[18] Although even here Grove does not drop his mask, he allows us a glimpse of the link between literary theme and personal experience. Obviously these emotional attachments to Germany may well be regarded as part of his 'ethnic' heritage. This heritage must be analysed in conjunction with other formative constituents of Grove's character.

Grove as an international writer

Frederick Philip Grove's work defies the categories of literary nationalism: he is modern because he is international. Grove—like Joseph Conrad and Katherine Mansfield, both of whom he admired, or, more recently, Vladimir Nabokov and V.S. Naipaul—occupies a position between literatures, which is both isolated and paradigmatic. The continuing interdependence between his work and contemporary developments in literature deserves closer attention. If we approach Grove from this direction, taking literary, rather than national or ethnic criteria as points of reference, a number of important problems might be explored more adequately than they have been so far: Grove's eclectic use of his cultural and literary heritage; the fundamental polarity of aestheticism and activism, of the dilettante and the settler as missionary; Grove's ambiguous concept of 'life,' not merely seen in its psychological implications but as a concept informing themes and structures of his fiction. Equally important seems to be a fresh study of Grove's reception in Canada: the paradox of his canonization as Canadian classic, the clash of his intention to establish what he saw as philosophical standards for Canadian literature, and the way he was—and still is—read and interpreted as a writer describing Canadian reality and voicing Canadian experience.

Even if few critics will be prepared to call Grove a very great writer, his contribution to Canadian literature at a crucial stage of its development remains as important as his re-definition of this literature from an international point of view. Frederick Philip Grove continues to be a mysterious figure—a Captain Scott of the prairies—but a comparative study may provide the basis for a better understanding of his isolation.

[1]"Thoughts and Reflections,' p. 326. The journal is in the Frederick Philip Grove Collection, Department of Archives and Special Collections, University of Manitoba Libraries, Box 22, Folder 2. It is an untapped yet important source for many of the problems discussed here because it offers a less literary, and more documentary view of the fundamental clash between universal aspirations and social and cultural conditions which forms the theme of many of Grove's fictional works.

[2]Malcolm Ross, Introduction, *Over Prairie Trails* (Toronto: McClelland and Stewart, 1957), p. v.

[3]Friedrich Michael, 'Verschollene der frühen Insel,' *Börsenblatt für den deutschen Buchhandel,* 28 (no. 17, Feb. 1972), A79-A82.

[4]T.D. MacLulich, 'Our Place on the Map: The Canadian Tradition in Fiction,' *University of Toronto Quarterly,* 51 (1982), 191-208.

[5]George Steiner, *After Babel: Aspects of Language and Translation* (London: Oxford University Press, 1975), p. 469f.

[6]Thomas Mann, *Tonio Kröger,* in *Die Erzählunger,* Stockholmer Gesamtausgabe (Frankfurt/Main: S. Fischer, 1966), p. 302.

[7]"Thoughts and Reflections,' p. 328.

[8]Unpublished lecture, ca. 1940, Grove Collection (Box 20, Folder 18), p. 5.

[9]F.P. Grove, Speech before the Professional Women's Club, 20 May 1940; Grove Collection (Box 20, Folder 7), p. 5.

[10]"Thoughts and Reflections,' p. 334 (27 January 1937).

[11]'Art and Canadian Life,' by 'Rusticus'; Grove Collection (Box 20, Folder 3).

[12]Unpublished lecture, ca. 1940; Grove Collection (Box 20, Folder 18).

[13]F.P. Grove, *In Search of Myself* (1946; rpt. Toronto: McClelland and Stewart, 1974), p. 11.

[14]*The Letters of Frederick Philip Grove,* ed. Desmond Pacey (Toronto: University of Toronto Press, 1976), p. 73.

[15]*Letters,* p. 371: 'I know Germany and admire and detest it at the same time' (To Lorne Pierce, 11 November 1939).

[16]'Thoughts and Reflections,' p. 329.

[17]Typescript of unpublished short story, Grove Collection (Box 17, Folder 41). The story begins in a thinly veiled autobiographical tone: 'Karl Amthor had come from Germany in the middle nineties, a young scholar disgusted with scholarship and a scholar's career.'

[18]'Thoughts and Reflections,' p. 328 (10 August 1936).

E.D. Blodgett

Ersatz Feminism in FPG's German Novels[1]

> Der Gegensatz erst lässt uns die Dinge erkennen.
> [The perception of things is facilitated,
> above all, by means of antithesis.]
> —Felix Paul Greve

How is it possible to think 'Grove' and not think of other names, casual metonymies perhaps, of Niels Lindstedt, Len Sterner, Abe Spalding, John Elliot, Ralph Patterson, Samuel and Edmund Clark, the allusively fictional Philip Branden, and other men haunting the margins of Grove's imagination? They are always men, with few exceptions patriarchal, archetypal, already somewhat stodgy when they first appeared, enveloping the victims of their vision with their tragic, male mythologies. They are all, as one of the sections of Douglas Spettigue's monograph laconically remarks, heroes.[2]

One of the problems with F.P. Grove—both his novels and the criticism they have inspired—is the dominant role his male figures enjoy. As a consequence of the power they possess, it is only a matter of time before they fulfil their aims, but it is not unusual that for all their vigour they appear static.[3] They have the vice of specialists: self-parody comes to them easily. One may, of course, excuse this as a generic flaw. It is very possible, for example, that Grove indeed confused drama and epic, and that he thought he could expand dramatic moment into narrative.[4] This would explain the simplicity of his characters, their tendency to become positions to be tested, as opposed to other attributes that would give them, as Roland Barthes would say, the effect of the real. What makes them baffling is their almost complete absence of background: in an almost theatrical sense they make débuts. But because they are not as solitary as they are made to appear, they form the background for their families, especially their wives and daughters. That they are themselves background lends them qualities not normally shared by heroes of epic. To whom would Achilles be background? Only temporarily does Dido stand outlined as bas relief against Aeneas. She does so only because her role, finally, is to heighten by contrast the hero's tragic destiny. To raise, of course, the heroes of antiquity who were, it seems, by definition self-enclosed, and, therefore, hermetic heroes, to raise them as paradigms in approaching Grove's patriarchs and romantic youths is to be, perhaps, unjustly ironic. But whether we speak of Grove's protagonists or the heroes of epic, there is no question that they share a certain innocence. Such innocence was, evidently, sanctioned by classical epic. It is, perhaps, the ideology of heroism to be untouched. Heroes move in a realm only accessible to other heroes, and women do not walk there. This may be what Grove calls an 'aristocracy of the spirit.'[5] Wherever such an aristocracy may be, it is that quality of innocence that makes his heroes appear as interlopers[6] in the modern world. This is particularly true when one bears in mind that mediaeval romance, to a certain degree, and the epics of the Italian Renaissance permitted women to move among heroes. Needless to say, as the hero of Ariosto's *Orlando Furioso* demonstrates, that is no proof against innocence. But what have Virgil and Ariosto to do with Grove? Precisely this: Grove's notion of the male character, when raised to epic proportion, at once engages a literary tradition and an attitude toward women (one implies the other) that not only calls the hero's innocence into question but also suggests that innocence, while not quite a vice, is only a heroic virtue, appropriate to heroic forms. I want to argue, then, that the heroic stature that Grove's male-figures may be said to possess, a stature characterized by innocence, is in fact their flaw and not, as in classical epic, a necessary habit. I want to argue as well that their flaw is an ethical background that invites the women who both oppose and support them to acquire other habits more necessary and more appropriate to domestic melodrama and comedy.

Innocence as a ruling passion in Grove's novels emerges in uneasy fashion because of the hybrid character of their form. Grove's protagonists move through climates that suggest the heroes of Norse sagas, and such temperaments as Abe Spalding's command the attention of that kind of power.[7] But the very fact that he possesses such an aura guarantees the irony of his function, for his role is displayed upon two stages, the timeless stage of the seasons and the historical stage of the pioneer family. As a result, his hybris, and the hybris he shares with Elliot and the others, is rendered problematic by the contradiction of agrarian ideologies that generate epic, idyll, romance, and historical 'realities' that modify epic into melodrama, idyll into complex pastoral, and make romance (Len Sterner's, for example) come perilously close to pathology. Repeatedly, narrators and protagonists assert that farming is man's highest vocation, and repeatedly it is demonstrated that farming, under specific historical circumstances, is not an agricultural pursuit, but an industrial occupation. John Elliot's celebrated apologia of the farmer's life as following Abraham's pattern, given the care with which Grove structures his novels as chronicles, can only be seen as a reification whose validity the novels formally question.[8] Thus the protagonists—little more than thematic *véhicules*—participate, indeed generate, the irony that the novels inscribe as tragic destiny.

That they are all, as I have suggested, innocents, seems to enhance the epic character of their irony. They are all to a fault inaccessible. Len Sterner is unquestionably one such character, and his name itself is a pun, that in English ('stern') relates him to Grove's patriarchs whose puritanism he displays, and in German '*Stern*,' (i.e., 'star') relates him to a symbolic purity not of this earth. Thus while his peculiar passion, so unearthly as it is, prevents him through suicide from ever becoming a son of the soil like his prairie counterparts, he nevertheless shares qualities with them and so provides a means of approach to the Grove protagonist.

By selecting Len Sterner as the archetype of the Grove hero, I wish to challenge a number of assumptions in Grove criticism, and primarily those that begin with an emphasis on the patriarchal, pioneer male. There is no question that Len Sterner is what his name suggests he is, whether he was raised near the 'Big Marsh' or not, and this fatal self-sufficiency of Grove's male protagonist is an inescapable fact of his fiction. Hence it is, as Desmond Pacey complains, 'from the real and tangible world of a pioneer district we are whisked to a strange unearthly lake which might have graced the pages of a novel by Mrs. Radcliffe or Monk Lewis.'[9] The gothic *décor*, whose literary implications are not explored, is criticized because of its lack of preparation. 'The laws of cause and effect and probability' are suspended and the reader must view Sterner through the opposition of 'a romantic super-structure' and a 'realistic base.' Such contradictions are, however, characteristic of Grove, and it is equally characteristic that he could almost blandly remark to Pacey: 'The end was suggested by the actual sight of the chattering rocks in Lake Winnepegosis.'[10] But what is important in Pacey's comment is that he saw the scene as gothic, for such a reading immediately projects Grove across a literary, and not a geographical, plane. It also reminds one that reviews of *The Yoke of Life* were quick to suggest Thomas Hardy's *Jude the Obscure* and Knut Hamsun's *Pan* as antecedents.[11] Grove has exculpated himself of the former charge (cf. Spettigue, *Grove*, p. 74).[12] The only novel of Hamsun's he appears to acknowledge acquaintance with is *Growth of the Soil* (*ISM*, p. 356) and once he went so far as to remark that he 'was a born Geissler' (p. 422). What is, in fact, striking about both *Pan* (1894) and *Jude the*

Obscure (1895) is not how two such dissimilar figures as Glahn and Jude could be perceived in Len Sterner, but that both should have appeared within a twelve-month period of Grove's youth, the same period that saw the initial productions of Villiers de l'Isle-Adam's Axël whose theme and conclusion seem to have a powerful resonance in Grove's novel. Such a filiation between the play and Grove's novel may only, of course, be conjectured, but the conjecture rests upon strong probability. For what was Grove's reading in the early years of the century if not such English writers as Walter Pater, Oscar Wilde, and Ernest Dowson, as well as French writers of like interests? But why precisely Axël?

Axël aims at an inevitable conclusion, a double suicide, and the preparation of the play's conclusion generates themes of the first importance to the period. First among these was, as it was called in German, Weltflucht, flight from the world. As the code of the play indicates, however, the flight is of a purgatorial character. Through their suicides, Sara and Axël participate in the alchemical 'work,' and so enter death as a purification process. The central metaphorical question of the play—what to do with the treasure, the gold—is answered as a problem for the spirit. As Titus Burckhardt observes of the alchemical gold, 'Gold is sun; sun is spirit.'[13] This is the gold Axël chooses. Immortality is possible only through a transmutation that would put him as microcosm in relation to the macrocosm:

> Pénétré de ton Idéal, passé toi-même en lui, trempé dans les flammes-astrales, renové par les épreuves, tu seras l'essentiel contemplateur de ton irridation. Inaccessible aux appels de la Mort et la Vie,—c'est-à-dire à ce que est encore toi-même—tu seras devenu, dans la Lumière, une liberté pensante, infallible, dominatrice.[14]

This would be a result of his master's injunction: 'spiritualise ton corps' (Villiers, IV, 194; cf. Burckhardt, p. 83). But the play is not all doctrine: it begins and ends with Sara whose arrival at the critical moment in Axël (whose name alone suggests the hub of the wheel around which the four essences revolve, thus the quinta essentia [cf. Burckhardt, p. 96]) leads him to the point where, as the master announces, 'l'Oeuvre s'accomplit' (Villiers, IV, 216). Sara—erotic, virginal, lunar sister of Axël the solar centre—generates the hieros gamos of sun and moon, soul and spirit, without which Axël's role as spiritual axle would be impossible (cf. Burckhardt, p. 106).

But what 'work' does Len Sterner accomplish? And how does he relate to Axël, the inaccessible centre of Villiers' humourless dramatization of the Hermetic doctrine? I have conjectured at Grove's knowledge of Villiers' play. The milieu of his formative years urges us to assume it as probable; and even more suggestive is his use of the name Axël for the man who first meets the heroine of *Fanny Essler* upon her arrival in Berlin, becomes her occasional lover, and plays a kind of buffoon. Fanny herself calls attention to the name by remarking that it is unusual, but pretty.[15] Her Axël possesses a character that is the reverse of the French Axël, and this only increases the special interest of his name. For Fanny it is a rare name, as it would be for the general German reader. But Sterner is no mystic. He moves, nevertheless, as an outsider through the Manitoba wilderness, and he seeks some way out of it, unlike both Hardy's Jude and Hamsun's Glahn, in the company of his soul-mate. It is the natural and symbolic resolution of his conflict with himself, as well as with what appears to be the unredeemable situation he faces. To die in the 'Lake' is tantamount to dying with the ideal, and so to achieve the perfection otherwise always eluding his grasp. That the quest is for purity, that it is purgative (suggested by the use of water as a cleansing element) and that it occurs at 'the Narrows,' calls to mind the biblical phrase, 'strait is the gate,' as well as André Gide's novel of the same title which Grove translated. The work accomplished, then, is implied in what Len perceives as a necessary passage out of the world, a *Weltflucht* of irrevocable implication. For to live united as they are at the novel's conclusion would be a sacrilege.[16] Thus the poignant discussions toward the end between Len and Lydia, frequently reminiscent of the dialogue between Sara and Axel, dramatize a sense of unearthly purity that make criticisms of Len's personality somewhat otiose. He shares with other Grove heroes a fateful propensity to do one thing, and to do it too well. The tragic consequence of this habit is an inability to see beyond the sphere of its own activity, and it is this very inability to see that prevents any release from the situation.

The intent of these introductory observations is to call in question the nature and depth of suffering in Grove's male protagonists. For this reason I have privileged Len Sterner in his innocence as archetypal of all these figures, and that is one of the reasons why I suggested an analogue between Sterner and Villiers' Axël. Wrapped as they all are in their 'visions,' they are in fact exempt from suffering. But isolated by these same visions, they are capable of causing much suffering and yet of remaining quite unaware of it. Only when their isolation is in some way breached, are they capable of suffering. Patterson is not portrayed as a man suffering because his will is not always accomplished. He suffers when he is finally brought to see how the limitations of his monomania have really hurt his family. The same is true for Spalding, and Elliot has an incredible habit of making life difficult for himself. His suffering, in fact, is certainly merited, but his refusal to see outside himself causes suffering everywhere. Had he been capable of such *anagnorisis,* he would have risen to tragic heights indeed. He cannot; and so he goes on, incapable of either comic reconciliation or tragic catharsis. Suffer he may within the limits of his vision and the isolation it induces, but his suffering is surely no equal to that of his wife, for example. Len Sterner, as well, is protected by his vision of purity, and nowhere do we find him at odds with such problems as Lydia's. *He,* in fact, is her problem, for she sees Len as *other,* someone to care for, and someone to share death with. She must fit his vision; she has none of her own.

So it is that while Grove's males are comic-figures involved in tragedies, the more frequent tragic-figures are his women who are usually overlooked or underplayed by his critics. Desmond Pacey's comment that Grove 'sees women predominantly in the role of temptress or succuba' is certainly excessive, and it clearly reflects a reading *through* the males.[17] As I have already suggested, the females are in a special sense, with the exception of *The Master of the Mill,* foregrounds moving against the male landscape and background; and where the males always seem to be who they are—unchanging, hopelessly teleological—it is the females who must act. What do they do but live, and, as we know from Axël's famous query, 'Vivre? les serviteurs feront cela pour nous' (Villiers, IV, p. 261).[18]

At first sight it would not appear that Grove's *début* as a novelist, *Fanny Essler,* is of the same pattern I have described, for the commanding figure of the text is a woman. Her function in the novel, however, would not be fully clear if it were not perceived that she stands in opposition to the values of the male world of her time. As a consequence, the ideologies of the German *Neuromantik* are at once satirically and bitterly examined and found to be thoroughly wanting. A full description of all the phases of *Neuromantik,* the German literary and social movement of Grove's maturing years (1890-1910), would exceed the limits of this essay. In a general way, it may be said to correspond to the French *Décadence,* not to speak of the English counterpart, both of which Grove knew thoroughly.[19] But it should not be forgotten that he was a native of Germany where, as it has been argued, the idea of *Décadence* was received with a certain reluctance and ambiguity.[20] It showed itself there as perhaps more reactionary than revolutionary, as an opposition to the Imperial Reich as well as official religious postures. Such a stance generated others, one of which is the opposition of generations; and another, the hyper-refined subjectivism that Hermann Bahr distinguished from earlier romanticism as a romanticism of nerves, as opposed to spirit (*Geist*) and feeling.[21] The seminal description of its German manifestation is Nietzsche's *Der Fall Wagner*, but it is characteristic for the period that Nietzsche's influence is everywhere as both its critic and master (Fischer, p. 38). Thus, while he stood against Wagner's *'Neuro-Mantik'* attitudes, Nietzsche, in his 'aristocratic' hatred of modern, industrial society, articulated an opposition, but it was an opposition that only exacerbated a situation Nietzsche would have desired to overcome.[22] His efforts to persuade his generation that culture was more than a 'Dekoration des Lebens,' that for the Greeks (that is, those who are not Romantics), culture was a higher form of nature where there was no decoration, no 'inner' as opposed to 'outer,' had the paradoxical effect of feeding the gradual sense of ego-disintegration of *Neuromantik*.[23] One of the classical manifestations of the larger opposition of *Neuromantik* is, of course, Thomas Mann's *Tonio Kröger*, but what is there dramatized as opposition is in *Buddenbrooks* exposed as a familial relationship: *Bürgertum* and *Künstlertum* constitute two phases of the same problem. The artist, too weak for 'life,' as both Nietzsche and Mann observed, possesses a weakness generated by the dominant class of the period. Thus their opposition was one of appearance only, for in fact one of their shared fears was, in Germany at least, the rise of social democracy and the coming of the 'barbarians' (Fischer, pp. 18-19). So it was not uncommon for the artist of the period to adopt 'aristocratic' manners and none more intensely than Stefan George and Rainer Maria Rilke whose origins are notably *petit bourgeois*. But an 'aristocracy of the spirit'[24] has no place to display itself but in the spirit whose apparent aristocracy, for contemporary critics, was viewed as a fundamental fear of life. The new Romantic was a 'noble youth' that refused to become a man.[25] A significant consequence of this refusal was his inability not only to relate to the present but also to the past. The past has no other reality than its result as artistic object, as line, rhythm, and ornament ('Dekoration des Lebens'), and especially as *Stimmung* or *état d'âme*. The past was not so much history as it was technique. So it is that Samuel Lublinski, who could initiate a discussion of *Neuromantik* with George and Hofmannsthal, concluded that, while there is a gap between literature and life, 'The man of today, in everyday life, is in no way a being in tune with myth, but a much more thoroughly rational being, that with cold and determined logic attends to his economy, his technology, and his business and politics.'[26] The 'man of today' complements the artist or, to put it another way, he is a man who needs the artist; each fails the other, the rationality of one and the 'mood' of the other always operating in distinct spheres by a 'logic' of their own. Neither, however, is shown to exist beyond the range of his own technical competence and each is shown to have reached a dead-end, each in his own, shared *fin de siècle*.

In Grove's English novels, the one may be seen in Len Sterner and the other in Edmund Clark. The particular relevance of *Neuromantik* to *Fanny Essler* is that not only is its ideology treated with continuous satire, but also it is the fundamental explanation of Fanny's pathetic failure to endure. This is significant, for the author of *Fanny Essler* was intimate with *Neuromantik* to a fault, and it would be difficult to demonstrate that such an essay as Grove's introduction to *Das Bildnis des Mr. W.H. [und] Lord Arthur Saviles Verbrechen* is satiric.[27] As a portrait of the artist, it is an indispensable document of the ideology of the period. What is important in the portrait is that it is of an artist, and not of his art. Wilde is typical of the modern because he lives artistically, which means that his very uprootedness roots him everywhere and makes him capable of perpetual self-metamorphosis. Not only heightened sensibility ('romanticism of nerve'), but also an ability to change his life through theatrical pose led Wilde to catastrophe: 'Pose became for him reality next to which real life grew pale, and where it did not pale, he confused dream and facts, and for that life took its revenge.'[28] To be an artist was evidently a dangerous game: to play it required that one abandon the unified role that life demands for a multiplicity of masks—at once Nero and Dandy—and his error as a player was to stray into real life.[29] The error was tragic, for playing against life, he was playing against impossible odds. He was, as Grove asserts, too weak for life. He should never have allowed the dream to be realized.

One thinks of Len Sterner, but to what extent does he enter 'life'? He is indeed too weak for life, but he has the sense not to live. Fanny Essler differs from the portrait of Wilde in one essential point: she only lies from necessity, and her virtue, pathetic as it is, is a sincerity through which the shallow kinds of tragedy of the decadent life are exposed. What makes the novel important for Grove is the irony by which this is accomplished. It would appear that Fanny is a kind of artist, a character at least striving to be an artist, who fails by straying into reality. The motif of the novel—to find a prince—is apparently beyond realization. Fanny begins by sleeping with a baron and then urging marriage upon him. Of course, both parents refuse for reasons of class, and so she begins her 'education' only to end up as the mistress of a man rich enough to be a prince and who is the last of all her disappointments. But such a motif—to realize a dream and find it illusory—is but the motif that runs through all the efforts of Fanny's life. One might reverse Grove's comments on Wilde—Fanny's error is to stray into dream.

The dream into which she strays is composed of all the commonplaces of *Neuromantik*. The first is the antinomy of the artist and middle-class society which comprises the first section of the novel. The second is the belief that the artist's life is in some way distinctive. As she discovers during her theatrical period, one cannot succeed without a private income to pay for a wardrobe. Thus to survive she must occasionally prostitute herself. To make matters worse, Fanny is often too shy to ask for money. By chance she moves into a Berlin artists' *Kreis* where she first encounters love. But while she is in love, she discovers that her lover—an effete poet—loves her but cannot respect her because of the life she has led. Through the one friend she makes in her life, she is drawn into a brief career as an art student in Munich where she meets her husband. Her husband, however, proves to be a man incapable of sexually satisfying her, and so she elopes with her last lover who satisfies her sexually but not as a woman. Mercifully she dies, 'une femme de trente ans,' of malaria. The novel is structured in five parts with an introduction—her flight from home—and so formally suggests the tragedy of her life through the phases of city, theatre, love, marriage, and death. Every phase is a disappointment, and in every phase she feels herself 'fremd' or, in modern jargon, an outsider.

Unlike Wilde, Fanny is incapable of posing. She is, however, capable of seeing through imposture, particularly that of the 'artist's life' and of the kind of impotent males it creates. By using Fanny as an object, the narrator readily projects these figures as satirical. The satire is of two kinds. Either the salons through which she moves are exposed, because of their uncritical seriousness, as fatuous, or the reflections that she excites are ironically treated. Fanny, fortunately, never hesitates to raise questions, and not to know the wedding march from *Lohengrin* (p. 300) underscores her freshness of spirit as opposed to the cliches of the salons where she is present. Thus what she lacks in *Bildung* (already ironic in, but characteristic of, a *Bildungsroman*[30]) she more than compensates for with 'her healthy common sense' (pp. 318-19). 'Healthy,' of course, is the significant adjective, for it immediately distinguishes Fanny from the 'sickness' of her decadent friends. It is this very health that urges her to challenge the repetitive discussions of Goethe (certainly a cliche of the period as an idol of Nietzsche), and the challenge issues in a discussion of one of Goethe's lyrics that she finds both childish and sentimental. The theme of the poem is the poet going into the woods to find nothing (childish), expressing a desire to enter his beloved's light on the mountain top (sentimental). This challenge is answered by saying that the task of art is to make the unreal real. Needless to say, Fanny triumphs, but it is the triumph of experience, rather than of her innocence (cf. p. 443).

The same critical sense is evinced in her thoughts when one 'master'—Herr Bolle, an artist of whom she is a sometime mistress—reads the work of another master. He reads it as if it were liturgy, and she wonders whether this is indeed inspiration or simply play (p. 307). Other ironies are more carefully woven in:

> Toward evening of the second day he sat for awhile facing her, exhausted and mute after having read quite a long time from Nietzsche's *Zarathustra* of which she understood not a word. Bit by bit his face began to assume a faint and tormented expression. Suddenly he said, bewildered, with the last breath of a pained sigh:[31] "Fanny. . . !" "What is it?" asked Fanny frightened.—"I am almost afraid of you!" he whispered.—"Oh, why?"—"There you sit, and you don't know me at all." (pp. 307-08)

Implicit in Fanny's ignorance is also Herr Bolle's for whom the style of reading the unreal as it becomes real always seems more important. Thus what is already more style than convincing ecstasy is ironically emphasized by the plain response that Fanny makes to Bolle's unmotivated fears. But in the midst of this little piece of theatre of ironic exchange Bolle's awareness that he is not understood puts one of Fanny's themes into a comic setting. For it is Fanny's charge to the males in her life that it is she who must always learn their Nietzsche and Goethe. Herr Stumpf is the only exception to this charge, and he is only capable of supporting her desire to be a painter. Her interests are not perceived as interesting.

Her best scene laying bare the sillier aspects of *Neuromantik* occurs on the night of her introduction to Bolle's *cénacle*. She retires to the library to smoke a cigarette and sits on a bench fashioned like a gothic choir stall. The woman with her suggests that all they need is someone to swing a censor to make the picture fully gothic. Unaware of the Pre-Raphaelite aspects of the image, Fanny laughs. Bolle comments in an almost greasy ('fettiger') voice that the woman is a scoffer, and he then proceeds to make a real *tableau vivant* of Fanny. Her puts her hands on the table, he calls other men in the room, he adjusts the gas lamp so the room lies in twilight:

> "Pity," he whispered secretively, "that no more daylight falls through the stained-glass window!"—Silence reigned.—"The hands!" whispered Herr Bolle in a voice from deep within: "just look at her hands!"—Fanny glanced at her hands astonished: they looked very white against the dark stained oak.—"Truly, Fräulein Essler," Frau Consul said quietly, "you really have Bolle hands!"—"What is it with my hands?" Fanny said, and removed one from the table.—"Oh, Fräulein Essler, please don't!" "Please don't!" cried several voices.—Fanny began to get embarrassed and stood up.—"But you really must come back here some afternoon when the light descends through the stained-glass window," said Frau Baumgarten, "and then the censor will have to be swung!"—"Certainly, Fräulein Essler," interjected Herr Bolle, "You will come tomorrow afternoon, won't you?" "How awfully perverse the short hair looked!" said one of the gentlemen, his words tumbling over themselves. (pp. 303-04)

Except for one comment, Fanny seems to have dissolved into the desires of her viewers, and the desires are controlled by the atmosphere, the setting, adoration for the 'master,' the stark contrast of her hands against the wood, and the foreign wood 'pervers' that focuses the tone. As satire, one is reminded of Arthur Symons' comment on Huysmans: it is 'delicately depraved.'[32] It is equally suggestive of the women in Ernest Dowson, whose *Dilemmas* Grove had translated in 1903, as well as Symons' *London Nights*, which he may also have known. *Pervers*, however, is exactly what Fanny is not, *demi-mondaine* though she may be. Sincere as she is, she finds the situation uncomfortable: to be a tainted madonna might have been a male ideal of the period, but Fanny would rather be Fanny, which is at once her strength and the cause of her downfall. Somewhat before this scene at Herr Bolle's she had in fact spent a year performing *tableaux vivants* simply to stay alive. It was a year, she felt, spent underground, in a vacuum, which dulled her blood and body (p.

278). It seemed a year in a foreign country ('in der Fremde') (p. 279).[33]

Her escape from Herr Bolle, foreshadowing her escape from her first love, as well as her husband, continues the satire on *Neuromantik*. She flees into the arms of her first love who spends part of an evening telling stories about bull-fights, a zone of experience entirely alien to the Berlin artists' *Kreis*. Bolle, thoroughly bored, decides to give a reading from *Zarathustra*, and as he reads, he swells up, turning blue-red like a mad bull. Thus her lover can play the role of a matador, saving her from Nietzsche in an hilarious parody of love at first sight (pp. 329-30). Typically for Fanny, her lover turns out to be as effete as, and certainly more contemptible, than, Herr Bolle whose name, incidentally, allegorically interpreted connotes 'bull' in English. But the satire sustains the attack on the artistic pretensions of the age, and neatly distinguishes them from Fanny. Simply through humour, the same point is made when Fanny embarks on a career as a student of landscape painting, and on her first day out places a fresh oil painting on the ground only to have her dog sit on it (p. 402). What Fanny cannot be, as she tells her last lover, is a 'Schablone,' a stencil (p. 522; cf. p. 378), and the pattern she refuses to fit is precisely that which corresponds to the artistic ideals of the time. Her life in the theatre and brief liaisons with officers can in no way be idealized in the fashion that Symons portrays dancers, nor can her desperate efforts to survive among artists in Berlin and Munich do other than expose the shallowness from which decadent attitudes spring. Part of that is made explicit in her own acquired contempt for artists, no matter how much it is affected by her love for the mysterious Herr Reelen (p. 473), and part is made perfectly clear in her exposition of the reason for prostitution while working in the theatre (pp. 312-13).[34]

It could, of course, be argued, that Fanny is a type of 'emancipated' woman. It is she who first proposes to the baron, her first lover; she who runs away to the city, working for a while for her aunt in a fashionable dress shop, but leaves because of her contempt for the bourgeoisie to seek freedom and 'her prince'; she who tries the artist's life only to be treated herself with contempt; she who marries a man who seems to support her work as a painter; and she who finally fails with her prince because she will not change her nature. I would argue that where she occasionally seems a feminist without knowing it, she is in fact a victim of a world that could not provide a woman with the same opportunities as a man. *Neuromantik* was a male ideology, and its worst characteristics were stigmata that women bore. Her first lover, Ehrhard Stein, a stereotype of the decadent poet, is as much dependent on richer men and women as Fanny—he is in fact as much a prostitute as Fanny—but Fanny bears the opprobrium of the ambivalent moral shape of the decadent world. The great merit of the novel is not, however, that it exposes what anyone can divine as historical truth, but that the articulation of that truth is done with a certain ironic skill. Never are we allowed to forget the fundamental distinction between Fanny's liveliness and self-awareness and the categorical view that males take of her. Herr Reelen acts for them all when the narrator says of him: 'He indicated to her what was to be indicated' (p. 545).

Fanny's virtue, then, whether she is emancipated or not, is her refusal to be stereotyped, to be as men want her to be, and to be as men are in the novel. Only Fanny, the novel argues, is capable of change; only Fanny learns from the world around her. Men arrive in her life as categories; and when she leaves them for their various inadequacies, they have not particularly changed because of her. The one exception to this may be her husband who plays two roles with Fanny. His courtship of her displays a man of overwhelming pedagogical logic. His marriage to her displays a man of impotent weakness. The first role, we are to assume, was a mask of courtship; and the second, the man he really is. In any case, neither role seems to be generated by his knowing Fanny. When she elopes with Herr Reelen, he admittedly commits suicide which is, on the one hand, a persuasive conclusion to his weak side and, on the other hand, may have been forced by the fact that Reelen was his best friend. In fact, it is made rather clear that his true companion is Reelen. The change of role may also be attributed to a structural principle of the novel which reflects invariably on Fanny's fatal inability to suspect the worst, and therefore underscores the candid nature of her character. It is she, then, to return to a point made earlier, who lives; and if her life as a part-time prostitute reflects on her morality (which it does not), it is, nevertheless, a sign of her being alive. Thus, she does not possess the pseudo-tragic virtue of Grove's males, whether they be German or Canadian, of existing within their closed worlds where women who do their will, who are absolutely necessary for their lives, are recompensed with a kind of blame for having lived. Grove's males, in a word, cannot be compromised. This is their flaw, but it is not tragic in the sense that Fanny's life is; for her education is but the loss of all illusion. It is her fate to feel foreign even in her native province, as everywhere else (p. 467). Only with Herr Stumpf, another outsider whose name ('stump') marks him as an outcast, does she form a friendship, for he needs a friend and she needs someone who cares for her (p. 379). That Stumpf is without a nose—a synecdoche of absence and otherness—is sufficient sign of his 'foreignness.' For Fanny it is enough to be a woman, to refuse the limitations of both *Bürgertum* and *Künstlertum*, to be an outsider.

Grove's second published German novel, as its title—*Maurermeister Ihles Haus*—suggests, has as its theme the family, and as its focus the father. It anticipates, therefore, more readily than his first work Grove's Canadian novels. It is, moreover, a comedy both in style and mode, but a comedy with cruel twists. The father, Richard Ihle, is the prototype of Grove fathers: self-made, strong, tyrannical. These characteristics alone make it clear that Grove need not be read as a novelist of the Canadian Prairie whose harsh conditions required that his males become the kind of men they become. Grove himself, of course, is responsible for this myth. As he comments in his 'autobiography,' 'pioneer conquest' requires 'dominant types, rigid types, of a single-minded pre-occupation with the specifically pioneering task' (*ISM,* p. 224). It is revealing, among other things, that, as he goes on to remark, he 'had had to suffer too much from [the] shortcomings [of such a type] to like it' (pp. 224-25). If he is referring to his own father, surely he is not referring to pioneers alone, but a type he knew only too well, and such relationships rarely elicit penetrating psychological analysis. Nor does Ihle receive any: we are told something of his rise to his current position, but not enough to explain his peculiarly nasty temper. His temper, in fact, is his 'humour' or ruling passion, and as such projects Ihle through the novel as a fictional, rather than a social, type. He is a comic blocking-figure, and his entry into the novel declares him immediately to be of that kind. He enters bellowing his wife's name three times, and then damns the whole household ('Wirtschaft'). 'The voice,' observes the narrator, 'sounded as if a madman were smashing the furniture to pieces.'[35] Frau Ihle's view of her husband, at least before her somewhat quickened awareness of him as a reality, is, we are told, romantic and idealized (p. 45; p. 47). Therefore, his behaviour is unexplained and best seized in an exchange between her and her daughters as they watch him from a window. She points him out running about in the yard simply discharging his anger for no particular reason. The mother giggles. Susie, the older, more precocious of her daughters, remarks that he is awful, and asks rhetorically for an explanation. The mother replies, ' "Yes, isn't he?" ' (p. 46; p. 49), which is somewhat of a *non sequitur* that at once supports the reader's bafflement and defines the father, as I have already suggested, as a background, as a kind of pall where their lives, the lives of women, are called into existence. The scene is also consciously constructed as a *pièce de théâtre* both visually and ideologically. It dramatizes the novel's central conflict which the narrator later makes explicit, observing that 'Basically, Master Mason Ihle despised everything female' (p. 98; p. 99). Needless to say, his attitude generates an appropriate response: 'In Herr Ihle's house everything female felt itself joined in solidarity against him' (p. 99; p. 100).

Although nothing explains the father's behaviour—he simply is a blocking character—he, by being who he is, is the explanation for the behaviour of the women in his house, and this is especially true for his daughter Susie. He is, in a word, her background, and it is from her perspective that the novel is told. Formally, the novel has a neatness that corresponds to *Fanny Essler*. Rather than five parts, it is structured in three parts, and each of these is further divided in three sections. Each part is respectively labelled 'Young Ladies,' 'Frau Ihle,' and 'Herr Ihle,' but the significant emphasis is Susie and her *Bildung*. Episodic as the narrative exposition may appear, some symbolic cohesion is sought. The first part is primarily useful as an exposition of character, particularly emphasizing Susie's boldness. The second is ordered in respect of the death of Emperor Wilhelm I and the mother's progressive 'insanity.' It concludes in her ironic abortive attempt at suicide. Subsequently, she is mentioned as dead. The last section addresses a change in the household in which all become betrothed, and Ihle marries. It concludes with a violent confrontation between Ihle and Susie in which she is almost strangled to death. It is strongly hinted in the final sentences that Susie will consent to marry a man she does not particularly respect, but a man whose life she can control. The marriage is clearly a false resolution of Susie's dilemma; and thus what might be considered a modal sign of comedy is ideologically an ambiguous decision. Susie survives her confrontation with her father and the values he thematizes by marrying a man of standing so as to escape the problem.

If the novel's conclusion is artistically and ideologically unsatisfactory (cf. Spettigue, *FPG*, pp. 147-48), the situation that is posed is Grove's own favourite, and it is addressed as a conflict of values between male and female. Since the world of Ihle's house is patriarchal, the fundamental conflict is the one that females face. Susie is clearly in opposition. Her sister Lottie is not strong enough to oppose; and the mother is divided between her 'retrospective' view of Ihle (and her hopes) and her awareness that her life has been suppressed. She stands, therefore, somewhere between Susie and Ihle as a 'tricky servant,'[36] but she cannot, finally, take any position. When she does—by running away from her husband—she fails to kill herself, and so is considered insane. Because the mother's position is itself transitional—divided between self-awareness and trained beliefs in the male—it is the most instructive. It focuses Grove's problematic and ambiguity: the female role is to correct, change, and call into question the male order, but how is it to be done? Her revolt anticipates comedy. Her dismissal to an asylum confirms the male order. We could call her a tragic victim, if Ihle were a tragic figure. He is not, and so her pathos is generated by a failure of the comic revolt; and revolt is to be stressed, for it is the central action of the novel.

Besides such exchanges as those that expose Herr Ihle's foolishness (e.g., the beginning of Part II, Section 3), Frau Ihle's true comic role is evinced both by her withdrawal from domestic activity and by her defiance of her husband's repression. The beginning of the change occurs in Part II, Section 2, the central section of the novel. Here she is described as always being a bit 'odd' ('wunderlich') and 'unsociable' ('menschenscheu'), but as time goes on her condition deteriorates (p. 95; p. 96). Her unsociability takes the form of abandoning housework to the maid and going to bed to read. The books she prefers have a markedly female orientation—Chamisso's *Women's Love and Life* and *Amor and Psyche*, Leves' *Female Figures in Goethe*, and above all Schiller and Heine—and it is her reading, I would argue, that gives a positive aspect to what appears to be her incipient insanity. It is also at this time that she begins to turn on her husband in violent episodes of screaming and door-banging. Correspondingly, Ihle is described as becoming more withdrawn. Frau Ihle's more overt revolt begins during her husband's absence to take a cure for rheumatism. She goes on a buying spree for her daughters and so strikes at the household power inasmuch as Herr Ihle's money is the source of his wife's subordination. One of the important expenditures is to have hers and her daughters' hair cut short, a possible sign of emancipation, and an act that strikes the father as unquestioned defiance. He sums it all up with a characteristic grumble, declaring he does not like girls who look like boys (pp. 131-32). Under slightly modified circumstances, he might have called it 'perverse.' It is a venture, however, that fails, and Frau Ihle, after another discussion on the budget, continues to withdraw until her attempt at suicide.

The ambivalence of the mother, who continually shifts loyalties from husband to children, is divided among the daughters. Lottie acquires the 'haughtiness of the autocratic German housewife' (p. 195; p. 192), and Susie makes every effort to become 'emancipated.' This is suggested to a certain extent by her venture into theatre, but her venture in no way corresponds to the necessities that Fanny Essler must face. Her strongest efforts do not become apparent, however, until Ihle's second wife moves in. Susie then becomes aware that she will become the spectator of the 'grotesque comedy' that Ihle and her stepmother will put on (p. 226; p. 222). Stepmothers are traditionally venomous, and this one is no exception. Thus, despite all of Susie's good will to befriend her, it is to no avail: the new Frau Ihle is everyone's tyrant. Susie's opposition follows the line of passive resistance initiated by her mother. Of course, in Ihle's eyes, her doing nothing is laziness, but for Susie it is a way of confronting the household power structure. It is also an 'ideal'—to read and enjoy herself (p. 226; p. 222). Ideologically, 'nichts zu tun' is an activity. For Susie it is her only means of resistance (*'Widerstand'*). Her method, directed against her stepmother, is to smoke. To do so provides her with feelings of emancipation; it is an 'ideal of liberated manners that hovered before her eyes as the antithesis of everything *petit-bourgeois*' (p. 237; p. 233). That this might have appeared to a contemporary as a cliche is apparent in the first exchange Susie has with her stepmother on the subject. The stepmother calls her a whore. Susie replies that Empress Elizabeth of Austria smokes a hundred cigarettes a day. The stepmother, not adverse to playing with syllogisms, concludes that the empress is also a whore. Despite being forbidden, Susie continues to smoke: it constitutes the sign of her revolt (p. 240; p. 235). She is not only perceived as a rebel, but feels that the intent of the parents is to subdue ('beugen') her, to rub her out ('ausstreichen') to the point where she could be cast in any role they wanted (pp. 241-42; p. 237). Their failure to treat her as someone of the same class ('ebenbürtig') makes it equally apparent that even her search for a little recreation in her life has brought her to the threshold of adulthood. Despite the irony that is generated by casting Susie's attitude into free indirect discourse, the rhetoric of revolt cannot be overlooked. Susie is seeking *cognitio*,[37] to be recognized as a woman, and in her own right free. It is somewhat paradoxical that she chooses to demonstrate this freedom by marrying a boor, but she knows, at least, that by marrying Consul Blume she can be master in her own house, and manage things to her own satisfaction ('nach ihrem Kopf'). This is a use of marriage that is not traditionally comic. It will not serve an integrating function, and it will probably turn out as *fabliau*. In that sense it is not fully consistent with her revolt against Ihle and his wife. It does not resolve the conflict—it sidesteps it. Nor can it be said that the energy directed against Ihle, despite her moral superiority over him (p. 225; p. 221), issues in a comic exchange of values, for Susie's role is to adopt the ideology of both father and stepmother by becoming master. Relationships are brought to a crisis, and the action is suspended.

In many respects Susie is a Fanny Essler in adolescence. Each woman in her own way refuses to adopt the limited life expected of her, and in each case the refusal is gradually shown to be of no account. Rebel as they will, it is either suppressed or not taken seriously. What is clear in both cases is their resistance to blocking figures, mostly male and called 'master,' thus suggesting a society of unjust relations. Blocking figures as humours do not require development: they simply block, and so represent, as Frye notes, a society of 'ritual bondage.' It is this society that is either exposed by ridicule or, if possible, subverted. Only the former occurs in Grove's German novels, but their structure as comedy is significant, for that is the structure that anticipates the Canadian novels. Action, further-more, is required of women, for it is they who are employed so as to expose the limitations of the moral ideology of either the *senex iratus*[38] or, as in *Fanny Essler*, the effete masters of the *Neuromantik*. The responses that both Fanny and Susie make to these figures constitute the elaboration of an ethical attitude. Their *Bildung* becomes the action of the novels, and it is they who incur moral risk and thus acquire moral magnitude.

An early reviewer of *Fanny Essler* observed that Grove was a student of both the psychological and naturalistic novel, 'but he left both schools not as a confirmed literary personality but rather wavering back and forth. . . .'[39] These, of course, were the temptations of the period, but the psychological novel was in the ascendancy; and had Grove continued to develop the inclinations of his poetry, *Wanderungen*, and the ideas expressed in the introduction to his Oscar Wilde translation, a Grove different from ours may have emerged. *Neuromantik*, Grove's origin, is stylistically opposed to Naturalism, and it has in fact been argued that Nietzsche's influence in the nineties not only weakened the reception of Naturalism in Germany, but also—by his attack on what he called the 'fait-alisme' of the Zola school—supported a growing sense of the importance of the subjective personality.[40] Grove's mixture of the two styles appears as somewhat ambiguous, for, on the one hand, he attacks the decadence in *Fanny Essler* and, on the other hand, he implies through repeated analyses of Fanny's *états d'âme* that certain kinds of subjectivity are to be respected. In *Maurermeister Ihles Haus* he uses naturalism for two ends: one is to set up scenes and the other is to bestow his characters with a certain sense of reality either through description or, frequently, through the use of dialects. Not only dialect, but also the descriptions so objectify characters as to make them appear subordinate to the things of their *décor*. A fine example of Grove's Naturalism is the entry of Susie's future stepmother into her field of vision. 'A black-haired, medium-sized, high-shouldered, rather strong, but tightly corseted lady of about forty in a correctly tailored, dark blue wool dress came quickly tripping along but firmly holding herself together with dignity, sliding along behind the table' (p. 204; p. 200). The paragraph continues in such a vein as to turn the character into object, heavily qualified, and more appearance than person. Dialect serves the same function, making minor characters only grotesquely alive. This is a style that reinforces, to be sure, the notion of character as theme and *actant*, and frequently all we need to hear is one of Herr Ihle's hilarious polysyllabic oaths to know of his existence. That is, in fact, all he is. The moral strength of both novels lies, however, in the analysis of the respective desires of Susie and Fanny. The ever-present need to be perceived as a human being shows itself in Susie, as I have already indicated, in the language of revolt, and as such is a manifestation of a certain will to freedom against the grotesque, inexplicable positions of Ihle and his new wife who simply are who they are as *actants*, as opposed to being creatures of free will seeking expression. The same insistence upon freedom of self-expression is evident in all that Fanny does, and her life seems governed psychologically by a rhythm of revulsion and new beginnings. Grove's sense of the psychological levels of his German novels seems governed by the subjectivity of *Neuromantik* in opposition to the implications of Naturalism.

As I have indicated, no resolution of these two styles is realized: Susie chooses to be master as a substitute for emancipation; Fanny succumbs to malaria. Just as there is a clear division of styles, so there is a suspension of the confrontations dramatized. This is particularly true of Fanny who always prefers evasion to the clarity of conflict, and so is condemned to repeat three times (perhaps four if one considers the novel's point of departure) a situation where she is involved with two men and depends upon one to free her from the other. It is not enough to say it is 'ironic' that she neurotically continues to repeat a pattern: it corresponds rather to the author's proclivity for unresolved repetition. Thus, if it is characteristic of Grove to imply that the psychological style tends toward self-expression, the elaboration of that tendency is either blocked or deflected. The subject is treated as object.

As I have tried to demonstrate, Grove's beginnings in the German cultural milieu of the turn of the century developed in his Canadian work. But while he employed a problematic Naturalism, his interest in the psychological novel waned.[41] His new sense of form appeared to be frustrated comedy. It is frustrated by the attention given to his male protagonists who are endowed to a man with attributes of a false nobility that corresponds to Grove's inclination toward an 'aristocracy of the spirit' (*ISM*, p. 423). It is difficult not to perceive this in both his patriarchal blocking-figures and his young princes, Sterner and Lindstedt. It is precisely this spirit that is attacked by those characters who intend a freer society. Patterson puts it succinctly when he observes: ' "Democracy's all nonsense, with Quarles and his black dog having as much of a vote as I." '[42] That the family itself is perceived as a political system is clearly articulated by Alice (*TG*, pp. 77-78), but with the exception of this novel it is usually unclear how Grove wants to implicate his reader morally into his novels. Because of the movement toward indirection that he prefers, all value-systems hang in suspense. Naturally, it is difficult to know whether Phil Branden speaks for Grove when he opts for either 'collective ownership' or 'limitation of wealth,'[43] but it is nevertheless evident that Grove was constantly exercised by political and economic issues that at once support the form and enter the narrative perspective of his novels. He preferred, however, to leave the implications of these issues hanging, and this is why, perhaps, he continually played with his conclusions or, as in *Two Generations*, he was planning a change in the relationship of Alice and Phil—always modifying, always trying a new detour.

So it is in a very deep sense that one cannot trust Grove. For while one can see the form of comedy emerge in his novels from the start, one wonders whether the sense of ideological change that is implied will be authentic. Or are the antagonists only aiming at more rational replacements of the old with the apparently new? There is nothing, of course, that prevents novelists from turning their narratives into ideological arguments, but an insistence on the arguments as the inscription of a form raises expectations to which the form, to achieve artistic wholeness, ought to give reply. This is the mark of Dostoevskij's novels; it rarely occurs in Grove. What is the point of Fanny's death? Mere irony? One may raise the question as well for Sir Edmund's death: his death is an arbitrary removal of a signal position by the author, and it frustrates with one shot the elaboration of the form as argument. It also, one infers, manifests an awareness of a kind of failure, for, as Birk Sproxton demonstrates, Sam and his son Edmund are only, after all, doubles.[44] The comic exchange is only an appearance of comedy. This is disheartening, but so are the implications of *Two Generations,* the novel whose comic form is most clearly realized. Alice and Phil oppose ' "sloth and prejudice and resistance" ' (p. 186), blocking motifs, but just as Edmund is his father's double, so Phil and his father are ' "exactly alike" ' (p. 190). What supreme irony is concealed in the sentence that confirms Patterson's comic conversion when it is observed that 'Here was the tyrant speaking to his slaves as to equals' (p. 257)? What does it mean that 'at the moment, he felt, for the first time in his life, at one with at least part of another's vitality, and that vitality Phil's' (p. 259)? Patterson's emerges from the cage of his inaccessibility only to be completed by what was his opposition. Thus in the instance when Grove refuses to evade, he neutralizes and so cancels a dialectic without transmuting it. So Susie becomes a master. As Grove remarks elsewhere, 'oldest daughters mostly resemble their fathers' (*ODB*, p. 252).

By a curious reversal of value expectations, it is evident that Grove does not want to get rid of his blocking-figures. They do indeed endure; and although his 'sympathies were always with the women,' he was 'no sentimentalist' (*ISM*, p. 224). It is perhaps impossible to find a single source for the aesthetic and ideological irresolution of his novels, but one might consider the popular political stance of his youth which is called in German *Edel-Anarchie,* a type of anarchy that attracted writers and intellectuals disappointed with Naturalism, among whom were Gide and Wilde.[45] It was, above all, a reactionary anarchy that stopped short of social democracy, that stopped short, finally, of radical social change. *Edel* ('noble') suggests Grove's 'aristocracy of spirit,' and one has little difficulty imagining Grove with all his talk of tragedy and tragic heroes being unable to disengage his sympathies from the greatness of individuals who appear noble—Nietzsche, saga-figures like Spalding, Old Testament heroes, Nero, Dandy, Oscar Wilde—to invest them with a nobility that is ambiguously conjoined with brutality. If one could remove the brutality, one could have comic correction and also preserve the aura of the tragic hero. Thus one's anarchical tendencies would never have to contend with the fact that such heroes as Grove's possess a brutality that is a function of their 'nobility.' But anarchy does not seek a change from the bottom up: it exposes, like satire; it delineates blocking-figures, like comedy. One of the best literary examples of such anarchy is Gide's Lafacadio, the hero of *Les Caves du Vatican.* Humorous as he may be, who is he attacking, 'ce monstre délicat,' but himself in other guises? But this is the implicit irony of making ideological struggles domestic comedies: since everyone is by nature 'ebenbürtig,' it only appears to be a class conflict. Circumstances may be arranged to make relationships appear feudal, but all that comic opposition may do is restore what is already an equality of class. Thus *Edel-Anarchie* is opposition within the same class. What kind of change can it pretend to realize? Thus the pathos—one is tempted to say gravity—that readers have attributed to Grove's work cannot be evaded, but it is the pathos of a comedy that cannot, because of the conditions of its elaboration, achieve *Aufhebung.* Ersatz revolution is, finally, ersatz comedy, self-reflexive and unchanging, never straying too far into reality.

---

[1]This is an abridged, revised version of '*Alias* Grove: Variations in Disguise' which originally appeared in my *Configuration: Essays in the Canadian Literatures* (Downsview: ECW Press, 1982).

[2]Douglas O. Spettigue, *Frederick Philip Grove* (Toronto: Copp Clark, 1969), Ch. v. All further references to this work (*Grove*) appear in the text.

[3]Cf. Edward A. McCourt, *The Canadian West in Fiction*, rev. ed. (Toronto: Ryerson, 1970), p. 59.

[4]Frederick Philip Grove, *It Needs to Be Said . . .* (Toronto: Macmillan, 1929), p. 29.

[5]*In Search of Myself* (Toronto: Macmillan, 1946), p. 423. All further references to this work (*ISM*) appear in the text.

[6]Cf. Laurence Ricou's development of this theme, *Vertical Man/Horizontal World: Man and Landscape in Canadian Prairie Fiction* (Vancouver: Univ. of British Columbia Press, 1973), Ch. iii.

[7]*Fruits of the Earth* (1933; rpt. New Canadian Library, No. 49, Toronto: McClelland and Stewart, 1965), p. 85.

[8]*Our Daily Bread* (1928; rpt. New Canadian Library, No. 114, Toronto: McClelland and Stewart, 1975), pp. 188-91. All further references to this work (*ODB*) appear in the text.

[9]Desmond Pacey, *Frederick Philip Grove* (Toronto: Ryerson, 1945), pp. 62-63.

[10]*The Letters of Frederick Philip Grove*, ed. Desmond Pacey (Toronto: Univ. of Toronto Press, 1976), p. 433. Cf. p. 500.

[11]Reviews of *The Yoke of Life* by William Arthur Deacon, *The Ottawa Citizen*, 11 Oct. 1930; and J.D. Robins, *The Canadian Forum*, Feb. 1931, pp. 185-86; rpt. in *Frederick Philip Grove*, ed. Desmond Pacey (Toronto: Ryerson, 1970), pp. 145, 147. To adduce *Pan* seems to me, at least, a trifle whimsical. Glahn nowhere seems to manifest the kind of chastity that would reflect kinship with Sterner. The name alone contradicts such a virtue. A very possible source for the theme of star-crossed lovers who commit double suicide is Gottfried Keller's 'Romeo und Julia auf dem Dorfe,' and that Keller was known to Grove is evident from his being mentioned, at least in passing, in *It Needs to Be Said. . .* , pp. 82, 122. Although it is most likely that he means *Der grüne Heinrich*, the novellae of *Die Leute von Seldwyla* could hardly have escaped his notice, particularly 'Romeo und Julia,' considered in the history of German literature a minor masterpiece.

[12]Grove, *Letters*, p. 316. *In Search of Myself* (Toronto: Macmillan, 1946), p. 356.

[13]Titus Burckhardt, *Alchemy: Science of the Cosmos, Science of the Soul*, trans. William Stoddart (Baltimore: Penguin, 1971), p. 78. All further references to this work appear in the text.

[14]*Oeuvres complètes de Villiers de l'Isle Adam* (Paris: Mercure de France, 1922-31), IV, 210. All further references to this work appear in the text.

[15]*Fanny Essler* (Stuttgart: Axel Juncker, 1905), p. 71. All further references to this work (*FE*) appear in the text. My essay depends implicitly on D.O. Spettigue's persuasive argument that the Canadian Grove is the German Greve (always referred to in the text as Grove), and therefore I include the two published German novels, *Fanny Essler* and *Maurermeister Ihles Haus*, in the discussion.

[16]*The Yoke of Life* (Toronto: Macmillan, 1936), p. 348. All further references to this work (*YL*) appear in the text.

[17]*Grove*, Pacey, p. 120.

[18]Cf. Grove's article, 'Gustave Flaubert's Theories of Artistic Existence' reprinted in this volume.

[19]Douglas O. Spettigue, *FPG: The European Years* (Ottawa: Oberon, 1973), pp. 50-58. All further references to this work (*FPG*) appear in the text. Cf. Anthony W. Riley's very useful introduction to the background of Grove's German novels, 'The German Novels of Frederick Philip Grove,' in *The Grove Symposium*, ed. John Nause (Ottawa: Univ. of Ottawa Press, 1974), pp. 55-66.

[20]Jens Malte Fischer, *Fin de Siècle: Commentar zu einer Epoche* (Munich: Winkler, 1978), pp. 78-93. All further references to this work appear in the text.

[21]Hermann Bahr's essays are among the most useful for the acquisition of a notion of *décadence* and its impact in German letters. Although it is important to bear in mind that Bahr was most influential in the *Junge Wien* circle, he is still of first importance as a transmitter of French literary attitudes into German literary criticism. He wrote a fine necrology for Villiers, and it is worth observing that in that essay he is more interested in the man as artist and poseur, than in Villiers' art. It is a view that corresponds to Grove on Wilde. The distinctions between the old and new Romanticism I have drawn from Bahr's *Studien zur Kritik der Moderne* (Frankfurt a.M.: Rüiten & Loening, 1894), pp. 19-26.

[22]For a discussion of the term and pun, see *Literarische Manifeste der Jahrhundertwende 1890-1910*, ed. Erich Ruprecht and Dieter Bänsch (Stuttgart: Metzler, 1970), pp. xxx-xxxii.

[23]The phrase, 'Dekoration des Lebens' is Nietzsche's and comes from the conclusion of his essay, 'Vom Nutzen und Nachteil der Historie für das Leben.' Cf. Fischer, p. 42.

[24]On the phrase and its homology with the political imperialism of the period in Germany, see *Literarische Manifeste*, p. xix.

[25]Samuel Lublinski, from *Der Ausgang der Moderne* (Dresden: Carl Reissner, 1909), p. 54, cited in *Literarische Manifeste*, p. 281.

[26]Lublinski, *Literarische Manifeste*, p. 286.

[27]See Spettigue, *FPG*, pp. 109-14. Nor are his *Wanderungen* (Munich: I. Littauer, 1902), a collection of verse that reflects Greve's attraction to the 'George-Kreis,' not to speak of his enthusiasm for Nietzsche. On the quality of the poetry, see Peter A. Stenberg, 'Translating the Translatable: A Note on a Practical Problem with F.P. Greve's *Wanderungen*,' *Canadian Review of Comparative Literature*, 7 (Spring 1980), 206-12.

[28]Oscar Wilde, *Das Bildnis des Mr. W.H. [und] Lord Arthur Saviles Verbrechen*, trans. and introd. Felix Paul Greve (Minden: J.C.C. Bruns, 1909), p. xxxvi.

[29]Greve, in Wilde, *Bildnis*, p. xxxvii.

[30]The negative significance that this term has for women is argued by Annis Pratt, *Archetypal Patterns in Women's Fiction* (Bloomington: Indiana Univ. Press, 1981), p. 36.

[31]The humour of this sentence is difficult to render because of insistent alliteration: 'Plötzlich sagte er mit dem Schlussatem eines schmerzhaften Seufzers verstört.' The sibilants cannot be overlooked, and so his sighing sounds somewhat like a steam-engine.

[32]The expression is from Symons' essay, 'The Decadent Movement in Literature,' *Harper's New Monthly Magazine*, Nov. 1893, p. 886; rpt. in *Aesthetes and Decadents of the 1890's: An Anthology of British Poetry and Prose*, ed. Karl Beckson (New York: Random House, 1966), p. 147.

[33]Riley's synopsis in *The Grove Symposium*, p. 60, is more reliable than Spettigue's in *FPG*, pp. 134-35. The latter's sentence, 'Busy reading Goethe, Ibsen, Tolstoy, she misses rehearsals and loses her job,' suggests that she is still with the Korso Theatre. Part of Fanny's problem at this point is her life as a mere body.

[34]Brief as it is, this kind of sociological, authorial intervention anticipates the Canadian Grove.

[35]*Maurermeister Ihles Haus* (1906; rpt. Dresden: Carl Reissner, 1909), p. 37; rpt. *The Master Mason's House*, trans. Paul P. Gubbins (Ottawa: Oberon, 1976), p. 40. All further references to this work (*MIH*) appear in the text. Although the second figure in parentheses refers to the English version, the translations are often my own.

[36]See George E. Duckworth, *The Nature of Roman Comedy: A Study in Popular Entertainment* (Princeton: Princeton Univ. Press, 1952), pp. 249-53.

[37]Frye argues that this is the mask of comedy. See *Anatomy of Criticism: Four Essays* (Princeton: Princeton Univ. Press, 1957), p. 163.

[38]For this expression, see Duckworth, pp. 243-49.

[39]*Der Kunstwart*, 2 Feb. 1906, pp. 549-50; cited in Spettigue, *FPG*, p. 139.

[40]The pun is Nietzsche's. See *Literarische Manifeste*, p. xix.

[41]On Grove's Naturalism, see Ronald Sutherland's useful article, 'What Was Frederick Philip Grove?,' in *The Grove Symposium*, pp. 1-11. One might also argue that Grove's negative obsession with sexual relations is a mark of his Naturalism, and Spettigue implies as much in *Grove*, pp. 110-11; but his interest in the *femme fatale* and *femme fragile* may also testify to Grove's other side as *Neuromantik*. See Fischer, pp. 59-65.

[42]*Two Generations: A Story of Present-Day Ontario* (Toronto: Ryerson, 1939), p. 155.

[43]*A Search for America: The Odyssey of an Immigrant* (1927; rpt. New Canadian Library, No. 79, Toronto: McClelland and Stewart, 1971), p. 380.

[44]Birk Sproxton, 'Grove's Unpublished MAN and its Relation to *The Master of the Mill*,' in *The Grove Symposium*, pp. 50-51.

[45]See Fischer's discussion on Kropotkin and Stirner, pp. 43-47. As Anthony W. Riley has observed, this may be an example of arrested ideological development. By leaving Germany precisely when he did, he 'retained . . . the cast of mind which had produced his early German novels.' See *The Grove Symposium*, p. 65.

D.O. Spettigue

Fanny Essler and the Master

The Introduction to the English translation of *Fanny Essler* refers to the 'strange inner drama of the author himself.'[1] Perhaps we shall never know much about F.P. Greve/Grove; he was secretive, and his native Germany was torn apart at the end of World War II, with consequent loss of records. But the glimpses we get of that inner man are fascinating, and I believe they have a very complex relation to the writings. The fictional characters relate to Grove the author in an unusual way, and that unusual pattern is nowhere more directly confronted than in *Fanny Essler*. In this sense, *Fanny Essler* is the key to characterization in the Canadian novels.

Some aspects of this topic have been looked at before, notably by E.D. Blodgett in his excellent study, '*Alias* Grove,' in *Configuration*.[2] There are relevant observations too by Walter Pache in 'Der Fall Grove,'[3] and by Henry Makow in 'Grove's Treatment of Sex'[4] and elsewhere. Makow emphasizes the Platonic in FPG's intellectual world, and makes a convincing case for it. From this perspective the conflict between and within Grove's characters may be seen as the age-old conflict between the material and the ideal, between those characters who are materialistic and those who, as Sam Clark describes himself and Maud Dolittle, are 'idealists.' In the dissertation lying behind that article,[5] Makow assembled instances in the essays that support the alleged Platonism, but what impressed generations of Grove readers is that the Platonism, if it is there, is so taken for granted as virtually to be left out of the fictions, which instead concentrate so heavily on the material and the mundane. Certainly Makow is right about 'The Canyon,'[6] and probably about *The Yoke of Life*. But is John Elliot an idealist? Only in the curiously narrow way Grove applies that term to the merely patriarchal; virtually everything in *Our Daily Bread* is either material or psychological, not ideal, unless 'ideal' is interpreted in a way peculiar to Grove. As Blodgett implies, it is not so much an idea as an *idée fixe*, and this is characteristic of Grove's protagonists. Of Niels Lindstedt the narrator of *Settlers of the Marsh* says: 'he must go on along the demarcated line . . . even though circumstances might have arisen which would make it absurd . . . It was his peasant nature going on by inertia. . . .'[7]

It seems to me that the real conflict is between the emotions and reason. There would be nothing unusual in that conflict—it is the stuff of both comedy and tragedy from *Antigone* to the present—if Grove did not so emphasize it and so specifically build his characters around it. Typically his male protagonists are rationalists who must undergo a painful initiation into feeling, or who find the rational structure of their lives betraying them. What is particularly interesting about Grove's characterizations is the equating of strength with reason, from his first novel to his last, while at the same time he undermines that strength and shows it hollow. The character of Friedrich Karl Reelen in *Fanny Essler* is the first and in some ways the most fascinating example. He reappears as Edmund Clark forty years later and the comparison deserves attention.

Fanny Essler was Felix Paul Greve/Frederick Philip Grove's first published novel. We do not know whether it was the first novel he ever wrote, but the publication date (1905) suggests that it was written during 1903-04, that is, during his imprisonment. *Maurermeister Ihles Haus*, published in 1906, presumably was written next, though this is by no means certain. A.W. Riley points to the 'unfinished' aspect of the latter,[8] as though it had been written first and finished hastily when the more comprehensive plan of *Fanny Essler* replaced it in Greve's mind. There is certainly some common ground between the two, though *Fanny Essler* is not so much a sequel as an alternative to *Maurermeister Ihles Haus*. Between them the two books say: either you marry for security, as Susie does, or you get out like Fanny. For women, at least in that time and place, there is no other choice. What the third novel would have said we do not know; *Der Sentimentalist* was advertised in *Maurermeister Ihles Haus* as 'In Preparation,' but apparently it was never finished. At a guess, it figured a male rather than a female protagonist. Was it the first, semi-autobiographical novel? One is tempted to date the composition of these novels in the reverse order of their publication.

Perhaps the 'Sentimentalist' did not need to appear, since the conflict between sentiment and reason was fought out in *Fanny Essler*. Fanny is on the side of sentiment—sometimes—and she gets the last word, on behalf of both sentiment and women, and against the rationalist. This is not to say that she wins; no one wins, but in her dying soliloquy she cries out for understanding, and rejects the rationalist Reelen who has left her alone while he observes the proprieties. (At the same time, this novel bitterly assails the masculine sentimental view of women which men use to oppress the other sex.) It is the figure of Reelen I want to concentrate on, but first, it is necessary to summarize Fanny's story.

Like Susie Ihle, Fanny Essler is one of two sisters in a household dominated by a tyrannical father who has no sympathy for or understanding of the needs or even the individuality of his daughters. Frau Ihle dies in the course of *The Master Mason's House;* Frau Essler is already dead when *Fanny Essler* begins; in both cases the husband is blamed for his wife's death in terms suggestive of *Settlers of the Marsh.* Nevertheless, the treatment of Mastermason Ihle and Mastersmith Essler is not unsympathetic. They are not whited sepulchres like Amundsen. They are not brutes, but they are physically powerful, peasant-stock, self-made, independent men who are proud of their standing in the community and believe in hard work, and careful but not harsh living, and who find themselves baffled and frustrated by the apparently unreasoning and unreasonable behaviour of their womenfolk. Frau Ihle dies after an illness, insanity and a last fling at a dance, events that readers of *Our Daily Bread* will recognize. After taking a second wife, who bullies him, Ihle deteriorates and becomes pathetic in his daughters' eyes. Fanny Essler recognizes early that her father is something of a paper tiger; his sense of guilt at his wife's death, and Fanny's resemblance to her mother, prevent him from punishing her.

The Master Mason's House ends with Susie ready to marry the effeminate Consul Blume whose social standing and weakness of character assure her of the maximum independence marriage allows. It is not an escape but an acceptable compromise. *Fanny Essler* begins with Fanny's stealthy return home the morning after her first seduction. At this point the intent seems to be the same: surely the Baron will marry her, and though he is rather inexperienced and dull, as Baroness she will have security.

Fanny, however, is stronger—or less pragmatic—than Susie. (Both heroines are the Marys of their respective households; their younger sisters are the Marthas.) In fact, Fanny is still sentimental in her attitude to love: she has an ideal 'prince' in mind against whom she measures the Baron and finds him wanting. Imprisoned in her room, Fanny escapes via a ladder, symbolically falls and is muddied, but makes her way to the station and thence to Berlin.

Obviously an innocent in the big city, she is soon picked up by an engaging ne'er-do-well named Axël Dahl who lives on her remaining bit of money.[9] When that runs out, she comes under the protection of a spinster aunt who owns a small boutique. Feeling herself virtually a prisoner in the shop, Fanny struggles again to escape, this time via the theatre.

Although she works hard as a drama student, and does well in her first few appearances, there is no future for Fanny on the stage because actresses have to provide their own costumes. Unable to provide hers, Fanny must refuse the better roles. Advised to find a sugar-daddy as the other girls do, she cannot bring herself to ask her occasional lovers for money, nor does she ever find a Maecenas, let alone the Prince. Although the others see her as snobbish, she sinks in her own eyes, and ironically she is the one arrested as a prostitute.

Only a chance encounter with a former shop-assistant of her aunt's, Bertha Grabow, frees her from the misery and shame of her role. Through Bertha she meets Nepomuk Bolle, a 'master' in Berlin art circles. Among artists, Fanny learns, it is possible for her to move freely as Bolle's mistress. Though Bolle is the target of Greve's satire, and Fanny comes to despise him, still he enables her for the first time to meet with more sophisticated people. One of these, Ehrhard Stein, becomes her lover, but their promised happiness quickly fades because Stein cannot excuse Fanny's past. He composes fairy tales in which he is the prince but she has become muddied during her search for him. Fanny is 'sullied,' and like the tragic hero of *In Search of Myself* Stein longs for 'purity.' He will marry a respectable girl in the interest of propriety and an income.

Humiliated by Stein, Fanny is saved by the first genuinely humane man she meets, a noseless Jew named Stumpf. He appreciates Fanny's honesty, and takes her to Rome with him, where they live as sister and brother. For the first time she is comfortable, even well-to-do, and sees herself as one of the arrogant ladies other poor 'Fanny Esslers' must envy.

On receipt of a small legacy from her father, Fanny leaves Stumpf—who gives her a Pomeranian pup as a parting gift—and begins studying art in Munich. Again the art circle is satirized, and again Fanny is prepared to escape, this time through marriage to Eduard Barrel. Unfortunately her husband, though intelligent and understanding, is weak and impotent. Fanny has always had a strong sexual drive which has never been satisfied—she has never met her Prince. This drive is reawakened, but unsatisfied, by her marriage, with the result that she torments her husband. Moreover, she has never had domestic training, and cannot cope with a servant, so her housekeeping is a disaster. A sojourn at a Pomeranian spa restores her love for her native land but cannot solve her problems. She has fallen in love again, almost unawares, and is quite unprepared when her lover invites her to run away with him.

He is the Prince—'*HE,*' a 'nordic god,' so tall, so blond, so elegant. Moreover, he also comes from Pomerania—more or less. And he is 'rich'; he has his own carriage; and he is the ultimate in sophistication. Not least, he is a super-efficient sexual machine; he makes love to her without emotion, and at last she is fully satisfied.

For a few erotic weeks Fanny and Friedrich Karl Reelen live in splendour in Hamburg, Paris and Coutances before sailing to Portugal for an international reunion with Friedrich Karl's 'friends and relatives.' There Fanny falls ill with malaria and while Friedrich Karl plays the perfect host downstairs, she sinks into a delirium and dies.

Friedrich Karl does seem perfect, except of course that it is hard to imagine any author creating a portrait of himself as perfect without being satiric about it. Reelen is not satirized—apparently his creator is too close to him for that—but neither is he idealized. His perfection as gentleman, rich man, sophisticate, epitome of elegance, is never undermined. But Friedrich Karl's cool rationalism initially intimidates and finally repels Fanny, who in her last conscious thoughts both loves and hates him—perhaps hates more than she loves him.

The reader of Grove recognizes the self-portrait in Reelen, and will assume that Fanny is a portrait of his first wife, Elsa. Elsa was born Elsa Ploetz, daughter of a Master Mason of Swinemünde, Pomerania.[10] She had apparently had some art training in Munich, and probably met her husband there, the self-taught architect August Endell, as Fanny meets Eduard Barrel. In a letter of 1902 FPG refers to Endell as 'my friend.'[11] He borrowed money from Endell, and ran off with his wife to Italy. *Fanny Essler* is Elsa's story, with Felix Paul Greve appearing in Part Five as Friedrich Karl Reelen. We make that identification as readers, but there is also of course Marcus Behmer's corroboration:

> Fanny Essler is really incredible: if Elsa Ti wasn't a whore before, despite her whorish nature, she has surely found her Louis now, who prostitutes her more [blatantly by publishing *Fanny Essler*] than if he let her be mounted at 50 cents a ride.[12]

That FPG was 'more or less' Pomeranian is acceptable if we consider the birth at Radomno and the infancy at Mecklenburg, however brief. As late as 1907 he was writing: 'I spent my early youth on a Pomeranian farm estate.'[13]

When Fanny first sees Reelen in the arty circle at Munich she is not favourably impressed. Granted that everyone defers to him, still Fanny dislikes his 'fishy eyes' and his rather mechanical politeness. At this point she has no interest in love or marriage. She accepts Eduard because he seems pleasant, and knowledgeable about art, and interested in her; he seems to offer security and a quiet domestic happiness. His subsequent function is to explain the causes of her hysteria, causes he finds in a premature adolescent sexuality that had never been satisfied, which experience had taught her would not be satisfied, and which therefore she repressed, becoming virtually frigid for fear her strong emotions would be aroused and again left unsatisfied. As Eduard is impotent, the hysteria grows. Moreoever, Eduard has no friends in Berlin; the two newlyweds are cut off from contact with anyone other than their unmanageable servant-girl and the censorious bourgeois neighbours.

Into this context Reelen reappears as Eduard's only friend and Fanny's only visitor. She lives for his visits, but remains devoted to Eduard, gradually acknowledging to herself her love for Reelen but never supposing that he could care for her because he is so far above the Barrels in wealth and sophistication. What she comes to identify as adorable in him is his blondness, his northernness, his deliberate coolness. He is 'like Balder, just like a young Nordic god' (II, 194).

Union with the god does not produce happiness, however. Sexual fulfillment, yes—for at last Fanny is physically satisfied, and for that she thanks his cool, businesslike lovemaking; there is no attempt at excitation, no sentimental pretence. But the basic conflict between her sentimentality and his formality is irreconcilable. He wants to play Pygmalion, creating her to fill the role of consort to him. Not that he needs her; to the end he insists even to her that he is totally alone, totally self-sufficient. She understands that her function is to be shown off, to complement his style, and she knows she is not equal to it. With heavy-handed tact he explains that of course she has much to learn, that he is not asking her to be other than herself but only that she not make herself too obvious to his acquaintances. She is not much better off than she was with Stein, who could not leave off reminding her that she was 'sullied.' The difference, Reelen carefully explains, is that he does not object to her having been sullied: her past was necessary in order to bring her to the present, to be here with him. But past is past; he does not want to be reminded of it. He lives in and for the present; the past means nothing to him. When Fanny, entering on her fatal illness, asks if she might be allowed to visit Kolberg, her birthplace, he changes the subject: home, family are merely sentimental—they belong to the past. (There are nice touches in this section: Fanny would like to have had her mother with her now rather than the snobbish, socially demanding Reelen—but mother would have to be a little better dressed, a little more sophisticated, to fit into Fanny's new milieu!) What Fanny is really presenting here is the feminist position: no man, not even the godlike Reelen, can give a woman the sympathy and support she needs—that can come only from another woman.

The godlike Reelen—'He!' I don't believe that Greve, any more than Grove, was capable of treating such a robot lightly. He could see what was wrong with this model of rational perfection—Fanny devastates that pompous image—but he could not make fun of it, laugh it away, or even satirize it. Grove could not, over a lifetime, escape from it; it was essential to himself.

A reviewer wrote, in 1906, that the novel represented a 'search for the self.'[14] Grove never forgot the phrase; he borrowed it for his autobiography nearly forty years later. In *In Search of Myself* the struggle is obscured by the need for secrecy, but in all the novels it is taking place. In none of them is the struggle between two attitudes to life more overt than in this first one and in those Grove reworked and published in the last years of his life. The closest equivalent to the sexual conflict of *Fanny Essler* is in *Consider Her Ways* and that between mind and heart is fought out in *The Master of the Mill*.

The famous interview with André Gide, the 'Conversation avec un Allemand quelques années avant la guerre,'[15] undoubtedly took place during or immediately following the composition of *Fanny Essler*. Here Greve plays in his own person the role he assigns to Reelen in *Fanny Essler* and to Edmund in *The Master of the Mill*, and plays it straight. He embraces the present, the world of action; he is the rationalist totally in control of body, of reflex—he has no reflexes, only calculated moves. What Fanny says of Reelen lighting a cigarette as though every gesture were deliberate, Greve says of himself to Gide:

> 'I experience the same need to lie, and the same satisfaction from lying, as another person would in telling the truth ... For instance: when somebody hears a sudden noise beside him, he turns his head.' (He grabs me by the arm.) 'I don't. Or, if I do turn, it is voluntary: I am lying.'[16]

What Greve is describing here is the creation of an identity. 'Lying' equals self-generation through absolute self-control. Perhaps because he had suffered emotionally from childhood in a divided home, from a sense of social inferiority in a class-structured society, from the lack of money and status at the middle-class Gymnasium and then at university (from which he had twice been a drop-out)—he had needed an alternative self, a fantasy life in which he would have the wealth, the elegance, the social graces and sophistication he may have admired and imitated in the Kilians and others. The elegance Gide admired in him was part of the 'lying.' No doubt the lying also served the practical purpose of impressing the people from whom he needed money or credit to maintain the 'elegant' role.

We all live in fantasy worlds part of the time, and for the same reason: in our fantasies we have security, self-assurance; we are perfected, idealized; we transcend our fears, weaknesses, inadequacies. What Mannoni says about Prospero's Island and colonialism is relevant here: that each of us creates an island-colony fantasy-world to meet our psychic needs, one in which we do not have to be responsible to anyone but ourselves.[17] FPG carried this common characteristic a step further, as imposters and confidence-men must do, and perhaps actors, artists and great teachers also, by creating an external self to match the internal one. This required self-control: in order to make himself into another person—even in his early life, let alone later in Canada—he had to be able to control his reflexes, his voice, his emotions. He had to be perfectly in command of himself in order to create the perfect image and persuade others of its perfection. He had also to be capable of driving himself, to work, to produce enough to sustain the image when borrowing and lying were not enough. In his lifetime he never succeeded in that, but it is remarkable how far he did succeed in Canada in living the controlled life. What Fanny says of Reelen in Munich or in the Berlin boarding house—all eyes were on him, all others were overshadowed by him— Arthur Phelps was to say about Grove a lifetime later in Canada. Grove 'towered' over others, Phelps recalled, but only because of his great height but by personality: 'he was a man, *the man*.'[18]

In Friedrich Karl Reelen Fanny finds her Prince, but only to learn that his perfection is not enough because she herself cannot meet that standard. In creating himself perfect, Reelen made it necessary also to create a help perfectly meet for him, and Fanny cannot bear the pressure of that re-creation. (Of course in practice FPG couldn't bear it either. Imagine the abyss of felt inadequacy as the necessary negative pole to generate the energy for Greve/Grove's self-creation! No wonder he suffered frequent breakdowns: 'I have been very sick, for months on end,' he writes André Gide in 1908,[19] and not for the first time.)

Psychologically this externalizing of the fantasy-self both satisfies one kind of pressure and creates others, but still must satisfy a need. Intellectually it has another function, one closer to the Platonism that Makow identifies. Reelen is both his own persona and therefore ideal in the psychological sense, and also an ideal of rationality, the triumph of the intellect over both flesh and emotion. When FPG describes himself to Gide as 'terribly strong' he means the triumph of his will over himself and over others. As Nietzschean Übermensch he could be above society. It is therefore odd that Reelen, the first fictional representation of this self-created rational being, is so bound by social convention. (So, of course, is Edmund Clark.) Fanny herself is largely free of this kind of self-imposed social slavery, and comes to scorn it in him. No doubt he would say that he is not bound by it because he uses it for his purposes: in the circles he moves in, decorum is all. (We may also wonder, as Fanny did, why so exalted a being would bother with Eduard and her, and this is never explained, unless you interpret the one-line coda of the book to mean that, had Fanny lived, the great disillusionment would be her discovery, no doubt Elsa's too, that that paragon of elegance was in some ways a fraud.)

As the rational ideal, Reelen has to be able to manipulate others. In this game, social presence, elegance, self-control are essential, even though in *Fanny Essler* there is no external goal beyond perfecting the role itself. In *The Master of the Mill* Edmund uses the same social savoir-faire to manipulate businessmen and politicians, ultimately to control society. Maud Fanshawe is Fanny Essler forty years later, as Edmund is Reelen, and both are aspects of Greve/Grove himself. It is remarkable how little difference there is in the portraits.

> About 40 people had been invited: ladies and gentlemen, singles and married couples from England, France and Germany . . . It had been a magnificent evening that had sparkled continually with lively conversation floating back and forth and which, in spite of the difficulties presented by the various nationalities, Friedrich Karl had expertly managed to meld during the course of the meal. The brilliance of the women's evening gowns, none of which outshone Fanny's in its special, simple elegance, added further glitter to the evening. After midnight they danced for several hours. . . . (II, 202)

The impersonal, abstract prose, asserting the brilliance of the affair without showing us how it was, will remind Grove's readers of

similar moments in *The Master of the Mill*. But for the names, this
could be the aged Sam Clark's reverie, or Maud's, as well as Fanny's.
In both books the scene distances itself and ceases to make any
impression except impersonality—which is both cases is just the
point. Fanny, on the 'divan,' in her 'boudoir'—this is comparable to
moving up from the first Clark house to the mansion—is crying
despite Friedrich Karl/Edmund's brilliance:

> She had continually marvelled at Friedrich Karl afresh: his
> understanding of how to arrange things so that there were
> always people surrounding her who knew enough German to
> be able to converse with her. And how he had presided at the
> dinner, and how he had danced, and how he had appeared now
> here and now there in order to enliven the entire party: and all
> this without any apparent effort, without even having to think
> about it. (II, 203).

Despite this display, Fanny is unhappy, because his formal
perfection appears to her 'almost as coldness instead of convention.
Only once had he danced with her' (II, 203).

The coldness is common to Edmund and Friedrich Karl. The
difference is that Reelen's is a personal thing, *his* perfection. Thirty-
odd years later Grove's interest is more overtly social: Edmund's
brilliance is directed toward an ideal—the realization of the worker-
less state as the logical end of industrial evolution. To achieve it he
needs monopoly control of finance and therefore of politics in
Canada. Having said this, however, we still can see much of the early
fantasy-persona of Greve/Grove in Edmund. Just as Friedrich Karl
Reelen directly reflects the elegant young Greve who takes advantage
of August Endell's hospitality to run off with his wife—whether or
not Endell's interest in him was homosexual and whether or not
Endell had invited him to be Elsa's lover, both of which Reelen says
of Eduard—so Edmund repeats on a larger scale that same elegant
young Greve, the emotional rationalist of the Gide interview and
Reelen the prototype. Even that 'on a larger scale' needs qualification: Fanny considers that Reelen is the ultimate both of wealth and
of social status—there is none higher. How that can be, in the Europe
of the time, is not made clear. There is mention of a royal palace at
Cintra, but we see Reelen and his guests only at the hotel. Somewhat
similarly, the master-plan Edmund Clark executes vastly over-
simplifies the North American industrial scene. These may reflect a
deficiency in the author's knowledge of high life on both continents,

but in the second case at least the intention must be not only personal and social but epical: to render the conflict between reason and emotion in the Canadian context on a heroic scale.

The female who looks for marital bliss and encounters instead male reserve and rationality is a staple of Grove's Canadian fiction: Clara Vogel, Martha Elliot, Jane Atkinson, Ruth Spalding, Maud Clark. Grove attributes life-giving, outgoing emotion to women, as least potentially, but characteristically his men are tight-lipped and withdrawn, rigidly puritanical, ruthlessly self-made. Self-creation is rational, a matter of work and of will. It requires a degree of self-indulgence that Grove's women do not allow themselves, the luxury of total absorption in the creation of one's own image whether in oneself, in a possession, or in another person. When, in the Prologue to *In Search of Myself,* Grove looks back on those times, the failure he refers to may be the failure to have become the self-created persona he tried to present to Gide. In that conversation characteristically he blamed Kilian for his arrest, blamed him in effect for a lack of faith in the person Greve had been in the process of creating.

Edmund Clark is the self-created man in *The Master of the Mill,* and significantly Grove bequeaths him such wealth that mere money will be no barrier to his success. Sam Clark, his father, is the one without faith in the creation; rather, he is the sensitive one, the man with the supposedly feminine virtues of aesthetic appreciation, sympathy, self-doubt and a tender conscience. Ironically it is his wife who accuses him of this last, and hopes needlessly that Edmund's conscience will be more 'robust.'

Many readers have felt uneasy with Edmund. He is just too precocious, a character from romance or satire rather than from a novel. At that first ball at Clark House he is described as 'brilliant'— at age fourteen! This is self-creation almost from infancy. But the skeptical reader might well ask what Grove is doing here. Why heap so much upon this character so early?

Grove is doing what he did in so many of his books: recording displaced versions of his own struggle to transcend the limitations imposed on him by his birth, his family circumstances, his financial and personal misfortunes, and his own nature. The first version of that fantasy-projection is Reelen who, by simple arithmetic, is seen to have been born in 1871 or 1872. Greve identified with his creation, became his creation later as Grove—who gave 1871 or 1872 as his own birth date. Of course Grove does not claim quite so glorious a past for himself (though not far short of it) as for Reelen, his fantasy-self, or for Edmund, the ultimate projection. If we accept Greve's words to

Gide, then the creation of the totally self-willed man began with
Greve's mother's death. In *The Master of the Mill* Rudyard's death,
Sam's discovery of his guilt, and the birth of the super-precocious
Edmund—all occur in 1898, the actual year of the death of Greve's
mother. All obstacles to Reelen/Greve's success were to be
surmounted by dint of a determined will, unbreakable resolve,
unwearied labour, the meticulous creation of a virtual super-being so
intelligent, so determined, so dedicated, so strong that nothing could
beat him. 'Society will beat you,' Gide warned him. 'No,' was Felix
Paul's reply, 'I'm terribly strong.'[20]

All Grove's major characters are strong, and almost all of them are
beaten. There is always a weakness to betray the intellect, and the
aging FPG saw that weakness in the emotions, in the flesh. Had he
not been seduced by the flesh to run off with Elsa Endell he would not
have been driven to ever more desperate ploys to borrow money to
keep her in Italy and ultimately to wreck thereby the relation with
Kilian that probably was to have been his path to fortune. Kilian
might have supported him until he was established; without Kilian,
imprisoned, forced to repay those thousands of Deutsche Marks,
trying to support Elsa on the pittance left over after mandatory
payments, undertaking unmanageably heavy commitments to publishers, he could not sustain the image of elegance, he could not hold
his head up among his fellow translators, writers, artists, he could
not even maintain the quality of his work, according to his Insel
publisher:

> A lot of his work, and I can say most of it, was excellent and in
> accordance with his great talents. Some of it, on the contrary,
> was not . . . The reason was not a lack of ability . . . but rather
> that he felt forced to take on more work than he could cope with
> adequately, in spite of his tremendous energy, as he needed the
> money to pay off an old debt, as he often told me.[21]

Great talents and tremendous energy betrayed by the flesh: that
would be Niels Lindstedt's story, and Len Sterner's, and that, in part,
the story of the narrator of *In Search of Myself*. Even Friedrich Karl
Reelen is not immune; Fanny observes that, when he comes to ask her
to run away with him, he is 'pale' and 'trembling.' This is the first
and last time she sees any emotion in him, however; thereafter his
concern is only to train her to be equal to him. As he says, 'You have
to have something to hit, or to tame—whichever way you look at it!'
(II, 146-7). He is disturbed only that Fanny takes so long to tame.

In fact, Fanny is never tamed. She is an Eros-type whose capacity for life gives the lie to Reelen's rationalism. Ultimately he cannot reach her and that is the source of his frowning impatience: only death will defeat her. (It is worth noting the change in FPG's attitude to Elsa from *Fanny Essler* to *Settlers of the Marsh*, from Fanny to Clara, though even Clara does have her moments.) In this respect, too, we should note the consistent association of Fanny (and Clara) with animal imagery, from the 'snake-like' movement of the young Fanny's head, her fondness for the Esslers' Newfoundland dog, for the horses at Pariek and even the sorry pair of nags Giovanni buys, to the Pomeranian pup Stumpf buys as his parting gift to her and which remains her last concern. Fanny is sentimental about all animals, and more than once we are told that she cries at the sight of any animal in pain. *She* would not hurt any animal; one of the reasons for being put out of the boarding-house in Berlin is that she cannot discipline the yappy pup.

Significantly his name is Troll, not in her case the kind one must do psychological battle with but a related kind that represents the irrepressible, the untamed in Fanny's nature. A number of times Troll is juxtaposed in the novel with Reelen's cold rationalism. Of course, Fanny herself can be pretty cool, but always on the side of the emotional life—or mere survival. In parallel incidents, Fanny tries to trick Bolle into paying for a few clothes for her, after he demonstrates his stinginess, and tests Reelen to see if he has enough warmth to be entrusted with Troll. In both cases, the trick is to lead the man to express his real self without letting him see what the real subject is, and in both cases he fails the test.

In the second case, Reelen fails for us, too, because the values he fails to affirm are associated with home, memory, mother, and animal affection, all of which the reader is bound to support. Dying of malaria, Fanny, whose recollection of fever as a kind of release into pleasant irresponsibility is mentioned early in the novel, recalls her mother and childhood, and wants to visit Kolberg, as noted above. Reelen is indifferent, and returns to his guests downstairs. Thus dismissed, Fanny can conclude that he is unfeeling. She almost courts her death, and in her delirium asks the loaded question, 'Who is Friedrich Karl?' and last of all says 'Troll . . . Giovanni,' bequeathing the dog to the lively Italian servant who is fond of animals as she is, not to hit or to tame, but to love.

The animal imagery reinforces Fanny's sentiment and sympathy; it contrasts with the artificiality of the worlds of art and convention, and it represents the untamed, even the cruel and indifferent in the natural world. In this respect the movement of the book is from the placid and obedient but affectionate dog Barry in the first scene to the sight of the seagulls on the voyage to Cintra near the end. On board ship Fanny is blind to the landmarks Reelen points out: he 'showed her what was to be shown'—the prose sufficiently expresses the mechanical tone of it—but unlike him, Fanny does see, in fascinating detail, the gulls:

> thick-set animals tapering off at the ends, not very elegant in form but agile as birds of prey, with red, merciless eyes and a cruel beak . . . but with almost childlike feet, dove-like, tight against the body when in flight . . . a small head perched on a squat neck that you hardly ever saw because it was retracted, lurking. Broad and strong shoulders: this was how Fanny saw them: each animal self-sufficient, roving, catching prey . . . every one for itself! Their calls not calls of communication . . . only shrill proclamations of triumph or greed. . . . How lucky they are, Fanny thought. What if I were like them? . . . She shuddered: she couldn't fly alone; she couldn't understand these animals! They were sinister in her eyes. . . . 'Just look,' she shouted, 'their eyes are completely red. . . . And they scream so beautifully . . . even more beautifully than peacocks . . . in comparison they almost seem to be lamenting. . . . And they fly all alone across the ocean and they don't get frightened! And it's true, isn't it, that there are seagulls that prey on other gulls? How awful!'
> Friedrich laughed. '*They* can live alone,' he said, '. . . just as I can.' Fanny looked at him. Why am I here then, she thought. . . . (II, 219)

Shortly after Friedrich Karl and Fanny elope, Eduard commits suicide. Reelen tells Fanny he had read it in the Berlin paper: she is astonished that he seems unmoved by it, though Eduard had been his friend. If Eduard could not live it is better for him to die, Reelen observes philosophically. We have no reason to suppose that Reelen will be any more moved by Fanny's death. (He must already have been embarrassed for his hotel guests, as they all fled at the word 'malaria.' Had she been conscious, Fanny might have been amused at having sent them all packing.) It is of the essence of Reelen's role that he must not admit emotion, nor concern himself with the past. It is not that he denies animal vitality—he chose Fanny, as he keeps reminding her—but that he is committed to its control. Fanny never denies his superiority to her, and to everyone else; but her past, and her love for animals, she defends against him. She loses, in the sense that she dies while still young, but her final challenging question asks whether Reelen retains a personality: 'Who is Friedrich Karl?' Is he the great lover, the 'prince'? Did Fanny ever meet her prince? Each of her would-be lovers failed her in some way. According to the coda, Reelen would have failed her worst of all. But would the disappointment be to find that he was not human, or that he was?

The conflict between reason and emotion is essential to Grove's art. In his German fiction it is fought out in feminist terms. When he begins again with *Over Prairie Trails* it is the same conflict, but this time the battle is with the world of nature and the tone is positive. The narrator is not trying to defeat nature; he is revelling in demonstrating the power of reason to withstand everything nature throws at it. Here the humane element is in the waiting wife and daughter, justification for the struggle, and its reward. *The Turn of the Year* is not only a weaker book, it is also darker in tone. The dramatic element is less apparent, the domestic element, the whole human element, is conventionalized, and the natural element is not battled but adjusted to or sombrely observed. The human is absorbed into the natural cycle.

This is still true when Grove returns to the novel form with *Settlers of the Marsh,* but the conflict between reason and the emotions is now overt. There is no weakness in Niels' program as a settler, no weakness in the performance except his humanity. That is not amenable to reason, and the very intensity of the struggle to subdue it guarantees the emotional blow-up. It's a nice question which self is ritually murdered: the rational by the irrational, or vice versa. In Blodgett's view, Clara is the female whose sacrifice is necessary to Niels' psychological rebirth. Her role, though much darker, is close to Fanny Essler's. A prostitute apparently saved by marriage to the ideal male who turns out to be less than ideal, she will be seen by the reader as another Elsa-figure. That is worth remembering when we read Clara's spirited defense of her conduct against Niels. Like Fanny, she has reason on her side sometimes, and the male is shown to be merely emotional when she exposes him.

It seems to me that the formal argument—that the Canadian novels represent a move to 'frustrated comedy,' as Blodgett puts it[22]— is interesting and has a point but should not be pursued too far. We can agree that when Greve began writing he was divided between the psychological and the naturalistic, the latter accounting for the repetitions, the cycles. In the Canadian fictions Grove assimilates the

psychological to the cyclical. The 'unresolved repetition' Blodgett
identifies is essential to the vision and is the form.

The point about Grove—and most modern writers—is that
neither comedy nor tragedy is particularly relevant except in a very
general way. The weakness in Blodgett's argument is that he uses
'comedy' and 'tragedy' as formal terms and forgets that, in the terms
he adopts from Northrop Frye, 'irony' is equally a form. Grove's
emphasis in the major works is on the cycle, the eternal round, which
in *The Master of the Mill* is seen in cosmic terms that render Sam's
conscience and Edmund's fascist idealism equally futile. But the kind
of endless cycle Maud Dolittle envisions, with or without the feeble
hope based on collectivity, is neither comic nor tragic but ironic. For
every Edmund there may be tragedy, but the perpetual cycle—
Professor Blodgett's 'unresolved repetition' on the grand scale—is
what in formal terms Frye calls ironic bondage. That is, in archetypal
terms, the blocking force remains blocking, the hero never breaks
through to get the girl and the fortune—or even the mill, in a sense—
or to re-integrate society around the happy couple.

Fanny Essler in this sense is ironic. Fanny has established a
pattern, a cycle—her metabolism is carefully linked to the seasons—
whereby she recovers from a winter of near-hibernation, having
stayed in bed day after day and lived on coffee and cigarettes, meets a
new lover or new situation, and then after a summer interval finds
herself alone and disillusioned again. This cycle is broken by her
death—she, like Edmund, has the luck to die before her last illusion
fails her. *Fanny Essler* is not a tragedy, nor is *The Master of the Mill;*
it is not the deep damnation, but the absurdity, of Edmund's taking
off and the meaninglessness of Fanny's that we respond to.

R.D. MacDonald's excellent analysis of *The Master of the Mill*
stresses the nihilism in this novel, and even more in *Consider Her
Ways,* whose action he sees as another use of the motif of the 'absurd
quest.'[23] I differ from this reading in that I would distinguish
between the pessimism in the judgment of man and the positive
representation of the heroic quest itself. This corresponds to the
positive elements in Fanny's personality, to the strength of intellect
and integrity in *The Master of the Mill,* and to the heroic life of the
artist in *In Search of Myself.* This is the ultimate conflict in Grove,
and what he means by tragedy: the conflict between the heroic life
that gives value to human action, and the meaninglessness of cosmic
existence which denies it. Formally this may account for the
inconclusive conclusions and the reworking of the fictions,
published and unpublished: art and the artist give form and meaning

to existence, and existence reasserts its formlessness and meaninglessness to deny them. Given the human dilemma as Grove sees it, this
conflict between order and energy is the reality.

[1]Transl. by Christine Helmers, A.W. Riley and D.O. Spettigue. Ed. and
Introd. bv A.W. Rilev and D.O. Spettigue. 2 vols. (Ottawa: Oberon, 1984),
I, 5. (First publ. Berlin: Axel Juncker, 1905.) Page references to the Oberon
edition in parentheses.

[2]E.D. Blodgett, *Configuration: Essays on the Canadian Literatures*
(Toronto: ECW Press, 1982), pp. 112-153.

[3]Walter Pache, 'Der Fall Grove—Vorleben und Nachleben des Schriftstellers
Felix Paul Greve.' In Harmut Froeschle, ed., *Deutschkanadisches Jahrbuch*,
5 (Toronto: Historical Society of Mecklenburg Upper Canada Inc., 1979),
121-136. See also his 'Frederick Philip Grove's Loneliness—Comparative
Perspectives,' *Annals* 4: CAUTG Publications No. 9 (1983), 185-195, reprinted in this volume.

[4]Henry Makow, 'Grove's Treatment of Sex: Platonic Love in *The Yoke of
Life*,' *Dalhousie Review* 50, No. 3 (Autumn 1978), 528-540.

[5]Henry Makow, 'An Edition of Selected Unpublished Essays and Lectures by
F.P. Grove Bearing on his Theory of Art,' diss., Univ. of Toronto, 1982.

[6]Henry Makow, 'Grove's "The Canyon," ' *Canadian Literature*, 82 (Autumn
1979), 141-148.

[7]*Settlers of the Marsh* (Toronto: McClelland and Stewart, 1966), p. 152.

[8]Anthony W. Riley, 'The German Novels of Frederick Philip Grove.' *Inscape*
11, No. 1, Symposium Issue (Spring 1974), 62.

[9]Professor Blodgett's argument for the influence of Villier's Axël as a source
may well be sound, but the supporting argument that Axël would be an
unfamiliar name seems odd, when the book was published by Axël Juncker.

[10]Desmond Pacey, ed. *The Letters of Frederick Philip Grove* (Toronto and
Buffalo: Univ. of Toronto Press, 1976), p. 552.

[11]*Letters*, p. 523.

¹²Marcus Behmer to Ernst Hardt (19 Feb. 1907). *Briefe an Ernst Hardt. Ein Auswahl aus den Jahren 1898-1947*, ed. Jochen Meyer (Marbach: Literaturarchiv, 1975), p. 53.

¹³*Letters*, p. 540.

¹⁴Quoted in Spettigue, *FPG: The European Years* (Ottawa: Oberon, 1973), p. 139.

¹⁵André Gide, 'Conversation avec un Allemand Quelques années avant la guerre,' *Oeuvres complets*, ed. L. Martin Chauffer (Paris: Nouvelle revue française, 1935), pp. 133-143.

¹⁶Quoted in Spettigue, pp. 122-123.

¹⁷O. Mannoni, *Prospero and Caliban: The Psychology of Colonization*. 2nd ed. (New York: Praeger, 1964), p. 108.

¹⁸The Search for Frederick Philip Grove,' CBC (Radio) Symposium (3 Dec. 1962); quoted in Spettigue, *Frederick Philip Grove* (Toronto: Copp Clark, 1969), p. 51.

¹⁹*Letters*, p. 548.

²⁰Quoted in Spettigue, *FPG: The European Years*, p. 124.

²¹*Letters*, p. 551.

²²*Configuration*, p. 147.

²³R.D. MacDonald, 'The Power of F.P. Grove's *The Master of the Mill*,' *Mosaic* 7 (Winter 1974), 91.

II
The Figure of the Immigrant

'Rebels All: Of the Interpretation of Individual Life' is the first of three 'Interpretation of Life' essays: in the second, Grove examines interpretations of history; in the third, interpretations of science. He begins the series, however, with an essay in personal interpretation and focuses 'Rebels All' on the events of his own life. This previously unpublished essay is thus one of the few instances, and perhaps the earliest, in which Greve, now Grove, writes about the events of his German past. He apparently never offered 'Rebels All' for publication. The only known copy is an undated and untitled manuscript in the possession of the novelist's son, A.L. Grove, who graciously consented to the publication of the essay in this volume. On the basis of internal references, Henry Makow dates the 'Interpretation of Life' essays 'from about 1919' and argues in his doctoral dissertation, 'An Edition of Selected Unpublished Essays and Lectures by Frederick Philip Grove on His Theory of Art,'[1] that 'Rebels All' is 'among Grove's earliest Canadian work.' The evidence he offers, however, is conjectural, and in the absence of more conclusive evidence, the essay cannot be dated with certainty.

Frederick Philip Grove

Rebels All: Of the Interpretation of Individual Life

I have lived through half a century and look back upon my life. Has it been anything extraordinary? Hardly. And yet, in thought as well as in actual range it has probably encompassed more than the lives of most men do.

I was born, so it seems, with a strange incapacity for action, or—as most successful men would put it—for success. A dim consciousness of this fact made me discard all consideration of other careers beyond that of the scholar. I shall never forget what a revered teacher said to me when, as a very young man, I consulted him as to my choice in an early dilemma. It seemed to me at the time that the supreme aim of human endeavour must be knowledge; and I was divided between two desires: on the one hand I wished to know the world as it is at the present; on the other I wished to know how it had come to be what it is. A strange, nearly uncanny facility at mastering languages seemed to point the way for me. My dilemma, therefore, was whether to choose the moderns or the classics for my especial study. 'It does not matter,' he said, 'you are sure to leave your mark on whatever you choose. Genius is bound to win.' I flushed with gratification. I had always adored the man: to this very day his life seems to me the embodiment of the highest there is in mankind; his estimation of my gifts and powers still whispers with subtle flattery. But have I justified it?

In later life, too, it was my fate to be surrounded by men and women who expected tremendous things of me.

For a while these men and women were younger than myself. They constituted me their spiritual or intellectual guide. They looked up to me as I had looked up to that great teacher of mine; for a while I swayed their destinies. As time went on, however, I became an episode in their lives: they lived beyond me it seemed. I suppose *they* were surprised to see how little I accomplished when they found success so easy; *I* was surprised that they contented themselves with the kind of success that came their way. At about the same time when they left me 'behind' a group of people older than myself began to gather about me: to them I was not the past but the future. To them it seemed that I was a 'coming man.' Some of them were men of power and influence, and they tried to shape my career by leading offers of position and office to me. They were astonished when I passed such offers by, or when, if I accepted one, I shortly abandoned the career this opened. They began to shake their heads in speaking of me: something must, so they concluded, be lacking in this man. There is no limit to what he, with his mental and educational equipment, might do. But he has no ambition.

Thus as last I became a hermit: intellectually, spiritually, actually. Still I meet from time to time and man or a woman who looks beyond my mask and who divines behind the exterior of the rustic a wider outlook, a deeper insight, a hidden power. How is it, these rarer people think—for their thought is quite transparent to me—that this man with his range of knowledge, with his experience of life, with his magnetism and power of speech became what he is. There must have been something in his life, so they conclude, some catastrophe which broke his career, which crippled his development.

I am an utterly lonely man.

My deepest thought is nobody's but my own; my dream is a dream and nothing else. Occasionally I meet one of the younger men who once associated with me; occasionally, too, one of the older men. When they see me they are astonished: 'Is that man still alive?' they think and wonder what they may once have seen in me. I read their thought in their smile and in their air of superiority. Am I so old? I ask myself. Have I really outlived my generation? Am I to those who lived a little this side or that side of my own age something like a 'revenant'?

Socially, the range of my life has been extensive. I have, in my youth, associated with royalty. I was known in the capitals of Europe. Later, I became the companion, and, at times, the oracle of the elite of its men of letters. Poets, dramatists, writers of fictions and of Utopias were not below taking ideas of mine and shaping them into the masterpieces of the age. Then I disappeared and began a new life in the New World. I have been a traveller there, a factory hand, a tramp. I have lived, on the one hand, in the reckless profusion of gilded youth, on the other, in utter poverty, lacking for weeks and months and years the wherewithall adequately to appease my hunger.

I have written books and published a few—under names assumed for the purpose—and I have lived to disown their authorship. Nobody ever has traced, nobody ever will trace them to me. I deemed at the time, of course, that they expressed my thought, but when a few years later, I read them again, I found that they did not, and even I myself have by this time forgotten even their titles. Strange are the ways of the human mind.

As for an actual career, I started out, as I have said, to be a scholar. There was a time when I read and spoke nine or ten languages. Then a disgust took hold of me, and I 'denied' whatever I had been. I became a writer, not without success. I became an agitator and saw the insides of prisons. In that I persisted longer than in anything else, because the mere fact that the authorities thought it worth their while to fight and to oppose me seemed to proclaim the value of my work. But I tired of it nevertheless. I took up farming and dropped it; factory work—and I became a foreman; tramping—and I made money at it; teaching—and a career which opened did not allure me.

Now I look back on my life as a man who has climbed a mountain looks back on the road which he followed. What I see, is not a straight path from the depths to the heights. It is a succession of devious trails, of a thousand starts soon abandoned, of manifold departures and retracings of steps. And yet I stand high—in my own estimation— surveying life from a point of vantage.

I have been a cast-away on the ocean of life.

But still I live: that is the astonishing fact about it. I live and have my dreams and opinions; desires and convictions, dissatisfactions and satisfactions. Indeed, it sometimes seems to me that I am the typical man of a period of transition. My convictions and opinions have embraced the whole range of convictions and opinions which have been prevalent in my time. I have often anticipated them. A few, perhaps, are original in an objective sense; but if they are, I do not know it. I have lived at random. I have read at random. Of my life I have forgotten more than I remember; in my reading I have, very likely, adopted many ideas; but where I found them, I cannot tell. I have many opinions for which I do not try even to account; the same as I cannot account for the general trend of my thought. A traveller going along the shore of the ocean picks up some shells to-day, and to-morrow, and the day after. Unless he labels them in a collection, he will soon forget just where he picked them up and why. Life has no system, and I am living.

Modern life I have come to detest. Modern life—that is to say life in an industrial community organised on competitive lines—treats man as a negligible quantity. Strange to say, its most ardent defenders base their defence on the fact that men are not born equal. But does not modern life make the impossible attempt to level all inequalities except one—and that one inequality not one of substance but of degree? No matter where I went in my life I found, superimposed upon an underlying real life, superimposed upon it, a surface life in which all men were equal by their desire for success, and success meant money. The inequalities underneath disappeared: the super-imposed surface became a hollow reality. The inequality of men which modern society recognises is not an inequality in what men are but in what they have. The few who dare to be instead of to have stand apart, aside, aloof. Life has flowed past them, unheeded. They are onlookers, like myself.

So; at last, I have retired from my many attempts at mingling with life and become a hermit. From the lives of those other onlookers whom I have met my own life was distinguished chiefly by this one fact that again and again I have taken hold: again and again I have tried to *live* modern life instead of merely looking at it and judging it. Every time I did so—in the verdict of those who witnessed my attempts—I have failed, failed in spite of the most promising beginnings. And yet I did not consider my tergiversations as failures myself. When success was difficult of attainment, I persevered. But when it was easy, I turned my back. To those who knew me, I was an enigma. To myself all my actions were perfectly clear. What was it that underlay them?

What is it that underlies the mediaeval myth of Dr. Faustus? Is it not the desire to know? Life is a mystery; all Religion is an acknowledgement of that fact. For all dogmatic Religion is an attempt to explain. But Religion demands belief and resignation; in fact, belief and resignation of knowledge of one and same: who believes is convinced that he does not and maybe cannot *know*. The justification through faith is a proclamation of defeat. Mystics are like the flagellants: they glorify spiritual suffering. But the magicians were in revolt against it. Real magicians, of course, there never were. But the longing for certainty, for real knowledge in place of belief, is attested to by the very creation of such products of the popular imagination as those insurgents. Magic tried to break through the barrier and to establish certainty by a short-cut. It is significant that Dr. Faustus according to the story first tried the study of all human 'knowledge.' Jurisprudence, Medicine, Philosophy and Theology, the four 'faculties' of mediaeval universities, he had studied 'from the ground up' and had found them wanting. So at last he sold his soul to the devil and found himself deceived again. Even the devil is life, and life cannot see itself. In this it is no less significant that the devil, misunderstanding Faust's ardent longing, interprets his desire to know as the desire to know the *forms* of life; and so he leads him through its various stages, its lowest depths and its highest heights; and Faust finds the same thing everywhere.

It was largely thus with myself. I found the same thing everywhere. The moving force in my peregrinations was a great curiosity, an insatiable desire to see the secret springs that make men go through the astonishing evolutions and gyrations of their lives. I had an inborn intuition of the great mystery; I believe, I was born a sceptic; but my scepticism was such that I doubted even *it*. Again and again I thought that perhaps merely some data were missing that would if hunted down change my whole view; and whenever I thought so, I at once proceeded to acquire these data. —By that, of course, I do not mean to say that I consciously guided my life. Whoever thinks he does, is self-deluded; for even desires which actually do fashion and shape our lives are not of our making or choice.

All interpretations of popular or personal movements are *ex post facto* and liable to the objection of *post hoc ergo propter hoc*. We must learn to discount the fallacy of cause and effect. Phenomena are links in chains of phenomena, and single strands of dependent phenomena cannot be unravelled. All interpretations are fallacies in themselves; but the most astonishing conclusion at which I ever arrived—astonishing to me at least—was this: that the fact of an argument's being fallacious is not necessarily an argument against that argument. The Ptolemaic system of the world was 'true' as long as no facts were known to contradict it. The Copernican or Newtonian system, on the other hand, is not necessarily true in an absolute sense either—as popular misconception assumes it to be—

because it works to-day. *We cannot know*. The moment facts are discovered—as no doubt they will be discovered—which contradict it—or, as popular misconception says, 'do not obey it'—it will become error though now it is truth. Nobody who is familiar with the intellectual history of the past can for a moment doubt that all our vaunted Scientific 'truth' is just error. Are we a chosen people living in a chosen age? Presumption of presumptions! Is history true? History is an interpretation and nothing else. But interpretations are useful nevertheless. All our lives are based on interpretations. We see a certain kind of light in our bedrooms at morning and we get up, presuming that another day has come. We might verify the fact before acting upon it, but we don't. The slender indication is sufficient for us to call forth an interpretation. We act on faith. A man who lives in America does not really know that there is such a thing in the world as Europe. In fact, it would be quite possible to find arguments to disprove the assumption. But he writes a letter to someone presumed to be living across the Atlantic and, after a while, receives an answer. And he interprets this fact by assuming that the letter he wrote actually did travel across the ocean and that his correspondent wrote the answer. Does it matter whether this interpretation is true or not? A child writes a note to Santa Claus asking for a certain toy. He receives it at Christmas. He interprets the fact by assuming that Santa Claus actually did receive his note and acted upon it. Does it matter whether this interpretation is true or not? I venture to say that three-fourths even of the interpretations of the common daily life of man are of just that nature; and probably ninety-nine hundredths of the popular interpretations of technical or scientific facts necessarily are.

If, then, I make bold to explain failure in the sense of the modern world as success in a life of higher significances, I am well aware that I am interpreting things the real connections of which escape my judgment. But that cannot deter me from putting my own interpretation on my own life and acquiescing in it. An interpretation is always a leave-taking. In studying the facts of our own lives or the facts of history who will say that he has really gone far enough to call a halt. But unless he does call a halt, judgment remains suspended. No matter at what point we arrive at a judgment, the facts upon which it is based are necessarily incomplete; yes, every single fact is necessarily incompletely seen; if for no other reason than that facts are at least linked up with the phenomena of life and change; and these phenomena are beyond human comprehension. Nor does it matter. For it is not the 'truth' that we arrive at so much which matters as it is that we strive for truth. What is the goal to us so long as we keep on and love the road? But with regard to the facts of our lives we *must* arrive at a judgment in order to free ourselves from the slavery which they impose upon us. Else we should live in death or die in life. The dead must bury the dead, and the living must face the now. So we interpret. Our lives are an everlasting saying of fare-well.

My mother died and her death left a wound. It was year and years before it ceased smarting. She was dead, but still she lived on. She lived on in a double sense: in myself who was part of her, born of her, flesh of her flesh and spirit of her spirit: but also as opposed to myself, as a foreign being, divided from me and as one who had met me in the battles of life and inflicted wounds which would not heal. She lived on in my sleepless nights as a 'revenant'; she lived on in my restless days as a critic of all I did or thought of doing but did not—on account of her. She lived on at all times as a judge passing sentence on my 'useless' life. My reaction to her was a mixture of love and hate, of accusation and glorification, of self-approbation and remorse. One day I started on the task of interpretation: I arrived at judgments: I put away that part of myself which was she, still consciously acknowledged her power and obeyed her: I freed myself from the bond of the past. And since this star no longer deflected my path—since I swung along in what I fondly imagined to be my own orbit, I could exult in the feeling of freedom which comes when you willingly submit to serfdom.

Astronomy calculates the orbit of a star and can henceforth predict its appearance or non-appearance in our skies with reasonable certainty: it has put an interpretation on a phenomenon. Is that interpretation truth? A planet revolves about the sun; but the sun himself perhaps revolves about some other star. And at any rate his motion is the resultant of many 'forces'—some of them known and others unknown to man. In fact, there is not the slightest particle of stardust floating anywhere—not in the remotest stretches of the universe—which does not influence the motion of even the largest body. And the orbit of the planet is doubly influenced: because it is part of the solar system and also because it is an individual star. Yes, for that matter, it is a thousandfold influenced; for every other body in the universe which influences it is itself influenced by that self-same particle of stardust that we have picked out for momentary consideration. And yet astronomy has the presumption to calculate the orbits of the stars. It arrives at certain limited facts and on them bases its calculations. But who will say where to stop in selection of facts? Does astronomy arrive at truth? Far from it. But if it did set out to gather *all* the facts it would arrive nowhere. Somewhere it draws the line and proceeds to its verdict. It calculates the orbit, as we say, with sufficient accuracy. It arrives at an approximation which will do for human life. But what is sufficient accuracy? Simply that which is not contradicted by the facts as discerned with our limited means of observation. Is it truth? What is truth? Truth is that which at any given stage of knowledge we cannot successfully contradict.

But we live, and in living we feel ourselves free. Our lives, like the orbits of stars, are the resultants of maybe finite, maybe infinite numbers of 'forces'—we cannot tell, for finitude and infinity are alike beyond human conception; they form part of that awful mystery surrounding us. What can be freer than our thought? And yet our thought is not undetermined. But it is only when two lines of thought are contending within us that we become conscious of a lack of freedom. 'Necessity,' as we call it, obtrudes on our consciousness only through revolt. And revolt ends only in judgment. Judgment, or interpretation, if we prefer to call it that, is a process of integration. We put a thing behind ourselves, below ourselves, we put it away, we bury it in the past; but we stand on it, nevertheless. It hold us in the place which we occupy although we do not notice it any longer. It, being a necessary condition of our being, has become part of ourselves. It has influenced our *orbit;* and since it *has* influenced it, our orbit can never again become what it would have been had that influence never been potent. But in our consciousness we ignore it henceforth and consider, instead of the influence itself, our judgment of it which is necessarily erroneous since it did not and could not consider all the facts. It is this which gives us the feeling of freedom which is merely the outcome of our interpretations or judgments.

The world of facts is unknown to us. The world of our interpretations is known. Even in our own lives, in looking back, we do not see the facts, but merely our interpretations of those facts arrived at *ex post facto*. But every fact that followed a given fact influenced us in our interpretation of it. Who has not gone through the experience that the interpretation of an episode changed as life proceeded? But what we call our past does not so much consist of facts as our interpretations of them: what lives on in us of any one fact is our judgment of that fact, the same as what lives on in our histories is not a mere record of fact but an interpretation of facts. Our past, as we see it, no matter whether it be the past of an individual or of a nation or a race, does not consist in facts at all but in such fictions as have become necessary through that which followed. Yet we call it 'the past' as if it ever existed the way we see it. Thus we arrive at the paradox that, as the past influences the future, so also does the future influence the past.

This is important in history, no doubt; but it is most important in autobiography. For the man who decides to live a conscious life—not that kind of life which modern masses lead and which is a continual search for sensations and a continual flight from insight and from judgment and interpretation—it is all-important that he arrive at such a view of his own past as does not involve a condemnation of self. Strange as it may seem, a condemnation of self, though rare, is possible. Yet, being so rare, we consider it morbid. In fact, we may take it as a rule that, with very few exceptions—which, being no true exceptions, on closer inspection confirm the rule—a man's interpretation of his own life will be such as to justify, not his past, but his present. Such a view may involve a condemnation of an historical past, illogical as it is.

My own life has been a series of what others call 'failures.' But since each failure has helped to make what I call 'me' I cannot view it in the way others do. But if I could give a complete record of the facts of my life, seen in the light of my interpretation, I should lead others to view my life as I do, and so they would come to see facts as they were not.

In order to make my meaning quite clear, I will fasten my view on some particular episode.

I was swimming—as a very young man—along my orbit—which was, as I said, the resultant of a number of forces to all intents and purposes infinite, though probably to a vaster intelligence than that of man it might have been finite—when I men another young man whose orbit approached mine for a while and then ran close and parallel to it. For a number of years no influence in his life was greater than mine, and—though I was the more active one of us two—no influence on my life was greater than his. For a number of years we lived close together, in body as well as in spirit. Then separation ensued. But still there was nothing to show that this separation in space might ever involve a separation in spirit. We met again, in space; and at once the separation in spirit became apparent. Both of us suffered; and, not being the kind that would simply drift along till we were quite strangers, we tried to bridge the gulf and thereby widened it. What might have been a simple ceasing of former relations became a catastrophal [*sic*] break. I do not see the necessity today—he might have yielded. Probably he does not see its necessity, either, and thinks I might have yielded. But there were facts, indisputable facts, which intervened and which were accessible to the judgment of the world in which we lived. I was made aware that a large proportion of our common friends condemned me without reserve; but I also found that as large a proportion of them condemned him unreservedly. I had to argue the case with the former group, and I gave it up in disgust: things that to me—and, as I found later, to many others—seemed perfectly obvious were flatly denied by them. If now we were both to give a record of what occurred, we might speak of the same facts, but no impartial reader of such records would recognize them as the same. For me, the facts as they were, do not exist any longer; nor do they for him: our interpretations alone exist. Our orbits have swung apart. Our later lives have changed our earlier lives.[3]

I have suffered; but like scar tissue my interpretations have overgrown the wound; and for the functions of my life the scar tissue is as useful as living tissue might be. In fact, spiritually speaking, our being consists of scar tissue.

I have become a hermit, I said. But we are all hermits, *if we live*. It is the curse of modern life—but in this sense the life of all ages has been 'modern'—that most people merely think they live: they search with their hands for a thousand things devised to keep them from living a life of their own. It is the curse of what we call 'individualism' that individual life becomes next to impossible; for individualism, as understood to-day, is strife; and in war all other desires, all other interests, are sunk in the will to win.[4]

This will to win, to excel, to own more than my neighbour, I have never had. Others condemn me on that account. They are even intolerant about it and have driven me into the voluntary exile of my hermitage. They have even made me unhappy through a considerable part of my life.

Compared with their 'achievements'—which were largely social and economic—my own have been modest to such a degree as to appear as failures. That has given me a feeling of insufficiency, or worthlessness which has weighed me down. But they and I started out in life with high dreams: both they and I began with the purpose of achievement. This purpose, as society is constituted today, necessarily works at random, at least for a time. But they found the niche into which they fitted or they fitted themselves into a niche which they found. Mostly it was the latter. I have never yet found the one into which I fitted; and though I found many into which I might have fitted myself, I never did so. A human being that has found his niche is considered grown-up. I still am essentially a child.

As I said, the knowledge of this made me suffer. Why should I be homeless when so many others struck root and cast anchor? Thus even the casual associates of various periods became a potent influence for me. I revolted against the feeling of inferiority. I accepted *their* view of my life and, taking their verdict as just and true, I came to condemn myself. I was like the prisoner in jail who repents: and I cannot help it, in my present view he commits the unpardonable sin: just as a wolf would do were he to envy the dog his slaving existence. The wolf was never meant to be a dog. It is his nature to rob and to fight and to fall in battle.

I felt like a child in the company of grown-ups. And in revolting I became conscious of bonds. Freedom is compliance with fetters. The dog is free as a slave; for slavery is his nature, and he not only endures it without revolt, he seeks it as the natural condition of his life. But revolt is the one thing unbearable: it warps all our being: it twists sentiment into resentment: and resentment is the sign of the unwilling slave. Make that your rule: if you resent, strike out: for there is no greater danger-signal than resentment. The man who harbours resentment is like an undercooled liquid which congeals at the slightest tremor: or like an overcharged boiler, full of internal stresses, for which there is vent in explosion only. But resentment never arises in a free-man unless he bears bondage of some kind.

My resentment arose from my bondage to the system of valuation imposed by others. So, being essentially a free-man, I struck out and annihilated that system by a revaluation. Childhood—in the sense which I gave it just now—is immaturity in the concerns of life; but childhood also consists in the capacity for growth. I weighed the 'others' and found that I measured up to them. They were not bigger, stronger, wiser than I; I had tried myself at their own game and seen that what they did, I, too, could do. If I did not care to go on doing what they did, perhaps it was because I felt that I could do more, or something which demanded a higher qualification. What that was I could not tell. But did that matter?

While 'they' lived past me, as it appeared to them, I persuaded myself that I had lived past them. What was their goal, was merely an experiment for me: a step aside which was soon retraced. And though a man who starts in goodly company, will be alone when left behind, he will be alone as well when he outmarches his comrades who stop by the way side. When 'they' look for me, they look back; when I look for them, I, too, look back. They fancy they see me far in the rear; I fancy I see them where I was long, long ago. Who is right? Am I? Are they? Who is there to tell? Quite likely neither!

And does it matter?

But then—does anything matter? I think so, yes. But, in explaining how and why, I must beg you to remember that what I offer is not living flesh but scar tissue only: it is not fact but merely a viewpoint: it is not truth but merely an interpretation. It is the subtle casuistry of the ego which will not submit to the consciousness of defeat.

I came to set myself up as the standard: the others had excelled in material things and had gained success: I had—voluntarily, so I persuaded myself—given up this success and striven after criticism. I weighed the others again and found them wanting. They had not reached my height of outlook, my sagacity in scrutiny, my sharp-sightedness in scathing contempt.

When man was a hunter, illness or bodily weakness was a disgrace. So long as those who had to be left at home with the women and children when the males went out for the hunt, had nothing to do but to share the work of the women and children, they valued themselves as such only, just as others valued them. But when the first among them found a way to carve delicate ornamental traceries on the blade of a bone knife, he had discovered a new justification for himself: he became an artist. From the point of view of the tribesmen his distinguishing trait was an incapacity: but from his own point of view it was a capacity: who was right? Who can even now say whether in the eternal scheme of things the tribesman or the primeval artist counted for more? There were always fewer of the artists than of the others. That alone tended to raise them in man's estimation. But the fact remains that, if in retrospection they rank higher than the rest, it is because they succeeded in instilling others with their own valuation of themselves which perhaps was not even sincere at first and merely a measure of defense; and at the very least such proceeding is not according to the strict canons of justice. Yet they have made civilization.

To this very day, however, all those who devote their energies to things other than the mere making of a living suffer under the tribal contempt of the masses. They profit by the testimony of the centuries which have made their work more enduring than that of the rest. But whoever starts out on a career of his own, has first to contend and to suffer. It is only when he has obtained a hearing or a following that he appears to be justified in the eyes of others. Till he reaches that point, he has only one thing to uphold him: his own 'avocation.' But this avocation is, first of all, a negative quality. Long, long before it is an achievement, yes, before it is a positive desire or a positive aim even, it is a negative aversion or inability. And many, many never win through to the positive desire. They simply suffer from the incapacity to live up to the demands of a humdrum existence which seems exacting and yet offers no thrill. It is these that furnish life with its victims, its derelicts, its thousand failures.

Yet, speak to one of them and see whether he acknowledges that he is nothing but a cast-away, a man lost in the maze of life. Wherever he is, there, for him, still is the centre of the universe, and he will cast about for an interpretation of himself, of his life, which justifies him, which glorifies his failure.

And seeing, as I said, that civilization, after all, has been made by such as them, who is going to say which verdict is the true one, theirs or that of the tribesmen?

So with myself. Even after I had clearly seen that from the point of view of the 'others'—of the tribesmen, as I began to call them now—I *was* a failure, because I started life with an incapacity which, under primitive conditions, would probably have been my undoing and which, among social hunters, would have relegated me into the same class with women, children, and old men. I still worked out an interpretation of my life which justified me, no matter whether I ever obtained success as a writer, or an artist, or an inventor, in short as a critic. I stood in line with those who, beginning with the first artist or thinker, have led mankind through such as Plato and Phidias to what it is to-day. No longer, it is true, could I acquiesce in the theory of 'great men.' I saw both sides of the question. Too profound was my insight into the futility of human interpretation and my despair of the accessibility of a higher one to raise myself upon a pedestal for self-adoration. If the world would none of me, I lacked the conceit to say, so much the worse for the world! But I saw clearly that, no matter what my degree of success as a critic might be, some measure of success was just as certain for me as it is for him who sets out to make a mere living. What is really needed for him who makes a living? A few acres of land, somewhere in the world, and the will to work: and barring rare accidents, all the essentials of life are his. A rare, a conspicuous success in that line is just as much, if not, considering numbers, far more the exception than a conspicuous success in the realm of mental activities. In either case, the conspicuous success does not nearly so much depend on the individual as on the vast conglomerate of surrounding circumstances. To talk of a 'self-made' man in any line, is non-sense. The error rises from incomplete knowledge.

Some measure of success? Even a life 'in obscurity' does not lack it. No person is ever so isolated but he preserves some points of human contact. No person is ever so insignificant but he exerts some influence on those who surround him. The measurements may be too coarse to detect it; or we may adjust them in too delicate a way to register differences in this man's or that man's magnetisms. But the influences are there; and the differences exist. Just as the most infinitesimal speck of stardust in the remotest heavens exerts its attraction on the mightiest suns through light years of distance. We, with clumsy fingers and senses and instruments cannot measure it, but it *is*; and it is measurable, though not to us.

Every thing depends on every thing. All things that ever were, had to be that I might be. Let one single, small detail in the chain of things, maybe thousands of years ago have been different, and I should have been different: perhaps if we could reason such things out, not measurably different as human instruments go, but different still, and measurably different for him who might be capable of absolute measurements. Thus, too, all things to come, even in the remotest aeons, are somehow and in some degree determined by me. And shall I, then, despair? Shall, then, I fell insignificant in the face of necessities beyond my power of remedy?

Even though I never attain to public utterance, a word dropped here, a hint bestowed there, and even my thought, that most intangible thing, in which there breathes a faint reflection only of my ego, will live. It may soon be forgotten, and yet it still lives on, because it influenced another's thought if only for a moment. That moment, however, is henceforth incorporated in the other's being: he can no more get rid of it than he can undo the fact of his birth.

There have been proposed systems of philosophy and religion designed to place our present conduct under the greatest restraints imaginable. Man, so their originators reasoned, is naturally light-headed and careless of consequences; in order to make him responsible we must attach tremendous importance to his every single act. Such systems were those of an eternal life to come which hinges upon man's pinpoint existence in the present world, and those of an eternal repetition of all things in which a life once lives has to be repeated an infinite number of times. Both systems to me seem utterly unfair because they presuppose logical absurdities: the conflict between free will and predestination: and indeed, they have produced nothing else but gloom. As a matter of fact, science, if worked out into a system of ethics, would prove a more cogent restraint than either; and it does not involve us in insoluble puzzles. Science proclaims us to be links in a chain and more or less irresponsible. But science itself is a link in a chain. It cannot, if it cares to be consistent, claim infallibility and absolute canons. Science changes from day to day, yes, from hour to hour: just as we do ourselves. Even the meanings of facts which are found, prove unstable. Science describes, it does not explain; and every description is always incomplete. From moment to moment we learn to see more: but we never see all and never shall. Science, too, is a mountain stream sprung from the heights of suffering, born under the oscillating flashes of the thunderstorm of pain. But finally this stream flows back into the river of life. If, at that point, one single human being could *know*, life would cease. But, fortunately for us, knowledge is not.

Ethics is of little avail. Ethics is a dream set up by those who fondle the thought of a definite aim. And a definite aim there is not as far as human knowledge goes. Which does not mean there is not a definite aim in the world of reality, beyond the mirror-screens of our understanding. There may be or there may not be one we do not know, we cannot know. But, if there is, it does not and cannot concern us, though our belief or non-belief in it may influence our lives. But belief or non-belief is alike beyond our powers of adoption. They, too, form a link in the chain of events.

So are the interpretations of our own lives and those of the historians who view human life in the mass. And since they are, they have their influence on all future things. Because we are we, we build them about us like a cardhouse to shelter us from the blast of reality. And they, in turn, determine reality, as far as the thoughts and inner lives of men are themselves reality. Yes, since realities have no meaning whatever for us unless they are first interpreted by our consciousness of whatever sides of them we comprehend, they are really the only thing which counts for human life. My life itself may be futile and nugatory as seen by others: and the life of these others may seem futile and nugatory to me; it is all a matter of standard and interpretation. But if my life in its final influence draws wider circles, then, in a human sense, it was the more important.

And thus we arrive at our conclusion: success is failure: failure is success: it is merely a matter of looking at things. We look at life through coloured screens; these screens are not of our making: they are we; and we are what we are and cannot help it. But since that which accepts and rejects in us is closely bound up with our fundamental being, we think we accept and reject; and we do: the only thing which is merely fiction in our conception of ourselves is precisely this that we assume an independent and spontaneous 'we,' which is as little of our making as the image we see in the mirror is of the mirror's making or assembling.

---

[1]An Edition of Selected Unpublished Essays and Lectures by Frederick Philip Grove on His Theory of Art, Diss. Univ. of Toronto, 1982, p. 103.

[2]As an afterthought, Grove adds: 'I am aware that this reasoning is not original in the sense that it has never been given before. Butler and Pearson— strange couple—join hands.' In the Introduction to *Letters from Eden*, Henry Makow discusses the influence of Samuel Butler and Karl Pearson on Grove's writing.

[3]As Makow notes in his dissertation (126), Grove here makes veiled reference to his relation with Herman Kilian. Concerning Grove's relation to Kilian, see D.O. Spettigue, *FPG: The European Years*, pp. 69-70, 90-99.

[4]In a note on the page opposite this paragraph Grove adds, apparently as a note toward a possible revision: 'My feeling of insufficiency, of unworthiness. How it has kept me from doing what I thought my task in life.'

'Of Nishivara, the Saint' was among the many manuscripts acquired by the University of Manitoba when it established the Frederick Philip Grove Collection in 1962. The work survives only in a handwritten faircopy; it is both undated and untitled. In the top left margin of the faircopy Grove has written 'Chapter 1,' suggesting that he conceived this work as part of a longer narrative. It appears unlikely, however, that he wrote any subsequent chapters; certainly, none are extant among the known Grove papers. 'Of Nishivara, the Saint' became the focus of attention in 1969 when D.O. Spettigue pointed to it in his first study of the novelist, Frederick Philip Grove, as a possible source of biographical information for the crucial years between Felix Paul Greve's 'suicide' in September 1909 and Fred Grove's appearance in Winnipeg in December 1912. In his second study, FPG: The European Years, Spettigue both reported that Greve translated Flaubert's La Tentation de Saint-Antoine and argued that Greve was led to Flaubert through Gide, whose work he was also translating. Noting the references to The Temptation of St. Anthony in Greve's Canadian writing and Margaret Stobie's assertion that Flaubert's text informs a crucial scene in Settlers of the Marsh, Spettigue remarks: 'perhaps we should see a chain of influence extending from Flaubert through Gide to Grove's "Saint Nishivara" ' (130). The text is reproduced here as it appears in the manuscript.

Frederick Philip Grove
Of Nishivara, the Saint
Chapter 1

1 This is the story of the birth and of the outward life of Nishivara, the saint.

2 He was born in the east, nobody knows exactly where and by whom; for he always observed silence on these points.

3 He lived in the countries across the great sea till he reached the age of maturity, concerning himself with the vanities of the flesh and of this world.

4 One day, while still a very young man, he had a great shock.

5 For it came to pass that he found himself entangled in sin and shame; and he bowed his head and thus spoke to himself,

6   I have done only what others do; but, being myself and not they, I did it more fearlessly and unrestrainedly.

7   Thus I have become entangled in the net of the world. Henceforth I must do the one thing which is needful.

8   I must seek my own life. I will cross the seas, so that I be among men unknown to me and such to whom I also am unknown.

9   And he guided himself and did as he had resolved.

10 But when he came into this great land where he who writes this treatise also lives, he forgot his purpose and once more sought for success after the manner of others.

11 Thus again he fell into the snares of the world and never strove to free himself.

12 In this way he spent once more as many years as he had spent before he crossed the seas.

13 But, when he had obtained that success for which the many crave he found that still his life was empty and his soul unsatisfied.

14 Once more he bowed his head and thought and spoke at last. And this is what he said,

15 Twice have I started life and failed. I must start a third time.

16 And he sold all he had and gave to the poor, keeping only such raiment as was needed for his journey, and then departed.

17 He travelled all through the land, crossing it from east to west and from south to north.

18 And wherever he stopped, he taught.

19 His teaching was this that life as it was being lived by the many was vain and without sense.

20 But how to live better he did not show except for the vaguest hints.

21 But although the chief word among his words was nay he found many followers who begged him to stay with them and to give them light on what they were to avoid.

22 For even then there was about his teaching that which convinces and carries men along.

23 But whenever any asked him this, he shook his head, for he saw the dangers of his own teaching which instead of leading to life lead to death.

24 Yet he could not refrain from speaking and he tried to justify himself, saying,

25 He that wishes to till the field must first clear it.

26 At last, however, he went into the wilderness, as he used to call it in later years. That is to say, he journeyed from place to place without touching the habitations of men, living on roots and bark and wild fruit.

27 Twice twelve months he spent in this manner.

28 And while he was going from place to place, he fought with God and was tempted by the evil spirit.

29 For God had laid upon him a task. And he appeared to him in daydreams and visions of his mind, commanding him to go among his kind and to proclaim his commandments.

30 Lo, he would answer God in his mind, thou hast sent thy prophets and even the Son of Man to proclaim thy truth. But the nations did not listen. Why should I, even I, be called to this thankless task.

31 But the evil that lives in man, tempted him and spoke thus: Peace is the sweet of life. Thou livest in peace as thou art living now. Hide thyself from God, and he will not be able to find you. Man is evil; going to him will only disturb thy peace of mind. He lives in darkness and loves not the light. If you show him the light he will be angry, for the light will reveal his iniquity.

32 And when Nishivara heard the evil spirit within himself speak thus, he turned to God who also was in him and spoke, crying to him in his utter need, and saying,

33 Oh my God why did you lead me into this land? In the nations where I was born and grew up there were the lowly [in] spirit whom I might have loved though I did not then know it. But here in this land pride abided, and lowliness cannot be found. What shall I do and whither shall I turn to escape the anger of my enemies?

34 For a long time God did not seem to answer his cry. He merely kept urging him to go and to proclaim His commandments.

35 At last, however, there came a day when Nishivara, having lain at night in the hollow of a river bank, and under the shelter of some sycamores, arose in the morning; and, as if by an act of grace, all his doubts were dispelled.

36   And he girded himself and once more set out on his wanderings. Outwardly his journey proceeded just as before; but in his innermost heart he knew that he was no longer stepping at random but with a purpose.

37   The direction of his journey was north and west; and he travelled for sixty days,

38   Till he came to a gentle hill reclining against a mountain the peak of which was covered with snow.

39   Between the mountain and the hill there was a shallow, wooded valley through which ran a stream of the purest water.

40   And when Nishivara came there, he started at once to build himself a hut.

41   And when the hut was finished, he spent many days in gathering a store of roots and bark and such fruit as could be dried to serve him over winter.

42   And he cut wood for fuel and built himself a hearth with the stones of the hillside.

43   Nishivara was at this time more than sixty years old; but his arms were strong, his eyes clear, and his heart joyous.

44   When spring came, he fashioned out of wood a rude sort of tool with which to till the ground; and he planted such seeds as he could procure in the wilds. He also walked more than thirty miles to his nearest neighbour's and borrowed from him a handful of the seeds of the Indian corn, promising to repay seed for seed out of his harvest.

45   Thus he lived for many summers, slowly bettering his circumstances, but never calling on anyone to help him.

46   At last he had a cow and several heifer calves, but he neither sold nor bought but kept his little flock as it increased, though for the beginnings of his husbandry he had occasionally recourse to borrowing.

47   But during the winter he travelled into the sparse settlements of men in the Northland and preached.

48   And since the settlers were simple folk, they recognised in his teachings the voice of the Lord and they found favour with him.

49   From that time on, though Nishivara avoided the talk of the world, the talk of the world sought him, and the fame of his teachings spread far and wide.

50 Often men even from the great cities of the plain, men who were troubled in spirit would come and speak to him, and sometimes women also.

51 Never refused he them an answer, though he often spoke in such a way that his answer would trouble them more than their question.

52 Slowly disciples gathered about him and lived in a village which they founded at the foot of the hill where the stream of the mountains by which his hut stood flowed on united to the great river.

53 Thus his fame spread over all the earth, for his disciples also went out to teach their master's words in winter time; but what will come of his teaching remains still to be seen.

54 The Great of the land, when they heard of him, feared him; but for many, many years they left him alone, seeing that they feared more even than him the multitudes that believed in him or rather the justice of his teachings.

55 It was only when he had thus, from a remote and nearly barren corner of the land, through his teachings conquered the spirit of all who heard them, whether from his own lips or through the echo of his followers, that they cared to interfere.

56 He was cast into prison for stirring up the people; and though his followers would have faced him, he forbade them and clearly signified that it was his wish to die a martyr to the cause of God.

57 Nothing, so he said, fertilizes the soil of the spirit so well as the blood which is spilled for the sake of truth. I am an old man, and the days of my usefulness are counted. Let them work their will, and that for which I care, the cause of the Lord, will conquer and live.

58 Thus, in a great city in the east of the land, he was put before a tribunal made up of the slaves of the world, and sentenced to die.

59 The times were troubled; and the law of war had been proclaimed; and thus he was shot by a band of soldiers who had not yet seen the light.

60 But his disciples, of whom he who writes this treatise was one, rejoiced for they trusted in his word that the cause would live through his death.

J.J. Healy

Grove and the Matter of Germany:
The Warkentin Letters and the Art of
Liminal Disengagement

Andreas Weidenhammer (1863-1925), born in Heidelberg, Ontario, editor of *Canadischer Bauemfreund* from 1903-9, gives Grove his first job in Manitoba. By the time he dies in 1925, as Inspector of Schools, he has changed his name to Andrew Willows. The anti-German hysteria of World War I, which changed Berlin to Kitchener, forced a man of German origin, born in Canada, to change his name in his sixties.

But there is a retention. Weidenhammer does not let his name go completely.

die Weid-e, fem. (pl. -en) willow.

Weiden: Willows gives a job to Greve: Grove.

How different is this kind of camouflage and disguise/fear from Grove's own predicament?

Of course, Greve-Grove had an earlier incentive. As someone who had faked his death a new name would be in order. As someone who had been in prison in Germany the only way past Canadian or American immigration authorities was another name. A criminal record spelled no entry.

Yet, like Weidenhammer, he stays as close to the core of his name as possible.

The act is one of translation, not denial or betrayal.

In the midst of the constraints of circumstance, there is personal and cultural integrity.

Grove was a German who became a writer. He was a writer who comitted 'suicide' and became, by this act, an anonymous person, an underground man. We say he was an immigrant, but this is a superficial, administrative category. He would probably have seen himself as an exile, in the beginning at any rate. Again this is a moral, psychological condition. Germany, being German, being a writer in German would have been the reference terms for him in the situation of exile, the positive poles of reflective concern in a place—North America—that had no reality for him. It was a negative entity: nowhere. Germany held Grove, attached him to its existence. By leaving it he left history; by leaving history he left his individuality.

The compact between history and society in Europe placed the identity of the individual into a concrete, metaphysically un-problematic world. What Grove's arrival in North America did was to destroy this compact. In *A Search for America* he put the matter succinctly:

> When I came from Europe, I came as an individual; when I settled down in America, at the end of my wanderings, I was a social man. My view of life, if now, at the end, I may use this word once more, had been, in Europe, historical, it had become, in America, ethical.[1]

This is an astute, and in its own way a remarkable statement. The quality of individual being, of being a shaped, coherent self replete with personality, background and prospect that *was* Frederick Philip Grove (as Greve) dissolved, became useless. His sense of himself became problematical. The recesses of a highly specific individuality that both Joyce and Proust examined with such curiosity became unavailable to Grove. He settled for himself as a proposition, reflective of man in his social (i.e. most general, anthropological) aspect; he settled for America as an abstract plain voided of history in which the ethical dilemmas of this universalized, social man were acted out. He was not alone in this and the large outlines of the European response to America are visible throughout Grove's work.

What is interesting about Grove is the *conscious* way he eventually negotiated the problem of an abandoned self in a strange world where disguise was always necessary and, in circuitous ways, betrayal was always possible. 'I must be I' is the constant refrain of his work. He negotiated his dilemma by redefining himself as a *writer;* that is, as a human being the primary aspect of whose personality becomes the degree of consciousness he brings to the world and to his experience. It is as if a Cartesian *cogito,* by distancing itself from the experience and the world as linked but separable items, overcomes the experience as a meshed-in aspect of the world, of the world as a meshed-in aspect of experience. In Germany, love, death, stealing, being in university, or prison, or Berlin are textured *into* Grove. They are the corpuscles of his subjective experience rather than categories of his existence as *homo sapiens.* Asserting himself as a writer became a shorthand and coded way of asserting his sense of self. And asserting such a self, even in a distantiated manner, was part of Grove's imperative for survival after his flight from Germany.

The other conscious program for survival in the early years was marriage. When Grove pulled the two projects together—marriage and writing—he found himself alive with the possibility, as he put it, of using the word *life* once more.

He may have lost the right, in his eyes, to feel easy with this world when he 'arranged' his death from a steamer in the Baltic. Apart from this, however, the early years of transition would have been sufficiently difficult for Grove to have withheld the full privilege of the term 'living' from them. Not being in Germany, for a young man who had stepped so messily and decisively from history, would have been the equivalent of not being in life. The attempt to re-enter a sphere of living with new associations in a new world on fresh ground rules involved a re-assessment of that core of his existence where being himself and being German were closely engaged.

When we first meet Grove in Canada it is against a German Mennonite background, on the eve of a World War. The underground man re-surfaces.

The most impassioned letters of his life were written by Grove to Warkentin on December 6, 1913, and February 10, 1914. Warkentin was now in Germany, soon to be interned by the outbreak of war.

The subject is Germany, abandoned by Grove only five years before, but still haunting his conscience and pressuring his consciousness.

Van Gennep defined *rites de passages* as 'rites which accompany every change of place, state, social position, and age.'[2] He divides the transitional rite as a process into three stages: separation, margin, re-aggregation. Turner uses the term liminal for the middle phase which inflicts a limbo, in-between condition on those who undergo it.

Grove's letters to Warkentin register the confusion of this phase in an instructive, and from the immigrant rite of passage perspective, classical manner. It is important not to dismiss Grove's utterances as psychological tantrum. Margaret Stobie does dismiss Grove in this way:

> As Grove's sense of injury grows, the tone of the letters changes. His world is now a smaller one, depending on small things that have suddenly ballooned to blot out distance, perspective, judgement, proportion.
>
> The detailing of the bottles of seeds, the mounting of insects, the cost of postage sounds like the cry of a man who sees a last chance slipping away. He is an outsider and unwanted. To ease

his mortification, Grove escapes into the legendary world that
he had already devised of the Swedish father and Scotch mother
and of himself as a sophisticated man of the world, a scholar, a
far-traveller.[3]

Margaret Stobie has given Grove the benefit of astute and
stubbornly honest attention. But here she gives him the benefit of
what Lawrence called the 'old stable ego' in a manipulative,
controlling, intentional relationship to his utterances. The case in
these letters is not so simple. Grove is writing in disguise, from
hiding, caught in liminal currents in which Greve and Grove caught
between Weidenhammer and Warkentin stands on transplanted
German Mennonite ground trying to sort out the complex terms of
his existence, to negotiate the difficult terrain between Van Gennep's
phases of separation from Germany and re-aggregation to North
America. These complex of terms will eventually become the themes
of his fiction. But in the letters to Warkentin they present themselves
with the ambiguity, the abrupt tendentiousness, the sudden insight
and the fit of irritation that goes along with newly discovered matter.
Grove wrestles with Warkentin, a man he hardly knew, who would
return to the Mennonite schools of Manitoba in 1918 and live until
1971. Warkentin was a symbolic correspondent in a symbolic place
who provided Grove with the ideal foil for a debate with himself. It is
from these letters that *In Search of Myself, A Search for America*
eventually spring. He is juggling with the terms Germany, America,
Europe, Canada, England. He is juggling with them as cultural
forces harboring conflicts and divisions that have to be exercised,
exorcised, sorted out. Grove would never allow himself to be either
this vulnerable or this revelatory about himself again.
   Turner speaks of the most characteristic midliminal symbolism as
being that of paradox, of being both this *and* that. He speaks of
masked figures invading the liminal scene. In Grove's letters we see
the paradox of a correspondent who is, as we now know, in hiding, a
masked figure enacting and exploring the paradoxes of being both
this *and* that, of being German *and* American. Within the masking,
by a process of rhetorical and fabular extrapolation, a persona, a role,
and a terrain of symbolic, ideal proportions are elaborated. By the
time we emerge from these letters a degree of fixity and assertion have
descended on Frederick Philip Grove. Many readers have sensed a
postulated quality to this assertion and perhaps like Margaret Stobie
have visited a degree of impatience on Grove and his work in
consequence.

A closer look at the liminal transitional phase of the Warkentin letters may be of value.

The first letter we have of Grove's, written to Warkentin from Winkler on September 7, 1913 is *in German*. It is a short letter, requesting three books on educational matters, beginning with a short introductory paragraph which one might be inclined to overlook in a more neutral, less deliberate correspondent.

Ich bin so froh, jemanden in D[eu]tschl[an]d zu haben der mir vielleicht behilflich sein kann, dass ich Ihnen möglicherweise lästig fallen werde. Vielleicht wird es Ihnen zur Genugtuung gereichen dass Sie ja schliesslich Ihrer Heimat helfen.

I am so happy to have someone in Germany who may be able to help me, that I may possibly become a nuisance to you. Perhaps it would be of some satisfaction to you that you are, after all, helping your country.[4]

The formal re-opening of lines of communication with his native land is in his native language. Subsequently, whether because Warkentin chose to return the correspondence in English or because a symbolic point had been made by Grove, the letters are in English. Yet, they are still written by a German, about Germany as a political, economic, social entity; about the relations of Germany to other nations, particularly England and the United States; about the mythologies and hostilities of nations that were becoming more volatile and fierce on the eve of the World War. The syntax, the tone and the subject place the Germanness of Grove and the German contribution to European civilization and history at the centre of this correspondence. The mood of his letters to Warkentin changes in response to Warkentin's own letters. We do not have these. But we can reconstruct from Grove's letters the temper of Warkentin's replies. We need to do this in order to develop a sense of Grove's initiatives in the exchange. He is glad to have someone *in Germany* to *help* him and he concedes that he may become a *nuisance*. Grove anticipated making demands but was clearly not expecting to have demands made on him. Warkentin's first six months at Leipsig University involved a good deal of culture shock for him and this sense of dismay and disillusion found its way to Grove in Winkler. The young man was homesick, disliked the drizzling weather, was impatient with the slow pace of the German worker. He gave Grove information about his curriculum in November 1913, but by

Christmas the correspondence from Warkentin had become a jeremiad. He hates Germany and is appalled by the rampant patriotism and the sense of superiority that is sweeping the country. The prostitution and sexual manners of a large city alarmed the young Mennonite from Manitoba. Grove quotes one sentence from a Warkentin letter: 'If we had waited for German philosophy to decide . . . where would we be?' It shows his impatience with the academic traditions of German idealist philosophy. None of this should be surprising. What is important for the reader of this correspondence, however, is the *reactive* nature of Grove's handling of the questions of German nationalism, German science, German philosophy, German claims to superiority, and of the Sexualle Frage in Germany. He deals with them because Warkentin has brought them up.

It is when we address the issue of *how* Grove handles these questions that one begins to get a sense of the negative and the positive aspects of his response to Warkentin. There is an objective and a subjective dimension to his replies. If Warkentin says that there is open prostitution in Leipzig Grove will point out that this is true of Paris and London and New York as well. If Warkentin says that Germans are slow and plodding Grove refers to trading figures which show that German exports are booming. That is the objective aspect of his defence of Germany.

When Grove is obliged to respond from his own subjective experience *as a German* the letters become agitated and, at times, anguished. At these points the exchange has turned around. Grove's contact in Germany has become a nuisance *for* Grove and in replying to that nuisance—a nuisance of conscience and consciousness for him—layers of his personality open up. The defence of Germany which began in a kind of negotiated and public manner suddenly, under the impress of Warkentin's lamentation, became a defence of himself. This was a private terrain which he suffered but did not yet control or understand. His writing career would take up this burden. But in 1913 and early 1914 Grove registered the weight and the confusion and could only begin to put out tendrils of explanation, of expiation.

The transitional rite of separation, margin and re-aggregation is carried through these letters with ambivalence and posture. Where the correspondence is most subjective it may often be least intentional. The tendrils of explanation are often called forth by the passion and issue of the moment and, in this sense, constitute a local and immediate explanation. Grove made an observation to

Warkentin in February 1914 which harbours an important distinction. 'I did not want you to like Germany—but I did want you to like the experience you are going through.' His own improvised explanations attach to the *experiences* he himself has gone through, somewhat apart from the anchor of place and culture that has accompanied those experiences. The correspondence juggles a series of defensive strategies: of Germany, of himself as a German, of himself as American, of himself as a self which is neither German nor American. The experience he is undergoing is filled with dilemmas but at the level of experience it is neither authentic nor inauthentic. It simply is. The local explanations that he calls up function to satisfy and reinforce the observations he is making to Warkentin. The purpose is pedagogical in relation to Warkentin, psychological in relation to himself and organizational in relation to the experiences from which the explanations emerge and toward which they eventually, having consolidated themselves, reconverge. By the time Warkentin is in Ruhleben Prison Camp and Grove has married Catherine Wiens, the future Canadian novelist has fabricated from the bits and pieces of this correspondence a fictional biography. He has moved from separation to re-aggregation. There are a number of ways we may phrase the reconstruction. We can say that Grove has reshaped his biography; that he has symbolically cut himself off from Germany; that he changed his idea of himself. He has tied the improvised tendrils of explanation to Warkentin into a fully fledged myth and it will be from the web of significance sustained by this myth that his writing career will grow.

In December 1913 Grove addresses Warkentin as an *American:* 'You American people are funny.' His affection for 'staid old Germany' is evident. Two months later, under the sting of Warkentin's hostility to Germany Grove retreats: 'Also, of course, I hate Germany. I hate America, too, but probably a trifle less because I am here.' Canada is an absent term in Grove's essential thinking. Europe and America, with Germany representing Europe, are the poles of his discourse. Yet although Germany has shortcomings it 'is the one really instructive country where Americans ought to go.' Grove cuts off the ambivalence with a declaration: 'Yes I am afraid, I *am* an American, always was one, sorry to say so. *I* could no longer live in Germany.' In a rhetorical sense this is sheer assertion, but if one looks at the italicized words one can detect the inner echo of a truth being spoken. He, Greve, cannot live in Germany; he, Grove, *is* an American.

It is between the difficult denial 'I hate Germany' and the bitter-sweet acquiescence 'I *am* an American' that we meet for the first time the great fabrication of Grove's new life:

> My father was a Swede, my mother a Scotchwoman, I was raised in Germany, I have lived in pretty nearly every country in Europe, in N[orth] A[merica] and Canada, I have travelled in Africa, through Asia, in Australia, I know India and China a little, the islands south of Asia fairly well—so I believe—speaking merely geographically—I can claim a certain 'many-sidedness.'

There is a Whitmanesque glow to this kind of utterance. Grove is certainly embracing global space and there is an arrogance to the manner which overwhelms the deception about his parents. It is simply one item in a self-generating exaggeration which pursues its own hyperbolic logic:

> Also as far as 'education' goes (the ' ' means that I think very little of what is commonly called education)—I speak English, French, German, Italian and Arabian—and I have a fair knowledge of Latin, Greek, Sanskrit, Spanish and Swedish with their respective literatures. . . .

This tapestry of universal claims is a mask of invention being produced at a great pace. The syntax bears this out. As a constructed fable it is amenable to a variety of contextual explanations and perhaps, more important for Grove, *usable* in his subsequent career.

The immediate context would be the value of the fabrication as an association-dissociation device for handling Warkentin (= Canada) *in* Germany by Grove (= Germany) *in* Canada. The mood of aggrandizement has an imperial outreach to it that has some echoes of the pre-1914, post Congress of Berlin German drive for colonies. This is the overseas German making a non-parochial non-Burger gesture: Grove as *auslander Deutsch*. The idiom of empire added to the temptation of the universal and the transcendental would naturally lead Grove into this language and the posture of self behind it. The shades of Bismark and Whitman hover around the re-making of Frederick Philip Grove.

The imperial omniscience he attributes to his putative self is a supportive fiction for his claim to 'manysidedness,' a claim necessary to *refute* the narrow-minded accusations which Warkentin directed at the Germans, and which Grove will re-direct at Winkler, and North America. But the main function of the imperial stance is to graft and neutralize a combination of opinion and experience that Grove needs to get under psychological, and subsequently, artistic control. Thus, in relation to the sexual question he makes 'an alarming statement' to Warkentin: 'I do not object to sexual intercourse without marriage—but I object to just those consequences. I also object to premature development of the sexual instincts.'

This is an *opinion* and as such is somewhat safe. We share our opinions with the world and they often derive from the culture or the group to which we belong. Rhoda Metraux, for instance, in her examination of German child-rearing books in the period of Grove's letter and of his own upbringing, noted that 'the greatest anxiety expressed by experts is connected with the idea that the child may be weakened and spoiled, may become unsocial and prematurely sexually aware (*frühreif*) through parental overattentiveness, overcarefulness, and overfeeding with foolish affection.'[5] Grove's sentences about sexuality, marriage and premature development are a mixture of the 'unorthodox' and the 'orthodox,' but they are so within the confines of a debate. Consequently, when he releases himself into that debate he has distanced his experience by making it an example of something.

> I have suffered immensely myself from that cause. I think I was 15 y[ea]rs old when I was "seduced" by a married woman.

Grove is placing cultural, historical and geographical frames onto his life (selected aspects of it) and by doing so thematizes it. Warkentin was a blessing in disguise. He gave Grove an occasion to 'place' his essential self (a hidden, previously secluded existence) into a manageable relationship to the various worlds he had endured, transgressed, betrayed.

After his confession Grove returns to the realm of opinion again, this time concerning the urban nature of German civilization. He is shuttling between the private and the public, between fact, fable and fiction. The shoring up of the first person continues:

> I believe I have been through every representative part of America with the exception of the extreme Northwest of Canada, and everywhere I found the closed mind.

Grove seems, at these moments, to be talking *through* Warkentin more than to him, to be talking *from* an extrapolated dimension of the immigrant experience. When he has detached the purely personal and subjective aspect of his experience, from his point of view, Grove can introduce his Winkler (echoes of *Winkeltum*, his synonym for ignorance and 'cornerdom') encounters. There is a genuine *cri de coeur* here which Professor Stobie finds irritating but which exemplifies a set of cultural observations which Grove believes to be true apart from their connection to him. A little later in this letter he speaks of himself valuing 'even one tiny little bit of found knowledge immensely more than all the deeds ever done.' The expression 'found knowledge' is particularly appropriate for the way in which Grove with naturalistic and almost pious industry *quarried* his own *literally* lived life for significance and meaning. His Winkler battles constitute such found knowledge and it is from this base (common to both Warkentin and himself in many of its aspects) that Grove can find a voice which is passionate, impersonal and of some philosophical seriousness:

> In the whole of life I do not see any sense. If I want to be truthful I must say that in our individual effort I see only a struggle to get over it in the best possible way. *I* stand apart, aloof, if you want to put it that way. It is a horrible thought to me that I am *acting*, 'doing' at all.

This is genuine speaking: it does not deal in paradox. He will develop the opposition of 'doing' and 'knowing,' of the active and the contemplative life. But after his faked suicide, his escape to America, his even now invisible years, the moving simplicity of the admission 'It is a horrible thought to me that I am *acting*, "doing" at all' is striking. Grove has found it possible to speak of himself with candour and a degree of freedom which is equally striking.

> Whenever you touch life you make a mess of it. When you are young you don't notice it so much.

Grove is not young in this way any more. He sees himself now as a spectator, someone who watches, observes, analyses, 'who wants to know.' In a most poignant phrase which we may take literally, soberly, he writes: 'That is my only salvation.'

Grove is writing at white heat at this point with a clarity and a despair that give one the impression of having been freshly minted.

His reading, his travels, his watching, his *being* find a bitter focus in which the asserted and hard-fought-for imperial self must sustain its existence against bleak odds:

> You say: "If we have waited for German philosophy to decide... where would we be?" But where *are* we!?! Is life one trifling little bit less raw, less cruel today than it was 10,000 years ago? Only the robust thick skinned people ever could endure active life: the rest of them went to the wall or into the wilderness. I am the latter.

This is a social darwinism imbued with the language of religious sadness and finding an almost existentialist habitation deep within Grove's mind. It will be a mood which will touch almost every subject that Grove sets out to handle. Like the slow, penetrating drizzle which discomfited Warkentin in Germany, the darwinian-apocalyptic pattern always seemed to emerge from the events that Grove scrutinized. But scrutiny, reflection, analysis was the only option open to an embattled species whose own version of what it ought to be, to be human, was so out of kilter with the facts of its own history and the evidence that was coming in from the physical universe and the study of animal behaviour. Mindless action was out of the question; actionless mind was not a visibly exciting alternative, but it was, like the penetrating drizzle of north Germany, more fruitful than the destructive downpour of sheer action. One can see why Grove was so reluctant to yield to Warkentin's impatience with German philosophy. Too much, beyond Germany and embracing the destiny of man at the outset of a brutal century, was at stake. Against this backdrop the Whitmanesque-Bismarkian posture of the imperial self becomes more comprehensible. There is no logical reason why the naturalistic assaults on the religious and humanist ambitions for man should not have overwhelmed one of the last bastions of these pretensions: a privileged almost sacred sense of a self in a rational, aloof, filtering relationship to its own existence. Where proofs could not be marshalled, assertion had to be invoked as an unconditional imperative. I must be I. Who, or whatever that I may be. It was an extraordinary dilemma for a man who wished to write but who had neither the euphoric, culturally sanctioned optimism of Whitman nor the stark, action-based but also culturally sanctioned *Realpolitik* of Bismark. Add to this his exile, his suicide, his changed name, his hiddenness in a strange land and his defence of his self becomes comprehensible.

There is a drama of introspective power going on in the italics of the first person in this correspondence, in the rhetoric, the emphases and the anguished nuance that Grove strives for whenever the occasion or the syntax of language requires that he write the most complex of all simple words: I.

The backdrop of his defence of mind is a raw, cruel one of 10,000 years in which the thin skinned among men—which includes those with intellectual, moral or compassionate natures—go to the wall or into the wilderness. 'I am the latter,' says Grove, a man who has been to a literal wall and who resides, from his point of view, in the wilderness. What he is fighting against is the terrifying possibility that the wilderness may indeed prove to be the final expression of the wall: extinction. Consequently, the intensity of his response to Winkler. A squabble with a fellow teacher is an either-or situation for Grove. He has no further ground to yield because all ground has become apocalyptic, holy. 'With our friend P.H. it is fight, I am afraid. It looks as if the issue will soon be: he or I.' From the detached perspective of history and if one isolates the educational politics one might feel that Grove has a kind of tunnel vision. But it is context and perspective that determine the significance of an event for its participants and Grove's response gives us a graphic glimpse of how he saw himself, the self that is attempting to negotiate a rite of passage out of chaos into a re-ordered world.

> But I am bleeding. The things said about me here are sometimes funny, sometimes they hurt because there is a kernel of truth in them. I cannot afford to pay any attention to that. I *have got* to win out.

Paradoxically, even in the wilderness one has to be thick skinned in order to survive, in order to direct questions at life—which it may repudiate or ignore but which still have to be asked. Grove's defence of the philosophical intelligence comes from a passionate association with the aspirations of that intelligence. He gives us, in his outburst to Warkentin, an *apologia pro vita suo*. The notion of the independent observer is one of the working assumptions of science; it becomes part of the functional assertion of Grove. With some irony and a little tiredness he points out to Warkentin that 'even Science never explains: it describes; describes more and more minutely—and I enjoy the spectacle.'

What one realizes at this stage is the sheer exhaustion of Grove's parrying with Warkentin and his stiff but eloquent juggling with his own thoughts and feelings about the host of issues that we have indicated make up the substance of these letters. We have suggested that the transformations going on apace in this exchange have the characteristics of the middle, liminal stage of Victor Turner's analysis of ritual. But the most remarkable utterance of this seminal and symbolic debate comes when Grove wants to disengage himself from the mess of assumption and emotion that the subjective pressures of their private situation has visited on both correspondents. Grove gets fed up with the terms of his defence and of Warkentin's attack on Germany. He gives vent to a surrealistic oath:

> Let the slow, careful German labourers of the mind work for me, and let the whole city of Leipzig go to smash, let the traffic be stopped and the fire department lift trolley cars!!

This is a vehement curse of dissociation. It is the *non serviam* of Frederick Philip Grove, the man who in another land and another language was a writer and who, in a new land and a new language, would be a writer, again, anew. The curse is also a prayer: 'let the slow, careful German labourers of the mind work for me...'—it is the world of Daedalus, of artifices of the mind, of exile, cunning, of the artist not romantic and lyrical in his intensity, but reflective, deliberative and, in his mid-thirties, no longer young.

The psychological distraction that Grove displays in part of this correspondence and which was a natural response to a fairly distracted life up to this point yields to a tougher, more impersonal conception of himself in relation to his previous German experiences and to his new role in Canada. The build-up of what one called the imperial self, the Whitmanesque dimension of rhetorical self-presentation, constitutes a mediating stage between the psychological reaction to his world and a more phenomenological, impersonal (in Eliot's sense of the word) reaction to found, known aspects of a world thematized by a reflective concern that gave it and his own efforts as a writer in relation to it, a deep seriousness. Grove has firmed up the interior uncertainties of his predicament. One might say that he circumvented the dis-ease of exile and immigration, which threatened to overwhelm him, by becoming the analyst of this dis-ease.

This is, of course, a private victory for Grove which gave him considerable subjective confidence. He has fabricated a host of allusions which enable him to write. And he will begin to do this in books like *Over Prairie Trails* and *A Search for America* with great power. It is not surprising that his first ventures, after having consolidated the fragments and aspirations of a difficult situation, will involve him in an examination of his new environment in its physical and symbolic aspects. The question that may be asked in the wake of his ritualistic interaction with Warkentin is this: is Grove, *from hiding*, performing Crevecoeur/De Tocqueville analyses of North America? It is an intriguing question.

Grove's reference, in the Warkentin 10.2.14 letter, to his former marriage is a parenthetical insertion. It comes as a bracketed comment after his espousal of the contemplative life as his only salvation and preceding his observation about the value of found knowledge. A general argument about science and the slow German mind has led to a side reflection of a personal kind:

> As for my marriage, that has gone to smash; something I have been working for for the last five years. I don't blame the girl—I merely don't understand her. Difference of age was considerable: she was my pupil before she went to college. At Christmas I went down to Arkansas—into the hospital!! And when I came out after a week of raging fever, I did not know my world any longer! I was so changed. Well, enough of that!

Why should Grove have introduced this item at this point! It is presumably an aspect of his biography. It suggests that Warkentin was aware of Grove's marriage although no one in Winkler saw the woman. Douglas Spettigue has canvassed the evidence around this relationship with what seems to have been an American girl. He came up with nothing. Yet, although Grove could fabricate in the grand Felix Krull manner or less grandly in the prosaic but crucial immigrant manner, he is unlikely to have distorted the kernel of truth that gave a quality of subjective authenticity to his fabrications. He was, in his own way, fastidious within the constraints of a predicament that circumstances and the botched antics of his twenties in Germany had created for him. Again, if we look at the passage with literal eyes, attentive to the masking that he was practising as the idiom of his contact with the world, we notice that Grove permits us to conclude that he has been working *for* a marriage for five years rather than *at* a marriage. So it may be *plans* for marriage that have gone smash and it could be that the fall-out of this smash explains his observation to Warkentin that he had nothing against sex outside of marriage, as long as one avoided promiscuity or issue.

The facts behind this passage are obscure. The tone and the attitude it reveals are not. Grove comes across somewhat like the bachelor of Henry James' first novel, *Watch and Ward* (serial publication 1871), who adopts a fatherless child and conceives of a the idea of rearing her in *his* image of the ideal wife, to be his wife. As Nora's cousin Fenton phrases it: 'It seemed to him an extremely odd use of one's time and capital, this fashioning of a wife to order.'[6] Grove had been working for the marriage for five years: it was a project. She had been his student before going to college. The difference in age was considerable. Roger Lawrence, the protagonist of *Watch and Ward*, would not have recognized his temperament in Grove; as a character he is quite different. But James would have spotted the fashioning, shaping intent and would have relished and probably polished into more astringent focus the phrase: 'I don't blame the girl—I merely don't understand her.' It is in the under-stated power of the 'merely' and the emphatic 'understand' that one explanation for the marriage parenthesis suggests itself. He has sandwiched his Jamesian 'scene' between his defence of the contemplative mind and his use of the term 'found knowledge.' The contemplative life he defines as 'the life of the spectator who wants to *know*, not to do.' The marriage project had all the ambiguous ingredients of watching, wanting to know and understand, wanting to do and not doing. Clearly, Grove would like the appropriateness of act to follow on a fullness of knowing the conditions and the consequences of action. He would like to get married but on his conditions with the relationship in his control, in the control of his *understanding*. In this way the element of design and intention is visited on what would otherwise be accident and mess. His letter to his future wife, Catherine Wiens, on June 29, 1914, in relation to the marriage festivities of John Enns, his fellow teacher, bears out this interpretation. Grove's Roger Lawrence passage is, then, his application of science and the slow German mind to a very private experience which has consumed his time and capital for five years and which he had hoped to be his 'salvation.' Grove would always bring the lens of the understanding to the volatile plastic world of emotion and imagination in his fiction. Here we see it in his life.

Just as the word 'understand' bears a peculiar weighting in the sentence we have quoted, so too does the word 'salvation.' A structural parallel is registered in this letter in which two items from different segments of discourse—marriage and the slow contempla-tive mind—are associated with salvational power. The form that the contemplative mind will take in Grove's life is that of writing.

Writing and marriage are, at this stage in Grove's career, redemptive channels, projects that he has to work at in order to survive. In a very dramatic was *Over Prairie Trails*, his first published book, brings both these salvific modes into crucial relation to each other, and together they connect up with the will to survive and the fear of extinction. The trail between Gladstone and Falmouth near the western shore of Lake Manitoba carried a man who had left the powerlessness of Roger Lawrence behind and now had both wife and child. But circumstances placed Mrs. Grove and their daughter apart and Grove's journeys through treacherous winter terrain were fraught with difficulty and tense with the possibility of his losing his way and perishing. The difference between his paradise regained and that paradise being lost depended on careful, often minute detailed observation. The scientific mind, the naturalist's eye, became an instrument of preservation for his self as an isolate entity and as something connected into other human beings through marriage and family.

Eugen Diesel in his introspective book *Germany and the Germans* (1931) has made the point that 'when particular eras of German history have run their course Germans have always felt themselves confronted with chaos.'[7] He contrasts this reaction to an English ability to manage crisis with less devastating despair. These matters of collective psychology are relative and it is quite possible to see the crisis engendering circumstances of the emergence of modern Germany as the explanation for a set of responses that are not innate to this or that people. But the evidence of Grove's work and life supports the Diesel observation although the exile-immigrant experience of the man would probably be sufficient stimulus to an intense preoccupation with order and an equally intense fear of chaos.

In the correspondence with Warkentin, order of an assertive fictive kind is visibly at battle with chaos. By the time we get to *Over Prairie Trails* the chaos has been placed outside the person of the narrator and beyond certain aspects of his predicament. Grove has withdrawn into a protective shell of shared humanity, *shared* with his family and community, *against* the power of nature. Chaos is placed in this book *outside* of men into a world of natural force. In an important way *Over Prairie Trails* is the product of the exile-immigrant come home. When he gave up on his Jamesian ward Grove spoke of finding himself at Christmas in hospital in Arkansas: 'When I came out, after a week of raging fever, I did not know my world any longer! I was so changed.'

On the road between Gladstone and Falmouth, he appropriated his world with remarkable detail and in doing so forged the link between his writing and his marriage. It was a fine homecoming for his talent and his situation. And it prepared him for what he knew he was especially prepared for: to be the novelist of the immigrant groups in Canada.

---

[1]Frederick Philip Grove, *A Search for America* (Ottawa: The Graphic Publishers Limited, 1927), p. 436.

[2]Cited by Victor Turner, 'Variations on a Theme of Liminality,' in Sally Moore and Barbara Meyerhoff, eds., *Secular Ritual* (Amsterdam: Van Gorcum, 1977), p. 36.

[3]Margaret Stobie, 'Grove's Letters from the Mennonite Reserve,' *Canadian Literature*, 59 (Winter 1974), 70.

[4]The text of the Warkentin letters is Desmond Pacey's, *The Letters of Frederick Philip Grove* (Toronto: University of Toronto Press, 1976), pp. 3-14. The references come from such a definable and limited body of text that I have omitted page details in favour of location by date of letter built into the flow of the article.

[5]Cited in Ethel Nurge, 'Some Depictions of German Cultural Character' in John W. Bennett, ed., *The New Ethnicity: Perspectives from Ethnology* (St. Paul: West Publishing Company, 1975), p. 237.

[6]Henry James, *Watch and Ward.* Quoted by S. Gorley Putt, *The Fiction of Henry James* (Harmondsworth: Penguin Books, 1968), p. 27.

[7]Cited in Nurge, p. 223.

Henry Makow, Editor

Letters from Eden: Grove's Creative Rebirth

A fascinating picture of Frederick Philip Grove's beginnings as a novelist in Canada has emerged in a recently discovered series of five letters to his wife. They were found in Mrs. Grove's personal copies of her husband's books too late for Desmond Pacey's edition of Grove's letters published in 1976.[1] The new letters not only help to bridge a large gap in Grove's correspondence, extending from his marriage in 1914 until 1923, but illuminate the critical period in the autumn of 1919, in Eden, Manitoba, when Grove began writing in Canada. Everything Grove did was dramatic and his recovery of creative power is no exception. After an interlude of ten years he was overcome by an inspiration so exhilarating and fruitful that he renounced his teaching career and henceforth devoted his life to literature. He wrote *Over Prairie Trails* in just seven weeks and began a new career which spanned three decades and established him as one of Canada's most profound and original novelists.

Grove's creative revival was the culmination of a long, difficult, and largely unconscious process. Thanks to D.O. Spettigue's research, we know that Grove had established himself as a writer in Germany under his real name, Felix Paul Greve.[2] Born in 1879, by the age of thirty he had published poetry, two novels, criticism, and scores of translations. In 1909 he disappeared from Germany in order to evade large debts. When he became a school teacher in Manitoba in 1913, Grove's plan was to save money by working for five years. He planned to become a recluse and devote himself entirely to writing. In his autobiography he describes what happened with an irony usually applied to his fictional protagonists who are diverted from their ambitions by circumstances. Instead of saving money to finance his retreat, Grove went into debt to buy books and equipment for his school.[3] Then in August 1914 he married the primary teacher, Catherine Wiens, and by December their first child was expected. 'From that moment on I renounced my old aspirations: I must concentrate my whole endeavour on a worldly career.'[4] Grove imagined that he must become a success in order to please his wife. When a future post with the department of education in Winnipeg was mooted, he took steps to become eligible.

In 1917, however, during his first period of leisure, unconscious forces began to stir. Grove felt 'out-of-sorts' for the first time in his married life. He writes that, 'while marriage had a great deal to do with it, my wife certainly had not' (*ISM*, 295). He had compared his life as school principal in Gladstone and future bureaucrat in Winnipeg with his original dream of artistic endeavour. Expressing his dissatisfaction to his wife, he said that he found town life 'profoundly repellent' because it implied a preoccupation with 'irrelevant trifles.' He was an 'outdoor man' with 'rural sympathies and tastes' and wanted a simple secluded life where he could give form to the 'essentials' in his writing. Catherine was willing to assist, and in the autumn of 1917 she accepted a one-room school at Falmouth in the bush thirty-four miles north of Gladstone. Eventually she would earn the living while her husband took care of their daughter May and wrote. Until they had some savings, Grove continued to teach in Gladstone and commuted to Falmouth on weekends. These, of course, were the trips which later served as the basis for *Over Prairie Trails*.

Circumstances again intervened in Grove's plans in 1918 when he was thrown from a buggy and suffered a back injury which raised fears of invalidism. Practical considerations were once more paramount; Catherine might one day be the family's sole support. Therefore, at the beginning of August 1919 Catherine enrolled at a Normal School in Winnipeg to study for a teacher's certificate. Meanwhile, Grove and May moved to Eden, 120 miles west of Winnipeg, where Grove became school principal. It was here that his creative reawakening took place. In his autobiography Grove writes that in mid-August, while awaiting Catherine's late-night arrival, '*I was seized with a sudden inspiration. I sat down at my desk and, in a veritable fervour of creation, wrote down, in its practically final form, the first chapter of Over Prairie Trails. No matter how severely, both in an emotional and physical sense, the next five months were to tell on me, as a writer I was to flourish amazingly*' (*ISM*, 332). This account must refer to a later visit from Catherine since the letters indicate that Grove did not start *Over Prairie Trails* until 10 October. The main discrepancies between the autobiographical account (written in the late 1930s) and the letters are in such instances of chronology.

Grove did not exaggerate the emotional and physical strains under which he worked. Despite its evocative name, Eden was an unlikely place for a creative reawakening. The town consisted of a line of commonplace shops and houses on the gravel highway eleven wind-swept miles north of Neepawa. Grove and May lived in the only available shelter, 'a small, tumble-down shack in the last stages of decay' (*ISM*, 328). Downstairs there was a single large room with a lean-to kitchenette while upstairs there were two rooms too dilapidated to inhabit. 'I had lived in worse places,' Grove writes, 'and my wife, whom I could not have asked to share such quarters, was not with me' (*ISM*, 329). Apart from physical conditions, Grove had his hands full as principal of the four-room school of ninety-five students and teacher of grades seven to ten. The letters indicate that there was constant friction with trustees, teachers, and students. Also, before and after school he looked after his four-year-old daughter, who did not adjust well to her mother's absence. After one visit from Catherine, Grove writes: 'The little girl was a changed creature. It was as though an almost adult realization of her plight had come to her . . . At times she became unnaturally thoughtful' (*ISM*, 335-36). The young wife and mother also felt the pain of separation. Despite their tight budget Catherine took every opportunity to visit and occasionally appeared by surprise. In addition to emotional strains Grove suffered recurrences of his back problem. Finally, the letters confirm that Grove was dogged by financial worries partly due to medical expenses and post-war inflation.

While Grove had been manipulated by such circumstances in the past, he was no longer their puppet. He had discovered an amazing creative capacity which gave him the confidence to overcome all obstacles. Rising at 5:30 a.m. to chilly room temperatures, Grove manages two hours of work before waking his daughter. During the lunch break at school he again snatched a few minutes to write, 'for what I was putting down on paper had become so vivid and urgent a vision that I should have liked to project it in one single, concentrated effort of the will. Often, when I had to tear myself away, I was in open revolt, damning the world and all its irrelevant exigencies' (*ISM*, 337). It was not until after supper when May was asleep that Grove had an uninterrupted stretch of four or five hours for concentrated effort. In spite of these conditions Grove wrote *Over Prairie Trails* in about seven weeks from 10 October to 28 November. It was accepted for publication on 19 December by McClelland and Stewart. Finally appearing in 1922, the book was a popular and critical success and launched Grove's new career in Canada.

The reader should be cautioned that the letters begin slowly and become more compelling as they proceed. Letter I, perhaps the least interesting, is none the less valuable because it establishes the importance of the series of five as a record of Grove's creative reawakening. It proves that as late as the beginning of September Grove had no immediate plans to write. The fears of invalidism had receded but they were replaced by a desire for material security. Grove calculates the amount of money they can save if both he and his wife teach school for a number of years. 'I believe under the circumstances we both should be quite satisfied to stay at work,' he tells Catherine. 'You don't mind working when you see you are getting somewhere.' But in letter III, written just six weeks later (21 October), Grove is determined to quit teaching altogether. He has started *Over Prairie Trails* and rediscovered his artistic ability. He will write 'even if it costs our last cent of savings and if I must go in rags to do it . . . My dear girl, I have started something, it is stronger than I am . . . It is like an illness that overthrows all plans. I only wish I had never taken this school!'

Grove also includes in these letters a lesson plan and some exercises in natural science intended to help Catherine meet her course requirements. They provide further evidence that the lyrical descriptions of nature in *Over Prairie Trails* were created by a man who also had a keen scientific understanding. A 'Nature-Study crank' by his own account, Grove kept records of weather for whole seasons as well as everyday observations of 'mere nothings.' 'I sometimes fear there is something wrong with my own mentality,' he writes in *Over Prairie Trails*. 'But to me it seems that the Kingdom of Heaven lies all around us, and that most of us simply prefer the moving-picture show.'[5]

The five letters are not dated, but their order and approximate dates have been established from internal references. Grove's peculiar use of commas and, in some cases, capital letters is a vestige of his native German. All the letters were handwritten except letter IV which was typed. The symbol *** indicates that there are omissions in the text because the page has been torn.

Letter I
[early September 1919] Saturday

[Last] night Mrs. H[ahn] suddenly asked whether I was going to stay. [I don't know,] I answered. It is too early to say anything. 'But,' I added, 'there is no way of getting around this, that Mrs. Grove and I shall both have to teach. Mrs. Grove has just been offered a position in the city [Winnipeg], I have often been told that I was wanted on the city staff. And though I do not wish to go to the city, yet the fact that we might teach together, may outweigh all other objections.' They did not say anything, and so I left it at that. But if they want to get Intermediate standing, they shall have to get second class teachers, *if they can get them*. Well, they *can* get you. Suppose they do take you—then, I think, we cannot do better than stay. We should have $80 to $90 a month for living + $150 to save. That would enable us to have ca $400 to $500 for a trip to the rockies and to Vancouver island + $1000 or $1200 saved by the end of the year. Besides, if we stayed another year, you would have your standing, and we should have $2500 in cash—half the sum that I should consider sufficient to consider some thing different. And that within 1½ years from now. If, as I think, they would, they raised both of us $50 each, we might even do better than that, for, I believe, if we had $1000 for living, we should be able to save a couple of hundred out of that. After that we should have, besides our salaries, ca $130 in interest the first year. Once you have the first few thousand Dollars, things become easier all the time. I do not see, why we should not be able to get somewhere near $3000 in a few years here or in a similar school. Then—with $5000 to $6000 saved, we could buy a farm and build. As long as things are agreeable, we could go on teaching. Should they become disagreeable, alright, we'd throw it up. We should be mighty independent. We could dictate our conditions. They will have to open the 4th room here sooner or later—I expect it in 2 yrs. Then—$1800 for me, $1000 for you. $1800 saved and $1000 for living, the interest on our savings for trips. I believe under the circumstances we both should be quite satisfied to stay at work: the same as I felt lots better when I heard that this year, it [the salary] was $1500. You don't mind working when you see you are getting somewhere. Of course, the house is a horror, but then—that could be changed in a short time. Somebody will realise that it would be good business to build.

[***] they would [***] on $1700 *if* they take me? Well, that would be no better [***] about it if you care to. I should like to have the residence, no doubt [***] small school, I believe I should prefer public school work, grades 5, 6, 7 and [***] If a large school, of course, I should not go except as principal. It's hard to say what may be best.

As for those outlines—I don't know at all what is wanted. You know I am the man of detail. I send you an outline for dog, horse, cow, chicken. I don't think it's of my best but it is in general outline what I should do or have done. I don't plan my lessons so very much; but I follow certain principles in developing them:

What I call the 5 formal steps

Preparation	(the working up to the new lesson from previous ones—sometimes in the form of review)
Presentation	(the exposition of the new matter)

Association	(the connecting up with what was previously taught)
Generalization	(the working out of the general principle underlying. In arithmetic f[or] i[nstance], the finding of the rule.)
Application	(Drawing the conclusions or consequences. In Arith.: hammering it home by additional problems involving the same principle)

1 Example of the whole thing as brief as I can make it.

Preparation	Review notation ones, tens, hundreds column read: twenty and 3 etc.

Presentation

46 x 23
───────
46 x 3

138

```
                  138
46 x 20           920
───────          ─────
   920           1058
```

Association:

```
3 ones   2 tens;       46
                       23
                      ────            of course,
                       138   46 x 3   several
                        92   46 x 2   examples
                      ────
                      1058
```

Generalization   Find rule of moving in one place. State it in words.

Application   *Drill* on just this.

I do not consider any one lesson well taught, in which any one step is missing: I am a Herbartian in this respect (Find Herbart in your Hist. of Ed.)[6]

Letter II
[29 September] Monday night

My dear girl—

Just in a hurry—because you don't know or rather remember the *name* Yellow finch which by the way I have always used, is no reason to reject the note—there is no wild Canary in Canada. People who think the name Yellowfinch is not pretty enough, call him Goldfinch. People who cannot distinguish a yellow *sparrow* living on or hailing from the Canary islands from a yellow Finch call him Canary. Canaries are kept in cages; they are *all* yellow, and they are grain eaters. Yellow finches are 50% seed eaters—thistle seed eaters, 50% insect eaters. You know the bird as well as I do. Yes, the Alder is monoecious. Yes the rounded buds are the pistillate ones, the others staminate.

Have just bought 26 lb of butter in a wooden pail. Am going to transfer to crocks on Saturday. The butter seems good.

Have not yet been able to cash Lange's M.O.[7] There seems to be something wrong about it.

Am frying a big pan full of tomatoes.

Gloves for May would be welcome. Don't know yet when and how much I can send you, old girl, so be careful. Saw Heeney[8] tonight and told him I needed every cent I could lay my hand on. I have only a few cents left now and have spent all I collected for books which I got from R.R. & Co. for the class. So I owe them quite a bill, I suppose.

Well, I've done a big piece of work: packed the butter in the crocks, working it down with my hands. I guess I'm still greasy.

Another general note:

Sept. 29. The first big snowfall last night. When I first went out this morning, I noticed that the snow was lying thick on all the grass, on the weeds and trees, on every bit of ploughed ground, and wherever there was a wooden sidewalk (as, I believe, in the corner of lumberland, if not, leave out or say, on a plank). But on the cement sidewalks and on the flat earthroads there was none. There are two possible explanations: either the specific heat of those places which held snow was less than that of the road and the cement. So the heat contained in grass, branch, wood, etc. would be used up more quickly, there being less of it. Or the conductivity of the hard beaten road and the cement sidewalks is greater. Now leaves and plant matter generally are mostly water, and the specific heat of water is the highest known. This eliminates the first consideration as a cause of the phenomenon. Remains the second. And indeed, it stands to reason that, as the deeper ground holds fast longest in the spring, so it will hold the summer heat longest in the fall. Through the hard beaten ground and the cement sidewalks this heat from below is conducted upward and so becomes available to melt the snow. In freshly ploughed ground the innumerable air spaces buried by the plow break this continuity of conduction; grass and weeds also hold non conducting air spaces underneath, and wood is a bad conductor of heat as the match burning at one end and cold at the other will easily prove.

Fall colouring:

Sept. 29 I noticed a very sudden change in the willows by reason of snow and frost. Without turning yellow, many leaves turned dirty grey and fell in a single night.

I happened to see that the Alder leaf, too, like the leaf of the Cottonwood, frequently shows green ribs and coloured blade.

Please do not forget to bring me a package of envelopes—I can't get them here any longer, and I have used mine nearly up.

I have no tobacco left and should appreciate it if I got some before Saturday. I shall allow $5 extra in whatever I can send you.

By the way, in order to save postage I shall transfer whatever I do not need in cash to your bank. So for what you need, you will have to draw a cheque. Tobacco—if possible, *Prince Albert* and *Fatima*. Together for ca $5.

Letter III

[21 October] Tuesday morning

My dear girl,

I read the two drives over in full last night. And I am now quite sure of it. It is not only great prose, but real poetry to boot. I am starting to condense my whole feeling of the North into them. And the seven drives must stand alone.[9] I am going to make them into a book by themselves with the title:

Seven drives on Manitoba trails

by

A Manitoba Teacher

I am beginning to be sure that they will go like wildfire. When I read them, I melted again by my own fire, if you know what I mean. There is not only Nature and observation, there is even a touch of greatness in them. The book will be about 200 pages and will cost $1 or .80¢

And I am quite sure now, even if it costs our last cent of savings and if I must go in rags to do it—I want my freedom for at least the six months of the second term. So I am going to give notice here and not listen to anything. And you go ahead. I am going to produce at least another book before summer. In spring this one must appear, even if I print it myself. If, then, we realize enough out of it by midsummer we'll have a trip. If not, we'll wait till winter, and my books must be the trip for you. But do not go for less than $900. If you can't get that we'll go to Sask.

This book, by condensation of facts and impressions, and also by unfolding to leafy branches what in reality was only a winter bud, will be about ¼ fiction and ¾ fact. That will make it all the better.

If I had a day job, I'd quit to-day.[10]

Bye-bye

Tuesday night

I am alright and so is May. I have written another 8 pages of ride no. 3. I am in for it now. This seemed the hardest one of them all, and I dreaded a little to start it. But May went to sleep, and I was off with the pencil. I cannot stop it. It is there and has to be written now or never. I know now that for 25 years I have wasted my time. I have done what I should not have done. I do not care one rap about school. I shall write, and if I cannot keep up the work in the school, I shall neglect it. I believe I could simply leave and go home if I feel a word that wants to crystallize into a sentence. My dear girl, I have started something, it is stronger than I am, and I cannot say that I like it. It is like an illness that overthrows all plans. I only wish I had never taken this school! Some paragraphs that I have written today, are the highest poetry I believe.

The remark 'for 25 years I have wasted my time' indicates that, five years after their marriage, Catherine Grove did not know her husband's true age or identity.[11] Shortly after May's birth in August 1915 Grove told Catherine that 'something might come up' at any time and he might have to 'pick up and leave.' He said no more and she was not to ask any questions.[12]

Initially Grove appears to have hoped to share the burden of his European past with his wife but he found that this was not possible. An unpublished poem, 'You and I,' expresses disappointment that a fusion of their lives had not taken place.

> O Come, o come to the woods with me
> Where the aspens' young leaves unfold!
> O that I could, that I could tell thee
> What will forever remain untold!
> . . .
> We have lived for years thus side by side;
> My wish it did not come true:
> It is long, so long since you were bride,
> But still we are I and you.[13]

The difference in their ages may partly account for Grove's disappointment. He was forty years old in 1919 and claimed to be forty-seven; Catherine was twenty-seven. 'My wife was something like a child to me,' he writes in *Over Prairie Trails,* 'I was old enough to be her father, older even in mind than in actual years.'[14] Grove generally oversaw Catherine's life, and even chose her clothes and hats.[15] He was tutor as well as 'father.' He told his class in Eden: 'I found a student with a mind as keen as my own and I married her.'

If Catherine was not Grove's peer, she was an exceptionally able and dedicated wife. Born of a Mennonite family in 1892, she began teaching in one-room rural schools at sixteen, and was saving money to go to university when she married at twenty-two. She recognized her husband's talent and supported his work by teaching and operating a successful private school. Grove realized that the marriage was the best possible for him. Many of his novels express the theme that romantic aspirations, like the fusion of two lives, are incompatible with artistic objectives. The artist must sacrifice worldly ties and devote his whole energy to his muse.[16] Nevertheless the years of shared sorrows and triumphs created a bond of affection and trust which enabled Grove at last to confide much of his European background to his wife. There is evidence that, over the course of the marriage, he told her his real name, nationality, and the facts of his imprisonment and first marriage.[17] Grove paid tribute to Catherine in his autobiography: 'There are many kinds of heroism; and it is not those that become spectacular which are the most inspiring' (*ISM*, 339).

Letter IV
[*7 November*]

My dear girl, no, I have not yet had time to write to those people. Nor shall I have time before Sunday. I'm pretty tolerably busy, you know, and I rather think that what I am doing, after all counts for more than that money, even though we need it badly enough, God wot!

But I'll write on Sunday sure.

As far as your school goes, I wish myself, we could get that settled, but I am afraid there is small chance before middle of December. That is when the vacancies open. Stratton—Pah! I don't even think he would take you. He is the biggest fool in Manitoba. But see Fletcher by all means.[18]

As for May, I am trying to keep from buying her a muffler here. She surely needs it. She has already caught something of a cold. You see, it is not as it was at Falmouth. Here she has got to go out, no matter what the weather is, and mostly it is beastly for town weather, no matter how nice it may be in the country.

Well, here the crash has come. Even if we did not plan what we do plan, I could not stay. I asked Heeney yesterday, whether he proposed to run the school. If so, I added, he might count me out right away. Of course, he backed down right away. Then I had the next crash with Miss Drysdale. I told her, that I was the principal, not she. As long as I was here, she would have to adopt my ways, not I hers. Well, she boards with Thompsons, and there you are. To night I gave my ultimatum to one of the trustees. I have just enough wood for to-morrow. And nobody wants to sell me any. Alright, I told this man, I want to get out. So, unless there is a load of wood on my yard by noon to-morrow, I'll take the afternoon train to Macreary. And I'll do so, too. Only, I feel sure that the wood will be there. They'll take the school wood.

No, my girl, it would not suit me at all if you came home a week sooner.[19] I have my plans laid out, and I want to get four weeks done with this time. As for your star-notes, I'll enclose another one, and I'll write still another one out on the reverse of this page. For that one you want to find a suitable date, because it is entire fiction, but true to fact. I simply have no opportunity of seeing the stars now. We have storm after storm. If you have unfavourable weather too, you must say so in your notebook. Orion is in the Western sky now, high up, at six in the morning. It's easy enough to see it. Nobody who sees it can mistake it.

There are two other brilliant stars nearby. As for Lidke's note, you must go to the bank and get the old note back and send it to him. I have subscribed only $100 V[ictory] B[ond]. Did not see how we could manage more without the money that is due us. Well, so long.

[*added in hand*] Have finished on the machine what I had in the book in W'peg. Have in the book what I had written—2 drives to be rewritten now. It's only exactly 1 mos. ago today [***] that I wrote the first line. First 3 drives [***]

[*reverse of letter IV*]
[in hand] This note holds good only, of course, for the *waxing moon*. Somewhere around Nov 4 or 5

[*typed*] My previous observations on the moon, broken as they were on account of unfavourable weather, have made it clear that the moon swings around the earth in an easterly direction. I wanted to determine whether the speed of its motion as calculated from daily observations, accorded with the time of a lunation as seen in the recurrence of the phases. So day before yesterday I went out and stood at a certain spot, so that I saw the moon exactly over a certain branch of a tree. This spot I marked. Yesterday I went again, repeatedly, till I saw the moon once more exactly over the same branch. It seemed to stand higher above it, though. The first observation was made at seven o'clock sharp. The day after the moon reached the same spot, as nearly as I could determine it, at 52 minutes past seven. Since there are 24 times 60 minutes in the day, provided that the moon moves at the same rate all through, which is likely and almost certain, it would get back to the same spot at the same hour in 24 times 60 divided by 52 days. That is 27-9/13 days, which is not very accurate but sufficiently so, considering that my observation was only approximate.

It appears that the school board had lost patience with Grove. In a meeting on 8 November his resignation was accepted.[20] Nevertheless he continued his duties until 12 December, when a replacement took over. Grove seems to have reserved his more human side for his family. In public his sense of alienated superiority made him appear austere and autocratic. 'He had a somewhat abrasive personality and a wit tinged with sarcasm,' a former student in Eden recalls; 'that and a certain aloofness, due to his background and education, made him none too popular in the community.' In the classroom he was a sharp-tongued disciplinarian whose appearance and knowledge inspired awe in his students. 'I can still see him striding up the aisle of our classroom, a tall, very slim, fair haired man, with penetrating blue eyes,' another student recalls. 'You just didn't try to put anything over on Mr. Philip Grove. The classroom prankster did once and his self-esteem was reduced to ashes by the blistering tongue-lashing he received in front of his classmates.' Grove demanded a lot and was usually disappointed. He attempted to teach in a university style with lectures and independent study but the twelve- to fourteen-year-olds lacked the necessary self-discipline. Grove sometimes compared them unfavourably with his four-year-old daughter whom he taught at home. Nevertheless, the students appreciated Grove's knowledge and his ability to make the subjects interesting. 'Mr. Grove was a complex character. But he was real. I guess I learned more under him than any other teacher. Perhaps I liked him in spite of himself.' The Groves were both accepted when in 1921 they applied again to Eden.

Letter V, written in instalments over a weekend, captures the grainy texture of Grove's life during this period, and reveals some new literary information. In speaking of his plans to write *A Search for America* (originally 'Immigrant') Grove gives the clear impression that he is approaching this novel for the first time. In his autobiography he often claims that he wrote the first draft eighteen months after arriving in Canada in 1892 (*ISM*, 193-94). The remark that he began *Settlers of the Marsh* (originally 'The White Range Line House') in German is a tantalizing one. Was there an early Canadian effort in his native language?

Letter V
[21 November] Friday night

I was half afraid and half I hoped you would step off the belated train today. I hoped because I hate this shebang so much by now, and I was afraid because it would then have been 4 weeks instead of only three.[21] I don't know. I am not going to quit so long as I feel I can do the work without endangering my book. We need the money too darn badly. But if I feel bad, I'll quit without a further word. My teaching does not count for very much, anyway. Today I simply forgot about a period which I did not like. I begin to hate the town worse than I hated Gladstone. There were at least *some* boys and girls there that did their work. There are none here.

Well, I do hope, everything is alright at Sarto,[22] as your letter of last night leads me to expect. The lonelier the better as far as I am concerned. I don't know much about you. If only we can get where we can spend a matter of $10 or so per month on books; then the more people will leave *me* alone, the better. They do not expect to close here before the 23rd, and if my health holds out, I'd be rather glad of the few extra dollars.

I did not mean to dissuade from Sarto at any time; only I come to believe that we must lay down our conditions *beforehand.* You are young and have no handicaps. So you can make your bargain. But with me, that is different. I have to take what I can get.—But I'll thank the Lord if my books will only bring what I could make by looking after a little country-school. I'll never want to go back to teaching.

I have the speed drive rewritten, no 6, and I believe it is good. I am copying it out into the last pages of the book. Then I'll read it once more, and if I still think it alright, I'll type it while starting on the last number. As soon as I have drafted that I'll start rereading the whole book for typing-mistakes, and at the same time send out inquiries to the publishers. If they answer promptly, the manuscripts will go out before Christmas. Then good luck to it!

Later.

Have just finished the clean copy of drive no. 6. It is exactly 6 weeks since I started the book. This is about 180 pages printed, Burroughs size.[23] That seems to be doing pretty well, considering that I am teaching and doing the rest of the things I do. I am utterly reluctant to start drive 7, though. I should infinitely prefer writing my 'Immigrant' first. That book becomes more and more plastic now. Tone, style and contents. It works itself into chapters, even. I do wish, these fellows here would get somebody in a hurry so I could start on the new book before Christmas. But I am afraid they won't. I shall need lots of time and lots of good humour for that book. I don't want to write it in a hurry. But I want to finish it before the summer comes, for I know, I never like to write in spring. A tinge of frost is needed. After that I have another book ready as to contents: The White Range Line House. The one that I started to work on in German. But of course, I'll remodel that if I write in English. I'll have to see first, whether my English will be a success. I am sure I can dash books down at a rate of two a year for a dozen years yet. In between there will fill out a couple more volumes of nature studies. But I want the connected story now. The large, monumental thing that takes building and careful planning ahead. I am tired of this essay thing of the first book. I am sure I can do better, too when I am entirely on fictitious ground. I don't like to be hampered by facts. I only wish that, to relax, I had something, or rather, lots to read, too. I am fairly starving for reading matter. Most of the Saturday Evening Post, after all, is mere slush. If my English is alright, of which I sometimes have grave doubts, I believe I shall break through at last into the open, even if these drives fall flat.—

[Saturday morn. 22 November]

A big hot dustwind all night. Snow is all gone, I have not even water to do what washing would have to be done. And every thing is beastly dirty. This is a place for pigs, not for men. I am so disgusted.

Eve.

Have finished the typing of no 6, too, now. So there remains nothing but all the work on no. 7 to complete the whole thing. But I feel kind of fagged out to-night with nothing to read unfortunately. That is the worst about living in the country, at least for me. If it was in the bush, I should go out at least—but here, walk on the grades? No thanks.

Just got 1 doz eggs—75¢ & ½ lb of cheese 25¢. Money is dirt these days. You don't get anything for a dollar any longer that amounts to anything. I made out a little order for Eatons to start next year on, and it ran up to $100. We shall have to sell another $100 worth of V.B. unless those buggers pay up.—On the other hand, just while I wrote these words, there came a knock at the door, and Jim brings me a big supply of head cheese. I had just been in at their house to return a dish they had sent with a little piece of head cheese the other day. When I handed it in, I said to her daughter, 'Please tell Mrs. Scott, I thank her very much, and that was the best head cheese I've ever eaten.' It was, too—so she sent me enough for 3 or 4 meals now. But nevertheless my bills will be about $40, outside of rent and wood. It is simply outrageous. As for that Eaton order and selling the V.B., I think it is better to do that, making a slight profit on the bonds and then freighting the whole order out, so as to get it simultaneously with our getting there, and then rather to save what cash is coming in than order in driblets, pay expressage every time etc.—Just totalled the order: $110.10 not including flour. But I think it would include three mos. groceries about. I'll let you look at it when you come here. There are only 12 doz canned goods in that, about half fish & meats, half vegetables, 1 ham, 1 bacon side, 25 lbs coffee.

But I'll be so glad to settle down in a decent new house that I should not care even though we had to salt in all our savings. I do hope things will run smoothly there.—Just had our supper, and in unpacking found a big bag of buns and doughnuts for May, too. It's nearly embarrassing. If they did *not* do that, however, what would my bills amount to, I wonder?

That blessed train never comes in before 6 p.m. now. Just heard its whistle now. Well, 4 weeks from now we'll be packing up anyway. I shall do the books before that.—Wood has cost me so far $16, and I am not going to buy any more. When this is gone, I'll go, that's all.—I feel quite stranded to-night—no work to do, nothing to do, no company—just loafing around. Too bad I finished that 6th drive so soon. 155 typed pages now—of Burroughs size, or rather a bit larger, because I wanted to see what it would amount to at the least, so every line (31 lines to the page) is 2 to 3 letters larger than Burroughs. 155 x 31 x 2 letters more:

155 x 62

310
620
─────
6510 letters

31 x 50

1550 letters to the printed page

1550   6510
       620
       ───

4 to 5 pages more will come out
of that

—Just got my mail. Well, no, I'm not counting on leaving here before Christmas at all—but I *wish* I could. No, I'm figuring on your coming *next* Saturday. When you have a writing husband, you don't want to spring surprises on him all the time. That upsets him. No matter when I'll quite, I expect you here next Friday. You better arrange for that. I don't care when I leave. I'll go if they get somebody. I'll go, if I don't feel right. I'll stay if they don't get anybody and I feel right. Whenever I don't feel like going to school, I'll stay at home, that's all. But we do need the money—so I'll stay if I can. But I do put my books ahead of everything else, now.

I only do hope those fellows with the ugly names will sign and give fuel, house, garden + $100 a month. Then we'll be a sight better off than we would be here on $150., especially if they'll put up a stable for chickens.

If Solomon doesn't pay up his note in a hurry now, I'll seize Jessie. Then we'll have a horse at least, though I'd rather have a different one after a while. I should like to get a bigger horse—one that I can ride horseback—with a saddle—you can go so many places on horseback where you can't go in a buggy.—Oh, as for Mrs. Wallace—if she sells I suppose you could make an arrangement with her successor. I should try to avoid moving if I were you—simply costs money. It's only for three weeks then.

Sunday, *[23 November]*

Everything is dirty, but I have no water. So I can't do anything. May & I had our bath from a cupful. Nobody has any left, either, except Heeney, and that is too far to carry. So things have to stay dirty till you come.

My goodness, how I hate having to start on that 7th drive instead of the 'Immigrant.' But unless I write that drive, that book will not be finished till next year, that's certain. The Immigrant will keep me busy for 4 or 5 mos continuous work—& will be a 500 page book, I'm sure, and since it has to be planned carefully, it cannot be dashed down as this one was.—

Sun. eve.—

Am writing away in a leisurely sort of manner on that 7th drive. Likely I shall have to rewrite it a dozen times or so—as is usual when I don't dash it down in one fling. Probably, at least, I hope so, I shall finish it about end of the week. Then that book is done, and I'll be mighty glad of it.

By-the-way, I had written to the Mayo Bros. and have received a reply. I was not going to tell you as yet. There may be a change in the diet after a while.[24] They also advise not doing anything that involves responsibility, nervous excitement etc. So that settles my teaching alright, especially here. There is hardly a day going by without my flying off the handle.—

Do you think if you draw $10 or $11 you could bring me some tobacco? Maybe 2 *tins* of Prince Albert and 2 or 3 packages of Fatima? I am out completely. There should be enough money left for that. I have not drawn anything except $10 for V.B. I believe this is the way it stands:

$128 from Hahn

$28	drawn in cash
$50	" for typewriter
$25	" by you
$10	" " myself
3.50	" for coffee

$116.50

- leaves $11.50 from that.

By the way—as for the cost of living: that cream is getting to be so thin that I shall soon prefer condensed milk. May is alright—alrighter than I.

Shortly before the new year Grove, May, and Catherine were reunited in Winnipeg. They proceeded to a district twenty miles north of the city where Catherine, who had received her formal certificate, taught in a one-room school. Grove was true to his vow to 'produce at least another book before summer.' By the end of April he sent a completed manuscript of 'Immigrant' (*A Search for America*) to a publisher. He also wrote two other novels. Throughout his life Grove's reward for his prodigious efforts was small. Nevertheless he did not depart from the course he set in Eden which he summarized in the words, 'I do put my books ahead of every thing else, now.'

I would like to thank Leonard and Mary Grove for making these letters available for publication and for providing pertinent information. Professor Margaret Stobie has kindly given permission to cite her research, which she has deposited in the Grove Collection at the University of Manitoba. Her material includes many extensive interviews with friends and associates of Grove which constitute an invaluable record.

[1] Desmond Pacey, ed., *The Letters of Frederick Philip Grove* (Toronto: Univ. of Toronto Press, 1976).

[2] D.O. Spettigue, *FPG: The European Years* (Ottawa: Oberon Press, 1973).

[3] In February 1914 he wrote to Isaak Warkentin: 'I spent the greater part of my salary on this school—that puts me back one year. Instead of being through in 1918 I shall have to work on till 1919 before I can retire' (*Letters*, 13).

[4] F.P. Grove, *In Search of Myself* (1946; rpt. Toronto: McClelland & Stewart, 1974), p. 287; henceforth cited in text as ISM.

[5] F.P. Grove, *Over Prairie Trails* (1922; rpt. Toronto: McClelland & Stewart, 1957), p. 99.

[6] Johann Friedrich Herbart (1776-1841), German philosopher and educator. For Grove's education views, see Margaret R. Stobie, *Frederick Philip Grove* (New York: Twayne, 1973), pp. 36-41.

[7] Lange is the name of a family in the Ferguson/Falmouth area (Stobie, 48). Presumably the money order is payment for back salary or a loan. Grove refers to an overdue loan in ISM, 340.

[8] Heeney is the 'Henley' of ISM, a minister and secretary of the school board in Eden (328).

[9] Originally Grove planned to include material which appeared later in *The Turn of the Year* (Toronto: McClelland & Stewart, 1923). See *ISM*, 337.

[10] A mysterious reference. Perhaps Grove is referring to a job where he could work by the day whenever he wished. Maybe he wishes to escape from the teacher's burden of evening preparation and marking to a normal nine-to-five job.

[11] Throughout his life Grove claimed that he was born in 1871 or 1872 and came to North America in 1892. He said he worked as an itinerant farmhand until 1913 when he began school teaching.

[12]Grove's daughter-in-law, Mrs. A.L. Grove, was kind enough to convey to this editor pertinent information from her conversations with Catherine Grove, who died in 1972.

[13]The Grove Collection, Department of Archives and Special Collections, Elizabeth Dafoe Library, University of Manitoba.

[14]*Over Prairie Trails*, p. 119.

[15]Catherine conveyed this information to a neighbour in Eden. For citations of Eden residents I am indebted to transcripts of interviews conducted by Margaret R. Stobie, Grove Collection, University of Manitoba.

[16]See Henry Makow, 'Grove's "The Canyon",' *Canadian Literature*, 82 (Autumn 1979), 141-48. In this novel a poet cannot create until he marries a woman who does not compete with his muse, a vision of ideal beauty. Grove also treats the theme in two other unpublished works, 'Two Lives' and 'The Seasons,' both written in the thirties.

[17]In 1969 Catherine told Mrs. A.L. Grove her husband's real name and nationality. She said her husband was apprehensive that the woman he left behind in Germany might make a claim on his property after he was gone. She reacted in a startled manner when she heard that D.O. Spettigue and her son were checking prison records at the early stages of their investigation.

[18]Robert Fletcher (1873-1963), then deputy minister of education in Manitoba, hired Grove (see ISM, 249ff.) and encouraged him to pursue a career in education.

[19]For reasons of economy and his work Grove did not want Catherine to visit more than once a month. Grove and May visited Winnipeg on 31 October so Catherine's next visit was not until 28 November. Catherine's request to come a week sooner may be the reason Grove half expected her on 21 November (letter V).

[20]Stobie, p. 52.

[21]Grove is referring to the amount of time before they will begin preparations to leave Eden.

[22]Sarto, a village ten miles south of Steinbach. Apparently Mrs. Grove was negotiating with the local school board.

[23]John Burroughs (1837-1921), American nature essayist. Grove refers to Burroughs in *Over Prairie Trails* (e.g. p. 100) and they corresponded briefly in the autumn of 1920 (see Stobie, p. 53).

[24]Grove says he suffered spinal lesions when thrown from his buggy in 1918. He says his symptoms were diagnosed as diabetes and he was put on a diet (ISM, 323-4). The 'Mayo Bros.' refers to the famous Mayo Clinic in Rochester, Minnesota.

W.J. Keith

Grove's Over Prairie Trails: *A Re-Examination*

The time seems ripe for a fresh critical scrutiny of Frederick Philip
Grove's first published book in English, *Over Prairie Trails* (1922).
In his 1969 study of Grove, Douglas O. Spettigue showed that most of
what we thought we knew about Grove's life, derived from his own
autobiographical writings, proves untrustworthy when checkable
clues are followed up.[1] The revelations concerning his 'European
years' as Felix Paul Greve have not only altered our view of his so-
called autobiography *In Search of Myself*; they also encourage us to
recognize that far more artistic patterning is present in all his
supposedly non-fiction works than has hitherto been assumed.
Grove appears, indeed, as one of the few Canadian writers intent, like
George Borrow or George Moore, upon remoulding his own
character on paper, one of those who, in the words of the late Lucille
Herbert, 'seem to confound the categories of autobiography and
fiction, because they think of subjective experience as itself a kind of
fiction, a perpetual proliferation of self-created attitudes.'[2]

Most affected by Professor Spettigue's embarrassingly thorough
detective-work is, of course, *In Search of Myself*, which must now be
grouped with *Lavengro* and *Confessions of a Young Man* rather than
with more conventional autobiographies. *A Search for America*,
though apparently based on Grove's still obscure American
experience between 1909 and 1912, was described by the author
himself as 'to a certain extent, fiction,' and has generally been
discussed as such.[3] But what about *Over Prairie Trails*, an account of
seven winter journeys in Manitoba during the winter of 1917-18?
While there is no reason to doubt that Grove made these journeys, we
are no longer obliged to approach the book as a 'mere' writing-up of
day-to-day adventures. Grove may well be employing his artistry no
less definitely—and perhaps even more subtly—in *Over Prairie
Trails* than in the later novels like *Our Daily Bread* and *The Yoke of
Life*. It is this possibility that I hope to explore in this paper.

Grove himself defined Art—not only the novel but all Art—as 'that
activity of the human mind and soul which awakens and directs an
emotional response to what is not I.'[4] It is a challenging definition,
and especially relevant to our present purpose, since nature-
writing—the category to which *Over Prairie Trails* clearly belongs—
is centrally concerned with this same attempt. Far from being
undisciplined effusions or the literary equivalents of unimaginative

sketch-books, the traditional classics of nature-writing depend upon the establishment of a clearly recognizable 'I' through whom images and impressions of the natural world can be filtered. Just as a landscape will take on a radically different character if created by, say, a Constable or a Van Gogh, so a verbal description is similarly reliant on the personal vision of the observer. The eyes of a Cobbett, a W.H. Hudson, a Thoreau will see different natural worlds.

In the case of *Over Prairie Trails*, however, the matter is considerably more complex. We are confronted with not one but seven word-portraits of the route between Gladstone and Falmouth, and although certain features are always recognizable, the descriptions vary radically. The trails are presented in thick fog, under virtually impassable snow-drifts, in dangerous winds and beneath the staggering beauty of the night-sky. The natural world Grove describes changes from day to day, even from hour to hour, with the meteorological variations of which he is so skilled and sensitive a recorder. But—and this is the important point—the changes in the natural world present new challenges and bring out new responses in Grove himself. Hence we are concerned here not merely with the writer's reaction to 'what is not I,' with a dichotomy between the subject seeing and the object seen, but with a complex series of inter-relationships between man and nature. On some occasions the landscape forces the man into fresh initiatives or even to display qualities he was not aware of possessing, while on others the man dominates the landscape through sheer strength of will and resourcefulness. It is the way grove builds up a sense of the ever-changing though ever-apparent connection between self and universe that gives the book its peculiar power.

Again, part of the book's complexity derives from tensions which were doubtless implicit in the autobiographical situation but which, I suggest, Grove chose to develop for his own creative and self-reflective purpose. Several commentators have stressed the 'epic' quality of these journeys—particularly those accomplished in thick fog and almost incredibly deep snow. In all but one of the seven journeys, Grove is travelling from Gladstone to Falmouth—that is, home to wife and child. Remembering his interest in Homer and the subtitle of *A Search for America*, 'The Odyssey of an Immigrant,' it is not difficult to fit the book into the pattern that Professor W.B. Stanford has christened 'the Ulysses theme.'[5] But, like so many recent treatments of the Homeric story, Grove is a distinctly modern-day Ulysses, and we cannot help recognizing in his situation an early example of the now familiar North American phenomenon, the week-end commuter. Admittedly, later social habits in Canada have pointed up the pattern, but it is not unreasonable to credit Grove with deliberately presenting himself as a Ulysses figure looking, like Janus, before and after.

But the image of Grove-as-Ulysses is itself in need of qualification. One of the oddest features of the book is the shifting emphasis between journey and goal, between *going* home and *getting* home. at one moment—it is itself a paradox—Grove presents himself as a curiously domesticated pioneer; at the next, the idea of wife and child seems forgotten in a fascinated and exclusive concentration on the Manitoba wastelands. The first paragraph of the 'Author's Preface' stresses the lengths to which he was prepared to go in order to enjoy the week-ends with his family; the second insists that 'these drives . . . soon became what made my life worth living' (xiii).[6] The narrative is ostensibly written so that his wife and daughter might enjoy it in later years (see 44)—yet they would be faced on the first page with the brusquely equivocal comment: 'I love Nature more than Man' (xiii). In fact, the moments of reconciliation between father and family at the end of the forward journeys are perfunctory in the extreme; even in 'A Call for Speed,' the chapter describing a journey undertaken in the belief that his daughter was dangerously ill, the emphasis is clearly on the soothing powers of the natural environment.[7]

A similar sense of the paradoxical, of an elusive chameleon-like quality that cannot be pinned down, is evident in Grove's self-presentation in this book. Our impression varies from page to page. He begins as an obscure but discontented schoolmaster, 'an outdoor creature' (xiii) given to dreamy meditations, yet he appears on later pages as 'a thorough-going person' (19), 'fatalistic in temperament' (72), 'something of a sportsman' (78), 'enough of a doctor to trust [his] ability to diagnose' (117), 'an aging man' (119). Such qualities are not impossible to fit into a credible and rounded picture, but it is a feat that readers are unable to achieve until they close the book. In the process of reading, they are constantly surprised—often, it must be admitted, disturbed—by the frequent introduction of unexpected traits and aspects. If they are expecting either the consistent portrait offered by traditional novelists or the reliable persona of the familiar essayists, they will be disappointed; if, on the other hand, they are schooled in the tradition of the semi-fictional confession, they will be less troubled by the devious methods of a cumulative self-portrayal.

The foregoing analysis, however, has failed to do justice to Grove's effect. This is because, in separating his response to the natural world from his portrait of himself, I have inevitably neglected his admirable synthesis of these two elements. 'Like the snow I obeyed the laws of my nature,' he remarks at one point (72), and the simile is not merely decorative, let alone 'clever,' but essential to his whole presentation. Here in a single sentence the relationship between self and 'what is not I' is firmly, if temporarily established. Perhaps the most important as well as the most dramatic example of this inter-relationship occurs in the memorable passage in which Grove realizes the height of the drifts over which he is travelling:

> I shall never forget the weird kind of astonishment when the fact came home to me that what snapped and crackled under the horses' hoofs, were the tops of trees. Nor shall the feeling of estrangement, as it were—as if I were not myself, but looking on from the outside at the adventure of somebody who yet was I— the feeling of other-worldliness, if you will pardon the word, ever fade from my memory—a feeling of having been carried beyond my depth where I could not swim—which came over me when with two quick glances to right and left I took in the fact that there were no longer any trees to either side, that I was above that forest world which had so often engulfed me. (86)

Here it is futile to try to separate individual from environment. We are offered a vivid impression both of the experience itself and of Grove's fascinated but tentative and untrusting response to it. At the same time, the sensation of looking upon his own adventure from the outside anticipates the reader's stance and openly reveals Grove's habitual method of observing himself from different angles. Moreover, the last few lines of the quoted passage, in boldly trans-posing imagery usually associated with the depth of the sea ('beyond my depth where I could not swim,' 'engulfed me') to his unique above-the-treetops situation, suggest a personal psychological landscape as much as a description of a 'real' experience.

This leads conveniently to a consideration of Grove's language since, as the extended passage just quoted makes clear, it is through his words, their rhythms and associations, that the necessary effect is achieved. Perhaps the most obvious effect in Grove's prose is his employment of 'pathetic fallacy.' Grove's awareness of this stylistic feature of his writing is evident from the following passage:

> Yes, the snow, as figured in the waves, *crawled* over the ground. There was in the image that engraved itself on my memory something cruel—I could not help thinking of the 'cruel, crawling foam' and the ruminating pedant Ruskin, and I laughed. 'The cruel, crawling snow!' Yes, and in spite of Ruskin and his 'pathetic fallacy,' there it was! Of course, the

snow is not cruel. . . . But nevertheless, it made the impression of
cruelty, and in that lay its fascination and beauty. (102)

He is, of course, protesting against the hostile implications of
Ruskin's term. For Grove himself, such an image is at worst neutral.
It is a way of communicating the subjective nature of individual
vision. Moreover, it is particularly appropriate for his immediate
purpose. One can readily understand why a solitary man, dwarfed by
the inhuman immensities of the vast Canadian wilds, should attempt
to humanize 'what is not I' by endowing it with domestic attributes
and characteristics. In the opening pages, this takes the form of
scrutinizing the scattered houses and farms that he passes and fore-
casting the personalities of their owners ('A house has its
physiognomy as well as a man, for him who can read it' (2), but this
habit is soon extended, by simile, to the natural landscape. The dead
wood in the forest is likened to 'gigantic brooms with their handles
stuck into the ground' and the underbrush 'lies like huge black
cushions under the stars' (16). These homely comparisons help to
bridge the gulf between man and universe.

This stylistic effect is developed throughout the book. What is
perhaps the most extended example occurs in the night-calm of the
third chapter:

> The stillest hour! But how much stiller than still, when the
> earth has drawn over its shoulders that morning mist that
> allows of no slightest breath—when under the haze the very air
> seems to lie curled and to have gone to sleep. And yet how
> portentous! The haze seems to brood. It seems somehow to
> suggest that there is all of life asleep on earth. You seem to feel
> rather than to hear the whole creation breathing in its sleep—as
> if it was soundlessly stirring in dreams—presently to stretch, to
> awake. (49)

Often, too, the forces of nature are tamed by being described in terms
of domesticated animals. The wind, for example, is seen as 'running
with breathless speed, with its tongue lolling out, as it were, and
probably yapping and snapping in mocking mimicry of a pup trying
to catch its tail' (82). And clouds partake of the qualities of both
animal and man: 'The clouds lost their sheeplike look again; they
became more massive; they took on more substance and spine, more
manliness' (134). Many other examples could be quoted. The
important point to note, however, is that this is not merely a stylistic
mannerism, or even a personal quirk. Grove's use of 'pathetic fallacy'

(and the phrase is obviously inadequate in this case) is justified—one might almost say, determined—by his subject and approach. The inter-relation between self and 'what is not I,' between human and non-human, is dramatically illustrated within the texture of the prose.

Lack of space precludes any extended discussion of Grove's other artistic effects. A whole paper might be devoted to the optical aspects of the book—the numerous ways of seeing that are both discussed and illustrated (how, for instance, Grove is forced in the 'Fog' chapter to imagine 'with [the] mind's eye' [35] what he had previously observed directly). There are, in addition, the varieties of formal patterning that reveal an artist rather than a mere recorder at work (compare the boy in the fog waiting for his father [38] with the father waiting for his children outside the school [126]). Readers may readily collect their own examples, but more important than the multiplication of instances are the artistic implications which are thereby made manifest. Grove, according to his own testimony, made thirty-six journeys each way between Gladstone and Falmouth and chose to re-create seven of the most memorable occasions out of the possible seventy-two. In such a situation, selection itself takes on the dignity of a creative act. Moreover, now we can claim to be a little more aware of Grove's creative methods, we can recognize that these seven journeys are not so much selections as accumulations. Whatever Grove may assert, it seems certain that the journeys presented in this book are careful conglomerations of scattered experiences, gatherings and mouldings of random incidents into what, once we come to examine them, emerge as a complex, intricate pattern. All this leads to the conclusion that, whatever Grove's earlier commentators may have argued, *Over Prairie Trails* is a *book,* a formal artistic unity, and not just a collection of descriptive essays.

One final point needs to be made. Although, as I hope to have demonstrated, the book is a self-sufficient whole that can be admired on its own terms, it takes on an added impressiveness when viewed within the context of Grove's later work, as an introduction to the total (English) 'canon.' In Grove's novels the main protagonists are always solitary. However traditionalist he may be in his technical and theoretical approaches to the novel-form, Grove is certainly modernist in his presentation of the inevitable loneliness of the human lot. Morever, his most moving and memorable scenes are those in which, as in *Over Prairie Trails,* a single figure is seen struggling homeward. One thinks of Niels Lindstedt making his way back to the 'White Range Line House' after his release from prison at the close of *Settlers of the Marsh,* or old John Elliot going home to die in *Our Daily Bread.* Viewed in this way, the basic structure of *Over Prairie Trails* becomes profoundly representative. Similarly, the ending is more readily appreciated when viewed in the light of his later work. The final chapter, 'Skies and Scares,' ends in failure. After a number of misadventures, Grove's nerve breaks; for the first time he fails to complete his journey and is forced to find overnight accommodation for himself and his horses. This may well seem, on first reading, a disappointing and arbitrary anticlimax, but some remarks in his later essays reveal its appropriateness to his total vision. 'The demand for the happy ending,' he tells us, 'is the demand of a childish mind,' since failure is 'the fate of humankind.'[8] Grove, like the Hardy he so admired, had a basically sombre world-view, and it would be false to experience if *Over Prairie Trails* presented a record of difficulties continually overcome. Ultimately, all his heroes fail; so must the writer, and so must Grove-as-Ulysses here. Much of the success of *Over Prairie Trails* as a work of conscious art lies in its representative function. It is, in fact, Grove's paradigm of the human experience.

<hr>

[1]Douglas O. Spettigue, *Frederick Philip Grove* (Toronto: Copp Clark, 1969), chs. 1 and 2, *passim.* Since this article was originally written and published, Spettigue has presented a detailed account of his discoveries in *FPG: The European Years* (Ottawa: Oberon, 1973).

[2]Lucille Herbert, 'George Borrow and the Forms of Self-Reflection,' *University of Toronto Quarterly,* 40 (Winter 1971), 152. A comparative study of Borrow and Grove might well prove fruitful. Both made literary capital out of an obscure and mysterious past; both exploited the no-man's-lands between fact and fiction, and between dreaming and waking; both distorted autobiographical fact to present themselves as types of the neglected genius—even to the extent of deliberately exaggerating the hostile reception of their early work. I have discussed Grove's relations both to Borrow and to semi-fictional autobiography at somewhat greater length in 'Grove's Search for America,' *Canadian Literature,* No. 59 (Winter 1974), 60-62.

[3]*In Search of Myself* (Toronto: Macmillan, 1946), p. 181.

[4]*It Needs To Be Said* (Toronto: Macmillan, 1929), p. 84. And cf. p. 117.

[5]See **W.B.** Stanford, *The Ulysses Theme: A Study in the Adaptability of a Traditional Hero* (Oxford: Blackwell, 1954). It should be noted, however, that Stanford confines himself to literary treatments of Ulysses himself and does not discuss analogues.

[6]Quotations from *Over Prairie Trails* are taken from the New Canadian Library edition (Toronto: McClelland and Stewart, 1957). All page numbers in the text refer to this edition.

[7]I have left this observation unrevised; readers should, however, consider Spettigue's qualification of my argument in *FPG: The European Years*, p. 200.

[8]*It Needs To Be Said*, pp. 89, 88.

*In September 1929 Grove and his wife, Catherine, left Manitoba to try
their fortune in Ontario. With him, Grove carried a typescript of 'Abe
Spalding,' a book on which he had been working for several years.
That spring and summer, fresh from the success of his third lecture
tour, he had completed what he hoped was the final draft of the novel,
but surviving correspondence indicates that he rewrote the book at
least once after he settled in Ontario. 'The Flat Prairie,' which
appeared in* The Dalhousie Review *in 1931, developed out of Grove's
revision of the opening chapter of Part Two, which in earlier
versions is titled 'Abe' but which in the published novel,* Fruits of the
Earth, *becomes 'The Prairie.' In that chapter, Abe is for the first time
made aware of the prairie landscape in which he has worked so long
and so hard. 'The Flat Prairie,' taken almost word for word from the
revised draft, is a fascinating attempt to gain a perspective on a
landscape that, Grove observes, is remarkable for its absence of
distinguishing features.*

Frederick Philip Grove
The Flat Prairie

The exceedingly slight slope with which the prairie south of
Winnipeg drains, in a northeast direction, to the Red River is hardly
perceptible; in truth, it amounts to less than a foot in a mile. To the
casual glance, this prairie seems flat as a table top. No native
irregularity, whether of soil accumulation or plant growth, breaks its
monotony. Whatever relieves the sky-line is man's work. The only
native growth is the long, slender prairie grass which, in a summer
breeze, gives the surface of the soil the appearance of a sheet of
watered silk.

Once the buffalo roamed here, supplying the eye with contours to
rest on; he has been replaced by the scattered homes of man. A
phenomenon characteristic of this prairie, though not restricted to it,
lends it some interest: the great frequency of mirages. Often a distant
strip of land is lifted above the horizon like a low-flung cloud; a town
or a group of farmsteads, ordinarily invisible behind the intervening
shoulder of the world, stands up clearly against the whitish sky
which only overhead shades off into a pale blue. The strip of featureless air between the mirage and the solid earth below is of that silvery,
polished whiteness which we see otherwise only in the distant mirror
of a smooth sheet of unruffled water.

On this prairie, near things often seem distant—a hay-stack no more than a quarter of a mile away looms gigantic as though separated from the eye by two or three miles. Far things, especially such as in themselves loom high—the huge storage granaries along the railways, for instance—seem near as though seen through the wrong end of the telescope. In certain states of the atmosphere, on the other hand, the layered air works like a huge lens: roofs five, six miles away show details of construction as though magnified by the glass.

Far to the west, a low, swinging line indicates the series of hills which, so geologists tell us, once formed the shore of the lake whose bottom has become the flat prairie. Occasionally, though rarely— mostly prior to one of the major storms of the summer season—these hills, too, seem lifted and drawn nearer, but without that silvery strip underneath which is characteristic of the mirage on unbroken prairie.

A traveller might go in an east-west direction for a hundred miles without finding the slightest change in the essentials of the landscape. Two railway lines branch from the international trunk lines which run roughly north-south from Winnipeg. Both turn west in almost straight lines, a matter of twenty or thirty miles apart, till, at the foot of the hills in the west, they join in a connecting loop. Both are strung with towns at intervals of ten or twelve miles. From a distance, all these towns look alike, their salient features consisting in the tall, spire-like grain elevators which dominate western landscapes everywhere; below them cluster a few stores, a few dozen dwellings, and such groups or lines of trees as the aesthetic sense of their inhabitants has impelled them to plant.

But if such a traveller chose to go from north to south, he would be arrested at regular intervals by enormous ditches, all running parallel to each other and sloping at a rate exceeding that of the prairie towards the river which bounds this steppe of the prairie in the east. To those who live in this district, these ditches are of importance not only because they are the only means which enables them to grow crops by carrying away the water which once flooded the prairie in spring for months at a stretch; but also because they often determine the distance which a settler has to travel when he wishes to go from one point to another not in exactly the same latitude. When full, they can be crossed only at such points where bridges are provided, which is, on an average, once in four miles. Two people may be neighbours, their yards separated by nothing but a ditch; yet they may have to travel four miles to get from one farm to the other.

These man-made diggings impress the beholder who comes from a distance, so that his perceptions are not dulled by familiarity, like the prehistoric remains of a drainage system devised by some mightier race gone to its accountings; so completely has the prairie grass obliterated the traces of tools used in their excavation.

Altogether it is a landscape which, in spite of the ever encroaching settlements of man, seems best to be appreciated by a low soaring flight, as that of the marsh-hawk so commonly seen in the open seasons. Wild life is little abundant. Gophers—even they are rare— field mice, an occasional rabbit, meadow-larks, blackbirds— especially the red-wing—and ground sparrows, in addition to hawks and burrowing owls, pretty well exhaust the native share of the vertebrate orders. Insects are represented by a few butterflies and enormous numbers of beetles and crickets, subterranean kinds, and clouds upon clouds of mosquitoes in spring and early summer. Birds that are recent immigrants congregate about the towns and such occasional farmsteads as are surrounded by wind-breaks of trees.

Owing to the peculiar difficulties of drainage with which the farmer has to contend, man remains distinctly an interloper; for the floods which come down from the western hills in the thaw-up, though tamed, have not been done away with by the ditches; and in places these ditches have furnished the soil for willow-thickets which are choking them up. It is true that, where the water once used to stand for months, it now stands only for weeks, at least in those elusive seasons which farmers call normal; but these weeks come toward the end of April and often the beginning of May when seeding operations are in full swing elsewhere; and the land, being the lowest, except in the far north, of the prairie provinces, seems to attract early frosts which hinder the due maturing of the grains when seeding was delayed by the flood in spring.

Such as live here—brought by those accidents of choice which determine location in a new country: the nearness to the western metropolis, the possibility of breaking large tracts of land without the previous labour of clearing away stumps or stones, the vicinity of friends or relations, or lastly a predilection for this peculiar, melancholy landscape, bred into the blood by some atavism or some inherited sentimental tendency—are developing what is so far exceedingly rare on this cosmopolitan continent with its ever fluctuating population, namely a distinct local character and mentality.

If they have lived here for some time, a decade or longer, and have stayed on in the face of all the inevitable and unforeseen discouragements and difficulties, so that the landscape has had time to enforce in them a reaction to its own character, they seem slow, deliberate, earth-bound. In their features lingers something wistful; in their speech, something hesitating, groping, almost deprecatory and apologetic; in their silence, something almost eloquent.

It is a landscape where, to him who surrenders himself, the sense of life as a whole seems always present, birth and death being mere incidents in the flow of an outwardly somewhat debilitated stream of vitality. It is not surprising, then, that physical facts notwithstanding, the difference in the mood produced by night and day, or by summer and winter, seems less pronounced than it is elsewhere. The average day, true enough, is hot in summer; and the night is cold. But the discomfort caused by the heat does not seem essentially different from the discomfort caused by the cold; the effect of both partakes of the effect of a lid placed over slow ebullition. Perhaps the time of day best fitted to bring out the characteristic impression of the landscape is neither noon nor midnight but the first grey dawn of day, especially a dull day; or the first dim dusk of night, that dusk in which horizons become blurred and the height of human buildings seems diminished. And similarly the time of year most in harmony with the scene is neither summer nor winter; but rather the first few days of spring, while the snow still lies in dirty patches and, from the heights to the west, the floods send down their first invading trickles which follow the imperceptible hollows of the ground; or the first drear approach of November days, with indurating winds and desolate flurries of snow in the air.

The prevailing silence—for, apart from man's dwellings, not even the wind finds anything to play its tunes on—is accentuated rather than disturbed by the sibilant hum, in early summer, of the myriads of mosquitoes that haunt the air, bred in stagnant pools, or the shrill notes, in the early autumn, of the myriads of black crickets that literally cover the soil. That silence, like the flat landscape itself, has something haunted about it, something almost furtive.

Camille R. La Bossière

Of Words and Understanding
in Grove's Settlers of the Marsh

But, for my part, it was Greek to me.
(Shakespeare, *Julius Caesar*, I, ii)

Ah. Jarl: an honest, earnest wight; so true
and simple, that the secret operations of thy
soul were more inscrutable than the subtle workings
of Spinoza's. (Melville, *Mardi*, Chapter 3)

Life is a foreign language: all men mispronounce it.
(Christopher Morley, *Thunder on the Left*, Chapter 14)

Michel de Montaigne, ironic assayer of perception and judgment, once observed that what may seem hot to one individual or group is not unlikely to seem cold to another. There is much in the criticism of the first of Frederick Philip Grove's published prairie novels, *Settlers of the Marsh* (1925), to suggest that the sceptic's ancient wisdom has worn well with time and much use. On the one hand, there is commentary such as Desmond Pacey's in the *Literary History of Canada: Canadian Literature in English* (1965): while admitting to 'some improbabilities' in the relations of the three main characters in that fiction, he finds in favour of Grove's 'acute and profound' analysis of the 'motives' of the protagonist Niels Lindstedt and praises the 'brilliant fidelity' with which the author describes the northern Manitoba bush country and the homesteader's life there.[1] In 1969, Ronald Sutherland also finds great virtue in the 'psychological depth' of the novel, judging *Settlers of the Marsh* Grove's 'finest achievement.'[2] More recently, a reader's guide restates the value of 'the psychological realism of Grove's characterizations and the naturalistic description of the farms laid precariously upon the northern Manitoba landscape.'[3]

On the other hand, some commentators have found Grove's work deficient in realism or truth to life and have assessed its artistic value accordingly. Edward McCourt, for example, in the 1970 revised edition of his *The Canadian West in Fiction* (1949), seems equally certain that 'Grove's knowledge of human nature was not, unfortunately, as broad or as deep as his knowledge of physical environment,' and that, consequently, he was 'not equal to the task which he sets himself in *Settlers of the Marsh*—that of making the central character . . . believable.'⁴ Margaret Stobie's *Frederick Philip Grove* (1973) develops a parallel thesis, criticizing the author for his 'reluctance to admit his limitations' and for his 'pretensions to experience or knowledge that he clearly did not have.' These deficiencies find expression in the 'often wooden and ludicrous' characters in *Settlers of the Marsh*, where, according to Stobie, the chastity of Niels Lindstedt borders on 'sheer stupidity.'⁵ It would seem that something of a critical tradition has raised itself up in the more than half-century of commentary on the novel. Warning of the collision of realities or understandings sketched above may be detected as early as November 1925, in some of the first reviews to greet *Settlers of the Marsh*: G.V. Ferguson, in the *Manitoba Free Press*, for instance, writes of Niels's 'simplicity' that it 'passes all reasonable understanding,' while Austin Bothwell, in the *Saskatoon Phoenix*, distinguishes the central character's innocence or 'denseness to certain implications' from mere 'stupidity,' to conclude that 'he is drawn with skill—is consistent, is real.'⁶

But there is a consonance, too, discernible in such a record of discordant voices. All seem agreed on the grounds for literary judgment in this case: Grove's (in)fidelity to the reality of people and/or places and things. And it is perhaps the harmony rather than the disagreement which proves the more instructive at bottom, for the commentary, taken as a whole in its broad lines, may be seen obliquely to mirror the 'problematic' of knowing, unknowing, and language acted out by the *dramatis personae* of *Settlers of the Marsh* and incorporated by the novel itself as linguistic artefact and investigative device. As commentators have implied, *Settlers of the Marsh* is 'about' knowledge and its articulation. Their responses help define, by extension, the fundamental issues at play in the fiction: the (in)vincibility of human ignorance and the (in)ability of words to grasp and convey whole truth. Each group of conflicting responses hits the mark, then, by focusing attention on the novel's intellectual and artistic centre, the nature of which the reader is encouraged to draw out and clarify. An inquiry into the agency of ignorance and words in *Settlers of the Marsh*, making explicit the grounds which the work offers for its own interpretation, would seem the next logical step in the critical conversation it continues to invite. The following words attempt an advance in that direction, by a search through the text to discern a way of reading the novel appropriate to itself.

The search begins in *terra incognita*—this is where the author immediately locates his central character, Niels Lindstedt. It is early November, and, in the gathering dusk, the twenty-four-year-old native of Blekinge, on the southeast coast of Sweden, is headed north from the Canadian prairie town of Minor. But he has no precise sense of where he is. Only three months away from home, he navigates by the faith he has in his companion's savvy: Lars Nelson, three years in the New World, 'knew the road.'[7] The 'engulfing dark' (p. 16) and a blinding snowstorm, however, deprive guide Nelson of his bearings. 'Danged if I know where we are,' he comes to admit aloud in English (p. 17), presumably to the added mystification of Niels, who knows little or no English. Only a stroke of luck and the laconic directions provided by a hostile old Icelander, partly in broken English, in response to questions in Swedish, permit Nelson, after an hour's groping, to find the way ('Now I know'; p. 19) to the Amundsen farm, where a job of well-digging awaits the two Swedes. What Niels makes of the Icelander's words is unsaid. At this point, the narration is less than five pages along, and, already, in two languages, each rendered as English, the author has framed the condition of a man enmeshed in translation, a stranger in a strange land.

The remaining thirty or so pages of the first chapter specify the lines of that stranger's entanglement in unknowing so compactly figured at the outset. 'The word of the Lord,' the hard facts of farm life, and the meaning of the world may seem 'perfectly clear' (p. 23) in the eyes of the self-righteous, prosperous, and self-deceived Amundsen, now seven years in the country. For this casuist, only the literal sense of the 'spoken word' is 'binding' (p. 20). It is otherwise with the uncorrupted newcomer Niels: unfamiliar as they are to him, the signs in his field of vision appear truly enigmatic. Finding himself 'somehow' (p. 21) attracted to Amundsen's only child Ellen, in her late teens, Niels cannot read 'any meaning' in the look she gives him (p. 22). What her general 'attitude spoke of' was a 'somewhat defiant aloofness,' as the narrator vaguely recalls of her effect on people (p. 21). Nor can Niels follow another kind of language, the German and English spoken by visitors at the Amundsen farm the first Sunday after his arrival there. That same day, at the Lund place, his sense of estrangement is all the more heightened when he is introduced to another group of visitors, including the vivacious and exotic widow, Mrs. Clara Vogel: names 'go past his ear in bewilderment' and the English sounds he hears are 'quite beyond his understanding' (pp. 29, 30). With reason does he feel 'outside of things' (p. 25).

But there is an important difference between these two kinds of languge. One is verbal, the other not. When, three years later, Niels encounters Mrs. Vogel a second time—the occasion is Olga Lund's marriage to Nelson, in English at a German church—the widow recalls with a nicely suggestive choice of word: 'When I first met you, you were dumb.' 'I did not know any English,' Niels ingenuously replies (p. 51). As Mrs. Vogel suspects, there yet remains a language foreign to him, of a kind untaught by the male teacher at the night-school in Minor. Now, as at their first meeting, when the nature of Mrs. Vogel's 'impression' on him 'did not become clear to Niels in articulate thought' (p. 30), he feels 'awkward, dumb' before the 'something in him' which this mysterious woman stirs up, a 'dumb, passionate longing,' 'a hardly articulate impulse' (pp. 46, 51). 'What did it all mean?' (p. 55) summarizes Niels' incomprehension before the innuendo in the widow's sly words of parting. While study over three years has given him some competence in one language, it has not enabled him to translate what 'words' leave unsaid or to give expression in 'words' to 'the mysterious powers' at work in his 'innermost being' (pp. 45, 46). The heart having its own reasons, the effect of this inability is to sharpen his desire for someone 'who would understand the turmoil in his heart without an explanation in so many words' (p. 54). His hope is to make himself known to others wordlessly. It is the only way he has.

The source of Niels' dumbness, however, goes deeper than a mere want of experience, for, even when he does understand something, he is unable to put his insight into words. Mrs. Lund's pathetic dream of the future, for example, confessed to him in Swedish during his first visit to her decaying home, sets off resonances in Niels' mind, prompting him to a recollection of his own life with his poor mother and a review of his own dream of prosperity as a man. Not only had he 'understood' Mrs. Lund, the narrator recounts, but he had been an acute interpreter, reading the tale of despair beneath the hope of her words: 'suddenly he understood far more than the mere words' (p. 33). Fully sensing as he does the unspoken truth of the Lund story, he does not need to explain it. And when, in his mother tongue, Nelson gives voice to his special feeling for land that he himself has cleared— not for him the buying of a ready-made farm with wage-money— Niels grasps what his companion's distinction really means, though he himself cannot express what that meaning is: 'Niels understood. That was his own thought exactly, his own unexpressed, inexpressible . . . ' (p. 36). The suggestion here is that the privation Niels suffers is beyond remedy. He cannot articulate what he really is and feels and believes, even when he recognizes what that is, because its truth is quite literally 'inexpressible.' What clarity is available to Niels comes in a motion as wordless and as sudden as that of a half-blind man's forked willow-branch divining a hidden stream below (p. 34). And so, as the last page of the first chapter transcribes, it becomes 'very clear' to Niels that the vague emotion he feels for Mrs. Vogel originates in that darkest and strangest of regions, where words cannot fully penetrate, 'his innermost self' (p. 56). Dumb as he remains at age twenty-seven, he has come to see clearly that what he does not understand is himself.

There is hardly a page in the second and third chapters in the history of Niels' progress along the way to enlightenment which does not directly advance the governing theme: the obscurity of the innermost life and the powerlessness of words to grasp and communicate the truth of that life. As in Chapter 1, Niels's 'powers of vision' (p. 60) are weak; 'his tongue' is 'tied' (p. 79). 'Searching for something,' he gazes into his beloved Ellen's 'inscrutable eyes,' puzzling over the code of her 'inscrutable look' (pp. 57, 58, 64). But no certain answer comes. Visiting Ellen shortly after her father's death by mishap, Niels looks at her, 'dully, incomprehendingly' (p. 64). On another occasion, he goes to her in 'a dull and incomprehensible excitement' (p. 68), completely at a loss for what to say. There are no words between them to make public what each privately feels: 'Always their intercourse had been full of silences' (p. 83). And when he hears the dying Sigurdsen's delirious utterances, 'trailing off into Icelandic,' raising up 'strange disquieting things' from a wild past at sea, Niels understands 'only half' of what the sounds say. Such speech is 'incomprehensible' (p. 84). What the garbled words from the lips of the former sailor echo, by analogy, is the voice of the 'hardly articulate impulse' (p. 51) in the man attracted to Clara Vogel.

Only vaguely articulated as well is Niels' sense of the 'things beyond the remedy of words' (p. 80) which separate him from Ellen and his dream of domestic bliss. Chapter 3 reveals what those 'things' are. After a chance meeting with Clara, during which her eyes seem 'to deprive him of his speech' (p. 88), Niels runs to Ellen, hoping to get from her an unequivocal expression of her feelings for him. None is given. 'Imponderable things, incomprehensible waves of feeling passed to and fro between them: things too delicate for words,' the novel states (p. 94). Ellen cannot 'understand' (p. 99) why she cannot help but not marry Niels, offering him no explanation; he responds to her incomprehension and his own with silence. 'He does not know what to do, what to say,' he does not 'understand' (p. 100). After the death of Sigurdsen, Niels returns again, this time desperate for enlightenment: 'I have got to know. I have got to get this clear' (p. 103). The thirty-year-old suitor stands 'in helpless incomprehension' before Ellen, who now struggles to compose her 'story,' not knowing whether she can 'tell' it, not knowing whether he will 'understand' it (p. 105). 'If you are to understand, I must strip my soul of its secret,' she warns him—she will have to speak those things which are 'skipped in silence' (p. 105). The story of the appalling cruelties inflicted by Amundsen on his wife, however, clarifies only the facts. Unveiling one secret, it is testimony to another, more profound: the inscrutable syntax of life, 'a dumb shifting of forces' (p. 101). Niels cannot understand that inarticulate shifting. He withdraws in silence, speechless before the testament of Ellen's life.

The figure implied, of Niels as a dumb and baffled reader before the enigmatic text of existence, is made explicit in chapters 4 and 5. He is perplexed, for example, by the 'abstruse phraseology' of 'a volume on National Economy' (p. 147) and discovers nothing in his search for 'something that might enlighten him' in *Madame Bovary* (p. 136). When he does find the "truths" of his own experience in another text, the Book of Ecclesiastes, what he reads, ironically, is that life is an enigma beyond human ability to solve (p. 172). In the mirror of Solomon's words, he sees the language of his own ignorance.[8] And while he is able to 'read in a glance and a nod' (p. 161) the truth of the Dahlbeck couple, he has 'no means of reading the mind' of Clara (p. 164), whom he has taken to wife subsequent to a passive and wordless obedience to 'strange, incomprehensible impulses,' 'dimly felt, not distinctly told off in thought' (p. 121). Niels cannot translate the hidden sense of Clara's 'words' that he not leave her for an instant (p. 125), since these only hint at 'dark, incomprehensible things' (p. 128)—'things unimaginable, horrors unspeakable,' as he comes to dread (p. 149). Beneath surfaces and words there are 'unsounded depths' he cannot 'fathom' (pp. 166, 145).

When he is eventually enlightened by the last word of the Dahlbeck woman's brutal taunt—'You married the district whore' (p. 177)—the words of Clara's repeated warnings and the language of her mystifying actions over the several years of their marriage are illuminated in 'a flash of real lightning' (p. 178). But if the fact is now plain enough to Niels—to characters in *Settlers of the Marsh* and readers less innocent it has been evident for some time before—it is another of those facts 'inaccessible to any reason' which make up the 'tangled labyrinth of his life' (pp. 168, 159). Again Niels is struck dumb. 'With unseeing eyes, unthinking brain,' in a speechless somnambulistic trance, he staggers home (pp. 182-183). In a world of almost 'utter darkness,' where what vision there can be is by a light 'very dim, almost divined' (p. 185), he obeys another impulse. A single shot from his hunting rifle ends the life of Clara. 'And he that increaseth knowledge increaseth sorrow,' Niels recalls the 'certain words' (p. 189) from Ecclesiastes (1:18). He has come to experience the truth of that wisdom in a tragedy of unknowing confirming the words of his earlier meditation on the invincibility of ignorance in this world: 'A dumb shifting of forces. Grass grew and was trodden down; and it knew not why' (p. 101). He still does not know the underlying why of things; he continues in his role as a perplexed reader of an inscrutable text. 'However much man toils in searching' after a complete understanding of himself and the world, writes Solomon, 'he does not find it out' (8:17).

It has been argued that the sixth and final chapter of *Settlers of the Marsh* is a *non sequitur* of sorts. The reunion of Ellen and a forty-year-old Niels, sending them off in search of possible happiness, detracts from the novel as an artistic and intellectual 'entity,' states Thomas Saunders. *Settlers of the Marsh* 'should have ended with the tragedy,' an end more consistent with the novel's internal design and more in keeping with Grove's view of life.[9] Read in the context of a drama of ignorance and understanding, however, 'Ellen Again' is a logical outcome of what has come before. From its opening page, the final chapter returns the reader to the question of 'words,' their agency and limitation, and the vagueness of human knowledge: at his trial, Niels does not utter 'a word which might throw light on the crime or his motives' (p. 192). What he does record before society is a written plea, 'guilty to the charge of murder,' set down in 'plain, unequivocal terms' (p. 192). Ironically—and perhaps even amusingly to the disinterested spectator—the very fact of the prisoner's impatient insistence on the certainty and veracity of his confession to a capital crime raises doubts as to its complete truthfulness, and Niels is found guilty of manslaughter 'with attenuating circumstances' (p. 193). While in federal prison, Niels is introduced to yet other ways by which mankind strives to unravel mystery. After four years, he begins to attend evening classes, learning 'something of French and Latin, of Algebra, Geometry, Science,' and acquiring 'a vocabulary which would enable him to read real books' (p. 195). He progresses in erudition, but his final lesson is in detachment: 'Finally he was amused. He learned to laugh at man's folly in puzzling out such curiosities of the mind' (p. 195). Having passed his examinations, he concludes with the Solomon-like query: 'What had it all to do with the real problems of life?' (p. 195). Niels, it would appear, has grown to a condition akin to the 'negative capability' described by Keats, 'when man is capable of being in uncertainties, Mysteries, doubts, without any irritable reaching after fact and reason . . . content with half knowledge.'[10] Content now with truth 'understood only half' (p. 84) and convinced of how little of life even his new learning and vocabulary can illuminate, he is in a position dispassionately to contemplate his ambiguous reality as a man who has both sinned and been sinned against. The less anxious Niels is now able to develop a more comprehensive sense of his entanglements in the moral life, of his guilt and innocence.

Nor are words said to speak more eloquently of the heart of the matter when the man who 'does not think in articulate terms' (p. 215) rejoins Ellen after serving less than seven of the ten years of his sentence. 'Words were not needed' (p. 213), the reader is informed. In a 'state of dusk,' Niels and Ellen converse in 'mutual wordless comprehension' (p. 213). 'Both know; and each knows that the other knows' (p. 214). And what each knows is that each is partly responsible for what has happened, that 'life has involved them in guilt,' and that 'never again must they part' (p. 216). Here the author repeats almost verbatim the sentence from chapter 3: 'imponderable things, incomprehensible waves of feeling pass to and fro between them: things too delicate for words' (pp. 214-15). Earlier, those 'things' had been 'somehow full of pain' (p. 94); now, they are 'somehow full of joy' (p. 215). If words are powerless to make up the deficiency which is ignorance, they are also powerless to express the plenitude which is knowledge. In the absence of words, there is silence to voice not only inexpressible ignorance and suffering, but also inexpressible understanding and joy. So comprehensive is the range of silence, in fact, that it can speak joy and sorrow at once: 'They stand and look, their feelings half joy, half sorrow. . . . No need for words' (p. 216). As the fiction nears its end, Ellen tells Niels of her belief that they can 'live down' the past, that the distance still between them can be bridged. But she is not certain: 'And whether we can or not, we must try . . . .' (p. 217). They have a chance, it is clear, and perhaps blind fortune will favour them.[11] In a dumb universe, beyond the ken of reason and words, they may by hap and by effort come to fulfil the promise of bliss. The reader last sees Niels and Ellen as they set off for home, hand in hand like Adam and Eve in the final lines of *Paradise Lost*, though without 'Providence' for 'their guide' (XII: 647). Where the remainder of their lives will take Niels and Ellen, whether to tragedy or felicity, is left to silence. They disappear from sight, bound for *terra incognita*.

There remains at least one other extension of eloquent speechlessness which the reader of *Settlers of the Marsh* is left to puzzle over once the story of the characters' lives is done. It is the conundrum set by the story-teller's persistent reflection on words, so often repeated as to encourage the reader to focus on the "written" nature of the tale: unlike his characters, Grove as author cannot limit himself to silence if he is to express what he understands of the "inexpressible." He is bound to find in words the least imprecise way of saying what he has to say. And what that language is has as much to tell of Grove's art and vision in *Settlers of the Marsh* as the story of Niels's life has to tell of the character's failure to see and articulate.

Perhaps what is most significant in the language of *Settlers of the Marsh* is the absence of knowledge it implies in its author, the partiality of his vision. The privatives repeated in the novel are a defining feature of Grove's expression, which draws heavily on the vocabulary traditional to negative speculation. 'Unseeing,' 'imponderable,' 'inarticulate,' 'unspeakable,' 'speechless,' 'inscrutable,' and 'incomprehensible' are examples already cited. Also, there are the limitative words to suggest a deficiency of comprehension. Of these, 'almost' is the principal, repeated no fewer than seventy-eight times in the two hundred or so pages of the novel, more than fifty times in the last hundred. 'Almost visible' (p. 50), 'almost transparent' (pp. 50, 88), 'almost dark' (pp. 55, 198), 'almost knew' (p. 84), 'almost palpable' (p. 91), 'imperceptible almost' (pp. 94, 215), 'almost forgotten' (pp. 120, 176, 177), 'almost complete' (p. 141), 'almost furtive' (p. 170), and 'almost happiness' (p. 199), for example, signal an ongoing search for the precise expression of what is known only in part, 'almost divined' (p. 185) but not quite. Only slightly less prominent by frequency is "something," with the ignorance such anonymous naming implies. As well, the wide deployment of subjective "as if" constructions—these number more than fifty—shows more a mind grappling with riddles, attempting to translate by supposition and hypothesis, than an eye certain of actualities. If Grove's semantics of privation may be heard to voice anything positive and certain, it is the author's understanding that his vision is unclear, his conviction that life is an unanswerable riddle.

Attention to the negative and limitative language of *Settlers of the Marsh* opens a way to a larger comprehension of this elusive writer. Since, as Pacey affirmed in 1965, Grove's novels show 'a thoroughly worked out and consistent philosophy and a technique . . . fully adapted to his intentions,'[12] the case of *Settlers of the Marsh* is not likely to be atypical of its author. Just how fundamental the semantics of privation is to the articulation of Grove's thought and art is suggested by the following passage from *In Search of Myself*, published more than two decades after *Settlers of the Marsh*. Grove here records the powerful feeling evoked in him by the imagined song of fictional Kirghiz herdsmen:

But, when we had left them a quarter of a mile behind, suddenly, unexpectedly, almost startlingly, the whole column broke into a droning song, with the effect of a ghostly unreality. It was a vast, melancholy utterance, cadenced within a few octaves of the bass register, as if the landscape as such had assumed a voice: full of an almost inarticulate realization of man's forlorn position in the face of a hostile barrenness of nature; and yet full, also, of a stubborn, if perhaps only inchoate assertion of man's dignity below his gods.[13]

This passage, read by Pacey (1965) and Sutherland (1969) as a summary of Grove's philosophy, is sonorous with the language of limitation, negation, and uncertainty.[14] 'Unexpectedly, almost startlingly,' 'a ghostly unreality,' 'an almost inarticulate realization,' 'yet,' 'if perhaps only inchoate'—such is the linguistic correlative for Grove's 'thoroughly worked out and consistent philosophy.' Understandably, the identity of that philosophy has never been easy to define in positive, unambiguous terms. 'What Was Frederick Philip Grove?' asks the title of Sutherland's contribution to *The Grove Symposium* (1974), in search of the 'highly complex and profound thinker.'[15] The riddling words of *Settlers of the Marsh* may serve as oblique reply:

Are there in us unsounded depths of which we do not know ourselves? Can things outside us sway us in such a way as to change our very nature? Are we we? Or are we mere products of circumstance? (p. 166)

Thomas Saunders offers this considered response to the interrogatives of *Settlers of the Marsh*: 'But there is no ready answer.' The reader's response echoes the author's; 'the novelist, through his characters,' Saunders goes on to say, 'arrives at no final answer.'[16] The negative confesses a degree of bafflement. But is there another answer, less ready, to the identity of Grove's intellectual creed? John Moss, in 1981, proposes a formulation consistent with the language of unknowing in *Settlers of the Marsh*: 'quasi-determinism.'[17] Man is almost free to choose, almost not; almost unfree, almost not. It might be argued that, in the Grove universe, there can be no knowledge more precise than this nor any syntax more articulate for an understanding of responsible man's lot below his grimly playful gods.

The Kirghiz-song passage also characterizes Grove's art, according to Pacey's affirmation in the *Literary History of Canada*: 'This is an apt description of Grove's own prairie novels.'[18] Each, then, is a 'song' 'with an effect of ghostly unreality,' a voicing of 'an almost inarticulate realization,' to repeat the words from *In Search of Myself*. But there is a difficulty when the historian goes on in the same paragraph to set the artist Grove squarely in the 'school of naturalists.' 'Like the novels of Zola and Dreiser and Hamsun, Grove's have strength and solidity, present masses of accurate sociological detail, and embody in plain prose a deterministic view of human character.'[19] Grove's 'apt description' of his own work, however, is hardly plain prose naming solid stuff, though it is very much like the prose of *Settlers of the Marsh*. Nor does it seem very much in tune with the language of *Sister Carrie* (1900), for example, Dreiser's literary imitation of what 'has been shown experimentally,' in its own words.[20] Some three times the length of *Settlers of the Marsh*, Dreiser's novel compels its author to "almost" about half as many times; it does not resound with the privatives of Grove's work. Clearly, there is a dissonance in the comparison.

In 1970, Pacey himself comes to suggest a corrective to the disjunction just below the surface of his earlier account. Introducing his collection of pieces from the history of Grove criticism, he remarks that commentators have not grasped 'the nature of Grove's symbolic art,' the fundamentals of which are not to be learned simply in the school of Naturalism.[21] 'Symbolic' is a valuable hint to the reader who would consider Grove in his relation to a tradition of writing more in harmony with the negative semantics of *Settlers of the Marsh*. The qualifier brings to mind a corpus of doctrine affirming the power of imagination, a faculty beyond reason, for the perception of essential, inscrutable truth, and emphasizing the role of silence and symbol as means of expressing that truth. Sceptical of positive science, it is a body of doctrine having *Sartor Resartus* (1833-34), not Zola's *Le Roman expérimental* (1880), as a cardinal text in the history of its evolution.[22] As Carlyle reflects in 'The Life and Opinions of Herr Teufelsdröckh,' 'not our Logical, Mensurative faculty, but our Imaginative one' can see into the underlying reality of this 'Universe of Nescience,' the nature of which is literally 'unspeakable' since hidden from our knowledge.[23] Silence, the argument follows, is the appropriate and complete expression of man's unknowing. The impasse of silence responding to nescience, however, is not entirely beyond solution: it may be solved, though only in part, Sartor Resartus proposes, by the action of symbolic utterance. The word-symbol, taking its vocabulary from the language of finite things, not only speaks of the world man can know but also expresses, by what it leaves unsaid, that which is beyond knowing and saying. By that 'doubled significance,' of 'Speech and Silence acting together,' writes Carlyle, the symbol allows a positive articulation even as it simulates 'the inarticulate mystic speech of Music.'[24] The analogy earlier suggested by Pacey, between Grove's prairie novels and his verbal account of an imagined song of Kirghiz herdsmen, an 'utterance . . . full of an almost inarticulate realization,' seems all the more apt when read in the light of the fundamentals of 'symbolic' art conceived of in this way.

If almost dumb, then, as Carlyle's account speculates and Grove's self-description reflects, the music-like symbol almost articulates as well. Symbol's agency, in this regard, is not wholly incompatible with a realism of the kind aimed for in La Fortune des Rougon (1871), 'a simple exposé of facts' by a 'scientist,' according to Zola's manuscript 'Plans.'[25] There is, in principle, no 'dédain de la nature' enjoyed by the symbolic artist's 'Néo-mysticisme,' in the words of an 1892 letter from the musician and poet Camille Saint-Saëns to the autobiographer and novelist Pierre Loti.[26] And practice has confirmed principle. Certainly, there is no disregard for surface reality or its language celebrated in the work of Conrad, for example, a reader of Sartor Resartus and one of Grove's favourite authors, who strove to render as much of 'the mystic nature of material things' as his art would permit.[27] As Conrad illustrates in Typhoon (1903), a tale exploring 'the mysterious side' of a taciturn literalist's 'stupidity,' words may serve to describe facts with 'perfect accuracy'; but, like facts, they may also serve as mute witnesses to the unspeakable underlying truth of man and the universe. 'Facts can speak for themselves with overwhelming precision.'[28] They can speak silently.

A similar "doubled significance" is present in Settlers of the Marsh. It may be found, for instance, in Grove's much-celebrated description of a sudden prairie storm, remarkable as much for its precise reflection of appearances as for its symbolic evocation of the unseen. Parts of the description follow:

The air is breathless: even the slight, wafting flow from the east has ceased [. . .] The wall of cloud has differentiated: there are

two, three waves of almost black; in front, a circling festoon of
loose, white flocculent manes, seething, whirling. . . . A
winking of light runs through the first wave of black. A distant
rumbling heralds the storm. . . .
[. . .]
The bush [. . .] stands motionless, breathless, blackening as the
sun is obscured. Birds flit to and fro, seeking shelter, silent. . . .
    Then a huge suction soughs through the stems. But already
the lash of the wind comes down: like the sea in a storm tree tops
rise and fall, the stems bending over and down and whipping
back again, tossed by enormous pressures. They dance and roll,
tumble and rear, and mutely cry out as in pain [. . .] A misty veil
rushes over the landscape, illumined by a bluish flash which is
followed by nearer and nearer growlings and barkings.
[. . .]
The first rain drops [fall], heavy, large, but few [. . .]
[. . .]
Down comes the rain in a cloud-burst, forming a wall [. . .]
Flashes of lightning break on the slough like bomb-shells;
rattling thunder dances and springs. (pp. 98-9)

The semantics of privation featured in *Settlers of the Marsh* figures
only slightly in this passage. There is continued absence, though, in
the form of what is unsaid, in the negation which is silence. The facts
of nature, their power to converse analogically with man confirmed
by the presence of simile and metaphor here, 'mutely cry out,' by
symbolic suggestion, what is unspoken and invisible in the
turbulent, conversation of Niels and Ellen as they sit and observe in
profound incomprehension of themselves before the storm. 'Niels
and Ellen still' are 'silent' (p. 99), a condition partially shared by their
author, who articulates from the appearance of nature images for the
mute expression of his characters' interior lives. Even as they mirror
knowledge such as the outward eye can give, Grove's words strive, it
seems, to translate what is beyond the power of words expressly to
say. As Dick Harrison remarks, Grove's sentences often have an
'opaque quality.'[29] Confronted by 'the enigmatical spectacle' of 'the
visible universe,' in the words of Conrad's Preface to *The Nigger of
the 'Narcissus'* (1897),[30] Grove finds what expression he can for his
vision of that universe in the speech and silence of symbol, or in a
language of partial or complete privation.
    What, then, is to be learned from the words of this teacher and
student of languages and self-professed quester after 'psychologic . . .
truth'?[31] Large claims have been made. The concluding sentence of a

paper read at the Grove Symposium (University of Ottawa, May 1973), Louis Dudek's 'The Literary Significance of Grove's Search,' for example, states that we may learn much: 'Through them you may learn to know yourself, and to know the universe and the gods.'[32] *Settlers of the Marsh* provides a clue to some of the particulars we may come to know, and the patterning of these hardly seems so positive. Specifically, as this reading has proposed, there is tuition to be found in the story of ignorance and silence that the novel tells, in the negative, limitative semantics of its author, a language fully adapted to the expression of what is know only in part if at all. It is instruction in a tongue somewhat foreign to the ear unattuned to silence, in a knowledge partly hidden from the eye unadjusted to obscurity. 'His mind was a lonely hunter through the intricate mazes of the words of seven languages, through the secret places of the human heart,' Kay Rowe eloquently commemorates Grove in the Spring 1949 number of the *Manitoba Arts Review*.[33] That Grove searched for the innermost truth through a labyrinth of words can be verified from *Settlers of the Marsh*. That he actually found that truth, though, is something less certain. A secret, after all, is a secret. Faced with the question of Grove's (in)fidelity to the reality of people and things in a fiction tracking the inscrutable ways of man in an enigmatic universe, the reader may understandably come to answer with the motto of another seeker after psychologic truth, Montaigne. 'Que sais-je?' is no unfit response to the truth of a fiction riddling in words of absence and uncertainty, signs of a fundamental privation also discernible in the mute speech of symbol. Here, perhaps, in a confession of reasoned doubt, not a certain profession of whole ignorance or knowledge, the reader is on solid ground. At bottom, the lesson of *Settlers of the Marsh* seems a lesson in limitation.

---

[1]Desmond Pacey, 'Fiction: 1920-40,' in *Literary History of Canada: Canadian Literature in English*, gen. ed. Carl F. Klinck (Toronto: Univ. of Toronto Press, 1965), p. 681.

[2]Ronald Sutherland, *Frederick Philip Grove* (Toronto: McClelland and Stewart, 1969), pp. 47, 51.

[3]John Moss, *A Reader's Guide to the Canadian Novel* (Toronto: McClelland and Stewart, 1981), p. 108.

⁴Edward McCourt, *The Canadian West in Fiction*, rev. ed. (Toronto: Ryerson, 1970), pp. 59, 65.

⁵Margaret Stobie, *Frederick Philip Grove* (New York: Twayne, 1973), pp. 189, 93.

⁶Cited from *Frederick Philip Grove*, ed. and introd. Desmond Pacey (Toronto: Ryerson, 1970), pp. 108, 109.

⁷Frederick Philip Grove, *Settlers of the Marsh* [1925], introd. Thomas Saunders (Toronto: McClelland and Stewart, 1966), p. 15. Further references in text.

⁸As John Keats writes in a letter of 1819, 'even a Proverb is no proverb to you until your Life has illustrated it.' Cited from *Prose of the Romantic Period*, ed. Carl R. Woodring (Boston: Houghton Mifflin, 1961), p. 541. His subject is the 'Agony . . . of ignorance.'

⁹Thomas Saunders, Introduction to *Settlers of the Marsh*, p. xiii.

¹⁰John Keats, in a letter of December 1817. Cited from Woodring, p. 525.

¹¹See E.D. Blodgett, '*Alias* Grove: Variations in Disguise, in his *Configuration: Essays on the Canadian Literatures* (Downsview, Ont.: ECW Press, 1982): 'It is perhaps impossible to find a single source for the aesthetic and ideological irresolution of his novels, but one might consider the popular political stance of his youth which is called in German *Edel-Anarchie*, a type of anarchy that attracted writers and intellectuals disappointed with Naturalism, among whom were Gide and Wilde' (p. 149). Unreason's governance of the universe is perhaps another source.

¹²Pacey, *Literary History of Canada*, p. 682.

¹³Frederick Philip Grove, *In Search of Myself* (Toronto: Macmillan, 1946), p. 153. This passage is from the 'exotic plant flowering imaginatively out of FPG's Swedish journey of 1908,' according to Douglas O. Spettigue in *FPG: The European Years* (Ottawa: Oberon, 1973), p. 188.

¹⁴Pacey, *Literary History of Canada*, p. 682; Sutherland, *Frederick Philip Grove*, p. 9.

¹⁵Ronald Sutherland, 'What Was Frederick Philip Grove?' in *The Grove Symposium*, ed. John Nause (Ottawa: Univ. of Ottawa Press, 1974), p. 10. In his 1969 monograph, Sutherland writes of determinism and free will in Grove: people 'are victims of forces beyond their control.' And yet, he continues, 'each human being is responsible for more than the working out

of his own destiny; he is responsible also for the influence of his own life on the life of others' (pp. 50-1).

[16]Saunders, p. xi.

[17]Moss, p. 110. Students are also informed that *Settlers of the Marsh* 'illuminates' the relationship 'between fate and free will' (p. 108). A.J.M. Smith finds less light in Grove's thought: 'his thinking, though honest and sincere, lacks the distinction of a great novelist' (*The Canadian Century: English-Canadian Writing since Confederation*, ed. A.J.M. Smith [Toronto: Gage, 1973], p. 286).

[18]Pacey, *Literary History of Canada*, p. 682.

[19]*Ibid.*, p. 683. In *Northern Spring: The Flowering of Canadian Literature in English* (1982), the first in the *Images of/du Canada* series of primers commissioned by the Embassy of Canada in Washington, D.C., George Woodcock observes that Grove 'applied European naturalism to the struggle of prairie farmers against both the land and their own passions. *Settlers of the Marsh* (1925) is the most darkly realist of his works, but Grove had too grandiose a mind to be a consistent naturalist, and his most ambitious book . . . was a symbolic epic on the onward march of mechanization, *The Master of the Mill* (1944)' (p. 4). Contributing to another primer, Sutherland comments on Grove's 'stark and clinical' technique of characterization in *Our Daily Bread* (1928) ('A Literary Perspective: The Development of a National Consciousness,' in *Understanding Canada: A Multidisciplinary Introduction to Canadian Studies*, ed. William Metcalfe [New York: New York University Press, 1982], p. 433).

[20]Theodore Dreiser, *Sister Carrie* [1900] (New York: Modern Library Edition, 1932), p. 362.

[21]Pacey, introduction to *Frederick Philip Grove*, p. 7.

[22]See William K. Wimsatt, Jr. and Cleanth Brooks, *Literary Criticism: A Short History* (New York: Vintage, 1967), pp. 456-60.

[23]Thomas Carlyle, *Sartor Resartus: The Life and Opinions of Herr Teufelsdröckh* [1833-4] (London: Routledge, 1888), pp. 148, 152, 146.

[24]*Ibid.*, p. 100.

[25]Cited from Matthew Josephson's *Zola and His Time* (1928) by Wimsatt and Brooks, p. 458.

26Camille Saint-Saëns, in an unpublished letter of 16 April 1892. Cited by Keith C. Millward in *Pierre Loti et l'esprit 'fin de siecle'* (Paris: Nizet, 1955), p. 326. Saint-Saëns is expressing to Captain Loti his fears for that mysticism. For an account of Felix Paul Greve, see Spettigue, pp. 50-7 in particular; and Blodgett, pp. 125-33, for a reading of the *Neuromantik* in FPG.

27Joseph Conrad, *A Personal Record* [1912] (London: Dent Collected Edition, 1946-55), p. 130.

28Joseph Conrad, *Typhoon, and Other Stories* (London: Dent Collected Edition, 1946-55), pp. 4, 3, 15, 9. See Camille R. La Bossière, *Joseph Conrad and the Science of Unknowing* (Fredericton, N.B.: York Press, 1979), pp. 48-50.

29Dick Harrison, *Unnamed Country: The Struggle for a Canadian Prairie Fiction* (Edmonton: Univ. of Alberta Press, 1977), p. 115.

30Joseph Conrad, Preface to *The Nigger of the 'Narcissus'* (London: Dent Collected Edition, 1946-55), p. vii.

31Frederick Philip Grove, 'Realism in Literature,' in *It Needs to Be Said* (Toronto: Macmillan, 1929), pp. 70-1: "Shakespeare was a realist; but his realism has very little to do with accuracy in such externals as historic or social custom. Art is not a matter of facts and figures. 'The aim,' said Lowell, 'of the artist is psychologic, not historic truth'." Cited by Harrison, p. 121.

32Louis Dudek, 'The Literary Significance of Grove's Search,' in *The Grove Symposium*, p. 99.

33Cited from Pacey, ed., *Frederick Philip Grove*, p. 199.

Margaret R. Stobie

An Innocent from Abroad: *Grove's* A Search for America[1]

A Search for America was by all odds the most popular of Grove's works during his lifetime, and deservedly so, for it is one of the best things he ever wrote. Yet it was seen by three publishers before it was accepted in 1926 by a fourth. All professed to admire it, one calling it an important work, another saying that he liked it and that it ought to be published; but all looked askance at what one reader described as 'a cartload of manuscript.' When the Graphic Publishers did accept it, they insisted that it be cut, and Grove wrote to Watson Kirkconnell, on November 25, 1926, that he had 'ruthlessly' cut it to half its original length. Half its original length ran to 448 pages in the Graphic edition. The publishers' diffidence is understandable.

The elementary attraction of this historical novel, which Grove set before the turn of the century, is the universal one of a good story, with a great variety of scenes, experiences, and characters, told with vigor. It has the attraction that the questing knight has always had, and the form of this romance is as inevitable as Chaucer's pilgrimage or Christian's journey: a beginning, many episodes, and a happy ending. The picaresque nature of the story of the road makes the addition or subtraction of episodes a matter of the taste or the exigencies of the moment.

The more specific attraction, when the book came out in the 1920s, was the timeliness of its interwoven themes which caught the attention of diverse people. Among the themes was the plight of the immigrant, disillusion within the New World, the disappearance of the hero figure, and the individual's transformation into adulthood—his finding of himself and of his life's work. The shifts of title (Grove always had trouble with titles) show that Grove himself was undecided about which aspect of the book to emphasize; or they may indicate his deepening awareness of the implications of it. In 1920 it is either 'The Immigrant' or 'The Emigrant,' each suggesting a different perspective; in 1923 he calls it 'The Search for America,' which has echoes going back at least to John Donne; but in 1927 he amends that to 'A Search for America,' which sharpens as it limits the application. Finally, he added a subtitle, 'The Odyssey of an Immigrant,' which calls up thoughts of another far traveler.

The story has two movements. In the mid-1880s, a young European dilettante, Phil Branden, aged twenty-four, who spends his time flitting about the continent and in and out of universities, is jolted out of his pleasant life by his father's bankruptcy, which is quickly followed by ostracism from his fair-fortune friends. Rejected, he sails for the New World to seek his fortune, docks at Montreal, goes on to Toronto where he gets a job as a waiter, leaves that to go to New York where he becomes a door-to-door salesman, discovers that all the world is a cheat and so, penniless and disheartened, starts west as a tramp, following the path of the rivers, in quest of Abraham Lincoln and virtue.

After a time of near-starvation and some hallucinations, the young Diogenes finds his honest man in a country doctor and in a farm couple who nurse him back to health after a bout of pneumonia. That part of his quest has ended. He says to the doctor, 'The Abraham Lincolns live all around. . . . You are one of them' (290).[2] The hero figure had not disappeared; it had simply been transformed.

The second part of Branden's quest is to find his life's work, his niche. The doctor gets him a job in a small veneer factory while he recuperates, and, grown suddenly mature, he trains the other workers, sets the business on its feet, and then once more takes to the road, this time as a harvest-hand hobo, to find 'the soil where I could grow.' He follows the harvest up the Dakotas, gets a job on a huge farm of over twenty thousand acres, instructs the young owner in his moral obligations, going farther north finds a shyster cheating a Finnish immigrant of his land and labor, is chased out of the village by a venal policeman, gets work running a railroad handcar, crosses into Canada, and gets to Winnipeg with his harvest savings of $249.35. He had realized that his niche, his part of the world's work, was 'to go to foreign settlements and help recent immigrants to build their partial views of America into total views' (392). In the last half-dozen lines, young Branden gets a job as a teacher and starts on his life's work. Two years after his arrival in Montreal, he has found America; he has found himself as 'a social man'; he has found his place: the quest is successful, and the ending is happy.

The double movement of the quest motif is reflected in a variety of schematic contrasts: the two restaurants in Toronto; the two book companies in New York, one diddling little old ladies and one gulling millionaires; the two social areas of city and country; the two moral and geographic areas of the degenerate East and the virtuous West.

What could become monotonous seesawing is averted, however, by an overriding pattern of ascending social values which determines the choice of episodes and their order. Book I, 'Waiterdom,' is the life of a menial, a form of slavery; Book II is the commercial world, the great con game, a corruption of human life and values; Book III ends with the veneer factory, which is desirable because it is the creativity of the industrial world, using human gifts, and is a proper outcome of education based on manual training and workshops; but of course Book IV comes, as it must, to the agricultural life, what Rousseau called 'the earliest and most honorable of the arts,' the root and crown of existence, from which all other forms take their being. Branden sees the vision of it as 'the ground-mass of the nation—the soil from which cities sprang, like strange, weird, sometimes poisonous flowers in the woods. For the first time I saw the true relation: the city, the town working for the country: the farmer, though not yet realized as such, the real master of the world who would one day come into his own' (310).

Within the section, the vigor of the narration overcomes any sense of a studied pattern. Individual episodes are carefully prepared, built to a peak, and gradually resolved. In the cheap restaurant, the waiters gather casually, exchange morning banter, and prepare their tables; a few customers enter, the tables begin to fill up, voices grow louder, the waiters' movements faster, the clash of dishes harsher until, behind the scenes, in the kitchen:

> a casual observer would have seen half-naked maniacs dancing and jumping about in crazy lunacy. In the corridor, waiters were bustling each other, reaching up into the dish-rack, flinging plates on the counter and bellowing orders at the top of their voices. From out of the reeking pit behind me came yelling shouts, repeating every order that was given. (52)

Gradually the fury of the noon hour rush subsides, and the waiters relax:

> In surveying the room, I was struck as by the sight of a disaster. Every table-cloth was soiled; every shelf of the central racks and the dumb-waiters was piled with a jumble of dirty dishes. The atmosphere reeked with the smells of the kitchen. The battle was fought; we were left on the field. (54)

In the episode of riding the rods there is the additional quality of tension and danger—fear of being caught, fear of injury:

> At last we were thundering along. The whole universe seemed to be one deafening bedlam of noise let loose. We swayed and swung as we were holding on for dear life, our hands getting sore from the pelting gravel, our eyes closed tight, our faces pressed down on our sleeves. The track seemed to be a succession of hills and valleys; the rods, a mere vibrating mass of whipping cords; our arms, springs now stretched to the snapping-point, now compressed beyond the power of re-expanding when the roadbed rose and pressed the steel-truck upward. I felt dazed and frightened beyond anything I had ever gone through. . . . (332)

But the action scenes are not the only effective ones. Grove often makes skillful use of silence, as he does in Branden's taking leave of the mute driftwood gatherer who had sheltered him:

> Then I stopped and said, 'I suppose, it's about time for me to be moving.'
> And something startling happened. The man spoke. He spoke with an effort, twisting his whole body in the act, the words sounding like those of an overgrown boy when he is changing his voice, hoarse, unexpectedly loud and husky. It looked and sounded as if he were heaving the words up from, let me say, his abdomen and ejecting them forcibly.
> What he said was, 'I reckon.' (259)

Another notable passage is the vivid account of the world's dropouts, of hobodom:

> It is characteristic of this unstable flood of floating labour that there is a great feeling of solidarity when they are together in a crowd. Then they are the hobos, as opposed to the great, contemptible mass of the respectable citizens. . . . But when we met them singly or in smaller groups, that feeling of solidarity was non-existent. Every individual feels himself better than his neighbour; his neighbour is a 'bum'; he himself is the Lord of Creation. . . .
> Gradually there formed in my mind the impression of a vast exodus, or rather a vast confluence of numberless multitudes engaged in a pilgrimage to some Mecca. (337)

The craftsmanship and the variety of such passages are admirable. The special knowledge of the cheap restaurant, of riding the rods, of the harvest hegira, give to this *roman vécu* that immediacy that places it in company, for instance, with Smollett's *Roderick Random.*

But it was not only the romance of the eccentric that attracted people to *A Search for America.* They also found in it familiar, popularly accepted myths, the Horatio Alger myth, and the innocent immigrant myth.

It is entertaining to place Grove's story beside that of Kafka's *Amerika,* for when Kafka 'conceived his novel in Prague in 1913,' Klaus Mann wrote, 'he knew no Americans at all and understood very little English.[3] Kafka's Karl, seduced at sixteen by a woman of thirty-five, is cast out by his family, breaks off his career in Europe, comes to America as to a rebirth, is cheated by swindlers, gets a job in a hotel, and is unjustly dismissed by a bullying head porter. The parallel between Karl and Grove's Branden indicates a recognized stock figure with stock experiences. And there is further affinity between the two books that has to do with the style or manner of writing. When Klaus Mann speaks of Kafka's personal style as one of 'dream-like romanticism and realistic exactness,' he could also be describing the style of *A Search for America,* for while there is plenty of realistic exactness, there is also a remarkable degree of dreamlike romanticism in the book.

In the European beginning, for instance, cities are named, countries are named, desires are fulfilled, and senses are satisfied, but though the time is July and the father is six-foot-five and in his seventies, time, place, and people are actually vague. As in many a medieval romance, the light is on brilliantly colored figures who are featureless. Thus it is with the father who says to his son, 'Don't let it for a moment enter your head that you should feel sorry for me. As I said, I am shaking off ill-fitting clothes in order to be better fitted. I see Paradise ahead' (8).

The New York interlude of Book II also has dreamlike qualities, though Branden calls it a nightmare. Again, hotels are named and addresses are given; the Flatiron Building, the Public Library, and Fifth Avenue are all mentioned. When Branden calls on an official in 'one of the most fashionable sky-scrapers of the city,' he is taken to 'the luxurious dining-room of a fashionable men's luncheon-club.' This New York is not more intimate nor more vivid than the one Kafka conceived in Prague.

As Kafka could dream up an America, as Coleridge could describe
tropic seas and icebergs neither of which he had seen, as Swift could
create convincing worlds that never were, as Grove himself could
recount, as he did later, a well-documented journey that he never took
from Venezuela up through Nicaragua to the Colorado Mountains,
so in *A Search for America* he used all his novelist's power in the
imaginative forming of experience for his creature, Branden. But
when the young novitiate starts west on his strange river journey in
search of Abraham Lincoln, the dreamlike romanticism of the early
part suffers a sea-change.

Having rid himself of his possessions, Branden starts west in the
clothes he stands in, with a raincoat, a few toilet articles, and in his
hip pockets, two slim volumes, the New Testament and, of course,
the *Odyssey*. On the level of actual behaviour, Branden presents an
astonishing sight as he purportedly seeks the soul of America by
creeping about, hiding behind bushes, shunning contact with men
'for whom I still had nothing but aversion' (239), starving himself,
suffering a fever fit, and finally coming down with pneumonia. It is a
curiously puzzling course of action which seemingly does very little
to advance the search.

But of course what the novel has entered upon is outright dream
vision, and Grove makes that apparent in any number of hints and
warnings. Apart from Branden's repeatedly saying that his search
might not be a geographical search at all, the opening pages of Book
III (225-34) are explicit as to the nature of what is to follow: 'the
chronology of events is confused. . . . The narrative must thus lose
some of its connections; transitions will be missing; apparent
contraditions will crop up; feelings, thoughts which are hard to
reconcile. And there are, especially in the beginning, detached scenes,
disconnected visions, like mere pictures flashed upon the screen of
memory, seemingly quite meaningless, and yet they belong into the
tale of my tramps. The very first memories are a series of mere
visions.' A little later, on his first day on the road, 'I feel strangely
weightless. I am cut loose, adrift on the world. . . . I seem to be
weighing the time, as if I held a certain mass of it in my hand.'
'Awakening is like a resurrection.' 'I got used to being silent.' 'I was a
wanderer in the hills. Soon after I became a wanderer in the valleys.'

What Branden finds in the hills and the valleys and the course of
the rivers in an interestingly literary world, the melding of old and
new, the legacy of European civilization, and its American
transmigration. An early encounter is with Ovid's *Metamorphoses*,
Baucis and Philemon somewhere in Pennsylvania but not yet turned

to trees; and there are some touches from Wordsworth's 'Michael.' In case we should miss the point, Grove wrote, 'oh, how I wished I could leave a "wonderful pitcher" behind!' (236). Unfortunately, Grove's prose deteriorates under the pressure of the highly sentimental scene; yet it is one which he was obviously proud of, for he transferred it, using much of the same phrasing, to the vignette of 'Love in Autumn' in *The Turn of the Year,* and it was at least an element in the creation of John Elliott of *Our Daily Bread.*

The rivers as usual are the flowing waters of life, of time; they are avenues of commerce: 'Water is nothing inanimate. . . . Water is company. . . . So long as I followed a river, I was sure of sustaining life' (237). And rivers are also currents of literary tradition. It is on the Ohio that two more literary works enter the dream vision of the outcase Branden. One is *Robinson Crusoe,* that one book needful according to Rousseau, but it is hardly surprising that in this geographical area Crusoe must jostle with his much younger American counterpart. Huck Finn-Robinson Crusoe-Branden shows great ingenuity in salvaging from the river a kettle, a ham, a pumpkin, and then a kitchen table and some logs with which he builds a raft and plies the river. It is almost obligatory, under these circumstances, that he should meet the driftwood gatherer whose face 'closely resembled the face of Mark Twain in Carroll Beckwith's portrait' (252). In his search for America, Branden *becomes* Huck Finn, and he meets Mark Twain on the river because 'America' is to be found in Mark Twain. It is a fine and wise stroke on Grove's part to make him silent.

But the literary vision is not over. The immigrant, too, is America, and on another 'strange trip along the river' (323), this time on the Missouri somewhere between St. Louis and Kansas City, Branden meets the hobo Ivan who reminds him of both 'Titian's painting of the Lord of Christianity,' and Tolstoy's Sergei Ivanovitch—the latter a rather curious association, for Tolstoy's self-righteous philosopher was a cold fish—but he later turns into Levin the agriculturist, the ideal human being, 'the man who stands squarely upon the soil, from the soil, from his soil, reaches out with tentative mind into the great mysteries' (384-49). Grove was enamored of that sentence, and he used it repeatedly not only in novels but also in the address that he gave from coast to coast in Canada on Nationhood. The culmination of the literary encounters is in the great gathering of the hobos, the lords of creation, each of them 'a coarser and de-sublimated Henry David Thoreau' (322).

Yet the search for America is not only the search for the spirit of a country; it is a search for, the discovery of, 'I, myself.' It is to this theme of the soul's purging and its renewal that chapter headings— 'The Descent,' 'The Depths,' 'The Level'—as well as various references to the inferno and to purgatory inescapably direct us. The long middle section of isolation is the trial, the testing of the novice, the metamorphosis from adolescence to adulthood, the rebirth of the individual. It is Rousseau's thesis at the beginning of Book IV in *Emile,* 'We are born, so to speak, twice over, born into existence, and born into life; born a human being, and born a man.' This twofold aspect of the book's structure is a characteristic one with Grove, repeated in various ways in later novels, and in this one of course a counterpart to the twofold movement of the quest.

The imagery of birth and transformation is diffused, implied in the coming to the New World as entering a new element, in the huge, womblike halls of the pier at Montreal and at Penn Station, in the chapter heading, 'I Submerge,' and in the strange water passage that Branden takes. It makes understandable the curious isolation from men as wet, cold, shrunken, Branden makes his way to the country of Abraham Lincoln. On the level of realism, of the actual story, this is incoherent, senseless; on the level of imagery it is the fetus making its way to birth. The birth, the leaving of the river, the time of fitful consciousness—the bout of pneumonia—the difficulty of emerging into human life, is quite fittingly attended by a doctor and a mid-wife.

Another image in the theme of self-discovery and associated both with the river and with the metamorphosis is that of the frog. As a waiter, having 'arrived at an undervaluation of myself,' Branden says, 'I lived, as it were, on the sea-level; I had the perspective of the frog; above him all things loom' (72). The same self-abasing image— 'I had to restrict my view of it [America] to the view from below, to the perspective of the frog'—precedes Branden's decision to become a hobo, independent and proud. The frog, of course, is amphibious, if humble; it is adaptable. Then, too, in its life course it is a dramatic example of metamorphosis, and so it serves to sharpen the implication of Branden's metamorphosis.

Also related to the theme of self-discovery is the clothing image. As Rousseau insisted, the essential man, the 'I, myself,' existed independent of the social order or of vocation. They are only outer clothing. This image begins in the first few pages with the father, a peasant's son who had married a wealthy woman now dead, and who, having all the fifty years of his married life in 'ill-fitting clothes,' proposes to cast them off, after 'a lifetime of disguise' (9). The image continues in the elaborate and unsuitable wardrobe that young Branden brings with him to the New World, particularly the 'stack of overcoats,' which are peeled off one by one as he loses his European dream and sells the clothing, 'suit after suit, overcoat after overcoat' (143). As with the fetus image, this image is ludicrous on the level of literal fact.

Closely connected with clothing and with the idea of transformation, of metamorphosis, is the motif of masks and masquerades. Faces, of course, are masks, and Branden had been trained 'never to betray an emotion, to keep his mask intact,' not to allow anything to alter 'the impenetrable mask of my face.' It is a strange reversal for him, an ironic masquerade, when he sees his face looking out of a newspaper at him and labeled 'Clever crook' (129). The masquerade permeates the New York experience, from the two con men who fleece Branden of his money to the book racket, 'a con-game on a gigantic scale,' of which he becomes a part. Branden's job as a waiter, too, though an honest one, was still to him 'bearable only when viewed as a lark, as something which you might do in disguise or for a very short time' (97).

Names are also a part of the masquerade. Hannan and Howard sound much more respectable than their aliases 'Han the Hook' and 'Big Heinie,' but not only criminals hide behind other names. At the beginning of the book there is 'The Hon.' who had returned from South Africa after making his fortune as a hotel keeper under an assumed name. At the end of the book, the Tolstoy figure says, 'Call me Ivan.' But the most protracted example of pseudonymous living is that of Branden's short-term Toronto friend, Frank the waiter, who turns out to have a remarkable flair for circumstantial lies in the false New York references and addresses he gives Branden. At one point the two discuss the subject of assumed names:

> 'Carrol's as little my real name as yours is Branden.'
> 'Just a moment,' I interrupted him. 'Is there no law in this country against assuming a false name?'
> 'No,' he said. 'There isn't. Not so long as you do it without dishonest purpose. Of course, if you do it for fraud . . .'
> 'Good,' I interrupted him once more. 'That settles that point. I don't see anything wrong in a man's changing his name if he cares to do so, law or no law. But since you've done it, I'm glad it isn't illegal' (80-81).

In the course of his search, Branden concludes that it is not family—a man's name—that is important; nor geography—where he goes; nor vocation—what he does. The important thing is what he is: 'Here I stood entirely on my own feet. Whatever I might have to go through, if finally I arrived somewhere, if I achieved something, no matter how little, it would be my own achievement; I must be I' (30). And in that resolution is the metamorphosis from adolescent to adult, to the man who, coming upon the Finnish immigrant being swindled, 'put the incident down for what it was: an incident. It no longer clouded my whole horizon for me' (391).

It is the passage from the world of Innocence to the world of Experience, it is the myth of the innocent immigrant, with the paradoxical turn that old Europe is the world of innocent and new America the world of experience. The paradox exhibits the essential theme of the book: the search is indeed not geographical but universal. We are all immigrants in a strange world.

The sense of perspective that Branden has discovered in himself, however, leads him to make other distinctions. The fundamental difference between this country and Europe is that 'The whole civilization of Europe is based on the theory of the original sin. . . . But here there is a profound suspicion that in his heart the human animal wants to do right and is good' (378). And he senses 'the great undercurrent of an evolution towards fairness, towards that which is morally right and true' (322). This evolution is accompanied by 'a fact of literary history: John Burroughs was coming into his own . . . . It was the movement away from the accidentals of life and towards the essentials' (218). In other words, the Romantic movement is triumphant, that movement which Burroughs carried on in the United States from his literary progenitor, Thoreau, who in turn perpetuated the European movement of Rousseau, Wordsworth, Froebel and others.

Yet the theme of the lost America undoubtedly added to the popularity of Grove's novel. The Age of Reform in the United States, goaded by the muckrakers, had given place to the Age of Disillusion by the time of Grove's revisions in 1926. Sinclair Lewis had already published chastisements of the middle class; Dos Passos was at work on his panoramic denunciation; and the Lost Generation were trying to see what they could do in a world they did not make—nor like. *A Search for America,* while it was fundamentally at variance with them, nevertheless seemed to be in accord with the widespread *mea culpa* mood.

---

[1]This excerpt is Chapter Four, retitled, of my book, *Frederick Philip Grove* (New York: Twayne Publishers, Inc., 1973), pp. 59-69.

[2]All page references are to the New Canadian Library edition of *A Search for America* (Toronto: McClelland & Stewart, 1971).

[3]Franz Kafka, *Amerika* (New York: New Directions, 1946) Preface by Klaus Mann, p. xii, p. 1

Although Frederick Philip Grove is best known today as a novelist,
he gained a nationwide reputation in his own lifetime as a public
speaker. He began his public speaking career in this country as a
teacher addressing other teachers; with the publication of Over
Prairie Trails, *however, he began addressing a wider audience and*
commanding a fee for his services. When Graphic Press published A
Search for America *in 1927, Grove came to the attention of Graham*
Spry, the newly appointed executive secretary of the Ottawa-based
Association of Canadian Clubs, who invited the novelist to
undertake a speaking tour of Ontario sponsored by the Association.
That tour was so successful that Spry quickly organized two
subsequent tours, a second through western Canada, and a third
through the Maritimes Quebec and Ontario. 'Here,' Margaret
Stobie points out, 'was an ideal subject for the Canadian Clubs—an
immigrant who had tried life in the United States, spurned it, and
chosen Canada; a New Canadian who could give voice to the silent
strangers, who could reveal their needs, trials, and dreams to their
would-be helpers; and a Canadian writer who had written a fine
book—in fact, who now had four books to his credit' (120). One of the
lectures Grove gave on his first speaking tour was 'Canadians Old
and New,' which appeared in Maclean's *even before he had*
completed that tour. In this two-part lecture Grove speaks to native
Canadians as a fellow citizen and to new Canadians as a fellow
immigrant.

Frederick Philip Grove

Canadians Old and New

Like the statues of the ancient Roman deity Janus, this article is
going to have two faces, one turned to those who, being born in this
country or having lived here long enough to be fully acclimatized,
invite through their recognized governmental agencies members of
all white nations to come and to make their homes among them; the
other, to those who have just arrived in pursuance of that invitation,
or who, having arrived some time ago, did not find all they may have
expected to find in the way of a welcome. It goes without saying that a
short article cannot do more than deal with the first principles of so
vast a subject as that which we commonly summarize under the
heading of the 'assimilation of the immigrant.'

Firstly, then, Mr. Canadian Citizen, let me tell you a few truths about yourself as well as about your guests; for, since you have invited the newcomers, they are plainly your guests, entitled to all the privileges which we commonly accord those whom we thus honor.

What, at the present moment, do you, the average citizen of this country, do in order to make the newcomer feel at home? Anything or nothing? First of all, you call him a 'foreigner'—a title of honor, indeed, since it implies that likely he has seen more of the world than you have seen—unless you have traveled. But it is well-known that this title, within the British Isles, has from time immemorial had a sinister sound. A strange thing to say, seeing that the population of Great Britain is itself a mixed population, compounded of many different racial strains. Yet, if the national status of Canada means anything at all, then it surely means this, that here, in Canada, we cultivate or at least mean to cultivate an attitude toward life and its various phases, economic, intellectual, spiritual, distinct from that of a mere British Crown colony. In such Crown colonies the foreigner may be tolerated; *we* invite him. In other words, the Britisher coming to these shores—in spite of the fact that we cherish our connection with Britain as the motherland and greet our British cousins as next-of-kin—is as much a 'foreigner' when he lands as any man arriving from Central Europe: both are citizens of this country only *in posse*. The Britisher has an enormous advantage over the continental European inasmuch as he speaks one of the two languages which have the right-of-way in Canada; but he is vastly less apt to have a desire to adapt himself and to acknowledge that the way 'we' do these things 'at 'ome' cannot be binding on the country to which he came in order to make his living. The present writer knows a good many districts in the west of this vast Dominion where there are 'little islands' of English or Scotch immigrants who offer as their contribution towards the evolution of a new Canadian mentality chiefly acrid criticism of the destructive kind. So-called 'foreigners' rarely make themselves obnoxious in that way.

Again, what, Mr. Citizen, do you do in order to welcome the 'foreigner' whom you invite? Oh, well, you assign him 160 acres of land in the bush or a job in a factory or work on the road-bed of a transportation line, and thereafter you leave him icily alone. He meets with other 'foreigners'; and if they are farmers, there is soon a 'foreign settlement'; if they are factory hands, there is a 'foreign quarter' in some city; if men of the pick and shovel, there is a 'foreign gang.' The adults in a settlement, quarter, or gang are very apt to hang on to their vernacular; they have little opportunity to acquire any other, especially the women. They have no desire for isolation; but it is forced on to them.

Their ways may be strange and even repulsive to you; so are your ways to them. In such a settlement I have heard a Russian farmer speak of Canadian farming methods as 'slovenly English ways.' He was, by the way, a better, more careful, more laborious farmer than most Canadian tillers of the soil in the west; many a native might have learned from him in that respect; he is to-day, in the midst of a bankrupt district, the only prosperous man. At the time, however, before the war, he might, but for his isolation, have learned a good many things from his Canadian neighbors, in addition to the English language. This particular Russo-British subject happened to be personally clean; but I have known any number of Ruthenians, Russians, Poles—as I have known some English people—who never dreamed that a head is not the proper recreation ground for minute inhabitants. I have never known any who did not at once try to rid themselves of them when they became aware that I, or anybody, objected to their sojourn there; and nearly always were these attempts crowned with success. These people are strange to you; but unless you overcome that strangeness, it is not likely that anyone else will try: the first step simply must come from you. If anywhere in this country a 'foreign settlement' remains as a foreign body within the tissue of the commonwealth, nobody is to blame but the Canadians surrounding them.

Another thing. We speak a great deal of 'Canadian Ideals.' But so long as we advertise our country abroad as a good place to come to, there cannot be anything that may properly be called a Canadian ideal; at best it is only a provisional one; for that ideal is still in the making; and when you invite anyone to become a new citizen of this country, you invite him also to help in the making of it. Nothing in this country is fixed; our economic status is changing from year to year, sometimes from day to day; our intellectual level is constantly rising—there is much room at the top; of a typically Canadian spiritual attitude towards life and the great mysteries we have at best the germs. Our invited guests will exert an influence on all three which we cannot suppress without making them frankly into slaves. I have often found that the total reaction to life of these new-comers was vastly more profound than that of many, especially young, Canadians who live largely for the three p's—profit, pleasure, preferment. Often these 'foreigners' come from communities with not only a vastly older but a spiritually richer environment than they find among ourselves. It could not be otherwise: our country is young, unfinished, crude. Many of them are readers in their own tongue—readers, that is, not of silly modern sex novels, but of the great literatures that have been indigenous to their own countries for thousands of years. I know a certain Scotch scholar—a member of one of our universities—who, in the declining third of his life, thought it worth his while to acquire a knowledge of Icelandic in order to study Icelandic sagas; he professes himself overwhelmed with their depth and significance. There are many Icelanders living in our midst, especially, of course, in the west, who have been familiar with that literature from their earliest youth. Yet these very men I have seen treated, by a Canadian-born station master who was a dunce, as if they were the scum of the earth because their English accent betrayed their foreign birth.

Do you, Mr. Canadian Citizen, think that these people have no contribution to make to our intellectual and spiritual life? Would you willingly limit the Canadian ideal to the exclusion of the wealth of meaning, the beauty, and the depth of view which these people can impart to our soul's picture of life? If you do, it is high time that you instruct your legislators to cut short all further immigration. These people are willing to assimilate themselves; but, if denied this outlet for their inner energies, energies that can contribute to the spiritual growth of Canada, they have only one alternative so long as they are here; and that alternative is to conquer you—not by force of arms, not by pressure of wealth, but by the strength of their unconquerable spirit.

Another example, one more from among the many which I might adduce. Is the western small town a thing of beauty? Has it such a wealth of loveliness that it captures our imagination and makes us revolt at the mere idea of change? Walk along Main Street, with your spirit's eyes open, in any of them. If you have any aesthetic sense at all, you will be horrified at the mess of ugliness, the utter absence of even any attempt at making the aspect of the town at least bearable. There is no planning for the whole or the detail; they make the impression of utter casualness; there is no attempt at disguising the often squint-eyed utility—I mean a utility deflected from its original purpose and twisted into a make-shift. In a large majority of rural villages we gather the impression of a premature neglect and decay, not that of a young but confident civilization that feels a reckless sap pulsing through its veins. It has been remarked by some of the most penetrating observers that, when we send our Rhodes scholars to

British universities, they by no means impress the old world as paragons of youthful manhood; one of them said: they all look and act and move as if they were preternaturally old. Their very gaiety is a sham. That is precisely the impression the majority of our western towns make on the immigrant; and thirty-six years of familiarity have not dulled my revolt. A barn that is half blown over by the wind and used as a warehouse; a dwelling sinking away in the mud, without foundations, its floors twisted and warped; a burnt-out store-building, with ruins never removed, two square-rods of billboard advertising a cheap tobacco leaning against one side, with, on the other, a similar poster, sea-green or cruelly blue or pink, screaming at a tender-tinted sky the vastly important merits of a certain baking powder.

That is your small town. But it is not the way the immigrant's old-country village looked. It may have been old-fashioned, quaint; but it had character; it had a history in the sense that every feature of it reflected centuries of endeavor—the endeavor of everyone, without exception, to assert the supremacy of the human mind over the force of destruction lurking in nature. We could not have given centuries of endeavor; but it is a reproach not to have given four decades.

Our guests come from Europe. Europe, as only he can know who has lived there as a poor man, is a bad place to live in; for Europe is crowded, and economic distress is the first and foremost enemy of freedom. Material things are high-priced in Europe; the only thing that is cheap is human labor. But in Europe even the poor man is profoundly impressed with the fact that the three eternal values—truth, goodness, beauty—rank far above any material values. Yes, beauty. These three eternal things are bound up with each other in such a way that the search for one cannot endure without the search for the other two. I, for one, feel that to be forced to look, day after day, on some piece of ugliness is as demoralizing as to be forced to listen day after day to lies. The Ruthenian comes, sees it all, and builds his log-shack in the bush, plastering it inside and outside with clay. He is poor; he has not the money to paint it all. He paints a small area around each window, bright-green, let me say. Into this bright-green field he sets his window frame in white or pink or red or blue. Do I hear you laugh? It is his protest against poverty and surrounding ugliness. His sense of beauty may be mistaken, crude, primitive. But he has that sense of beauty. Have you? Or, have you ever seen Easter-eggs prepared by what we must now, I suppose, call Czecho-Slovakians? Some have impressed me as works of art, a popular art, if you wish, but a true art nevertheless.

And now the crucial question. Do you, Mr. Canadian, want to assimilate these people? Do you want them to give up what is theirs and to adopt your vaunted 'high standard of living' which is only a high standard of waste? Do you want them to eclipse themselves and to drop their good as well as their evil? But the question itself is sheer nonsense. It posits as possible what is an impossibility. There is no such thing as a one-sided assimilation. Every action has its reaction. Don't forget that these people who come among us have pluck and enterprise; or they would not be here. Do not forget that they have brains; for most of them were the underdogs in Europe; and it is precisely the underdog who develops his brains. Look at your rural schools in mixed districts: which children lead their classes, yours or those of these 'foreigners.' No, assimilation can only be mutual. Only if you take from them, will they take from you. The friars of the thirteenth century became a power in England, not because they made themselves the hosts, but because they consented to be the guests of the poor. Have you sat down at a Ruthenian table? If so, you have done more to change the hostess's ways than by inviting her to a banquet in a palace. The thing, however, which I wish to underline in this connection is that these 'foreigners,' little as most of us realize it, have something to give as well as to receive; and what they have to give is vastly more than the motive power of arm and back: they bring a spiritual heritage as well as their brawn which is at best an economic asset.

But I must cease and let the other face of the Janus-head speak.

Mr. Newcomer, we invited you to come among us, and you followed the call. We bid you welcome. We are bound by a promise. We wanted you to help us till our soil; to swing the pick in order to release the ore that lies buried in the depth of our rocks; to turn the wheels of our industries. In return we promised you freedom.

You have lived in Europe; so you know that there is no freedom without law. Your freedom depends on your attitude toward that law. You must, for the moment, accept and obey it; or the very machinery that is set in motion for your protection will continue moving to your enslavement. That is fundamental, here as in Europe; we have no longer, perhaps we never had, any wild west. But freedom involves opportunity. We are wasteful, you are thrifty; if you were not, you would not have survived; in that lies your opportunity. Do not become Canadian in this one point. The wages we pay in this country offer an ample margin over and above the necessities. What you do with that margin is nobody's business but your own. If you spend it on moving-picture shows, candy, or 'smart' clothes, it will not be available to give you a start as an owner of land, a merchant, or a producer of industrial goods. If you don't, it will do so. Could you have become the owner of a quarter-section of land in Europe? If so, you would not be here to-day. This is one thing we offer. Retain your thrift, and you will prosper.

We offer more. We offer you a partnership in the business of 'running this country.' Live among us for five years without wilfully destroying your opportunities by coming into flagrant conflict with the law, and we will give you a share in forming that law. If there are details of that law as you find it which seem strange, which perhaps seem oppressive to you, you will be able to do your share to change them; and if, in a given point, you do not succeed, you will learn to bear with it because it is part of that law which you helped to shape. In school district, municipality, province, dominion, we want you to contribute your share and your vote, for, after five years, we will consider you as one of ourselves; till then, you are our guest.

Perhaps you will meet with a man or a woman here and there who will turn away from you because you have betrayed by your accent that you were not born among us. I will give you a piece of confidential advice. Put that man or woman down, in the depth of your heart, as belonging to the riff-raff of this country; you will find such a riff-raff wherever you go. Should you happen to meet them in the mass, as will happen, hold on to this great truth: these people, as a nation, invited you to come; as a nation, therefore, they bid you welcome. They wanted you; they will want you; they are merely momentarily hidden behind that screen of riff-raff. If you doubt, make this test: go to the most prominent, the best educated man—or woman—in your district and ask for sympathy or help; I feel sure both sympathy and help will be given.

Still more. We offer you brotherhood. We do not only want your strong arm or your special skill. We want *you*. If you have knowledge which we lack, we want you to give us that knowledge. If you feel emotions which are strange to us, we want to share those emotions— do not forget those trees whose name lies hidden in the first two syllables of the name of your native Bukovina, nor the ash that is called Ygdrasil in Icelandic sagas: if you long for them, we honor that longing; tell us about it so that we can share it. If you have curious dreams, let us see them with you; to those who know, your dreams seem greater and more precious than the brawn of your muscle. I know there lives a song in you: do not forget your language. We may not know that language, as likely you knew no English when you came. It was your own experience that your powers grew as you learned a new tongue. Be proud, then, of the fact that in the knowledge of your native tongue you have a power withheld from many of us. In our high schools and universities we teach our own youths one or two foreign languages—Latin, Greek, German, not to mention French which is not foreign to Canada; we do so for the sake of the mental power such knowledge imparts. It is true that most of our provinces bid you send your children to a school where they learn English. That is as it should be; there must be a common medium of communication.

But the best thing we offer you lies perhaps in this that we offer you a soil in which you yourself can grow. If you think we want you to become in all things like the rest of us Canadians, you are mistaken. By becoming absolutely like ourselves—if such a thing were possible—you would lose the greater part of your value to us. Seventy-five per cent of the population of our west—more in the east—is Anglo-Saxon in origin; that is, they are a blend of Celt, Briton, German, Scandinavian, and Norman-French, not to mention Spanish and colonial infusions. The blend is old; it has stood many tests; it has been successful in history; it has built a not inconsiderable empire. It is a lusty blend, still full of the exuberance of youth. It will stand further blending. The Anglo-Saxon is constitutionally opposed to the narrow theory which places a value on pure racial strains. We consider the admixture which you bring as a useful leaven. Learn our language, obey our laws, and help us to make them when you have qualified for that function: that, Mr. Newcomer, is all we ask of you. Apart from that, remain what you are, except in as much as the newly changed environment, the freer, less crowded air of this continent exerts its unavoidable influence. That unavoidable influence you must not resist, or your own growth will be stunted. But if you withhold from us what you bring—the example of thrift, the ancient viewpoint which sees in life more than the opportunity to accumulate dollars—you stunt *our* growth.

Above all, hold your head high. This country does not claim to be a 'melting-pot.' What it does claim is that in it there 'are many mansions'—and one of them, undoubtedly, is the mansion that has been waiting precisely for you.

Only weeks before Grove received Graham Spry's invitation to tour the country on behalf of the Association of Canadian Clubs, he had himself been considering—and not for the first time—the possibility of earning money as a public speaker. He was thus predisposed to accept Spry's invitation but he worried the choice of topics for his lectures. ("What in the world could I lecture on that will draw people," he asks in a letter to his friend, Watson Kirkconnell (L, 78). Spry himself suggested only that Grove lecture on the ideas expressed in A Search for America, *and for Spry himself the most important idea was that the author professed to find some "spiritual satisfaction" in his choice of Canada. Grove's good friend and mentor, A.J. Phelps, advised him to restrict himself to literary subjects and suggested topics such as 'the Art of the Novel,' 'The Function of the Canadian Novel,' 'Tragedy in Canadian Life and Art,' and 'The Tragic Motive.' Although Grove did lecture on literary and aesthetic subjects, he appears to have been drawn to the issues of immigration and national identity. If, as he stated in* In Search of Myself, *his ambition was to be the 'spokesman' for a race, he perhaps came closest to realizing that ambition, or, at least, to gaining public recognition for that role, on the speaker's platform. In such lectures as 'Canadians Old and New' and 'Assimilation,' which also appeared in* Maclean's, *he entered a debate on immigration fuelled by such works as J.S. Woodsworth's* Strangers Within Our Gates *(1909) and fought out in magazines and journals throughout the twenties.*

Frederick Philip Grove

Assimilation

We should let the immigrant grow as what he is;
not as what we think he ought to be.

We are worried today over ethnic problems. By certain persons—or shall I call them interests?—a formidable-looking indictment has been drawn up against the immigrant. A great deal is being said about preferred and non-preferred nationalities. I wonder with how much justification.

According to the reasons stated for the attitude adopted, these opponents of unrestricted immigration fall into two classes. One bases its objections on purely economic grounds; the other, on grounds political, social and spiritual.

Let me deal with the former first. Many of our mid-European agricultural immigrants stubbornly decline to adopt what those involved in the argument choose to call Canadian ways of dealing with the land. When you enquire more closely into the matter, you find that these Canadian ways are not Canadian at all but originated in the United States of America. The mid-Europeans refuse to farm on as large a scale as the average Canadian; they refuse to use machines to the same extent; they refuse to avail themselves to the same extent of the system of credit. We can readily admit that this indictment is true.

The most powerful counter-argument consists in the fact that these Poles, Hungarians, and Ukrainians can move into a district abandoned or on the point of being abandoned by Anglo-Saxons and succeed where the latter may have made a failure. This fact nobody who knows conditions will dispute. It may well be that the reason consists not so much in their using better methods, as in their thrift and their ability to get along contentedly with a lower standard of living. Whatever the reason is, the fact remains that they contribute to the national wealth and that they are building empire.

It has been said that while on the American continent less wheat is produced per acre of land than in Europe, more is produced per man employed in the industry. I will frankly admit that this is the American trend; nor will I deny that it runs counter to the whole European peasant tradition. To the European peasant, and more especially the mid-European peasant, the land is a sacred thing, more important than the individual on whom its ownership has for the moment devolved. The question arises: which of the two trends is from a national point of view the more desirable one? For him who views things from year to year, or from day to day—in other words, for the hand-to-mouth view—the most important thing undoubtedly remains that every man employed in agriculture should produce every bushel of grain which he can possibly produce, even though he may thus occupy more land than he can do justice to. The moment we view the matter from a point of view of a settled country—the result of such a policy is plainly disastrous. It is beginning to be apparent in such a relatively new province as Manitoba. Already we have abandoned farms there. Already, a few years ago, I counted, within a radius of six miles around a once-prosperous town, no less than fifty-three quarter sections so fouled with weeds that it had become impossible to farm them. Already, too, there are districts which are being invaded by a thriftless and, by the way, purely Anglo-Saxon tenantry. And that in a province which is in its infancy.

While there is plenty of free land available, as there was up to a few years ago, the disastrous effect of such a policy does not show on the national balance sheet. An empire like the Canadian West, a province like Manitoba, may plainly be prosperous as a whole because it produces the grain, while every single individual composing the agricultural population may very conceivably be insolvent. I do not say that such is the case; but there are districts where we are marching straight toward such a condition of affairs.

There is a further danger. The West is essentially an agricultural country. Agricultural countries depend for their welfare less on prosperity than on stability. I know a Canadian farmer who has moved from one place to another four times in a single lifetime. I know scores who have changed farms once or twice. Migration seems to their children the natural thing. Their apparent prosperity resolves itself in the last analysis into a voluntarily assumed slavery to implement and loan companies. Consequently, young people crowd into cities and towns. I am, of course, well aware of the fact that these are the growing-pains of every young country.

Does such a policy breed happiness? Does it breed men? So far it has produced wheat. But land has been consumed rather than farmed; crops have been converted into dollars; dollars into first payments on machines and motor cars. May we not question the ultimate wisdom of exporting the fertility of the soil in order to keep the machinery of a so-called up-to-date life lubricated?

I have so far accepted as true the assertion that we produce more wheat per man employed in agriculture than does Europe; but even this assertion may be questioned. We must count in all those who are employed in the implement trade, in the manufacture of implements, in the making of cars, in the transportation of the crops to distant markets, in the handling of these crops; all these are, though indirectly, employed in the production of our grains. Nobody will for a moment deny that their number vastly exceeds not only that of the farmers on this continent, but also the number similarly employed in Europe where, after all, our so-called up-to-date methods are deliberately repudiated by a peasantry that knows what it is about. If we divided the total yield of the country not by the number of our farmers alone, but by the number of all directly or indirectly employed in producing it, I wonder whether the yield per man would still exceed the yield per man in any but the poorest districts of Europe.

We speak of peasants as if the very word made us shudder. Let us not forget that it is the peasantry which, so far, has enabled every civilization evolved in the past to survive as long as it has survived. The peasantry of Europe has always fed the cities not only with bread and wine, but with new blood and new manhood. Is Canada—evolving as it is a great material civilization imitative of the great material civilization of our neighbours to the south—is Canada reproducing that manhood which did the pioneering work of a hundred years ago? Is it not a fact that the Canadian-born in Western Canada today, in the country and in the small towns, are becoming soft, mentally and physically; that in certain kinds of hard, manual labor there is an imperative demand for the immigrant, that education, though it is being spread far and wide, is also being planed down to the thinness of a mere veneer? And further: is it not a fact that while we improve the 'plant' of life, as the mechanical equipment is commonly called, we sorely neglect the fundamentally human qualities which we sum up in the one word 'character'?

But though, through the improvidence of the last generation we have alienated the greater part of our land, and have allowed it to pass into private hands, it remains none the less true that the sort of people we need on the land is still that class which we call the pioneers.

European civilization has in the last 2,300 years become essentially urban; that is, it has neglected all the ruder virtues except the martial ones. If we want to find settlers fit to do our sort of work, we must go to the poor districts of Europe, to the districts where the hardships of poverty have trained the population for the hardships of pioneerdom; to the districts where thrift has been enforced by hard necessity rather than by a long schooling in ironic wisdom; for ironic wisdom does not presuppose to emigration: we must go to those parts of Europe where there is still an indigenous and rude sort of peasantry.

With wide-open ports and unrestricted immigration something resembling a natural quota law has just re-established itself. Last year we had 75,000 British immigrants, 25,000 from northern Europe, 50,000 from what we call the non-preferred nationalities of central Europe. I will not deny that these figures are perhaps, too high—not because they represent a national menace, but because we have been unable to place that many on the land. The remedy consists in a releasing of the high-pressure, rapid-fire salesmanship used by our transportation companies rather than in any governmental restriction of immigration. Yet, even at that, the fact remains that a higher percentage of the third class of immigrants has found its way to settling permanently on the land than of the other two classes.

How are they fitting themselves into the national life of Canada?

In this connection, other objections are being raised. It is being said that as soon as they are naturalized, they lend themselves to partisan exploitation by adroit politicians. I have lived among almost all classes of immigrants; in the open country; and I have lived among them in such a way as to be mistaken for one of their number. It is true that among those who are unable or but scantily able to speak the English language, at election time politicians would come in, their cars loaded with cigars and tobacco, their pockets bulging with bright, shiny half-dollar pieces to be distributed among the children. It is true that when they left, the Ukrainian farmer, often unable to judge between parties, would cast his vote for the man who had been most friendly to him and his. If you will think for a moment, I don't believe you can blame him. He is concerned with establishing himself economically and spiritually. His daily bread is more to him than political institutions; his inner adjustment to a new country, a new world, means more to him than a law that may be passed or voted down. Political opinions, unless inherited—and that is the least intelligent mode of acquisition—are even for him born in the country the last thing he evolves in the process of fitting himself for life: few of our adolescents have political opinions of their own before the age of twenty-eight. Political opinions of his own cannot be intelligently evolved by the immigrant before he has established himself economically and spiritually in his new environment. Politically, the immigrant is necessarily indifferent for at least a decade.

If that is true—and you may take my word for it that it could not be otherwise—on whom does this political exploitation of what is called 'the foreign vote' reflect: on the so-called foreigner or on the native politician? I myself refused to vote for the first twenty years of my stay in the country; and I could not convince myself that I was doing anything but the intelligent thing in thus refraining; for I refused to be exploited, as, had I voted, I should have been, in spite of the fact that the English language was almost native to me. For such exploitation remedies are at hand. I am not concerned with them here. But any group of reasonably sympathetic men can work them out in an hour. What I am concerned with here is the fact that this exploitation does not argue against the immigrant. If he were left alone, he would do, as a not inconsiderable fraction of Anglo-Saxons do voluntarily: he would refrain from voting. Even though we forget only too often that, having invited these people into the country, we are their hosts, they are not so apt to forget that they are our guests: left alone, they would almost think it rude or undutiful on their part to interfere in matters which they consider our business. As a matter of fact, many an immigrant neglects naturalization proceedings when he is entitled to claim citizenship in this country, not because he does not wish to become a Canadian, but because he feels himself to be, at least in desire, so much a Canadian that he rests content to accept any political measures which his hosts may care to impose upon him. 'That,' he virtually says to those born in this country, 'you had better settle among yourselves.'

Closely connected with this objection to the immigrant is another: he settles in what is called 'solid undigested lumps.'

Now I was tolerably familiar with Europe as it was before the war. In nearly every large city of Europe—in Paris, Bordeaux, Marseilles, Antwerp, Amsterdam, Stockholm, Copenhagen, Moscow, St. Petersburg, Munich, Dresden, Berlin, Athens, Rome, Madrid, Barcelona, Lisbon—I used to know Anglo-Saxon colonies. Certain streets were solidly English. There were English shops, English restaurants; English librairies, English churches, English papers. Why should that have been? Why, indeed, except because these people, for one reason or other, chose to live in foreign climes and clung to each other in 'solid, undigested lumps.'

Well, if they did it, can we blame the European settler in this country for doing the same? Consider for a moment. He finds himself suddenly transferred into a world which is alien to him. The less of an education in his own language he brings with him, the more alien this world is to him, alien in speech, manners, morals, economic conditions, spiritual outlook or lack of it. Is it anything but natural that these people should congregate in 'foreign districts' or 'foreign quarters'? Why! It could not be otherwise. The point is, what in the world is the objection to it?

It is being said they will not mingle. Let me assure you from actual experience, repeated again and again, that it is the other way around. The British will not mingle with them. Why not? From one single reason: from racial conceit. It is a very strange and, to us New Canadians, very incomprehensible, but none the less indisputable fact that the average Anglo-Saxon considers himself superior to all the other races of the world, individually the more so the less reason he has. The fact is the more incomprehensible to us when we reflect that the Anglo-Saxon himself is a blend of Briton, Celt, Roman, German, Dane, and Swede, not to mention the infusions of French, Spanish, Jewish and West-Indian Creole blood. I have lived in mixed districts where small Anglo-Saxon minorities sat like an army of occupation in conquered territory within solidly Ukrainian, Russo-German, or Scandinavian settlements. It was they—that is, the first generation of British immigrants—who held aloof, not the foreigners, unless they were provoked. It was they who expressed indignation when their sons married Ukrainian, German, or Scandinavian girls. This second generation of Britishers were often anything but slow in recognizing that these girls were clean, pretty, intelligent, thrifty and good cooks to boot.

I am coming to a point of the utmost importance.

If assimilation means the absorption of one race by another, the absorbing race not to undergo any change by the process, then there is no such thing as assimilation. You can extinguish a race by preventing it from propagating itself; but, if you want the immigrant to survive and yet to become what you are, you are aiming at an impossibility. Two races living side by side can do one of two things: they can mingle and blend, thereby giving rise to a third race: thus Angles and Normans blended in England; Scots and Norsemen in Scotland; Franks and Gauls in France. Or they can define themselves against each other, as on the whole the continental Europeans have done. This definition may be peaceful or martial: it has, on the whole, been martial in Europe. Yet it does not need to be martial; in fact, I cannot convince myself that such a martial definition of races against each other is the natural thing; for who would deny that the whole trend of civilization, in spite of disastrous recrudescences of the warlike spirit, has been one toward peaceful methods.

But in order to make peaceful definition possible on the large scale, we must first of all learn one important lesson: namely, that no racial strain is intrinsically superior to any other. To learn that lesson should be easy for us who are members of a great empire in which only eleven per cent of the total population is British. Some bond must hold that empire together. What is it? What should it be if not mutual toleration—a toleration perhaps not yet shared by the ignorant, by what we may call the riff-raff of the nations, but stubbornly upheld by those who have learned lessons from history.

Politically, toleration expresses itself not in subordination, but in federation; this is a lesson which it has taken even the mother country centuries to learn. Subordination results in rebellion: force breeds resistance. For an example, look at the American Revolution! Federation, on the other hand, is merely another name for what I have just now called peaceful definition of the races against each other—races which have learned to consider each other as being of equal value and which, therefore, are willing to consider each other as having equal rights.

In order to prepare the way for my ultimate conclusion, I must for a moment speak of these 'foreigners' in our midst as perhaps nobody has ever spoken of them before. Don't forget that I am one of their number.

You want to Canadianize them. What does the word mean? I have already said that you cannot 'absorb' them, in the usual sense which thoughtless people attach to the word assimilation. If anyone had told me before I came to this country that a majority of its citizens might want me to cease to be I, I should not have come. In fact, to turn black into white is impossible. But black can be overlaid with a veneer of white. Overlay a Ukrainian with an American veneer, and underneath he must necessarily remain a Ukrainian. Black can also be destroyed and white substituted for it: that process the United States has tried during the last twenty years—in fact, since the United States executed its great change of front, with what I believe to be disastrous results. The theory of the Melting Pot is exploded today.

How do you want to Canadianize them? Politically, economically, spiritually? Politically, you can win their loyalty by giving them, economically, a square deal and by leaving them spiritual freedom. Economically, you can force them to adopt all the externals of American civilization: the high standard of living, the facile manners of an apparent democracy, the lack of respect and reverence for achievement and experience, the devotion to the mechanics of life, with an obliteration of all that lies beyond these mechanics. Spiritually . . . well, spiritually you can kill them; you cannot conquer them.

Here is an essential point: politically, when they arrive, they may be in the nature of minors; economically, they may be backward—I do not say they are: they made a living under conditions vastly harder than conditions are in this country; but they may appear so to you. But spiritually they are, to say the least, not inferior, class for class. They came from countries where the spiritual realm was the only one in which they could assert their individuality. This spiritual realm can be divided into three provinces: the mental, the emotional, the religious. In the mental province we must distinguish between information and intelligence. Why is it that in mixed schools the children of our immigrants almost invariably lead their classes? Where do they get their mental endowment? In the spiritual province it is they, not the native Canadians who bring a tradition. According as they come from various parts of Europe, their endowment varies. The whole Slavic race is astir with music and poetry; Finns and Scandinavians with critical thought. In the religious province . . . Oh, well, why talk about it? Religion means something to them which governs their lives.

Assimilation? You can shear them of the finest flowers of older civilizations. You can destroy; you cannot assimilate. The principle of the melting pot has proved to be a failure in the United States. Are we going to prove it a failure once more?

What other principle is there? I have already named it. There is federation. What does federation mean?

The British Empire is a federation; so is Canada. One-fourth of our population consists of French-Canadians. Are they loyal? If so, why? Why, indeed, except because we have left them their own language, their own religion, their own ideals, their own aims, their own art? Because we have found means to leave them that spiritual freedom, of which to deprive them was fortunately beyond our power when the question arose.

Suppose we tried something similar with our later arrivals? Instead of forcing them into that conformity, spiritual and economic, which has been the aim of unsuccessful endeavors in the United States—a conformity which can be brought about only by destroying their true strength and by making them into hollow standardized masks—suppose we encouraged them rather to retain their religions, their standards of family life, their reverence for the land; and to develop their often remarkable artistic, mental and mystic gifts; thereby to grow among us as what they are, not as what we think they should be; and suppose we cease laughing at them because they are different—shall we secure their loyalty?

Let me answer that question by another question. Have we or have we not won the loyalty of the French in our midst? Let us cease to standardize; let us individualize them rather! Let us go and learn from them; they have much to teach. It is true that they scoff at our standard of living, that standard of living which means that we feed our transient appetites with costly foods and live like Lucullus in the midst of a multitude crying for bread. We scoff at deeper things. Let us cease to do so. Let the Icelander explain to us the marvellous depth and significance of his sagas. Let the Slav give us of that music whence the symphonies and the chamber music were distilled to which we listen in our most cultured concert halls. Will they be loyal to a country which allows them to grow as if they were still rooted in their native soil? What is more blessed, to give or to receive? Only by giving can anyone grow.

And now just a word of a great historical mission which may or may not be assigned to this country, according as we interpret events. One thing is an accomplished fact, whether we approve of it or not. Already all the nationalities of Europe have met on this continent. In

Europe they had lived side by side for centuries. They had not blended. They had defined themselves against each other; and they had done so in a martial way. For centuries the United States of Europe has been the cherished dream of advanced minds. That dream has failed in the past. These nationalities, defined against each other in a martial way, meet here in America on common ground, in peaceful intercourse. Ultimately they may blend; perhaps in the course of millennia; perhaps not till the white race as such is forced to close its fronts by the menace held over it by a colored race; merging its national quarrels in a common enmity: it has been that way in the past; more than once, alas. Meanwhile there is a shorter way of arriving at a *modus vivendi*; the way of peaceful definition.

That, as I see it, if there was providential guidance in the course of history, must have been the intention of that providence which withheld the western continents from the nations of Europe till modern times. That, if we formulate a reasonable aim of geo-politics, would be the mission assigned to America.

Suppose a supermind had, in 1492, foreseen the rush that would throng this continent within four centuries. Suppose that supermind had also had the power to determine events, thinking along purely human lines and fired by the desire for an ultimate good. What would that mind have done? How would that mind have reasoned? Thus, I believe.

These many nationalities have tried in Europe to find a way of peacefully living side by side; they have tried to do so by arming themselves; they have failed. I will make them repeat their great experiment here in America without allowing them to arm themselves. But suppose they still choose the wrong way; suppose the first-comers attempt to force the late-comers to conform, to assimilate themselves to those who arrived ahead of them? Then they will fail again; and instead of evolving a great new civilization to which each unit contributes its own particular virtues, they will meet on purely economic and material common ground and merely evolve a high standard of living to which each unit contributes its own particular vices.

I will provide against that, too, such a supermind might have said. I will divide the continent into two great political divisions, the settlement of one of which I will retard. Then, if the first attempt, in the southern division, fails again, the northern division will be able to learn from its mistakes.

Yes, I will go still further. I will make that northern division part of a great empire in which slowly, slowly the principle of federation is to work itself out among distant nations that have no immediate contact, among nations which are too different to admit of even the dream of assimilation: Hindus, Kaffirs, Afrikanders, and Malays. Then, perhaps, they will learn, not only from the mistakes made in the southern division, but also from the success of that great federation of nations. Still more. I will hand that northern division over successively to two racial strains, so that the one coming later shall find the older one present, unable to assimilate it and forced to define itself peacefully against it whether it wants to or not. If with these three lessons before its eyes, that northern division, under the rule of the second racial strain, with many other grades coming in, still persists in the European principle of 'conform or fight'—then it will deserve to be wiped from the face of the earth.

That, it seems to me, might have been the reasoning of such a supermind. That, in my view, is the mission of Canada in geopolitics. You may see it that way or not. I am one; you are many.

Canada is the meeting-place of many races. Only through such a meeting-place where Slav rubs elbows with Anglo-Saxon, Teuton with Frenchman—and where they can learn, not only to respect each other's various gifts, but also to recognize that they have more that unites than separates them—only through such a meeting-place of all its children can Europe be redeemed. The children must reconcile the parents. That, I repeat, is, in my opinion, Canada's misison in geo-politics.

Let us assume that task until with Pericles—for I always revert to antiquity, and there is nothing new under the sun—we can say: 'We have no black looks or angry words for our neighbor if he enjoys himself if his own way; and we abstain from the little acts of churlishness—a sneer here, a shrug there—which, though they leave no mark, yet cause annoyance to whoso notes them.'

Then, perhaps, we can make this great dream of federation come true.

I believe this is a new principle to be worked out and to be recognized in this our country. As I have said, it is a principle of far-reaching importance for ourselves as well as for the world at large: this principle of federation and good will, respect and mutual recognition. For what, at bottom, does federation mean? It means free intercourse between men and women of many different races, each of them variously endowed, and each entitled to equality within a common loyalty. 'The very word,' exclaims Herodotus, 'is beautiful, *Isonomia!*'—a word which we may equally well translate by 'equality before the law,' by 'federation,' by 'unity in diversity,' or by 'fair play.'

III
The Figure of Estrangement

Grove reached the height of his popularity as a novelist on his three Association of Canadian Clubs lecture tours; his best-selling books were the two promoted while he was on those tours, A Search for America *(1927) and* Our Daily Bread *(1928). He moved to Ottawa in December 1929 as 'President and Editor of Ariston Publishers Limited,' a division of Graphic Press, in the hope of building on that success and making a place for himself in the social and cultural life of the nation. That was not to be. Grove no sooner moved to Ottawa than he discovered that he was simply the figurehead president of Ariston and that the company had 'nothing to sell' (L, 278) and no money with which to negotiate for books or agency contracts (L, 279, 281); and, of course, he arrived in Ottawa on the heels of the Depression. To make matters worse, reviews of the two books with which he followed* Our Daily Bread, *that is,* It Needs to be Said *(1929) and* The Yoke of Life *(1930) were, at best, mixed, and royalties from his earlier works rapidly declined. Moreover, Grove was soon forced to realize that the doors which had opened to him during his lecture tours had opened only temporarily. In a letter to Lorne Pierce on April 1, 1940 Grove describes his life in Ottawa as 'an isolation comparable only to that of an Arctic explorer, one afflicted with smallpox at that, lost on the Barrier who, at the best, meets a scavenger gull' (L, 383). It was in this state of mind that Grove wrote 'Apologia Pro Vita et Opere Suo,' an apology for his life and work published in* The Canadian Forum *in August 1931. Writing to Watson Kirkconnell shortly after the article appeared, Grove announces his imminent departure from Canada and described the 'Apologia' as 'a sort of valedictory to his friends and enemies' (L, 296). Although the Groves decided finally against emigration and moved instead to a farm outside Simcoe, Ontario, the article marks a turning point in Grove's career.*

Frederick Philip Grove

Apologia Pro Vita Et Opere Suo

Both my way of living and my way of writing have been bitterly, even venomously attacked. I have never answered any individual, waiting for some opportunity to say a few words in a less personal and more generally valid way. I will deal with the two in their order, as far as it is possible to separate the two.

For, after all, my way of living is conditioned by my aims in writing; or, in other words, I am a writer first and a living being only secondarily. It remains, of course, true that the total of the writer's work is necessarily determined by the sum of his experience, but with me, who am in my sixtieth year and have been writing and publishing for over four decades, though only recently under my name, the time has long since arrived when I deliberately limited experience in the horizontal, so to speak, and sank my shafts perpendicularly into the depths.

What are my aims in writing? What I have to say will sound presumptuous to many; it is not meant so, for nobody realizes more profoundly than myself how much achievement has fallen short of the aim in the past, and, seeing what life has made of me (a stunted growth, starved, by a relentless struggle for the daily bread, of intellectual food and of leisure), how much it is bound to fall short in the future. But my aim is still what it was at eighteen; and I would today rather live and work with that aim in view, knowing that I must fail of attaining it, than lower the aim and reach a lesser goal.

I aim at building the sort of work which, while like the pyramids, taking time to build, will also stand for some little time after being completed. But since time is a commodity of which few except myself seem to have a supply on hand these days (I have saved it for thinking and writing by the expedient of not spending it on either living or amassing wealth), how could I possibly exist except under conditions of almost total retirement? Metaphorically speaking, I live in the wilderness and cannot afford to take part in the activities of my fellows. Necessarily, in my way of living as well as of my writing, I am a member of the opposition; and whether I belong to a party of yesterday or tomorrow remains to be seen. Thus, though I am a lover of music, I abhor the gramophone and the radio; though I love to talk to my neighbours, I will not tolerate the telephone in my house; though I am keenly interested in the events of the world and the thought of my contemporaries, I read neither the daily press nor the average magazine and very few books (though, truth to tell, I read about as many good ones as I can lay my hand on—a thing which is more fully explained in a little unpublished work entitled *In Praise of Poverty*); for exercise I resort to walking without carrying steel-tipped sticks with which to drive a hard little ball before me; for entertainment, to almost anything but games. Otherwise I claim to be 'normal.' In a single word, I do not 'conform'; and that, I take it, is the unforgivable sin in this our America of today.

We artists—for, whether my work will prove to be art or not, I am that psychological phenomenon, an artist who cares much for his work and little for himself—we artists need solitude above all. Unfortunately, we also need books and life; and in that contradictory need lies our peculiar dilemma. We need solitude because only when we are alone can we penetrate to any kind of truth—to that reality which, in so-called real life, is disguised by thousands upon thousands of inessentials. Not for nothing is the muse of female gender: like any real woman she needs to be wooed in a fury of concentration, not in the intervals of relaxation between the pursuit of a dollar and a dinner party. We need solitude, further, because only when we are alone can we abstain from the narcotics of a social life; we dare not use any stimulant but one, and that is sleep; like women during gestation we care too much for our offspring not to refuse all others, no matter how much we may crave for them. For let it be said that ours is a strenuous task. In the complex, involved, manifoldly conditioned 'appearances' of this kaleidoscopic world we have to find what is common to all of them, what is simple and typical: the component parts of all those many patterns in the kaleidoscope which, to the casual observer, constitute the essential pictures. We abhor what makes up nine hundred and ninety-nine per mill of the current imaginative reading matter: all that is exceptional, pictur-esque, and baroque—the steep gesture, the exaggerated emotion, the florid phrase, the 'queer' in character as well as in situation; these are the opiates of a nerve-racked 'public.' We artists grope for the stars; and perhaps our grasp will not reach them any sooner than the light of some of them reaches the earth; perhaps it will never reach them. We cannot help ourselves; we do not choose our themes nor our methods of treatment; they are imposed upon us. Nor are we greatly concerned about our failure or success. But we have the consuming desire of that grasp. What, then, could we have in common with those whose dream is of the next movie-ticket or a more expensive radio set?

Our lives, I said, are conditioned by our work. What about that work, since it seems so important to us?

First of all, though we are the children of our day, we are not concerned with any sort of literary school or tradition—which, paradoxically, is our way of fitting ourselves into the so-called great tradition. Nor are we concerned with depicting, realistically or otherwise, the life of modern Canada or of any section of it. We believe that a good deal of truth about Canada may be culled from our books, and of a kind not commonly traded in; but to depict such truth does not enter among our aims. We are concerned with something more fundamental which we might just as well have propounded with a setting of ancient Greece or mediaeval Europe had we happened to live in such surroundings; for only then could we have been sufficiently familiar with that setting to use it. We are concerned with showing, in the casual disguise of whatever setting we have happened to be thrown into, some of the universally valid and generally human, and, we opine, therefore tragic or comic (according as you look at them) conditions of man's life on earth. (Is it not striking how soon mere 'humour' becomes obsolescent so that a commentary is needed to expound it? And what is more barren than the expounding of humour?)

It has been said that our work, being stark, is fundamentally ugly. That may well be, though we do not believe it; ideas of beauty change according to the capacity of finding it. We are the heirs of two thousand years of Christianity and of half a millennium of science; and, though, in our aims, we go back into the past beyond both science and Christianity, we are profoundly influenced by both in our methods; meticulously we find a peculiar sort of happiness in finding knowledge: we are very conscientious and refuse to be bribed into compliance with the demands of our day: that is our Christian and scientific heritage which we may curse but which we cannot escape. On the other hand, just as Homer, Aeschylus, and Simonides live today, in spite of two thousand years of Christianity, so we aim at creating that which will live beyond Christianity and in spite of whatever sublimation may take its place. We shall most certainly fail in that; for, as I have explained elsewhere, this is not a time for the production of great art; but we are content to be the forerunners of such a time; and, to say it once more, we are not much concerned about our ultimate failure or success. Failure may be tragic; but we do not shrink from tragedy; we are not loose-lipped women.

Secondly, we consider even such achievements as that, let us say, of Dickens or Thackeray as mere preliminaries, as mere foreground achievements: quite likely their achievement will, in the long-run, outshine any achievement to which we may even approach; but the point is that it was won on a territory which we deliberately repudiate. They were the masters of mixed styles and the heirs of romanticism. The public calls us realists; we call ourselves classicists, perhaps in a merely epigonic sense, to borrow a term from German critics; time will have to tell; we are in no hurry. Much might be said about this opposition between romanticism and classicism; I have tried to say some of it elsewhere; but at the bottom of it all is this: romanticism places a right against a wrong: God against the devil; and we have long come to suspect that there is no devil; or that, at least, he is only one of God's degenerate children and god-like still. It may be well to state expressly that we do not limit the term romanticism to that comparatively insignificant (though, in a lyrical sense, extremely splendid and iridescent) fraction of the movement which, in England, found it supreme expression around the turn of the last century. Romanticism was a European movement and found more typical expression in continental Europe than in England: forms that continue to dominate much thought today. Classicism opposes a right to a right; and we, too, believe that there is no need, in order to arrive at a conflict—the life-blood of narrative art—to resort to a falsification of life. Life swarms with conflicts; in a sense it is conflict; and in every conflict both sides are right, for both sides are human.

The Victorians, I said, were masters of mixed styles. A mixed style softens matters down for a debilitated taste: it is the proper food for a pessimistic age (but, I am afraid, the diagnosis of pessimism has still to be made for that period of British history). We are just beginning to take courage again and to place ourselves beyond pessimism and optimism, where the ancients stood and a few of the moderns. Only ages of real courage, able to face life as it is, have enjoyed tragedy and its unmixed style. Tragedy is the proper food for men with masculine tastes; and so, by the way, is comedy, taking the word in its strictest sense which excludes both irony and humour. The mixture of the two is the food of a feministic civilization: the tear in the eye and a smile on the lip; and the reader divines that, in spite of its antics, the present age is trying to rid itself of the apotheosis of the 'eternally feminine.'

It has been said that our work is inconsistent in itself. That, too, may be, though hardly in the sense in which the charge has been made: we shall see by-and-by; there is no hurry. We choose *milieus*, so-called critics assert, in which problems are simplified because they arise in their lowest terms: our characters, they say, are primitive, unrefined by the conventions of a complex civilization, and inarticulate; yet, the moment it suits us, we let them express themselves with amazing lucidity. Primitive? Perhaps. But what is meant by the term? Birth is primitive; death is; and all of life between the two except in the inessentials of the methods by which its needs are satisfied. The charge of inarticulacy is, of course, simply nonsense. In a new country nobody is primitive if the word is to convey a lack of complexity in emotional experience. In that sense, the so-called sophisticate is more primitive than the transplanted peasant. The latter is merely silent under ordinary circumstances. That, in an emotional crisis, he shows his complexity with amazing lucidity is due to the fact that he has thought more, and more deeply, than the average dweller in cities. Like ourselves, the artists, he has had time to explore his own complexity. We, of course, assume the right to correct his spelling and grammar; we are artists, not phonographs. That, ordinarily, he does not speak without hesitation and seeming uncertainty, especially of himself, is due to his reticence, his disinclination to reveal himself, his pride. It is not true that what is commonly called education, except in its highest forms, makes for articulacy in a deeper sense; it merely makes for readiness of expression in inessentials.

Another point needs to be touched on here. National characteristics, and therefore the distinguishing features of national civilizations, do not primarily arise in urban centres; they merely crystallize there, provided they are strong enough, developed as they are elsewhere and transplanted to the city, to withstand the levelling and 'shallowing' (*sit venia verbo*) influence of city life. Urban civilizations (except where they were urban merely in appearance, as in pre-Periclean Athens) tend to become alike in all countries. Even distinctions of language tend to disappear: see the Europe of, let us say, 1800. But the European peasant remained what he had been: German, Dutch, Swiss, Italian, Spanish, French. When the superficially unifying influence growing out of the cultural predominance of France in Europe, before 1789, had been overthrown (strange to say, by Napoleon), the capitals of Europe became national again, forced into their new (or old) moulds by pressure from below, not from above. Above, in Germany, f.i., stood Goethe, aloof from national aspirations (again, strange to say, this is even today made an indictment against him). We do not mean to say that national differentiation is necessarily a desirable thing; too often it is not; but the cry is today, 'Let Canada be a nation,' and therefore we repeat the differences in national character are most pronounced in those who are in immediate contact with the soil they sprang from; for they rest on geographic, topographic, and climatic conditions.

Again, I do not mean to suggest that rural civilizations are more desirable or of a higher type; I merely wish to point out that in them the origin of national differentiation has to be looked for. In Canada, the fundamentally new things, a new attitude towards life and its mysteries, arise in the country, not in the city. In contradistinction to older countries, the city stands here for the conservative tendencies: the country is in a cultural revolt; the city tries to impose upon it some semblance of a cultural continuity. Between the two tendencies individuals are being ground up as between the upper and the nether millstones. This needed to be mentioned because it, too, is one of our topics.

One of our topics? Oh, the weariness of it all! For, what we are trying to do cannot become clear till at least a trace of the walls of that edifice becomes visible which we are trying to erect: so far, we have put down only a few of the foundation stones. And so we come back to this: either our day has been, or our day will come; we only know that, in our aim, we are not of this day of false fronts and shoddy. But we also know that, if our lives and works are to be of any value whatever (and we sometimes doubt it), they will be so precisely on that account.

The title of Grove's article, 'A Writer's Classification of Writers and Their Work,' published in the first volume of The University of Toronto Quarterly *is misleading; it might, in light of the Greve essay translated for this collection, more accurately be titled 'Frederick Philip Grove's Theory of Artistic Existence.' In the article Grove is concerned with classification; however, he classifies writers on the basis of their relation to both world and text. The views he expresses are not new. He reworks here ideas set forth not only in 'Gustave Flaubert's Theories of Artistic Existence' but in several of the essays collected in* It Needs to be Said, *most notably 'Realism in Literature.' Here, however, the ideas are more clearly articulated and more carefully developed than in the earlier essays. The result is that 'A Writer's Classification of Writers and Their Work' is perhaps the most succinct statement we have of Grove's vision of the writer.*

Frederick Philip Grove

A Writer's Classification of Writers and Their Work

I

Nothing is in itself either beautiful or ugly, but seeing makes it so. I believe it was Croce who first said that or something to the same effect. It is undoubtedly true that we see beauty to-day where two or three centuries ago few people saw anything but horror or ugliness. The Alps of Europe furnish a convenient example. Creative minds had to see and to interpret that beauty for us before we could see it. They saw harmonies where previous observers had seen confusion; they saw significances where previous observers had seen chaos; and mankind at large has learned from them. What they actually did was, of course, an act of interpretation. In other words, they arranged these mountain landscapes in conformity to human predispositions: and lo, terror became awe; the desire to close one's eye became unconscious selection: the result was picturesque perception.

Picturesque perception of the kind hinted at is a special case of a wider phenomenon which I venture to call creative perception; and it is the purpose of this first section of the present article to elucidate what I mean by the help of a figure of speech. It is my fundamental belief, as I have more fully explained elsewhere, that all our precious knowledge consists in metaphors which are designed to make the universe around us capable of being grasped by the constructive imagination. Truth, as again I have said elsewhere, is what we can grasp. So, in the general dearth of aesthetic insight, I may be pardoned if I attempt to break new ground by labouring a perhaps rather crude figure of speech in order to find some approach to obscure phenomena.

What, then, any person sees when looking at a simple object, as, e.g., the flower-vase on my desk in front of me, is in itself a construct arrived at by the unconscious comparison and composition of two separate images. It is only by this process of comparison and composition that we are enabled to see things with the proper distribution of their parts in space or, as I shall call it in the sequence, 'plastically'; this word I use in the very sense in which the plastic arts are distinguished from the graphic arts. You can walk around a statue and look at it from all sides; but even if you look at it from only one point of view, you remain conscious of the fact that the various parts of it are not represented in a single plane. We cannot, so, walk around a painting, no matter how skilfully the painter has tried to force upon us the illusion of plastic vision.

To apply our figure of speech we may explain what is involved in ordinary plastic vision. In judging the relative distances from the eye of parts of the same object, complex processes of induction and deduction are employed which, in the case of objects within the range of ordinary vision, remain unconscious only because, with the help of a lifelong experience, they are carried on with lightning speed. Whenever the object looked at is either farther or less far removed from the eye than the distance which I have just loosely called the range of ordinary vision (and which varies considerably according to the variation of many factors), that ability fails us: sun and moon we see as flat disks instead of as hemispheres; we need a conscious, and that means an unusual, process of deduction and interpretation in order to decide which of two ships just within our horizon at sea is the nearer and which the farther from ourselves; provided, of course, that it has not been, for long periods, our business to arrive at such decisions quickly: in other words, the greater, in any given decision, the extent of our previous experience has been, the less time will the process of deduction and interpretation take and the less shall we become conscious of it.

Now it is a familiar fact that, within the range of ordinary vision, we see a different aspect of any object according as we look at it with our right or our left eye; and it is no less well known that, the farther the object within that range is removed, the more nearly will the two images be alike, till, when the distance exceeds that range, they become identical. Ways and means have been found to increase the range at which, by using both eyes at the same time and artificially increasing the distance between the points from which they look, we see objects plastically. If it were possible—as, no doubt, it will be some day—to combine, in one human vision, images seen, let me say, of the constellation of Orion, from points separated from each other by the diameter of the earth, then that vision would, at a glance, see the various stars composing the constellation in their true distribution through space, not only in a graphic sense, or as that distribution is at right angles to the path of the light proceeding from those stars, but also plastically, or along the radii of vision. In other words, a very complex process of computation in spherical trigonometry will be reduced to an act of spontaneous and instantaneous perception.

If what I have said about the importance of the fact that our two eyes do not occupy the same point in space, is true, how much more would it not be true if two distinct observers looked at the same object and were yet able to combine, in a single mind, the process of interpretation of what was seen by the two separate sets of eyes. I lay special stress on the process of interpretation conducted by a single mind: for a mind able to do just that, by some mysterious gift, I contend, has what I call creative perception.

So long as the interpretation is carried on by two separate minds which are served by separate sets of sense organs, the best we can hope for is the combination of these interpretations by a process similar to that used by spherical trigonometry in interpreting two observations made from antipodal points of the globe.

If, instead of limiting ourselves to the observation of a single object, we admit as the object of perception complex sets of facts or human relationships, such a process of interpretation of separate observations by a third mind, and the consequent computation of their relative merits, is, by the way, nothing uncommon in daily life: it is the function of the judge or the jury in our courts of law; two people or groups look at the same set of facts or human relationships and cannot agree; they refer the case to the arbitration of a third person whom they supply or are presumed to supply with all the data of their own perception and whose task it is to interpret the two different aspects in the perspective of the law.

Now let the things looked at be as complex as they can be: let them embrace any two or more sets of data in the infinite number of combinations or permutations of human relationships; till we arrive at the vast complexity of human life which forms the subject matter of artistic creation, at least in narrative and dramatic art; and we arrive at once at a critical distinction between at least two sets of artists or writers.

For this is the strange thing about it that every observer of any such complex set of circumstances as is presented by any aspect of human life almost invariably thinks the aspect seen by himself, not only the one correct aspect, but also the only morally justifiable one; he, therefore, quite conscientiously condemns the man who sees a different aspect, not only as blind to obvious truth, but also as morally perverse: as not only unable but unwilling to see what is so clear to himself.

Similarly, there are among writers of narrative or dramatic works of art those who refuse to see the conflict (for every true work of narrative or dramatic art deals with some forensic case) which forms the object of their narrative or drama (I intentionally do not say 'subject') from more than one point of view—that point which is usually the one of their 'hero'; and, on the other hand, there are those who see this conflict simultaneously from the points of view of all concerned.

This distinction might perhaps be expressed in a somewhat naiver way thus: there are writers who look at human life from the moral point of view (their hero being the representative of morals); and there are writers who look at it from the purely artistic point of view (which would be the creative way). Tentatively I have, in a different context, called the former group romanticists; the latter, classicists (for the word 'realist' has, in Anglo-Saxon parlance, assumed a narrow and misleading connotation; though, strictly speaking, it would be the better term).

In trying to determine (quite internationally, of course, and with complete abstraction from domestic conditions; for, as far as the general public goes, Canada is a non-conductor with regard to any kind of spiritual current)—in trying, I say, to determine the trend of present-day art in narrative and dramatic literature, I have come to the conclusion that we are slowly once more approaching a period of classic art. It goes without saying that there is much in the world's literature which does not admit of a rigorous classification in one or other of these categories. Shakespeare's work, e.g., is a mixture of the two kinds: Percy Hotspur and Henry IV are differentiated classically; Edgar and Edmund romantically. But that does not affect the validity of the fundamental distinction which depends on the analysis of work at either of the two extremes: let me say of Scott and Aeschylus if I may eliminate questions of rank for the moment; Aeschylus, e.g., in the Oresteia where Clytemnestra commands throughout as much of our sympathy and understanding as Agamemnon, Cassandra, Electra, Orestes.

By this time we have reached a point where our initial figure of speech—that of the actual observation of objects by means of eyes removed from each other to a more or less considerable distance—ceases to serve as a clarifier of thought. For in moral vision the observing organ is not a mere eye, alike in all, at least in kind of vision (though not, perhaps, in the degree of accuracy with which it sees), but itself a whole moral complex and organism with likes and dislikes, passions and powers, blind spots peculiar to itself and similar perspicacities. Above all, every human being sees the human world surrounding him in the perspective of his own experience of life; just as the judge is at least supposed to see the matters at issue between contending parties in the perspective of the law.

Nor do we look, through the medium of narrative or dramatic art, at mere objects which release sensations and emotions in the beholder. Conflicts, such as form the subject matter of narrative or dramatic art, are conflicts between human beings or between human beings and sets of conditions and circumstances created by human beings. And human beings are our kin and, in life, our friends or enemies, our rivals or helpers, our admirers, perhaps, or detractors. No doubt there has been a time in the evolution of mankind when one human being was to the other little more than an object; just as to-day animals are to many men, less highly developed than others, no more than objects. But by a long and painful process, by no means ended, a good many men have come to see a common substratum of humanity in all of their brethren: and in this process art has played a far from subordinate part. After all, as Longinus puts it, 'it was art that has made gentle the ways of the world.'

Yet the fact of individuality remains. In life, it dominates our relation to the surrounding world of men; we hear only their words, which are not our words; we see only their actions, which are not our actions. But it is one of the functions of art to break through that barrier of individuality and to make us understand: to show up that common background of humanity—or, as we may metaphorically call it, 'the divine'—in even those who, seen superficially, seem farthest removed from ourselves because we did not happen to live under the circumstances under which they lived; because we were not burdened with their heredity; because, perhaps, we were not exposed to the same temptations; because ours was a different *Moira* or 'share of life,' and therefore a different destiny.

Now it is the artist's task to understand and to make us understand; and, therefore, the rank of the artist is necessarily conditioned, among other things, byt he range of individuals potentially contained in his own common humanity; or, to fall back on our initial figure of speech, by his ability to shift the point of view from which he sees, with at least one of his two eyes, to that point from which other individualities look upon the circumstances conditioning a given conflict. This has been expressed by saying that the dramatist or novelist must successively feel with, think with, act with his various 'creations': he must successively 'be' every one of the characters whom he presents to us. This, it has also been said, will be the easier to him the less he is himself individualised; the more nearly his whole being coincides with the common substratum of humanity (or divinity) which pervades us all; that is, so they say, why, in life, the artist is so rarely what is called a strong character; or one who sees the world and acts with regard to the world as though he were he by divine right, entitled to impose himself upon a reluctant environment and to force it to adapt itself to his demands upon it. That is also why the artist, the true artist—not the sham variety so common all about us—so often finds himself unable to cope with the ordinary problems of life, as, e.g., that of earning his living, in spite of the fact that, on the other hand, it is the very reason why, in a well-ordered civilization, he is an indispensable factor in the life of the commonwealth, one with which only immature civilizations think it possible for themselves to dispense.

But, of course, no artist ever is completely merged in the common substratum of humanity. If he were, or rather if any two of them were, the individuality of their work would also disappear; and, apart from accidental differences in subject matter, their work would be indistinguishable.

No true artist of the first order will ever emphasize his own individuality: it will pervade his work in spite of himself; and, strange to say, by his very failure in completely merging himself in that substratum, he adds a new interest to his work; for, after all, it is a fundamental peculiarity of that common substratum of humanity that it 'appears' never as a 'pure culture' in the biological sense, but only in the disguise of individuality. Yes, more; it is precisely through this disability of the artist that he becomes truly creative.

Let us take a concrete example of a conflict enacted between two characters who are at issue because each is wholly individual. Let us take Agamemnon and Clytemnestra. Let the artist be Aeschylus, that is, an individual who fought at Marathon and whose significant life was lived between 499 and 456 B.C., now at Athens, now in Sicily. Let us suppose, as Aeschylus' contemporaries probably supposed, that Agamemnon and Clytemnestra were historical personalities who had their actual being at the time of an actual Trojan war and between whom a tragic fate enacted itself. According as we look at the conflict brought about by that fate (that is, by the reaction of character to a given set of circumstances and events) from the point of view of Agamemnon or from that of Clytemnestra, we side for or against one or the other, and we feel that one or the other was a hero or a villain; one or the other was human or inhuman; we can never inwardly participate in, or be reconciled to, the fates of both at once. Life consists of judgments; without judging, all action would cease; but while we are under the influence of art, that judgment is suspended, and, if art is a potent factor in the life of the spectators, some tempering of ordinary judgment is carried beyond the brief spell of art's direct influence. In the first part of Aeschylus' trilogy enough is said, though only just enough (and that is the artificial part of the art in it) to make us understand, and sympathize with, both these great characters. Neither is such that our sympathies readily flow out to it (and this is one of the great secrets of the powerful effect of tragedy). But both are fused with Aeschylus himself in such a way that we look simultaneously at the issue between them from both their individual sides, seeing it, to revert once more to our initial figure of speech, 'plastically' as a cosmic event in which human lives are ground up: similar to the other cosmic events all of which are in a very deep sense symbolical of human life as such—of a life which, though one and the same in all, yet, as it were, ties itself up in the knots of individual destinies. The common substratum lies dormant in the characters who can not see beyond themselves; it lies dormant, but it is there: and Aeschylus calls it Zeus, that Aeschylean Zeus who learns by suffering, and the truth of this statement remains unaffected even if we presume that Zeus was to Aeschylus, as an individual living his significant life in the first half of the fifth century B.C., a personal god who had his dwelling on Mount Olympus in Thessaly. In other words, Aeschylus had looked at the data which legend offered, and he had perceived them creatively.

II

I will now shift my ground entirely and look at the same problem (more or less) from a different point of view, drawing some conclusions from my data.

Unfortunately, writers are also living human beings, not gods placed outside of life and endowed with the power of making men's souls transparent. One understands that I am speaking of writers of imaginative literature only: of epics, lyrics, drama, and of prose narratives such as we call 'novels.' In order to make clear why I group these various, heterogeneous types together, opposing them to writers on history, science, and other subjects which have to be approached, at least in part, by the reasoning faculties, it may be well to state my belief that all art which is truly art has an ultimately lyrical aim: that is to say, only where that lyrical aim can be clearly traced—whether it be in a work of fiction, or the arts of painting and sculpture, or architecture, or of music—do I acknowledge that the result is entitled to be classified as a work of art instead of being the product of a craft. In just what that lyrical aim consists may be a matter of controversy. I have expounded my personal view elsewhere, and, for reasons of space, do not intend to enter upon the question here.

Writers, I said, are 'unfortunately' also human beings: unfortunately for themselves, not necessarily for those connected with them in daily life, and not at all for those who read their works. Whether, for the outer universe, we accept the hypothesis of a benevolent creator or not, the only purpose of life that we can discover is that it be lived; but if life were simply lived as the vegetative and animal creation lives it, it would resolve itself into a succession of generations without history, science, or art; and the slow evolution of mankind, if such there be, has precisely proceeded through history, science, and art. Besides, there is this contradiction in any theory of life as purely mechanistic or vegetative process that the differentiations of pain and pleasure have led within life and, therefore, within nature, to a fundamental criticism of values which, in turn, has led to the position of many 'ifs'; and thus life, itself created, whether by a personal creator or by such processes as evolutionary science tries to trace, has become creative in turn, though the word creative here assumes a somewhat modified sense. Whether we approve of it or not, creative it is to-day. Creation, however, means at bottom simply a reconstitution of given elements in new combinations. Even in Genesis there was chaos before the creative process began. But the creator's position is, there, imagined to be outside the elements from the recombination of which he fashions the new creation. Where, on the other hand, man becomes a creator in an artistic sense (that is, where the writer is a great writer; and the same applies to all other arts though it is, perhaps, harder to trace the process in arts other than literature), the trouble is that he himself forms at least one of the elements out of which he creates: in fact, every single element which he uses (be it an element of sensation, emotion, or pure observation) assumes, in art, its significance only by that relation to the central ego which gathers them and recombines them, tinged by that admixture of itself. It is in this very circumstance that the ultimately lyrical nature of all art at bottom resides. Now the process of life consists fundamentally in a passive or active reaction to all that is not 'I'; and certain philosophies would reduce even the active reaction to a passive one, denying free-will. The 'I,' in life pure and simple, remains, at any rate, almost unconscious of itself, except in as much as all reaction is either pain or pleasure or a combination, in varying proportions, of the two. But the process of artistic creation, as I have pointed out, consists in a conscious or unconscious relating, of everything that touches the creator, to his ego; in a reconstitution of its elements with himself as one of these elements. That we do not know just what this ego is, need not enter into the discussion. At any given moment of creation the artist treats at least part of himself (mysterious as that 'himself' may be to him) as something objective and outside of himself, as though it were a matter of observation. In other words, he reconstitutes himself, as it were, in two planes, one of these reconstitutions watching, the other watched. With regard to all his reactions he has, in a sense, lost his innocence; and thus the spontaneity of life is lost to him: a tragedy which all great artists have, at one time or another of their lives, profoundly felt as a curse afflicting them.

In the artist, the very process of external observation is vitiated. Let an artist and a trained reporter listen to a conversation and write out what they have heard. Let them both do their best to reproduce what, in such a conversation we may, for the present purpose, call nature. And compare the results. The artist, so the average critic will say, saw and heard more than the mere reporter. In reality, it is very likely to be the other way around. But the reproduction of the artist is certain to be richer in connotations: it carries the utterances of the conversants to their final conclusions; it interprets gesture or expression of face or hands; *not,* it needs to be said, in the sense of the conversants; but in the sense of himself, or of a third being mysteriously come to life, as though he and either or any of the conversants, at each successive moment, had become one and the same person, or rather a person which might be the resultant of a subtle mixture of their two essences.

Incidentally, it might here be noted that, the farther this process of a subtle replacement of at least part of the personality observed by the personality observing goes, the more we approach, in the resultant reproduction, to a truly creative process and to an art which I would call classic, in contradistinction to an art which, correspondingly, I call romantic. That is the reason why romantic art, in narrative, knows angels and devils, whereas in classic art both sides to a conflict (and a conflict of one kind or another is the inevitable theme of narrative as well as dramatic art) are right because both are human and, therefore, more or less cognate to the artist; and why, in Milton's *Paradise Lost*, e.g., Satan engages our sympathies: he is as much of Milton's fibre as Adam or God. That is also the reason why Dickens' 'charming' young ladies fail to charm us, for Dickens, being at bottom a romanticist, failed to make them human or to mix into the stuff of which he made them some of the ingredients of his own coarser nature.

From what I have said, writers, then, may be classified according to the share of themselves which they put into their creations. In all creations of the great writer that share will be considerable; and the greater the writer, the more various will be the creations which he thus shows himself able to fuse with himself. The greatest of writers will be man, woman, and child at the same time; god, angel, and devil; and they will live simultaneously in youth, in the prime of life, and in old age; in poverty and wealth, power and impotence.

But the share of themselves which they put into their creations will vary even within their own work; occasionally it will vary through very considerable gradations; and according to these gradations the value of their work will vary. Thus, strange to say, the strong personality, the one that, in his life, aims at nothing less than a complete conquest of the outside world and of himself: the objective, highly disciplined, much embracing personality (Goethe, Shakespeare) will produce work the value of which is almost directly proportional to the degree in which his own intensely human and subjective nature penetrates it, perhaps in spite of himself. It takes very intense emotions to stir such personalities to their depths so that they surrender themselves to that fusion of which we have been speaking. But once they are stirred, their souls glimmer and shimmer in a thousand colours never seen by mortal eye before; and the result is a Hamlet, a Lear, or a Tasso or Faust. Then they succeed in revealing to us lesser men hidden potentialities of ourselves and of human life, and they enlarge our own personalities by enforcing in us a fusion of ourselves with their own *'Erlebnis'* (a Goethean word so charged with Goethean meaning that it has become untranslatable by the colourless English word experience). Whereas others, of the second order, more readily swayed themselves, but nearer the surface (Heine or Shelley), rise in power, the greater the share of the objective world becomes in their creation. Occasionally we find an artist who, like Ibsen, produced work of *his* first order (though, as a personality, he may rank considerably below such encyclopedic beings as

Goethe), no matter whether in that fusion of object and subject (to use these outgrown terms) the one or the other prevails; and the reason will be clear in a moment.

I have indicated my belief that the life of the creative artist is fundamentally different from that of the non-creative person that merely lives. In order that art may live, the artist must, at least temporarily, die to life. That, by the way, is one of the reasons why it is dangerous to live with artists: to the artist, everything and every-body they come in contact with is neither more nor less than what we may call, very imperfectly and almost indelicately, a model. But though an artist is, in a sense, always an artist, he is so, at different times, in varying degrees; and consequently he is, at different times and in varying degrees a non-artist and lives the life of ordinary folk. The more intensely he does so, and the longer the periods he does so, the greater will be the volcanic pressure, the eruptive vehemence with which he creates when the degree of saturation with life at last forces him into the process of creation: the time will come when, whether he wants to or not, he *must* create. The 'it' in him, whatever it be which forces him to create has been at work all the time, unsuspected even by himself; and suddenly, like a flood, it forces it way, perhaps bringing ruin to the landscape and the human habitations that have grown up along its hill-slopes. Thus Goethe left Weimar and Frau von Stein. The creation takes on an uncanny life of its own, like a child in gestation, with rights of its own, rights so imperative as to impose themselves on the creator. A book produced under such circum-stances is what I call a book that 'has grown': it will always outrank, in any scale of ultimate values, any work produced under circumstances of greater control. It will, perhaps, show flaws; and dead matter may be embedded in it. But it will carry those flaws and that dead matter as a flow of lava may carry whole masses of unfused rock or debris which it has swept before its onset.

Such are the greatest works that constitute the true classics of all times and climes.

There are other great works, near-classics, that were not grown but made. By far the greater part of what constitutes the world's abiding literature consists of them; and there are two ways in which such works may originate.

In the first place, the great artist has, as I have hinted, his periods of uncreativeness. Suppose such a one has ordered his whole external life with a view towards creation. When his truly creative powers have gone into a sort of hibernation, he will feel as though all meaning had gone out of his life, as though he were living in a great void; and almost unconsciously he will search for something to write about. If his art be that of narration or of the drama, he will perhaps take to a more intensive observation of the life about him and will there find conflict which he needs to exercise his plastic powers on. If he be sufficiently great as an artist, he will bring about an artificial fusion between himself and such characters as figure in that conflict, till they are imbued with a semblance of life sufficiently striking to impose themselves on reader, hearer, or spectator. There are rare cases where such a process of artificial creation is so successful as to deceive all but the finest critics. There need be no false note left in the product; but the real critic will detect a subtle difference between the work that is 'made' by such an artist and the work that has 'grown.' Some last fusion is missing; some last power, therefore, of carrying away the reader, surface and subsoil and all. Thus Ibsen created his 'Hedda Gabler,' whereas the same author's 'Ghosts' was 'grown.' It might be well to add that other artists (the greatest among them) are apt, in such periods of dormancy, to produce the utter inanity, the hopelessly mediocre and uninspired; and that for the very reason that they have never ordered their external lives with a view towards that creation which has always overtaken them like a catastrophe—as, so it often seems to them, a *by-product* of their lives which, to themselves, becomes the redemptive factor of their existence only in their old age when, to their own surprise, they become a problem to themselves, so that they speak and almost think of themselves in the third person: the case of Goethe.

In the second place, there are those who are in love with art and yet are not, fundamentally and by a psychological necessity, artists. Let me mention Lesage or Walter Pater or Gustave Flaubert. In their productions, these are inevitably stylists. They scrupulously avoid the trite (which the great artist imbues with a new life); they will never fall to the level of the mediocre; but neither will they attain the heights. They are the only ones among those that count who are at bottom capable of 'objectivity.' They are often clever (the great artist never is, just as a mountain-range is never clever, though a landscape-garden is nothing unless it is cleverly done). They may offer us an entertainment of a very high order; but they do not write the last chapter of Hardy's *Jude* nor the second fragment of *Sappho;* they do not even reach out for an *Eroica* or such lines as 'Lasciate ogni speranza voi ch' entrate.'

And there it stands: one has the choice whether he will live among the peaks of mountain ranges or in the pretty walks of terraced gardens.

Kenneth C. Dewar

Technology and the Pastoral Ideal In Frederick Philip Grove's Writing

The literary vision of Frederick Philip Grove is dominated by two images in tension with one another: an image of pastoral society, characterized by harmony and wholeness, and an image of modern technology, characterized by dissonance and alienation. The tension between them remains unresolved throughout his work. Grove tends, however, to judge their relative value and his pastoral images verge at times on the sentimental. The tension is not, then, between two equal concepts of society, but between an ideal of pastoral and the reality of the triumph of technology. An analysis of these images suggests the existence of a garden myth in Canadian culture; certainly such a myth is to be found in Grove's work, in both his Ontario and prairie writing.

The conflict appears in its least subtle form in *Two Generations,* a novel set in southern Ontario and concerned with the development of a rural family, the Pattersons. One of the two family farms belongs to Mrs. Patterson and is situated in particularly beautiful natural surroundings. Its name, significantly, is Sleepy Hollow. It is presented as a sheltered paradise, a haven from the vicissitudes both of nature and of human life. The reader's first glimpse of it is indeed idyllic: the entrance lane is lined with trees, the grass heavy with the dew of early dusk. 'Under the westering sun the whole place, sunk in the hills, had an air of breathless and uncanny quietude.' A sense of natural harmony pervades the scene. Inhabited only intermittently, the farm has become 'a veritable sanctuary of wild life,' and numbers of birds and small animals are all about. The boys arriving from the home farm are affected by a sensation which is central to Grove's writing: 'Now something of the essential isolation of all human beings came home to them.'[1]

In this bucolic setting, one of the boys goes off to fetch the mower to cut the long grass. The activities of the others in the farmhouse are described in a tone continuous with the above. Suddenly, 'as with a profanation, the hollow in the hills vibrated with the clatter of the mowing machine.' The harmony of the pastoral landscape is destroyed by an instrument of the mechanical age. This is of particular significance since nature holds a mysterious force for Grove, with which man must come to terms, a force which is knowable only if one achieves harmony with it. For two of the young Pattersons, Phil and Alice, Sleepy Hollow represents freedom and innocence, and an escape, moreover, from their father's oppression. Its essence is silence, 'a pocket of silence in the roaring traffic of this so-called modern world.' Here they contemplate the meaning of life; Phil quotes some anonymous lines of poetry:

> Far in a western brookland
>   That bred me long ago
> The Poplars stand and tremble
>   By pools I used to know.
>
> There, in the windless night-time
>   The wanderer, marvelling why,
> Halts on the bridge to hearken
>   How soft the poplars sigh. (*TG*, 161, 62)

The machine is alien to this setting and to this contemplation—it is a 'profanation.'

The conflict here dramatized is of course a conventional one in art and literature. Its role in the literature of the United States, for example, has been traced and analyzed by Leo Marx, who argues that there has been a unique American version of the conflict and that an understanding of it is key to an understanding of the American character.[2] Yet one is struck by the similarity between Grove's Sleepy Hollow and the Sleepy Hollow of Nathaniel Hawthorne, which Marx uses as an introductory motif for his work. Marx's concepts have a usefulness beyond the boundaries of his particular study: I propose to employ them here in analyzing the work of Frederick Philip Grove.

Marx described the conflict between the pastoral and the technological as one between 'two cardinal images of value':

> One usually is an image of landscape, either wild or, if cultivated, rural; the other is an image of industrial technology. Sometimes, of course, the cardinal image is not actually present but is represented by lesser or associated images. In any event, the common and distinguishing feature of the motif is the sharp conflict of meaning and value evoked by the clash of images. The contrast between them arouses a sense of dislocation, conflict and anxiety. All established ideas are called into question.[3]

While this clash is not the key tension in every work in which it appears, Marx argues that, taken as a whole, it constitutes 'a supreme metaphor of contradiction' in American culture. The image of the machine, signifying an entire civilization, contradicts the wholeness and harmony of the pastoral. The machine 'is to the ideal society what a hideous noise is to a delicate sonata.'[4] This clash of images, then, evokes two concepts of man's relation to nature.

Two important distinctions emerge from Marx's analysis. In the first place, the theme of pastoral is not the same as the theme of romantic primitivism; it implies no rejection of civilization or the idea of an ordered society. 'The traditional landscape of pastoral,' Marx points out, 'occupies a middle-ground somewhere between raw nature and urban civilization.'[5] Secondly, the concept of pastoral is further refined by a distinction between the pastoral ideal and the pastoral design, design referring 'to the larger structure of thought and feeling of which the ideal is a part.'[6] That is, the pastoral ideal refers to the sentimental 'wish-image of happiness' which we associate with the popular culture of TV westerns and beer advertisements. The pastoral design encompasses the total artistic conception of reality expressed by a writer through a complex literary structure. Sophisticated pastoral literature, in other words, does not leave the reader with the simple affirmative attitude which he experiences on encountering pleasant rural scenery. 'In one way or another, if only by virtue of the unmistakable sophistication with which they are composed, these works manage to qualify, or call into question, or bring irony to bear against the illusion of peace and harmony in a green pasture.'[7] Within the design the more 'real' world of industrial civilization acts as a counterforce to the ideal. 'Complex pastoralism, to put it another way, acknowledges the reality of history.'[8]

In Marx's terms, the idea of pastoral is broadened beyond simple nostalgia and the desire to return to some sort of lost childhood.[9] It becomes sufficiently complex to incorporate conflict, the potential source of creative power for a new resolution. In the case of Grove, as suggested above, the conflict tended to produce a regret for the passing of agrarian society. The regret was not for that society as an end in itself, but for the opportunities it afforded for man's spiritual development. A consideration of Grove's treatment of nature and of man's relationship to nature forms a necessary prelude to an analysis of his pastoral design.

Grove paints nature in a somewhat paradoxical fashion:

> Those woods were mild, soft, lovely; they were the adequate
> setting for spring; these were gloomy, elemental, terrible in
> their gloom, with the terror that attaches to all origins; but also
> beautiful—with the beauty of Nature in the raw—no less so
> the desert, or the sea in its anger, or barren mountain ranges of
> rock and snow.[10]

This passage in *The Turn of the Year,* a series of sketches based on
Grove's rural Manitoba experience, expresses his ambivalent view of
nature. On the one hand, it is harmonious, and on the other, harsh
and foreboding, a 'hideous wilderness.' This ambivalence is seen also
in his description of spring's war against a cruel winter; in the
contrast between the soft, rumbling thunder of a spring shower and
the harsh, blasphemous thunder of a summer rain storm (*TY*, 24, 32,
52, 109); and in a scene at Sleepy Hollow, when, in a furious
snowstorm, the Hollow represents peace and order amidst chaotic
nature (*TG*, 237). The apparent conflict between these two sides of
nature is resolved within man himself, for nature in its wildness
presents an opportunity for him to prove his worth, and indeed
challenges him to do so. In *Over Prairie Trails* Grove portrays
nature's wilder side in a number of ways, notably in his description of
the aftermath of a violent northern blizzard and his battle to conquer
the drifts. After a while, he begins to enjoy his ordeal.[11] Wildness as
much as the tranquillity of Sleepy Hollow provides opportunities for
spiritual development.

Mankind's response to nature, however, is by no means uniform.
Grove's experiences in the United States, described in the semi-
fictional *A Search for America,* had shown him that the American
'population' was crude. The 'country,' however, was different:

> But here, in the hills and the woods, there was something
> strangely at variance with that population. Here there was, not
> a church, not a society, not a man-made institution; here there
> was God; but God, too, sometimes seemed cruel.[12]

Nature's ambivalence was not resolved by all people; some
Americans were untouched or touched adversely by this environment; others were profoundly influenced by it. Where, then, was the
'real America,' the America of Lincoln, Lowell, and Thoreau? This
was not a geographical question. The answer seemed to lie in the
man who stood foursquare upon the soil.

It is important to note that, like his landscape, Grove's yeoman of the garden is not a one-dimensional sentimental ideal. He is not Kenneth Harvey, in *Our Daily Bread*, attempting to revive the romantic picture of the cowboy of the Old West, complete with six-shooter, bucking bronco, and the boast of being a 'regular son-of-a-gun.' The tall tales of the West Grove heard in his travels in America stood in 'flagrant contradiction' to the 'squalid reality' he saw all about.[13] Nor is his picture that of Woodrow Ormond's leisure in 'A little cottage in the country, with a garden and trees all around; or better still, a field!' (*ODB*, 178). Grove's yeoman is somewhat more complex.

In the first place, the rural man is rooted in the soil, doing 'actual work,' in his own employ, with primary produce. Farming, to John Elliot, to Ralph Patterson, to Abe Spalding is the only honourable occupation for man. Trade, commerce, speculation are impure; farming is not a question of dollars and cents. Elliot's objection to Woodrow Ormond's courtship of his daughter is that Ormond, a university professor, is 'unanchored in the soil.' To the suggestion that his son Arthur work as a clerk, he declares angrily that cash is dirty and that in commerce you don't *make* anything (*ODB*, 77, 176-77). The soil holds an intrinsic goodness. At one point in *A Search for America* the problem facing Grove is to find a spot of humus, where he can 'take root *in order that I might grow.*' (*SFA*, 115).

The man of the land, moreover, is close and therefore attuned to the cosmic force of nature. Grove saw this sensitivity in Ivan, his hobo companion in search of harvest work in the Dakotas. He saw it in the nomadic Kirghiz herdsmen of the Russian steppes, whose song seemed to merge with the landscape, expressing man's forlorn position in a barren nature, yet full of a 'stubborn, if perhaps incohate assertion of man's dignity below his gods.' And, somewhat more romantically, he saw it in the face of the harvester in *The Turn of the Year:*

> He became to me the man who stands squarely on the soil and who, from *his* soil—his, no matter whether he owns it or not; and likely he was no more than a hired helper on this particular farm—who from *his* soil reaches out with tentative mind, and with a great seriousness—far beyond that of a mere thinker or scientist—gropes his sure and unmistaken way into the great, primeval mysteries which are the same today as at the dawn of history. (*TY*, 211)[14]

The yeoman's role is to supply the essential produce for the rest of mankind. It is in the country that food is grown for the 'seething world,' the 'teeming millions.' One of the reasons Abe Spalding refuses to change from wheat to flax is that the former is food for mankind.[15] It is bitterly ironic that in the stock market crash of 1929 'those who furnished the essentials of life were, illogically, the principal sufferers' (*TG*, 219). By virtue of his role as food-producer, the farmer is master of the world. The city acts for him as a 'mere agent,' and is dependent upon him. The urban masses, indeed, think of the farmer as their servant, but he has only one master: God (*TY*, 206; *SFA*, 356, 435-36).

This picture is, of course, complicated by many other factors, as a reading of any of Grove's novels will show. In attempting to depict real life, Grove did not deal in bloodless stereotypes. Forces other than nature impinge upon his characters, and as individuals they respond in varying ways to nature itself. Grove found 'much that is horrible in modern life' and figures such as Frank Bramley, whose farm was a 'picture of desolation,' appear throughout the novels (*ODB*, 83; *SFA*, 421). Most significant, two forces inherent in rural life have deleterious effects on people like Spalding, Elliot and Patterson. The first of these arises from man's ownership of the land. In *Fruits of the Earth* Abe undergoes a loss of independence and control over himself and his family, and although part of this is attributable to the changing world around him, much of it is due to his bondage to the soil. Grove himself came to the conclusion that 'property you own, owns you' (*ISM*, 418). That this phenomenon is not unique to the farm will be seen later in the discussion of *The Master of the Mill*.

The second force at work is the self-defeating role of the pioneer. His role, indeed his duty, is to reshape the very condition in his environment which gives him economic and historic justification (*ISM*, 225). The pioneer role involves a further complicating factor in man's relationship to nature, for its aim is to tame the wilderness. The aim, it should be noted, is to tame rather than conquer. The process is an often tragic one, involving the 'age-old conflict between human desire and the stubborn resistance of nature' (*ISM*, 226-27). It is a struggle of the soul to build order out of chaos. At its successful end, however, the pioneer is unable to settle down and enjoy the fruit of his labour. Even if his life is not over, he cannot remold his purpose. 'Nothing to do. . . . Pioneering, that was the task of the Pattersons: a settled existence, with nothing but living for its aim, went against their grain. . . .' (*TG*, 19).

Technological society impinges on and conflicts with rural society on a number of levels. The image of the machine is not a narrow one, but expands to encompass a number of aspects of technological civilization, from a specific area such as higher education, to a general area such as the city, to the essential characteristic of the 'so-called modern world,' the 'externalization' of human values in the form of materialism. In other words, many scenes and images not specifically technological nevertheless are variations of the image of technology in its clash with the pastoral.

Grove maintained a profound distrust of modern civilization. He saw it as a movement away from the essentials of life to materialism, artificiality and insecurity. In the wilderness of Manitoba, 'so-called civilization, with its feverish chase after treasure, seemed infinitely far away' (*TY*, 140; cf. *OPT*, 118). There, a primitive but dignified man was neither dependent nor helpless; his only two concerns were Nature and God. In Grove's most extreme view, the very presence of any man-made work in nature had a certain incongruity about it (*OPT*, 56, 9). Modern civilization, furthermore, with its great material expenditures, was for him the 'consolidation of barbarism.' It consisted of selfish waste:

> Put the case this way. In an arctic expedition so-and-so much food is taken. If one of the members surreptitiously uses more than his share, all the others may be in serious danger. But so long as there is not an absolute surplus in the production of mankind, mankind as such must be considered as a unit embarked on the expedition of life; and mankind includes every Siberian, every Indian, every Chinese who may starve in a famine. (*ISM*, 451)

Modern society lacked the essential universalism of Grove's ideal.

Grove did not always present higher education in conflict with rural society. He himself was university educated and it is obvious that, in *Two Generations*, Philip and Alice will find their years at university of immense value. He did not, in other words, agree with Ralph Patterson that university education *per se* was nonsense. But at the very least he saw a tension between the college sophisticate and the uneducated rustic. This is reflected in Abe Spalding's feeling of awkwardness toward the manners and conversation of his sister Mary and her husband, Dr. Vanbruik, although this declined as, in his meditative old age, he came to know the doctor more intimately (*FE*, 18-19). The tension is also seen in John Elliot's visit to his daughter,

Cathleen, who had married Woodrow Ormond. In this situation, however, the education is coupled with an acceptance of urban materialist values more clearly in conflict with those of agrarian society (*ODB*, 163-87).

The city, of course, represents the greatest concentration of the artificial qualities of modern civilization; it is but a bubble on the sea of life. In its relationship to the garden, it appears in a number of different guises, some of which are of an apparently ambiguous nature, and thus again emphasize the complexity of the pastoral design. Grove himself felt that the city was foreign to him. When John Elliot visits his daughter in Winnipeg, she picks him up in her car at the railway station: 'He felt as if he were being kidnapped into things unknown and unheard-of.' In Regina, he spends a night alone in a hotel room:

> Already he felt sorry that he had left Sedgeby and the security of his house; nobody knew him here; he was just a silly old man. Down there, in the street, motor cars honked and street cars thundered by. (*ODB*, 269, 164)

Yet, for the younger generation, the city holds great attraction. Henrietta Elliot wishes to marry a man from the city; Lillian Flaws dreams of urban luxuries. Jim Spalding abandons his father to become a mechanic (*ODB*, 48, 51; *FE*, 218-22). The point, of course, is that what attracts the young is the false, debilitating goal of material gain. Moreover, their education had brought them into contact 'with *what appeared to them* to be a world wider than that of the farm' (*FE*, 219; italics mine).

Containing real ambiguity, reflecting a tension between the ideal and reality, is another set of attitudes which sees the city in its relationship to the farm both as a parasite and as a servant. Ralph Patterson, for example, always looked on the town as a parasitic force, sucking the blood of the farmer. To take his revenge upon it was one of his reasons for embarking on the retail dairy produce enterprise which was to bring him close to ruin (*TG*, 143, 146). In *The Master of the Mill*, Rudyard Clark embodies that force, and in *A Search for America*, Mr. Kirsty of Pittsburgh is an exploiter, not of the farmer, but of the poor inventor.[16] At the same time, as has already been indicated, Grove saw the rural producer as master of the world. The purpose of Toronto was to serve the country; it was a means, not an end. 'The moment it becomes an end, it falls heir to all the evils that attend overcrowding' (*TG*, 257).

The city, however, clearly had become an end, and the resultant evils clash with Grove's conception of the American ideal. At the very least, cities were only superficially American. 'In order to catch the real trend of American thought you have to get your ear to the soil to listen. Then you will hear the sanity, the good sense, and the good-will which are truly American' (*SFA*, 112). In more extreme terms, they were 'Black sores . . . on Nature's beautiful skin.' This attitude is evident in Grove's description of his train journey to Pittsburgh. Passing through an industrial town, he saw 'dingy huts and smoke-blackened houses,' when a few minutes before he had seen green hillsides and a swift-flowing creek. Then again, mountains rose, and budding trees 'spoke of spring in the world, of hope, of innocent life' (*SFA*, 219). The inhabitants of these towns, when they appear in the countryside, appear as interlopers: 'poor, depressed, and almost lachrymose victims of our cavernous modern civilization' (*TY*, 221).

These cities contrast in a partial but not insignificant way with the cities Grove claimed to encounter in Siberia. These also offered a contradiction to their environment, in the sense that they appeared as fragments broken off from western civilization and scattered over an alien, barren land (*ISM*, 147-48). The tragedy of North American cities, as Grove saw it, was that they were indigenous, yet still contradictory.

At the core of Grove's image of urban industrial society was the growth of technology. While the city strongly affected the country-side, the machine went much further: it invaded it. The machine itself appears in somewhat different aspects. In *The Master of the Mill*, it is often seen as a living thing. As Samuel Clark gazes out his window, 'another thing became clear: the mill was not a man-made thing: it was an out-growth of the soil, the rock, the earth, subject to laws of its own, independent of himself' (*MM*, 60). This quality of animate existence, however, has a sinister, mysterious aura, particularly evident in relation to the mill at Arbala. It is this type of being which enslaves man. Throughout Grove's other works, the predominant characteristic of the machine is its inanimateness. Abe Spalding prefers 'the response of living flesh and bone to the spoken word' to the 'unintelligent repetition of ununderstood activities which machines demanded,' although he recognizes mechanized farming as necessary to his goal. In response to John Elliot Jr.'s assertion that machinery is taking over, his mother declares that machinery will never produce milk and eggs (*ODB*, 108; *FE*, 41).

Grove develops the idea in the concluding pages of his auto-biography. In comparing the horse and the car as a means of transport, he argues that domesticated animals 'up to a point' recover from expended energy and, in addition, they reproduce. Machines, however, do neither. They need 'upkeep, repair, and replacement.' 'They are the bottomless pit.' This applies to all material things, for they need 'more labour in their preservation than in their production; and at the best even the preservation is only provisional' (*ISM*, 455-56).

In nature, the semi-inanimate object is an alien force. This is graphically presented in *The Turn of the Year*, when the narrator and a farmer approach the machine at sunset atop their loaded rack:

> We came from the east; and as we approached, it [the engine] and all accessories stood outlined like black monsters against the white of the western sky. The swinging belt that ran from engine to separator seemed to be alive and to embody the force of strange underground helpers in league with black human figures that hurriedly pitched off the last few loads. (*TY*, 209-10)

The words 'monsters,' 'underground' and 'in league' convey the essential evil of the machine. In sharp contrast are the picturesque setting and, more especially, the yeoman seated beside the narrator. He is the very embodiment of all that is 'fine and noble in bodily labour' and in the joy of actual work.

This clash of images recurs throughout the novels in episodes similar to the one at Sleepy Hollow. In *The Turn of the Year* a screaming sawmill pierces the quiet while in *Fruits of the Earth* the sound of the ditching machines breaks the evening silence (*TY*, 130-31; *FE*, 33-34). These intrusions act as a disturbance in the garden, and also as a reminder of the existence of another world.

The essence of the machine's relationship to man, however, is that it erects a barrier between him and real life. It is inseparable from the debasement of human values by the quest for material gain. Together, technology and materialism are, in Grove's view, forces essentially destructive of the human spirit. The motor car and the airplane had as their consequence the 'acceleration and shallowing of all life processes' (*MM*, 189-90). The 'catastrophic development' of Grove's own life, leading to materialistic degeneration, was his purchase of a Ford car. With that 'disastrous departure,' he embarked on a process of 'externalization' whereby his thoughts and actions became less concerned with his internal self, and more concerned with material comforts. As a result, he suffered a loss of contentment and failed to achieve his spiritual goals. It is the concluding lesson of his autobiography (*ISM*, 369-70, 377, 397, 447-57).

Similarly, Abe Spalding comes to the realization that machines will bring no millennium. The attention required for the so-called labour-saving devices built into his new home brought exasperation and frayed tempers. The machine itself was nothing. 'The use of machines may "pay" in a money sense; it did not pay in terms of human life. The thing done is nothing; the doing everything' (*FE*, 132). That Grove saw mechanization as a debilitating influence upon the urban worker as well is evident from the fact that he once admitted the possibility of partial spiritual fulfilment for the pre-mechanized industrial craftsman (*SFA*, 346-50).

These themes and images appear in their most developed form in the industrial setting of *The Master of the Mill*. Here one finds in close interrelationship technology, materialism and the unethical, dictatorial world of finance. The class relationships of capitalism constitute an important theme in the novel, but one which is nevertheless subordinate to the theme of technology; moreover, the significance of the latter is unclear when approached in isolation from the pastoralism of Grove's other novels. In other words, Grove's pastoral image is not brought directly to bear on his image of technology in *The Master of the Mill:* the story unfolds itself and is itself a judgment.

The mill dominates the novel. Two views of it are presented in the opening pages. In the first, it symbolizes the capitalist world order:

> . . . a ruthless capitalism which had once been an exploiter of human labour but had gradually learned, no less ruthlessly, to dispense with that labour, making itself independent, ruling the country by its sheer power of producing wealth. (*MM*, 21)

This view forms a continuous theme throughout the book. The mill has a tradition and that tradition is profit; not the profit of any particular person, but profit in the abstract (*MM*, 90). The unethical, indeed criminal, beginning of the mill's rise to industrial supremacy haunts Samuel Clark to the time of his death, and William Swann, the blackmailer, repeatedly plagues his existence. Yet it is made clear that the mill's beginning would have been condoned by the business class, for it is 'the American game to "put one over on the other fellow" ' (*MM*, 101). Each character, moreover, experiences his own particular tragedy or ruination as a result of the materialist value system of capitalism.

The second view Grove presents of the mill is that it is 'a monument of a first endeavour to liberate mankind from the curse of toil; for it produced the thing man needed most, bread, by harnessing the forces of nature' (*MM*, 21). If he does not know at the beginning, the reader knows by the end that this hope of liberation through the conquest of nature is futile. All who come into contact with the mill are enslaved by it. Samuel Clark is able to shake off its oppression only with death. Its effect on the men who labour in it is vividly portrayed in terms of its subjugating, dehumanizing power. Its slavery is mental, not physical. Within less than a year, a new man succumbs to it:

> Whatever he does, he seems to do automatically; in reality, the pace forces him to be constantly on the watch; it isn't that he becomes a machine; that would be tolerable if undesirable. What he becomes is the slave of a machine which punishes him when he is at fault; the machine seems to watch for the chance. All the time. The men are tempted to yell and to curse at it. And then he is spoiled for anything else. (*MM*, 193)

Grove's vision of the ultimate end of the mechanization process is seen in the horrible brave new world of Edmund Clark. It was Edmund's ambition to create a state within the State and thence to control the whole country. There would be 'only one master, one god: the machine' (*MM*, 287). It was an empty and barren vision. During the transition, possibly violent, to that society, he would act as a dictator, 'in the Roman, not the mid-European sense.' Significantly, however, Edmund is killed by a striker's bullet.

Thus Grove paints a picture of technology and modern civilization which, taken with his image of the garden, seems to despair of any reconciliation between the two. Rather than describing the conflict between the garden and mechanized civilization in a way which admits of a possible resolution, his books judge the latter in terms of the former. *Fruits of the Earth* ends on a curious note of optimism, not for the continuation of Abe's pioneering achievement, but for the continuation of his rural, pre-war values. He breaks up the dance in the old school house, symbolic of the decadent morality of post-war society. 'The news of his action spread throughout the district that very night; and there were not a few who breathed the traditional sigh of relief' (*FE*, 266). Grove evidently did not intend this comment to be ironic. In the last resort, despite its complexity, his pastoral conception of the twentieth century was an idealized one.

This conclusion is inescapable in the context of the ultimate vision of Grove's work: the insignificance of man in the universe and in eternity. A recurring theme of his writings is the never-ending processes of decay and regeneration, of death and life which nature reveals. The examples are numerous in *Over Prairie Trails* and *The Turn of the Year*. In *Fruits of the Earth*, Abe finally sees for the first time the landscape about him. The aging trees would 'die and decay; unless they reseeded themselves as they seemed to do; then they would spread and conquer his fields and the prairie, converting it into a forest clad plain. Yet, if that prairie were capable of bearing a forest, would not the forest have invaded it long ago?' (*FE*, 134). The mortar of his new house begins to crumble; even the mechanical age is bound to end. *The Master of the Mill* concludes with the contemplation of technology's growth and decay in the context of eternal time.

This theme appears again in its least subtle form when Ralph Patterson comes to self-realization at Sleepy Hollow, sheltered from the chaos of a winter blizzard. 'We are born, and we live, and we die,' he said, 'And that's a pulse in the history of the race.'

> 'Of the race?' Phil cried. 'The life of the race is no more than a pulse.'
> 'A pulse of what?' his father asked shrewdly.
> Phil was still standing. 'Hear the wind?' he asked as if that were an answer. (*TG*, 258)

The man whom Grove felt was aware of Phil's meaning was the yeoman of the garden.

It was in Canada that Grove saw the continued existence of the garden, or, in other words, the 'American ideal' actualized. In the years subsequent to his supposed travels in the United States, he came to believe that that country had abandoned its ideal. Canada, however, was still inhabited by a simpler people of 'peasant mentality,' whose homes contained worn Bibles, and whose values were spiritual and unmaterialistic. Part of his Canadianism derived from the continued tie with Great Britain; as a former European he felt less alien in Canada than in the United States. More important, 'my own final interests had come to define themselves as bound up with pioneering conditions which, in Canada, existed in a purer culture, as it were, than in the country to the south' (*ISM*, 217-18; *SFA*, 435, 436n.). As the years went on, the locale became even more closely defined. Eastern Canada, in its worship of money, became for him an outpost of the United States, which in turn had become an economic and social outpost of a 'misunderstood Europe.' The garden lay in the West.

The image of Canada as a harsh, rather barren land demanding unremitting toil from man has often been regarded as dominant in Canadian culture, particularly in prairie literature. This image is common to the United States as well.[17] The writings of Grove, however, evoke a somewhat contrasting image; they are permeated by a vision of the garden. To the extent that Grove, a German immigrant, is a representative figure, this essay has demonstrated the existence of a garden myth in Canadian culture. It is a myth which qualifies rather than contradicts the image of harshness. Grove's version of the myth does not conceive of an 'agrarian paradise' in the sense of material bounty; rather it conceives of it in the sense of a higher morality.

---

[1]Frederick Philip Grove, *Two Generations: A Story of Present-Day Ontario* (Author's Limited Edition, 1939), pp. 29, 30. Hereafter referred to in the text of the article as *TG*.

[2]Leo Marx, 'Two Kingdoms of Force,' *The Massachusetts Review*, Vol. 1, No. 1 (Fall, 1959), pp. 62-95; *The Machine in the Garden; Technology and the Pastoral Ideal in America* (New York: Oxford University Press, 1964).

[3]Marx, 'Two Kingdoms of Force,' p. 77.

[4]*Ibid.*, p. 80.

[5]*Ibid.*, p. 70.

[6]Marx, *The Machine in the Garden*, p. 24.

[7]*Ibid.*, p. 25.

[8]*Ibid.*, p. 363.

[9]These are the terms in which Northrop Frye defines pastoral in his 'Conclusion' to Carl F. Klinck (ed.), *Literary History of Canada: Canadian Literature in English* (Toronto: University of Toronto Press, 1965), p. 840.

[10]Frederick Philip Grove, *The Turn of the Year* (Toronto: McClelland and Stewart, 1923), p. 137. Hereafter referred to as *TY*.

[11]Frederick Philip Grove, *Over Prairie Trails* (Toronto: McClelland and Stewart, 1965), pp. 59-90, 78. Hereafter referred to as *OPT*.

[12]Frederick Philip Grove, *A Search for America* (Ottawa: Graphic, 1927), p. 153. Hereafter referred to as SFA.

[13]Frederick Philip Grove, *Our Daily Bread* (Toronto: Macmillan, 1928), pp. 38-40. Hereafter referred to as *ODB*. Cf. *SFA*, p. 235.

[14]Cf. Frederick Philip grove, *In Search of Myself* (Toronto: Macmillan, 1946), pp. 152-54, hereafter referred to as *ISM*, and *SFA*, p. 399.

[14]Cf. Frederick Philip Grove, *In Search of Myself* (Toronto: Macmillan, 1946), pp. 152-54, hereafter referred to as *ISM*, Cf. *SFA*, p. 399.

[16]Frederick Philip Grove, *The Master of the Mill* (Toronto: McClelland and Stewart, 1967), p. 27. Hereafter referred to as *MM*. Cf. *SFA*, pp. 220-21.

[17]Lewis O. Saum, 'The Success Theme in Great Plains Realism,' *American Quarterly*, XVIII (Winter, 1966), pp. 579-98; Cole Harris, 'The Myth of the Land in Canadian Nationalism,' *Nationalism in Canada*, ed. by P. Russell (Toronto: McGraw-Hill Ryerson, 1966), pp. 27-43.

Margaret R. Stobie
Grove and the Ants

'Go to the ant, thou sluggard; consider her ways, and be wise.'
That is the epigraph of the last book Frederick Philip Grove
published; and in the few revisions he made in the introduction,
shortly before he suffered his final stroke, the book contains the last
writing he ever did, and therefore it is of special interest. It's different
from anything else he ever wrote in that it's an animal fable, a
journey undertaken by ants from the Orinoco Valley in Venezuela to
New York City, in the course of which they observe and judge the race
of men. Grove said of it, 'Perhaps there is as much laughter in it as I
shall ever evoke.'

The Ant Book, as he called it for years, had a long history and a
number of titles. It was published in 1947 as *Consider Her Ways;* in
1940 he had submitted it to Lorne Pierce as 'Go To The Ant'; and the
earliest manuscript we have of it, about 1925, is called 'MAN, His
Habits, Social Organization, and Outlook.' The radical difference in
between that title and the other ones indicates the radical difference
in content, style, and perspective between the first version and the one
he wrote shortly after settling in Simcoe. That manuscript is dated
1933. The only thing he left unchanged was the introduction, the
framework of ant wisdom. Otherwise it is the published version.

The first mention we have of this work is in a letter from Grove to
Kirkconnell, January 11, 1927, when he comments on a volume
Kirkconnell had lent him of essays of Dean Inge, known as 'the
gloomy dean.' He says, 'I have read parts of it to Mrs. Grove who says,
"Sounds as if it were in your 'Ant-book' "'—I don't know whether
you've ever heard of my "Ant-book" which, for 20 years or so I used to
consider *the* book of mine, till one day A.L.P. [Phelps] knocked the
conceit out of me by saying, "A pretty good sermon, that." Since then
I haven't read any of it.' A couple of months later, and again to
Kirkconnell, Grove writes, 'Generally speaking, I'm not so sure
about instinct. My own, very limited observations—the only ones I
have made under scientific conditions were made on ants—lead me to
the conclusion that you may just as well ascribe the building of the
city hall at Winnipeg to instinct as, for instance, the careful and
scientific fungus-farming of the oecodoma ants of Central America
and South America north of the Amazons. I have not found anything
new, but I have seen observations of Bates, Belt, and others
confirmed, and they seem to point to the fact that education, among

ants, plays at least the same part as with us—though, as you know, I do not call it education but induction.'

The 1925 manuscript is over two hundred pages, typed single space, and it consists of the fantasy Introduction and a mass of dull, stodgy sermonizing. Phelps was quite right. But its genesis is a fascinating journey into Grove's mind, and an interesting example of the way in which he created his fiction.

For the introduction, the framework, Grove borrowed freely from a book published by Jonathan Cape (Nelson handled it in Canada) in the summer of 1924, by Professor Arpad Ferenczy, a professor of sociology and jurisprudence at the University of Budapest, called *The Ants of Timothy Thümmel,* and sub-titled 'A Satire on the History of Mankind.' It is, in effect, an allegory of World War I and the Russian Revolution, tracing the development of ant society through the rise of parasitic clergy, landholder, and warrior classes, with the subjugation of the workers, until a World Ant War came when the workers overthrew their rulers and established a harmonious egalitarian society under a new divine revelation that work is the only title to life. Grove followed closely the details of the machinery for this narrative. Ferenczy chose for his exemplars the Aruwimi ants, living in a forest glade in Central Africa north of the Congo. Grove chose the Atta Gigantea ants living in a valley in central South America, north of the Amazon. The fictional scribe in the one is Professor Thümmel, a renowned zoologist; in the other, F. Philgrove, an amateur myrmecologist. Thümmel deciphers his history in ant tracings on certain leaves; an ant scholar communicates with Philgrove by dotting letters on a page of his open book. When Thümmel returns home he is put in a madhouse where he commits suicide; Philgrove admits, 'I knew I was living at the very edge of the dreamland of insanity.'

Grove also takes over most of the bibliography of the literature on ant life which appears at the end of Ferenczy's book, compiled for him by two (non-fictional) Fellows of the Entomological Society of London; for the incidents in Ferenczy's were founded on scientific data in the works of such authorities as Forel, Latreille, Huber, Emery, and W.M. Wheeler—the last of whom Ferenczy quoted on the comparative age and sophistication of ant and human societies. Wheeler says, 'Our ancestors were probably just forsaking that life among the tree-tops which has left its ineffaceable impress on all the details of our anatomy. A large part of the diet of these early Hominids probably consisted of those same ants, which had already developed a co-operative communism so complete that in comparison the most radical of our bolsheviks are ultra-conservative capitalists.' Grove even takes over a detail from Ferenczy's appendix on the foresight of the ants in storing food. Ferenczy says, 'The ancients were quite convinced of it . . . Aristotle, Virgil, Horace and Pliny held a similar view of the ants.' Grove's version, 'My study of ants went back to a time when the science was just developing into something like a systematic survey; and, I being by training a classicist, it had taken its starting-point from such ancient observations as those of Pliny and Aristotle.' To Ferenczy's bibliography, Grove adds Thomas Belt's *The Naturlist in Nicaragua*, and Henry Bates's *A Naturalist on the River Amazon* (he notes that both works are available in the Everyman editions), and from them he borrows freely for authoritative detail on the geographic setting he chose. But nowhere does he mention his considerable indebtedness to the professor of sociology and jurisprudence of the University of Budapest.

However, the title of the 1925 manuscript, which obviously could not have been written before the publication of Ferenczy's book, is "MAN, His Habits, Social Organization, and Outlook," and that is a close parody of Wheeler's remarkable study published in 1910, *Ants, Their Structure, Development and Behaviour*. In his introduction, Wheeler notes, 'Some anthropologists like Topinard, distinguish in the development of human societies six different types or stages, designated as the hunting, pastoral, agricultural, commercial, industrial, and intellectual. The ants show stages corresponding to the first three of these—the hunting, pastoral and agricultural stages—the three great phases in the history of human development.' But ant society, like human society, can degenerate, and in one of his later sections, Wheeler enumerates the seven permanent social parasites (among them one species that corresponds to the warrior class), and he goes on to say, 'The zoologist, as such, is not concerned with the ethical and sociological aspects of parasitism, but the series of ants we have been considering in this and the four preceding chapters cannot fail to arrest the attention of those to whom a knowledge of the paragon of social animals is, after all, one of the chief aims of existence. He who without prejudice studies the history of mankind will note that many organizations that thrive on the capital accumulated by other members of the community, without an adequate return in productive labor, bear a significant resemblance to many of the social parasites among ants. This resemblance has been studied by sociologists, who have also been able to point to detailed coincidences and analogies between human and animal parasitism in general' (502-503). It's easy to see the basis for the allegorical satire of Ferenczy the sociologist, and for Grove's dark denunciations.

On the other hand, as Thomas Belt, another of Grove's authorities, says in *A Naturalist in Nicaragua*, the ants are a measure of civilized society: 'When we see these intelligent insects dwelling together in orderly communities of many thousands of individuals, their social instincts developed to a high degree of perfection, making their marches with the regularity of disciplined troops, showing ingenuity in the crossing of difficult places, assisting each other in danger, defending their nests at the risk of their own lives, communicating information rapidly to a great distance, making a regular division of work, and all imbued with laboring not for itself alone, but also for its fellows—we may imagine that Sir Thomas More's Utopia might have been applied with greater justice to such a community than to any human society' (25-26).

The ant world, then, affords not only a vehicle for Ferenczy's political satire, but in its life pattern it presents a social structure, a biological structure, which gives an alternative to the human one; and this alternative is a matriarchy. The anthropologists, the biologists, the sociologists, and Grove suggest, hint at, possible mutations in man's societal development—an inescapable theme with Grove.

The body of the 1925 Ant Book is the report of the delegation this ideal world had sent on a long and dangerous journey to determine whether human society had any saving vestiges of reason. The report has been considered and sentence passed: man must be exterminated to save creation, for man is too destructive. In this fictional framework, the venerable scholar Wawa-quee, who had communicated the report to the human scribe, dies; and Philgrove has the responsibility of warning his race of their doom unless they change their ways.

Following the fictional introduction, however, the ant world disappears almost entirely, except for a few references and scattered footnotes, and what is left is some flat-footed preaching which is very heavy going. Yet this mass of material is important, I think, because it is a repository for Grove's ideas and convictions, which by this time were fixed. They change very little in the twenty years of his writing life that follow, as they imbue what he had already done. By 1925 he had completed *A Search for America;* he had published *Over Prairie Trails* and *The Turn of the Year;* and *Settlers of the Marsh* came out in the fall of that year. The 1925 Ant Book gives a valuable and central view of Grove's intellectual equipment.

For the most part, it's a mélange of Rousseau and Thoreau with a fair admixture of Goethe's scientific thought. Grove had already done homage to Rousseau in a paper 'Rousseau as Educator,' and to Thoreau and indeed Goethe in *Over Prairie Trails* and *The Turn of the Year*. Now he organizes his arguments and elaborates them. The work is in four divisions: Part I, Man as Part of Creation; Part II, Man's Organization, Economic; Part III, Man's Organization, Social and Political; and Part IV, Man's Higher Life, Spiritual and Intellectual.

In a general way, the first book, Man in Nature, is in sympathy with the views of Goethe (who read and admired the botanical writings of his contemporary J.J. Rousseau) in such works as his *Comparative Anatomy* and *The Morphology of Plants*. Here Goethe emphasizes the logic of nature, the great diversity within a system of unity, the rigid laws that govern particular form ('no animal can burst the bonds of its type'), the mutual interdependence of all organic life, and the function of reason given us to discover a mental and spiritual unity. Nature is god—the pantheism characteristic of the nineteenth century. But Grove insists, following Rousseau's declaration at the opening of *Émile*, that Man has fallen away from that ideal, has enslaved nature and destroyed universal unity.

In Part II the economic views expound Thoreau's slogan, 'Simplify, simplify' and follow his dictum that the needs of man are few beyond food and shelter, that artificial needs and desires are wasteful of life. And here Grove gets carried away in an evangelical outburst against women's dress, and he plods mercilessly through the chemise, the corset, the corset-cover, the blouse, and the folloy of importing such. (Sybil, in *The Master of the Mill* is put through a similar strip-tease at the hands of a raging mob.) Luxury begets trade, and as Thoreau thunders, 'Trade curses everything it handles,' and creates the injustices and artificiality, in terms of real wealth, of supply and demand. Grove proposes a measure of wealth which would have a real base, and here in large part is the argument later in *The Master of the Mill:* 'In a civilization like man's, where property is private and dependent upon trade, another property of wealth becomes even more important than these two; and this property is exchange value. . . . Let us probe for some fundamental and unalterable measure of wealth. Nobody can doubt for a moment that such a measure consists for man, as for all animals, in food. In America, wheat comes nearest to such an ideal standard. . . . The real values of this wheat would be fixed and determinate as the sustenance for so-and-so many heads of population and for a given length of time. . . . [wheat] would form a practically unchangeable standard of all values . . . [the value of other commodities] relative to wheat would then be determined by the amount of wheat consumed during the time required for their production.' Other implications in this scheme, of course, are that Commerce and Industry, the two stages of development beyond that of Agriculture, are virtuous insofar as they grow out of agriculture and serve man's basic needs. Thus the work of the master of the mill is 'The world's work,' as Grove called it, and entirely virtuous in its fundamental nature. But there is still a dubious element: 'all private ownership is unjust. That is the real cause of the evils prevalent in the so-called civilization of man.' It's not hard to see why Grove ran for the CCF.

Moving from economics to Part III, man's social and political organization, Grove begins with what amounts to a paraphrase of the opening of Rousseau's essay, 'The Origins of Inequality,' in which Rousseau distinguishes two species of inequality among men and explains that there is 'one which I call natural or physical inequality because it is established by nature, and consists in the difference of age, health, bodily strength, and the qualities of the mind, or of the soul; the other which may be termed moral or political inequality, because it depends on a kind of convention . . . and consists in the different privileges, which some men enjoy, to the prejudice of others, such as that of being richer, more honored, more powerful, and even that of exacting obedience from them.' On this subject Grove—or the scholar ant—becomes quite emotional: 'And this leads me on to the darkest of all those features which make human life the inexorable, bitter, and contemptible thing it is: which makes it that image of crime and folly which I have tried and am still trying to depict. Inequality there will always be among all animate things: but that inequality is one predetermined by Nature or God. In the last resort, he who wins the great prizes of life, namely real achievement and real greatness, will do so by no virtue of his own, for even the industrious own their industry to things beyond their control . . . one will with or without effort, turn the thoughts into immortal treasures of deed or word; the other will strive and struggle and yet, by some freak of heredity, always fall short of the highest achievement, the one will reap where the other merely sowed. Such in Nature's relentless law.' But man has added a system of artificial inequality to the natural one, 'economic inequality becomes social inequality,' and so the basis of subservience in one degree or another, what Thoreau calls 'unofficial slavery.'

In this section Grove depends heavily also upon Rousseau's other well-known essay, 'The Social Contract,' with its famous opening line, 'Man was born free, and everywhere he is in chains.' Following Rousseau, Grove says that civilization was a 'transition from pure and undisguised individualism to a state of organized interdependence by his 'peculiar way of holding property . . . which is held by private individuals' and so inequities arise even by a failure in crops, which can make a man slave either to the land or to another; and he repeats the idea, 'The violation of the conditions of a fundamental social contract . . . though such a contract was probably never entered upon in so many words, yet brings about a very real inequity. . . . The misfortunes of one is the opportunity of another.'

And here perhaps it's worth remembering that Grove was then working on a novel published several years later as *The Yoke of Life,* but which in the first manuscript he titled 'Equal Opportunities.' It's of the farm lad, Len Sterner, shackled by the needs of his family and their land, thwarted in his desire for education and a chance to develop his talents, a novel in which the first part is permeated by Rousseau. Even the final title comes from 'Origins of Inequality'— 'All gladly offered their necks to the yoke, thinking they were securing their liberty.'

However, out of the inequities there does come another phenomenon—one that Lincoln Steffens had explored—the 'good bad man,' who also appears later in *The Master of the Mill:* 'There is another consideration worth mentioning. The single, enormously rich man is rather apt to be conscience stricken at his own enormous inequity, and thus in a futile attempt at expiation, he may devote at least part of his wealth to worthy purposes; to the large-scale endowment of charity or education.'

The last section, Man's Higher Life, leads back to the anthropologists' outline of the stages of civilization: hunting, pastoral, agricultural, commercial, industrial, intellectual; and links up with Goethe's rejection of theological theories of the origin and metamorphosis of animal life and with his view of Mother Nature as 'a single great organism.' Grove argues that leisure is needed to release the powers of reason to try 'to understand the underlying laws and to find out how to conform to them,' and with Thoreau he says that such leisure can be achieved only by 'reducing necessities to a minimum.' And all of this leads to a consideration of education (with monotonous repetition of the education/induction slogan) in which he repeats most of what he had said in the paper 'Rousseau as Educator' and adds theories of the German educationist, Froebel.

Grove summarizes the various views: 'in a reasonable as well as natural view, education consists, not in the repression of powers, nor in their creation, but in the awakening of directing instincts which in the individual lie dormant. . . . This education ends only at the point of death, of course, but it consists essentially in the 'drawing out' of latent powers.' Unfortunately, current methods discouraged the desire for knowledge in children: 'They are "inducted"; that is, broken to the yoke of human insanity.' In this section can be found the talks that Grove gave in Simcoe ten years later on the need for practical education, the destructive influence of the school room, and so forth. It's something of a grab bag. But his lasting convictions are here, and the sources from which he drew them.

After the triumphal tours, after the move east, after the peculiar experience in Ottawa, after the destruction of hopes of either a sinecure from the government or a highly paid post in the publishing world, after he settled in Simcoe in fact, Grove reshaped, redirected the whole body of the Ant Book while retaining the framework of the ants of the Orinoco Valley. In place of the pulpit-thumping jeremiads in which Grove cried 'Repent ye!' to everybody else, there is an amusing, entertaining work of wry humour and mature perspective, even though it has a sombre ending. The manuscript is dated October, 1933.

This is the version, retitled 'Go To The Ant,' that Grove sent to Lorne Pierce saying, 'This is the Ant-Book so often mentioned on which I have been at work since the fall or early winter of 1919. It has had even more rewriting than "A Search for America" or the "Life"; in fact, I believe it is the most laboriously-produced book of mine, the plan of which reaches back to 1892 or 1893. . . . Perhaps there is as much laughter in it as I shall ever evoke. . . . It has one merit—that of utter originality. And I think it contains a few things which are important.'

The purpose of the ants' journey, and with it the tone of the book, has changed. It is no longer to examine, judge, nor condemn man; rather it is to undertake a scientific expedition 'to complete a survey of antdom . . . a cataloguing and classification of all forms of ant life on earth,' and to trace 'the definite scale of development up to our own race . . . the very apex of creation,' the Atta Gigantea ants. It's obvious from this remark that ants are not ideal creatures, not super-human, for they share the human weakness of vanity. They also share human skepticism of new ideas or of different people. Even the great scholar Wawa-quee says, 'I cannot imagine a state of affairs in which, the animal in question having reached the stage where a social life (as distinct from a herd life) become impossible, as man has, the male is the dominant sex; and it is with man. This is against all reason. Every male is capable of fertilizing many females unless it dies in copula (male man does not); yet, the seminal fluid discharged in a single copulation suffices (at least with us) to fertilize thousands of ovules;—even where the male is not restricted to a single copulation (as it is with us), it is the rule that, after having fulfilled its proper function, it serves for such menial offices only as defence or the labour of procuring food, etc. I cannot think of any other animal which has developed to the social stage—distinctly an achievement of the female—and which nevertheless supports its males in a dominant position. I therefore conclude that, in the past, man, too, has lived under matriarchy as we do today. . . . Man is a degenerate type.' Grove's views and those of the venerable ant coincide.

But the ant world harbors not only vanity and incredulity; it is also capable of treachery. This comes from Assa-ree, the ambitious military commander, and it is her nature and actions that give a quite remarkable degree of suspense to the narrative.

There are vestiges of the earlier version, but they are properly subordinated to the new purpose. For instance, a long dissertation on man's perverse waste of the bounty of nature in the burning of forests is here limited to a sentence, 'The native vegetation on which the rest of creation depends for shelter and food they destroy by fire or otherwise' (23). The exposition of Goethe's views on the unknown and the unknowable is given dramatic force when the views are expounded by Anna-zee, botanist and philosopher, in the course of the great exploration. Azte-ca, the recorder, dilates on the insanity of English spelling, but fortunately only for about a page. More entertainingly, Wheeler, the renowned myrmecologist, enters the narrative as a character, The Wheeler (because he rides a bicycle), a monster, a source of terror as he goes about scooping up ants. The real and the fictional merge.

Grove's narrative, like Ferenczy's, is firmly based on the findings of reputable scientists, and some of the seemingly impossible incidents come from scientific accounts. For instance, Bissa-tee, the zoologist, gathered twelve Eciton army ants that had been decapitated in her presence by a human physician, and brought them along to observe 'the protoplasmic vitality of the Eciton body as such.' These ants kept on marching, and 'never discovered that they were not with an army of their own kind. . . . It was sometimes ludicrous to see how they begged for food, palpating us with imaginary antennae and lifting the stumps of their necks as though

they were opening shadowy mouths. . . . They lived for 39 days and
kept up sufficient energy to continue marching to within the last but
one day of their lives.' That tale comes, according to Grove's
footnote, from an article in *Scientific American,* 1893, on 'Tenacity of
Life in Ants,' by Miss A.M. Fielde. With it, Grove gives a beautiful
satiric touch about the military mind—or lack of it. By such means he
presents his fantasy as completely credible and at the same time
makes us newly aware of the remarkable phenomena in nature. It is
an excellent fictional technique.

Sometimes satire and allegory mingle. On one occasion the
explorers became aware of a peculiar odor. 'It was the scent of death
and decay, uncanny, alarming.' As they went to investigate, they saw
'an enormous heap of dead ants. . . . There were hundreds of
thousands of them, piled to the height of a hundred ant-lengths; and
all were stark-dead. It was a scene to shake the stoutest heart. Far in
the east the grey of dawn stood in a sky of featureless cloud; a sloping
plain stretched away to meet it, without a tree, without a shrub,
without even a tall weed, featureless like the sky which it seemed to
reflect. It looked like chaos before the creation.' Iridescent germs of
pestilence were floating in the air, and yet a long line of ants were
hurrying to join the pile of dead. Grove holds the suspense well, and
at length reveals that the scent which has created the havoc is 'the
perfume of royal favour'; it is called Money. An ant once perceiving
it, 'She will follow no matter where it leads; for it seems to promise
power and everlasting satisfaction of all desires. . . . She has, from that
moment on, no other desire than to inhale this money. Nothing will
hold her back; no consideration of honour, no love of kind; no sense
of formicarian dignity. Have it she must should it lead her to death.'

Then, among the honey-ants were the repletes, 'strange spherical
bodies,' filled with honey from which the others fed, and attached to
the roof of some of the inner galleries, 'suspended above the common
herd, unable to take part in their pleasure and diversions except as
lookers-on; debarred from all friendly and intimate intercourse.'
These were the authors, who 'first of all were required to fast for a full
year, or for a quarter of their lives, many of them dying during this
period of their training. Next they were, for a period of from two to
three moons, exposed to all sorts of practical jokes, expressions of
contempt, and an utter isolation, only critics or minims having
access to them. . . . and they had to be at the beck and call of even the
humblest of their fellow ants who, no matter how excellent the honey
they furnished might be, thought themselves entitled to nag at the
food they received; and that in the exactly inverse ratio of their
qualifications as judges.'

The narrative which the scholar ant recounts is, like the expedition itself, a command performance from the queen, 'it pleased Her Majesty to ask me to compose a popular account of the whole undertaking, to serve as an introduction to the detailed study of special subjects.' The great expedition began in 1925, led by Wawa-quee at the head of the cream of Atta Gigantea scholars, a Supreme Command of 162 specialists in five divisions—zoologists, botanists, geographers, communications experts, and recorders—and protected by an army of 10,000 under the separate command of Assa-ree. The journey took eight years, and of all the host only Wawa-quee survived.

They went up the isthmus by night marches for it was the territory of their deadly enemies, the Ecitons; they crossed the Panama Canal with great ingenuity; in the mountains they found the pastoral, aphid-keeping ants, and in the fifth summer (1929) they came to the Garden of the Gods and the honey ants with their repletes. Taking winter quarter in a human barn, they lost some of their number to The Wheeler, and more to barnyard animals—a hen demolished the geographer-in-chief. On the Slope they met the agriculturalists, 'the great harvesting ants, most interesting and civilized in their habits,' with storage chambers filled with 'carefully husked and cleaned grains'; and on the Plain they found the slave ants. But 'it proved much harder to descend the mountains than it had been to ascend them,' and they fought a continuous battle on the march east. Great disasters befell them. The Wheeler scooped up twelve soldiers and eight scholars; the terrible red ants, advancing 'in twenty-five ranks twelve abreast' cut a swath of death through them and 'our total number was now reduced to less than 1,800'; an automobile roared along the road and 'sixty-six great scholars, everyone a leader in her field . . . were reduced to a greasy smear on a highway!' Crossing the Mississippi many more were killed when lightning struck a metal cable they were clinging to. Assa-ree mutinied and she and the rest of the army were destroyed. Only three scholars were left—the botanist Bissa-tee, the recorder Azte-ca, and Wawa-quee. They reached the seaboard in the box car of 'a space machine,' and found refuge in the New York City Library, where they lived on molds and devised a way to read the human records. After a year or so, fumigators came one morning, and Azte-ca, who was a flighty soul and had become addicted to detective stories, perished because she couldn't tear herself away from the whodunit she was reading. The other two escaped through a broken window. On the arduous way back Bissa-tee died that Wawa-quee might live.

There is yet another facet to this prismatic work, and that is its analogy with Grove's personal life in the years 1925 to 1933. The way up to the mountains was hard, the Garden of the Gods (if Ottawa can be called such) was reached, but the stay was brief and the descent was much harder. What the ant calls 'the disastrous march east,' is echoed in *In Search of Myself:* 'what happened to us . . . was done by the east.' The analogy is kept light, but it glances in and out all along the way. Occasionally Grove brings it forcibly to our notice. When the pathetic threesome remnant of the great host reaches New York City, they are in constant danger of being stepped on by the great throngs of humans, but they escape because these callous creatures simply don't notice them. However, 'suddenly I *was* observed. A human hurrying along, with his head bent low, saw me and stopped. He stopped and, deliberately lifting his near hind-foot, he brought it down on top of me in order to crush me out of existence. . . . I was furiously digging myself into the snow before the enormous flat sole of that foot descended. No longer as nimble as I had been in my youth, I was not quite fast enough and so I felt my carapace crack and nearly swooned. I don't know how I know, but that man's name was Ayr; and I want to hand at least his appelation over to the everlasting condemnation of antkind.' The reference is to Robert Ayre's article about Grove in the *Canadian Forum* April, 1932, in the series 'Canadian Writers of Today.' It was not particularly laudatory.

And there is the extraordinary scene between Bissa-tee and Wawa-quee, the two wretched survivors on the way back, in which there are repeated references to 'six years ago,' which would have been the time of the death of the Groves' young daughter. The narrator says, 'Every now and then I caught Bissa-tee, now recovered to a point to which I, being so much older, could not recover any longer, looking wistfully across the brook and scanning the horizon; and I know that she was blaming me in her heart.' A quarrel comes: 'For more than an hour we indulged in mutual recriminations. Both of us were partly in the right; and that fact blinded us to that other fact that we were both wholly in the wrong. I retired to our temporary quarters, angry and despondent, but at the same time longing for comfort and companionship, longing for Bissa-tee to come and make it up. She did at last; slowly and shamefacedly she came in. . . . Both of us felt stirred to our depths; and we begged forgiveness from each other, blaming fate, blaming the state we were in; feeling sorry for each other, feeling sorry for ourselves.' I don't know of any other passage in Grove that is as intimate, compassionate, and self-critical as that.

The Ant Book, then, provided Grove first with a storehouse for his ideas, and later with a vehicle for science fiction, satire, and a record of his own recent life. It seems also to have given impetus to another work. In letters to Dent in March 1934, Grove says, 'It took me eight months to hammer the "Ant-Book" into shape;' two days later he is proposing a novel about 'The Rise and Fall of a Small Western Town: the rise as a consequence of growing industry (flour milling)—the fall as a consequence of ever-increasing mechanisation (automatic machinery)' and by March 28, 'that confounded novel of mine, the one about the Rise and Fall of Langholm, Manitoba, has actually gripped me.' The ant world and the conceptions of the ant world glint in and out of *The Master of the Mill*.

There is the very structure of the mill 'which towered up, seventeen stories high, like a huge pyramid . . . [with] the wide ground floor with its eight cavelike openings through which led the tracks of the trains that carried the wheat in and the flour out, day and night, never ceasing, year after year.' Here is the mound of 'the great harvesting ants' with the chambers filled with grain, which 'like those of most ants, must have taken its inception from a single and unattended queen who, having excavated a tiny chamber and piled the matter removed in a fan-shaped mound north of the entrance, at once proceeded to rear her first brood of minims.' So the mill with its layout in units, at present with 170 units, 'yet the lower part of the present north wall is still the original one.'

Of course there are the slave-owners. In the insect world, the proportion was 'at least three Subsericeas for every Rubicunda,' but with the mill owners the proportion is much greater; even in the mansion it is something like ten to one. Then again, the small Clark men in successive generations have served the mill and a matriarchal society—the three Clark queens, 'tall and full figured,' who were all named Maude. And in this book, as in the latter part of *Consider Her Ways*, Rousseau's question of who is slave and who is master permeates all relationships, and has its ironic presence in the title, *The Master of the Mill*.

Overall is the conception of wheat as the foundation of trade and commerce, that Grove expounded so enthusiastically in the 1925 version of the ant book, here becoming also the power of government: 'the issue is whether ignorance or knowledge is to govern this country, and, wheat being its principal product, control of the mill, in the long run, means control of the country.' And of course the enterprise connected with wheat forms a transition from the agricultural phase of human development to the phase of commerce and industry in a worthy way, because it is founded on agriculture which, according to Wheeler, is the highest stage. There is also present, in the highly cultivated Jew who admires Baudelaire, the final, intellectual stage of development.

In this world as in the ant world (after Rousseau) justice is relative. Wawa-quee can put down a mutiny ruthlessly; with the mill owners, fraud can be a virtuous act: 'It was against man's law; granted. He obeyed a higher law. No great man has ever hesitated about breaking man's law when a greater purpose was to be served by its breach. . . . Consumed by flames it could be fertilized. The end justified the means; it has always done so; it will always do so.' Thoreau with his I/not I query is here too, as Sam Clark ponders, 'Who are we? What is the reality in us? That which we feel ourselves to be? Or that which others conceive us to be?'

At the end, the women are left alone, the matriarchs. Man being now degenerate will go back to the beginning, and then rehearse the anthropological stages of development. There is just room enough left for a little Goethe on the unknown and the unknowable: there will come 'some entirely unforeseen thing. Some development of which we cannot even dream yet. It is useless to try to divine it.'

There are, of course, other themes in *The Master of the Mill* but few, I think, that do not occur in 'MAN, His Habits, Social Organisation and Outlook.' The Ant Book, in one version or another, encompasses most of Grove's convictions, and those convictions are remarkably consistent, even monotonous, throughout his books. It was on August 17, 1939 that Grove wrote to Richard Crouch, 'The Master is finished, thank the Lord.'

After Ellen Elliott had accepted *Consider Her Ways* for publication in December 1945, Grove wrote to her, 'I want to cancel the appendix of the ant-book and replace the first 23 pages with a few changes, for which I need another few days.' By April 21 he had received galleys for the autobiography which she had also accepted for Macmillans, and a sample page of Ants. The changes he had made in the introduction were his final writing. The second stroke came at the beginning of May.

The ending of the introduction is changed. Whereas the aged scholar, Wawa-quee, having completed her task of passing on her knowledge, then died, and the human scribe said 'Peace be to her dust' and dropped a tear, now the pathetic disappears and so does the ant, 'I never again saw my friend,' he says. And that shift is a shift in tone consonant with the tone of the new body of the work. The other changes have to do with the human scribe, and grow out of the means of communication between ant and man.

In the first version there is an elaborate scheme, following Ferenczy, a sort of parlor game, taking up seven or eight pages altogether, in which the trivial machinery is as painstaking as it is tiresome, and its effect is to underline the impossibility, the unreality of such a happening. In his final revision, Grove cuts all the ingenious devices. In their stead is a conception that was a profound reality to him from the time of our first knowledge of him in Canada. It is that of the unity of nature. The astonishing thing is how simply this is done, and once done, how logical it seems to be. There is no need for devices. All nature is one. There is a communion too deep for words.

The effect of this change is to create once more a figure of multiple oneness, a conception that underlies the persistent autobiographical elements in so many of his works, from *A Search for America*, written in Rapid City, to *Two Generations*, coming out of Simcoe. This time it is a fusion of authors. There is the I-narrator who is the ant-scholar, and there is the I-narrator who is the amateur myrmecologist who traveled to Venezuela, the obedient human scribe to whom the adventure happened. This narrator signs the introduction F.P.G., but F.P.G. is both fictional and real, an embodiment of the life of the man who called himself Grove. He is man-traveler and ant-traveler, fictional narrator and Frederick Philip Grove, the name that appears on the title page—and someone beyond that.

The change begins with a kind of mental metamorphosis as the ants mesmerize the man intently watching them, until 'Moments of clear but vacant consciousness were obliterated by lapses of an absolute mental void.' He falls and strikes his head. 'On awaking I had had a very peculiar sensation. I had not seemed to be I.' Up to this point, Grove had cut about two pages of devices, and had succeeded in focusing attention on the I/not-I theme. By cutting another five pages of contrivances and substituting a new ending of less than four pages, Grove details the movement from general metamorphosis to a complete fusion of man and ant, 'By some mesmeric action I, my individuality, had been sucked up or down into an alien mass-consciousness which communed with me through channels other than those of the senses. The moment I surrendered myself, my consciousness was that, not of my former self, but that of ants, and of no individual ant, so far, but of all antdom.' The unity of nature has triumphed, and F.P.G. goes on to the 'mesmeric transposition of personality' with the ant-scholar of 'extreme old age.' 'I walked and acted like a human being; but my mind was that of the ant: I had lived her life; and her memory was mine.' The identification prepares for, establishes the element of personal analogy within the narrative.

In the tone of the revised introduction, as in the tone of the revised body of the work, Grove seems to be even amused at the I/not I frenzy that had preoccupied him. If 'life in all its forms is one,' if one form of it flows into another and can take the mind of another, if society is in transition and individuals are mutants, what price the individual, or the pose he assumes, or his name? 'I surrendered myself.' Has Thoreau given way to Goethe—'Surrender is the ultimate joy'?

But this is Frederick Philip Grove—and we have to remember that at the time he was making these changes, he was also reading proofs for perhaps the most unsurrendering and unrevealing of all autobiographies, *In Search of Myself*.

In 1938 Morley Callaghan published an article in the University of Toronto Quarterly *titled 'The Plight of Canadian Fiction.' The problem, as Callaghan saw it, was that 'a young Canadian writer who had an authentic talent for creative prose, and wanted to develop it honestly, had little or no chance in this country.' Canada, he noted, lacks the 'quality' magazines in which young American writers can make a start. What is more, a Canadian publisher 'can remain in business as a distributor of fiction and never publish a work of fiction by a Canadian writer'; indeed, he concedes, it would be economically unwise for them to publish Canadian books for the Canadian market alone. Consequently, he concludes, fiction writers in Canada 'need not expect to be nursed along in their own country.' Callaghan's article struck a responsive chord in Grove. 'The Plight of Canadian Fiction' appeared in the January issue of the* University of Toronto Quarterly; *within weeks of reading it, Grove had completed 'The Plight of Canadian Fiction? A Reply,' which appeared in the July issue of the* Quarterly. *While Grove agrees with many of his contemporary's arguments, he disagrees profoundly with Callaghan's view both of the writer and of his reading public.*

Frederick Philip Grove

The Plight of Canadian Fiction? A Reply

I confess myself as among the admirers of Mr. Callaghan's work, his novels as well as his short stories. And I also agree that there is a deal of truth in his statement of 'The Plight of Canadian Fiction'; but I cannot chime in with the conclusions he seems to draw. More, the statement seems to me, in spite of Mr. Callaghan's obvious desire to be fair to publishers and editors of magazines, to leave the smudge of a blame where it does not belong: it is much too lenient in its appraisal of the Canadian public; it ignores the critic; and, finally, it views the Canadian writer in far too rosy a light.

The failure of any considerable body of Canadian fiction to impose itself on any considerable Canadian public is indeed monumental; it assumes the proportions of a natural phenomenon. We have a book-shelf reaching from Halifax to Victoria; and on it stands one single book, written by a Frenchman transient in Canada. That, in sober fact, is the situation; and to me it is appalling; for a book is a book only when it is read; otherwise it is a bundle of gathered sheets of soiled paper.

There are four agencies that may be responsible; any one, any two, any three, or all four of which may be responsible. In what follows it is my contention that the responsibility must be shared by three.

The four agencies are: the writer, the publishers, the critic, the public. I shall discuss them briefly in turn, leaving the case of the writer to the last.

I

In order to get at the publisher as one of the possible agencies at fault, let us, for the moment, assume that the writer has done his work carefully, faithfully, and not without that talent which is indispensable as a prerequisite for his work.

Being, by hypothesis, a Canadian, he wishes to submit it to a Canadian publisher.

Right here he is due for a surprise. He will find that the per capita number of publishers in Canada is amazingly small. Being a man of sense, he would not, of course, expect to find in Canada the multiplicity and variety of publishing enterprises to be found in Great Britain or in the United States. What he might reasonably expect is to find them as numerous as they are, let us say, in Sweden and Norway combined. If he has listened to the average Toronto business man who blindly vouches for it that there can be no country to equal Canada in cultural opportunities—Canada being, thank the Lord, still largely 'a white man's country'—he might even think that it should excel, in the number of publishing houses, the queer and outlandish nations to be found in the Scandinavian peninsula. But such is not the case. The Canadian publishers who are publishers, properly speaking, can be accounted for on the fingers of one hand.

Is it the publishers' fault? Every now and then a new publishing firm opens its doors, bent upon arresting the decline of the race. Its career is usually brief and inglorious. It seems that the existing small number is fully able, and more than able, to saturate the market and to take care of what production there is. The reason, to be looked for later, is very likely the same that accounts for the appalling scarcity of retail book-shops or the deplorable plight of Canadian broadcasts. A book-shop, by the way, is, in Europe, a place where books are not only sold but discussed, analysed, and quarrelled about as well.

As Mr. Callaghan has pointed out, a second surprise awaits the young writer when he finds that not one of these publishers makes the publishing, that is the printing and marketing, of Canadian books his exclusive business; just as there are no book-shops that sell only books, of which there are several in every fifth-rate town in Czecho-Slovakia.

In Canada, publishers rely for their bread and butter, and occasionally for trips to Europe and Cadillac cars, on the business of distributing throughout the Dominion books printed and published elsewhere. If, then, the Canadian writer finds a Canadian publisher favourably impressed with his work, he is, more likely than not, faced with the necessity of first discovering a publisher in England or in the United States who will print for, and sell sheets to, the Canadian publisher; and, naturally, the publisher in England or the United States prefers his authors to have been born in his own country instead of in the Canadian wilds.

I repeat: Is it the publishers' fault? It is not. The reason for such an extraordinary state of affairs must be sought in one of two things. Either there is a scarcity of books written in Canada or there is a scarcity of buyers of Canadian books.

I have been in the publishing business myself; and I can testify to the fact that, as far as mere numbers go, Canada excels other countries in the number of books written. In fact, I soon realized, when I became a publisher's reader, that I could no longer trust even my apparently most harmless and respectable-looking friends, male or female; they sat by my fire-side, chatting most charmingly; and then it came out: they had all written books and looked to me to have them published; and not my friends only. Under the avalanche of manuscripts the sorrowful conviction was forced on me, that in my youthful innocence—I was not yet sixty—I had been mistaken all the while: the chief industry of Canada was not agriculture; it was writing; six out of its eight million English-speaking citizens dreamed of literary fame. If a publisher had printed all these books, on condition that every author he published should buy one copy of every other book published by him, he would soon have been a multi-millionaire capable of lifting the national debt.

If, on the other hand, he had had to rely on the remaining two millions to buy the books, the story would have been different. It might be argued that, by the single fact of their abstention, they proved that they should have been the ones to write the books—which, of course, could have been only satires in Praise of Folly. I believe I am rather quick in detecting even a spark of promise in a manuscript; but had I depended on the sparks which I detected in the welter of manuscripts for lighting my furnace, I should have had to sit in the cold.

There is such promise, of course; among eight million people there must be at least eight promising young writers; they did not come to me. As Mr. Callaghan says, they took their wares to the United States; he might have added that very few of them ever even offer their books in Canada. Being aware of the wider market and the unlimited opportunities in the country to our south, they send their manuscripts there in the first place; and if they get an acceptance, they usually follow them in person. Anyone who has watched matters, as I have done for close to fifty years, knows that. Even 'tripe,' as everybody is aware, finds a market and a public across the border; where should we be without tripe? In Canada, it is true, many of the manuscripts would never have got an acceptance; being an agent as well, the Canadian publisher would have had to put them in direct and immediate competition with the best-sellers of two great markets at once. I shall all but state it as my opinion, lower down, that such a success of a Canadian writer, especially if won in the United States, means almost certainly the ruin of that writer as a writer, though not, perhaps, as a business man. It also means incidentally the loss of that writer to Canada.

Yet even Mr. Callaghan admits that occasionally a Canadian book finds its way into print in Canada. Is it as rare as he tries to make out? Apart from my brief excursion into the publishing business—in the course of which I gave two writers who had not submitted their wares to me the chance of seeing themselves in print—my experience is limited to myself. And if I presume, for a moment, to speak of my personal experience, the fact should be taken as a sign of my modesty; I do not mean to advance exaggerated claims for my own productions; nobody knows their short-comings as well as I do.

Well, here is the sober fact: fifty per cent of my books, so far published, were first printed in Canada; thirty-seven and a half per cent have never been printed elsewhere. Yet this thirty-seven and a half per cent has brought me more applause—not money, mind you—than all the rest of my books together. In every case I myself predicted that, in Canada, these books could be published only at a loss; but outside of Canada nobody wanted them; they were considered as too exclusively Canadian. And that does not hold good only for my published work, which represents a very small fraction of what I have written. A great English publisher recently sent me his readers' reports on a book of mind dealing with the industrial development of Canada; and in these reports I found such amazing statements as that the book was 'a book on the grand scale,' the work 'of a distinct personality'; but that it was feared it would find no public in England. 'For Canada,' one of the readers added, 'its importance is probably very great.' Which seems to show that at least this English publisher had no confidence in the Canadian market as such, for I had offered him the rights for Canada as well as for England. I feel convinced that one day I shall see it printed in Canada—pehaps not till after my death, but I am in no hurry.

For whenever, in the past, I prophesied that a certain book of mine could be printed in Canada only at a loss, I found, to my surprise, that such a prophecy acted on the Canadian publisher as a stimulus rather than as a deterrent. Three different publishers, during the last fifteen years, cheerfully accepted the prospect. In only one case were the negotiations conducted orally; and I can, therefore, vouch for the publisher's attitude in that case only. 'I know,' he said when I warned him, 'but this is a book which should be published in Canada; and I am going to publish it. It will be worth the fun.' I admired that spirit then; I still admire it.

Though the point properly belongs in a later section of this article, I may add here that my prophecy was fulfilled: the book failed to cover expenses. What is more, to this day, ten years after its publication, I have not yet heard an appreciative echo, from among the public or the world of critics, that came from Canada; but more than one such echo has come to me from continental Europe and from the antipodes.

As far, then, as my personal experience goes, if my writings have not made me wealthy I cannot blame the publishers. I must look for the fault in one of the other agencies.

II

The critics are next in line; and there the story is very different indeed.

A great deal of excellent critical work is being done in Canada, though not yet enough; unfortunately, nearly all of it is academic and deals with the dead. It appears in book form, in England; or in the university quarterlies. Among the many hundred Canadian reviews of my own books, to which my attention was drawn, I can think offhand of only one which went behind the letter-press to essentials. It was the only review that detected the presence of (what, according to one of our most popular reviewers of books, is almost completely absent from Canadian fiction) political and social criticism, in one of those books which, if I remember my intention aright, ought to have consisted of little else—though, as a novelist, I naturally expressed that criticism in the form of human experience rather than in the form of extraneous argument or social agitation, underlining the tragedy, not the need for reform. Characteristically, that one review came from the pen of the president of one of our universities, himself an accomplished writer, though not of fiction. I also seem to remember a long and brilliant review of Mr. Callaghan's work—a review which proved that at least this professorial critic was not handicapped by a purely academic outlook.

Unfortunately, the influence of our universities is narrowly restricted. The three great Quarterlies which should be found in every house whose inmates lay claim to a liberal education, yes, in every public library in even the smallest town, are read largely by university men. I do not think that the review of my own book to which I referred was responsible for the sale of a single copy.

Next come the lay periodicals.

I believe it to be axiomatic that the general level of mental aliveness within a nation can best be measured by the spirit of intellectual adventure displayed in the critical activities of weeklies and monthlies. I have asked Europeans from three different countries, men who are keenly alert to anything going on in even the remotest corner of this globe, what they thought of our weekly and monthly periodicals as media of public enlightenment. Their only answer was a brief laugh and a scornful shrug of the shoulders. One only, on second thought, singled out, like Mr. Callaghan, the *Canadian Forum*. But look at the circulation figures of that solitary exponent of intellectual integrity!

There remains the daily press. It does not take a great deal of perspicacity to see that book-reviewing, not to say literary criticism, is treated as the Cinderella of the press. The space allotted and the salaries paid tell the all-sufficient tale. The field is a desert. I once ran across a brief notice of a new edition of *The Brothers Karamazov* in English translation. It contained nothing but a contemptuous reference to readers who may want that sort of thing. It was obvious that the writer of that notice had never heard of Dostoievsky.

I know of hardly one book-reviewer in Canada who, in judging a book not previously heralded by discussion in Great Britain or the United States, does not hopelessly flounder. The best that can be expected is a brief 'I like this' or 'I dislike it'; and almost invariably the reviewer likes what he should dislike and dislikes what he should like. Almost, I say; for even in drawing a card from a deck the chances are one in thirteen that you draw an ace; but the chances are only one in two hundred and twenty-one that you draw two aces in succession.

If, among the reviewers, there is any kind of established background from which to arrive at a considered judgment, I have failed to find it.

And the public stands for it: there was no outcry against that notice of *The Brothers Karamazov,* no demand for the head of its writer on a platter of brass.

III

And that brings us to the public. In a sense, Mr. Callaghan seems to defend that public. I cannot agree. The Canadian public is ignorant, cowardly, and snobbish; it is mortally afraid of ideas and considers the discussion of first principles as a betrayal of bad manners.

Unless they are very sure that it is socially disgraceful not to own a given book, they refuse to buy it. If it is imperative, socially, that they be able to talk about it, they borrow it. Even in order to own it, you don't necessarily have to buy it: you write to the author, and if the author knows what is what, he will send it to you with his autograph!

To how many people in Canada are books the daily companions they ought to be? Shall we say five hundred? Or is that too flattering? I mean, of course, outside of educational institutions.

Here is the point: any nation has the literature which it deserves; and no false enthusiasm, such as Mr. Callaghan treats to his scorn as one of the 'boosting' activities of this country, can alter that fact. More appallingly, Canadians are at bottom not interested in their own country; I honestly believe they prefer to read about dukes and lords, or about the civil war in the United States. They are supposed to be born explorers; but they have not yet heard that the human heart and soul are perhaps the only corners in this universe where unexplored and undiscovered continents are still abounding.

This lack of mental aliveness is fundamental. Canada is a non-conductor for any sort of intellectual current.

I am the last person to assert that the writer is entitled to a reward in the form of money; I shall have to say more about that in a moment. The trouble is that the Canadian public recognizes no other reward. The money standard, being the only one which it knows, is the only one by which it judges. Any writer who has made a success in terms of money, even though he wrote for the mentally immature, is a great writer; anyone who has failed to make such a success, even though the best in many countries applaud him, ranks among the riff-raff of the world.

Granting, then, for a moment, that 'money talks,' even if in a sense different from the commonly accepted one, permit me once more to give my personal experience.

I have written two books which sold widely in Canada: *A Search for America* and *Our Daily Bread*. Why did they sell? Because they happened to appear, one shortly before, one shortly after I made three consecutive lecture-tours through the country, which placed me, for the moment, under the lime-light. Wherever I went, people made much of me; I was mentioned in head-lines; I was interviewed; my entirely uninteresting opinions were abundantly misrepresented: in one word, I was a social lion. Not to know me, not to display my books would have argued a lack of ability to keep 'in the swim.' My own weariness, my frequent disgusts remained unnoticed or at least disregarded. Had it not been for these facts, thousands who bought one or both of the books would never have done so. I have written other books; I have written better books; they remain unknown in this country.

What is the financial result to myself? Actual figures will tell the tale. But before I give them I must add one word, to place them in the proper perspective.

The book of mine which has made the greatest sales-success in this country—significantly, it is artistically the weakest—was first published in Canada, then in the United States, and last in England. The English publishers led the dance: less than four weeks after the date of publication they went into bankruptcy. The publishers in the United States followed; and at last even the Canadian firm which had bravely published it bit the dust. Whether these successive failures were causally connected with the printing of my book I cannot say with any degree of certainty; but those are the facts. Before the American publishers went to the wall, they dumped thousands of copies of my book, at cut-prices, on the Canadian market, illegally. In order to stop that—for naturally they paid no royalties on these sales—I stepped in and bought up the remaining American copies as well as the plates, to enter the business of selling over the bargain-counter in this country on my own account. Of course, for the good of my pocket-book I should not have done so.

If then, to-day, I total up royalties received on all my books and expenses incurred in behalf of the one most successful of all, the difference is close to eighteen hundred dollars in my disfavour. To that extent, the Canadian public has short-changed me.

Or let me leave out my losses and consider transactions only which resulted on the credit side; what reward, in a monetary sense, would that have given me? Perhaps I should say that I am a slow worker, that it takes me years to put a book into a shape in which I care to publish it. Well, my remuneration for the work which I have done in the field of Canadian writing, take it for whatever it may be worth, has been a trifle less than two cents an hour. If I am correctly informed, that is less than the law prescribes as the minimum wage for a married man.

Do I complain? I do not. The thing amuses me; perhaps it may amuse others.

IV

With that we come to the writer; and it is here that at last I take serious issue with Mr. Callaghan.

Mr. Callaghan puts the case as if the writer should make his living by his pen. To him, it appears, a writer is necessarily a professional writer. I part company from him.

'In my time,' said the painter Degas to a young man complaining or boasting, I forget which—'In my time, monsieur, we did not *get on.*' That was putting it neatly.

Or let me quote Nietzsche. 'For the attainment of greatness'—and, like Mr. Callaghan, I am talking only of writers who aim at greatness—'For the attainment of greatness a man must first become acquainted with profound self-contempt, with the martyrdom of self-distrust, with the misery of the defeated.'

I wonder how many of the great works of literature would have been written, how many of the great works of music, composed, how many of the great canvasses, painted, if writer, composer, painter had even expected to make his immediate living by them; or, worse still, if he had actually made it.

I believe that the very expectation would have warped his outlook. It is the work of art that matters, not the artist. At least he matters only in one single aspect of which I shall speak at the end.

Mr. Callaghan himself admits that for those who have their eye on the market there is as good a chance in Canada as anywhere else. It is true, our magazines do not pay the fees which the *Saturday Evening Post* pays. Perhaps, if in their own fields—which are neither Mr. Callaghan's nor mine—they were as good as the *Saturday Evening Post,* they might command an international market as well as a national one; and it is my belief that it would be entirely within the possibilities to make them as good, though hardly with a purely Canadian staff of contributors.

But Mr. Callaghan and I are not talking of the writer who writes in order to supply the quite legitimate demand of a more or less illiterate public with such reading as will enable it to close its eyes to the things that matter. Admittedly we are talking about the writer 'who goes on, year after year, doing the thing he loves, never yielding, and maybe taking a bad beating now and then. . . .'

For that matter I should like to lay it down as axiomatic that no 'living' is in sight *in no matter what country, at no matter what time.* That writer may have a chance success which will place him beyond all worry and care; it has happened; but he will not owe it to the excellence, he will owe it to the weakness of his work. As matters stand, and as they have stood for the last few thousand years, the presumption must *a priori* be against the best-seller. But why, you ask? Because the writer worth his salt plunges into the unknown; and he has, of necessity, first to create that taste by means of which he expects to be appreciated. Such a task may take a decade, as Mr. Callaghan suggests; I am inclined to think that, more probably, it will take a lifetime or longer. Look into the history of literature and you will have to admit that I am right; look into the history of music or any other art.

When I first listened to the first movement of Beethoven's Ninth Symphony, I felt dimly that here was a giant of whom I was a pigmy replica; and then I asked myself whether, had Beethoven not been 'too poor to be respected' (to quote one of his biographers), he could have written that Ninth, or the Third, or, for that matter, the Fifth, or the Sixth, or the Seventh. It is a deplorable fact, but it is a fact nevertheless, that success does not stimulate man to his highest endeavour; it is defeat which does that.

And there are compensations. In my own writing life—modest as my efforts have been compared with those of the great—I have, through my books, made a dozen friends, half of them in this country, whose applause, whose often qualified applause, has not only given me happy moments but has spurred me on to ever-renewed endeavour and to that spirit which made me feel and say, 'I shall get there yet!' And, I believe, I am exactly twice Mr. Callaghan's age.

'I shall get there yet!' Where? Arrive at a material success? No. Emphatically no. But at the point where I might be able to say that, in the form of fiction, I had definitely expressed what I had set out to express—a tremendous task. Taking things by-and-large, the writer who, his book finished, feels that he has embodied his vision without residue has very likely not aimed high enough; not, at any rate, as high as he might have aimed. Had he aimed higher, he would perhaps have failed in reaching his mark; but, in an undefined and indefinable direction, he would have gone farther than, as a matter of fact, he did go.

Many things might be said; Goethe and Homer might be quoted; things might be said which I have tried to say in the past; things which others have tried to say before me: Galsworthy, for instance, in the preface to the omnibus edition, *Caravan*, of his short stories. I will refrain.

But let me repeat that the writer who wishes to do what Mr. Callaghan outlines so eloquently, whether he live in China or Canada, in France or Brazil, has no business to expect a living from his books. Grillparzer was a clerk in a government office; Goethe, a minister of state in a fifth-rate principality; Flaubert and Galsworthy had private means. Yet they wrote *Sappho, Faust, Madame Bovary*, and *The Man of Property*. Would they, could they have written them if they had looked to their books for their living?

Many who have done things have starved; no doubt many who are doing things are starving. Does it matter? What matters is that the things they do be done.

What should worry the writer is not whether his work will bring him success. What should worry him is whether his work is what it is humanly possible to make it. Meanwhile let him shovel coal if he has to.

That is the trouble with us: living in a great material civilization not of our making, not fought for, not evolved out of the sweat and blood of our limbs, not paid for with our suffering, our lives, our triumphs—living in such a civilization, I say, we crave material comfort rather than spiritual achievement. If there were more Canadian writers 'shovelling coal,' to remain in my metaphor, perhaps we should feel that, no matter what we have done in the past, there is glory to come in the future for what to-day we fatuously call Canadian literature; and the plight of Canadian fiction would not exist; for, whether a work of art be printed in Canada or in Timbuktu, it is, to-day, bound to conquer the world that has shrunk—though not, perhaps, within the lifetime of its maker.

You know how, towards the end of the third century A.D., the Caesar Galerius went against the Persians under Narses in Mesopotamia and was disgracefully defeated, so that he had to flee to the feet of Diocletian at Antioch. But his defeat steeled him; and the victory demoralized the Persians. Within the year, Galerius retrieved his lost honour; it was not victory that made him strong; it was defeat.

And so, having had my say in this haphazard fashion, let me conclude with a parable.

Let us assume that there is some being resembling Hardy's Spirit of the Years in the *Dynasts*; and let us figure that Spirit viewing the arrival of Xerxes' armament in Greece.

Against that armament Leonidas is sent, with the task of holding those hordes in the narrow pass of Thermopylae. To hold the Persians, no more, that is his ostensible task.

But in his omniscience I like to figure that Spirit as musing.

'Yes,' he might be presumed to say to himself, 'I picked the right man. He will fall at Thermopylae—he with his three hundred. And if he knew my deeper purpose in sending him there, he would be the man to approve that purpose.

'For these three hundred must die, not because it is of any importance that the Persians be held for a day or two—though it is. They must die so as to set an example of the devotion to a cause which will ring through the millennia; so that, in a higher sense, they can never die.'

Yes, and may I repeat? 'In my time, monsieur,' said Degas, 'we did not *get on.*'

R.D. MacDonald

The Power of F.P. Grove's The Master of the Mill

Grove's power as a novelist is strangely related to his heroes' failures of vision. In so many of his novels, a protagonist strives mightily to realize a heroic dream, and paradoxically creates (and becomes the victim of) a reality which is a distortion of his original purpose. This is as true of Niels Lindstedt, the Swedish immigrant of *Settlers of the Marsh* (1925), who dreams of carving a large farm and vast farmhouse out of the raw bush, as it is of Len Sterner, the sensitive homestead boy of *The Yoke of Life* (1931), who dreams of leaving the bush to become a great scholar. And it is true of the scholarly persona that Grove projects in *A Search for America* where his immigrant hero turns his back upon the past and sets out to discover the archetypes of the new world spirit, the Lincolns, Washingtons and Thoreaus, in the life of the common people. Here the wide search does not give birth to any consistent or profound discovery, or to any significant image—the disillusioned narrator abruptly ends this autobiographical account and heads North to Canada because somehow to him Canada has remained more true to his original dreams of North America.

A similar kind of large ambition can be seen in Grove's *In Search of Myself* where again one sees the cultivated immigrant, this time asking the question why he has failed to realize his youthful promise as an artist. In the background of both these *Searches* is a shadowy and remote past, a romantic European past . . . the great universities of Europe, wealth, large mansions and tyrannical fathers. Against this past is the aspiring, sensitive, rebellious son, the Byronic prodigal who leaves and does not return to be reconciled to his old world. This motif of youthful aspiration becomes very telling in *A Search for America, In Search of Myself* and in *The Master of the Mill* where the men who are remembering their past are doing so from the saddened and diminished perspective of the older man who has failed to realize his early dreams: the failed hero attempts now to discover the roots of his failure, where or why he went wrong, and then to discover his justification.

Though none of the above works brings forth a very clear explanation of the failure, in the introduction to *In Search of Myself* Grove does present poignantly the mood of the older man who sees now his failed promise and sees too its correlative in front of him, the vast, empty and drab winter landscape, as he sits waiting and musing on a floodbroken road. He is about to pick up a young domestic who is to help himself and his wife in their new farmhouse, a home which it is suggested is already too much for them, a house which will demonstrate once again man's grandiose aspirations and his insufficiency. Musing in this way, Grove describes himself blowing his car's horn dismally through the empty winter landscape, calling perhaps the young girl from the farmhouse but more so giving vent to his sense of waste. Indeed what he brings forth unintentionally is a pitiful apparition of old age, the girl's grandfather physically ravaged by time, a man not much older than Grove himself, but a man who has already passed over into gleeful and energetic senility. This painful caricature of man's 'end' shows up the absurdity of the questing man because, once again, we do not arrive at what we set out to find. In this 'light,' life becomes a heroic illusion, a Sisyphean quest with no appropriate end or purpose beyond itself.

The wisest and perhaps most precise realization of this painful idea is to be found, not in *The Master of the Mill*, though it is there, too, implicitly, but in Grove's epic chronicle, *Consider Her Ways*. Here a heroic band of ants sets out on an ambitious and disinterested exploration of Central and North America. When Anna-zee, the ant-philosopher, attempts to persuade her fellow questors to go no farther, she propounds one of Grove's fundamental motifs, the absurd quest. Though her argument is immediately attacked as an expression of 'rank nihilism,' for our purposes her speech is useful: it epitomizes the pointlessness of all heroic endeavour, and it is a variant of Maud Dolittle's 'wisdom' in *The Master of the Mill*, namely doing little:

> Man, it is true, from what she had seen of him . . . does not strive after knowledge for the sake of knowledge; he strives after it for the sake of increasing his power. Ants, who have long since abandoned that aim, seeing clearly that material progress—which means no more and no less than the increase of power for the achievement of material ends—would side-track them in their essential task which was to live this life of theirs fully—ants could never be satisfied with so low an aim; and that for the very reason that they see themselves as thinking, exploring, feeling and reasoning beings—not as slaves of material ends. What, then, stands at the end of a complete exploration of the knowable world? What, if such an end there is, stands at the end of science? At that end stands neither more nor less than a

complete realization of our ignorance. For, since it is ant-
nature, since it always has been and will ever remain ant-nature,
to ask that question 'Why?' we shall merely find ourselves
confronted with the whole realm of the unknowable; in other
words, the best that science, even on the basis of our
assumption, can achieve is the conversion of the vast knowable
universe into an unknowable universe.[1]

Despite Anna-zee's argument against searching farther, the ants
continue their collective quest and prove only the various potentialities which have been in them from the beginning—the quest
becomes its own noble meaning. The book itself becomes an epic
celebration of their heroic endeavour and a chronicle of their
remembered impressions and metaphors. Appropriately the tale
itself does not move to a single end or moral: on the last page, Wawa-
quee, the narrator, has come almost full circle in her return, but she is
represented finally as not yet returned, but still returning.

Although the ending of Grove's *Consider Her Ways* is more
directly consistent than *The Master of the Mill*, in its *apparent*
weakness and dishonesty *The Master of the Mill* paradoxically
emphasizes the basic power of Grove's narrative structure, especially
as that structure is determined by the absurd questor. Sam Clark, the
'master' and 'questor,' seeks lucidity; he seeks to arrive at a final
judgement regarding his responsibility or guilt in the creation of the
mill before he dies. Despite the indictment before his imagination of
the long lines of unemployed, he returns to his original vision of
labourers freed from the drudgery of work and of benevolent masters
who would make their work 'the supreme fulfilment of their being,'
this in man's 'garden-cities.'[2] The violent upheavals of the past, then,
are finally to be justified as the inevitable means to a humane end.
And so, remembering Grove's hint that 'every creature on earth must
be justified to itself' (p. 386), the reader can believe that Sam can die
seeing himself, his father and son 'justified in his [Sam's] eyes' (p.
387). To this point Grove maintains an obvious control over his
ambiguities, but at the close the ambiguities become almost self-
contradictory or self-cancelling. The two women who survive the
Clark males act as a chorus and speak 'truths' which must be
questioned. Responding to the final judgement of Miss Charlebois
which is proclaimed through the sardonic image of a wheel
'return[ing] to every point at which we have been,' Lady Clark insists
that the 'wheel does not rotate in empty space: it moves forward. At
least let us hope so,' and she places her faith in 'some entirely

unforeseen thing,' 'some development' related to her 'great confidence in the capacity of the collective human mind' (p. 392).

But these last words are contradicted and made ridiculous by the thrust of Grove's book. They become a false summary. As a misreading of events, they can be seen to be consistent with Sam's earlier false final judgement and in accord with Grove's nihilism. Grove' motif of the absurd questor, and his narrative design powerfully suggest a pessimistic meaning completely opposite to Lady Clark's hope: man, individually *and* collectively, moves in circles or creates what he did not intend.

Though it has been suggested above that Sam's quest is not genuine in that he is seeking self-justification, not truth (p. 386), the source of the novel's design and meaning is to be found in that quest. The first six chapters, then, dwell upon the origins of the mill, the grandfather who chose so wisely the site of his mill, a point half-way between what would become the great wheat fields of the West and the huge markets to the East, a site adjacent to water power and fated to be on the line of the Canadian Pacific Railway. Sam's primary focus in this opening, however, is upon the re-discovery or re-living of how his father, Rudyard Clark, managed to achieve his amazing expansion of his mill. As Sam approached closer and closer to the criminal act of his father (the burning of the mill and the collecting of the insurance for thirty thousand bushels that had not been delivered to the mill) the novel reads more and more like a detective novel, especially as Sam becomes more and more impatient because his memories and inferences do not take him directly to the solution of his mystery.

Sam has inherited the mill and has become the master of the mill in the middle of the book, chapters seven to sixteen, but he has become a false master, one who must protect the reputation of his dead father, one who must protect the past and the status quo. He no longer dreams of releasing the labourers from their drudgery and of bringing the benefits of the mill to society as a whole. He strives instead to gain absolute control over the milling business so that no one else can uncover the shameful source of his father's power. Throughout this part of the book Sam is presented as a secretive, preoccupied man, a man who has lost any spontaneity that he may have had before. Sam becomes a man living in an alien world, a man looking on almost like a peeping Tom as his more unconscious and spontaneous fellows, a man who becomes an envious onlooker watching his fourteen-year-old son charm the woman who is meant to be Sam's wife. This section of the book closes as Sam deliberately leaves Langholm and the mill in the hands of Captain Stevens, the general manager, knowing that Stevens, being ambitious, will make a mistake and thereby bring about a strike that is inevitable anyway.

This closing is significant because in the next eight chapters, which reconstruct the shift of control from Sam to his son, Edmund, the latter very decisively arranges matters by himself. In a very intricate, even diabolically precise way, Edmund deliberately takes upon himself the responsibility of creating the second strike. Edmund, unlike his father, Sam, has been no juvenile dreamer; he is a determined man who has a very specific understanding of history, and who conceives the mill as a technocratic utopia which will eliminate political forms of government, the majority of mankind, and human labour itself, except for the few 'masters' who will paradoxically become the slaves of the machine. As Edmund appears on the very scene of the battle between the strikers and the strike-breakers, he is killed by a stray bullet.

It is obvious in this reconstruction of the story that *The Master of the Mill* is not a tragic work: it does not uphold the nobility of man against the indifference of the natural order. This become partially apparent as the story shifts away from Sam himself: the action is displaced from Sam to his more potent father and son. Just as the action is displaced from remembering man himself, the actions of the father and son are displaced into the mill itself. What remains in the reader's memory, then, is not a tragic work, but a blighted representation of man objectifying himself, losing his powers of joy and will, as he creates an alien world in which he has no real or necessary part. Man becomes like Old Sam himself, stumbling through his own self-created darkness, looking peevishly for his flashlight or for a way out.

The ending (the last two chapters) is a post-mortem which presents little more than the message of a shrug—that is, a denial of meaning: who can know the final truth? And what wisdom can there be except indifference or 'doing little'? The women who have survived have apparently, like the three male Clarks, inherited a world which is too complex to understand, and they are aware of a vastness of space and time which intimidates the imagination itself.

Grove's creation of this belittling and be-numbing vastness is the source of his novel's power. What then does this vastness imply for man? And how does Grove make this vastness formidable? The central image, one which is presented in many different forms, is the image of the wheel, or more abstractly the idea of change as pointless, directionless rotation.

Before looking at the overpowering images of the wheel and the mill with its suggestion of rotation, it will be useful to examine the human perspective that is over-powered by these large brooding images—in this diminution of human perspective one may see once again that there is no 'master' or that the master is only a false master. Grove's narrative technique goes far in bringing about this diminution of the human being: there is no single omniscient narrative viewpoint; instead that viewpoint is shattered into the multiple and unreliable perspective of several weakened survivors attempting to pull the fragments of their past into a meaningful whole. The principal seeker, old Sam Clark, has gone so far in his old age that he has lost what little control man has over his memories; memories, often trivial ones, appear unbidden, much to the frustration of this man who seems to be seeking self-revelation but who (we are told) is seeking what even murderers and thieves seek, namely self-justification. The hopelessness of Sam's condition is implied from the opening page of the novel, especially in those images which suggest a tremendously complex reality not reducible to human terms. The fragmented light of the chandelier in its intricate organization, 'broken by the cascade of prismatic crystals' (p. 5), is repeated by the reflected water-image of the mill 'shattered and broken into a million luminous shards' (p. 7). The enlarging mill becomes as complex as its reflected image, and its ultimate origin, destination and meaning become almost entirely shrouded in an inchoate symbolism which seems to open out without end into unresolved possibilities of meaning. And there are those strange passages in the book where time itself becomes an inchoate complexity as Sam, willfully reliving his past, becomes incapable (just as his reader momentarily becomes incapable) of distinguishing the different degrees or levels of the past from each other and from the present.

This complexity is accentuated as one sees its effect upon Sam and his daughter Ruth. The two experience a separation from reality, which is repeated by an inner disassociation. In Sam this leads to an atrophy of will; the stillness in Ruth, to an excess of will. In her nihilistic rage against the emptiness of life, she would rather will nothing than have nothing to will.

On the opening page, Sam is presented looking through glass at the mill. Elsewhere, the dark evening and the rain are represented as a veil between the musing Sam and the object of his meditations, the mill. His daughter suffers an even more imaginative sense of her removal from reality. Living in her luxury, she feels the glass barrier between herself and the outside social realities, and she desires to break through that barrier. Ironically, just before she leaves Langholm for good, repelled by the sexual advances of a boyfriend, she drives off suddenly leaving him behind, turning her back in disgust upon this human or animal impulse, careening through the night with a malfunctioning car until finally she smashes through the plate glass window of an automobile showroom. Leaving Langholm then and marrying an Italian duke old enough to be her grandfather, she enters into an unconsummated marriage, a business arrangement which permits her a new immunity from the eyes of the world, thereby paradoxically re-creating the glass wall between herself and the world. Her nihilism is most completely expressed in her declaration that if she were a man, she would 'make a bomb big enough to blast such abominations as this town into nothingness' (p. 244).

The disassociation of Ruth is repeated in other characters. Rudyard, the founder of the Clark mill, has no conception of how complex, how incredibly interlocking the various components of the mill have become. His 'action' of burning the mill down and then claiming compensation for undelivered wheat is represented by Sam not so much as an act of will but a weakness of will as Rudyard is seen yielding to temptation. Even the brilliant and powerful Edmund proclaims that his actions are not really his own, that he is merely a small part in a vast evolutionary drama, that man is not great except when he confronts problems that are themselves great. The unreality of 'character'-in-action is emphasized even more as Grove resorts increasingly to the metaphors of the stage: at the crisis of the book where Edmund is manipulating the Prime Minister, Sir Arthur, to call off his investigation of Montreal Timber Limits, and where Edmund is getting rid of Mr. Cole, the various performers in these machinations are presented as if they were putting on costumes in preparation for a party which is really a highly contrived play. The Clark house itself (or the setting) has already been presented in its synthetic makeup as being little more than a real-estate showroom or an hotel; Maud Clark is made to play an almost immoral role in the 'wooing' of Rosenbaum; Edmund 'puts on' his impersonal 'fate'-voice for the benefits of his wife. The heavy artificiality is made all the more apparent when Cole, approaching his nemesis, is described as having a head like a 'football balanced on a five-foot post, waiting to be kicked off by some giant' (p. 340). The histrionics of the following passage are quite obvious:

> Everybody falling back, to make room for Lady Clark, the
> group opened up; and this, the senator retarding his step, made
> the impression as if, like the actors in a Greek drama, Maud, Mr.
> Cole, and Mr. Birkinshaw were isolated on the stage, to the
> choral accompaniment of the music filling the house.
> Meanwhile, through the wings, Charles Beatty was making his
> entrance, moving rapidly to take part in the scene, impersonat-
> ing the *deus ex machina*. (p. 342)

The deliberately theatrical style is brought to a vicious climax in a
Huxley-esque exchange of wit. Cole is vanquished once and for all by
Beatty's malicious and heavily literary sarcasm: 'It is better to have
had a head and lost it than never to have had a head at all' (p. 345).

It is obvious in these images that Grove's presentation of
impotence and disassociation takes on not an unreal but a surreal
quality—Sam, the master, who is little more than a peeping Tom
watching the actors in a farther room; Sybil and Maud Clark
attempting to outdo one another in gymnastic feats, performing in a
glass-walled private gymnasium; Maud telling her stolid husband
that she might run off and join a circus because she must do
something meaningful; all the central characters being almost
entirely without distinguishable phyusical characteristics while the
minor characters are represented with a heavy geometric and
grotesque precision; the nightmare images of a sterile past, Sam
searching through empty drawers for things that have been disposed
of decades ago, the vast and empty mansion itself, the burnt-out
workers' cottages, the boarded-up Clark house, the fishbones that
Sam spits out in peevish anger; the growing stillness and indifference
of Sam and the others as he approaches his death and as in his
memories he approaches the death of his son, both their deaths being
presented with an atmosphere of a cold arctic vastness which
accentuates the smallness of this human drama.

The cold vastness is closely allied to Grove's symbol of the mill,
especially as the mill becomes the embodiment of a vast supra-
human power and as its very size dwarfs the human being. From the
opening pages, the mill is a strange amalgam of science fiction and
fantasy. It is a pyramid, self-illuminated, having a specific size and
specific number of units, yet built in such a way that it has been added
to while keeping its original pyramid design intact. The Langholm
mill becomes a futurist building, having such a magnificence of size
and sweeping line that it both thrills and dwarfs Sam Clark and
Maud. The Arbala mill, built by Sam's son, Edmund, is even more

advanced: it becomes the culminating epitome of the self-operating, cybernetic whole, a structure so powerful and efficient that its shape is reduced in size and changed from a sweeping pyramid to a compact cube. It is paradoxical that the power of this smaller mill is greater than the larger, and it is strange that the smaller mill is more awesome when its machine movements and noise have been perfectly self-enclosed. This forbidding stillness, much like that of an arctic silence, anticipates the setting and mood of the novel's ending, 'white, spotless, silent, and seemingly motionless. I half thought they had stopped the machines for my benefit. In reality, all motion was internal and enclosed' (p. 230).

The description below, spoken by Inkster, catches as well as any passage the empty and cold heartlessness of this cybernetic system:

> "The place was like an enormous well into which all sorts of puzzling machinery had been suspended. Here and there a man with a mop of cotton waste was hanging in mid-air; here and there another was crouching in a grid, wiping flour dust. Everything glittered; everything felt and smelt oily. At various points, far overhead, pipe-like tubes entered and, from minute to minute, discharged, with a sound, first of hissing, then of rumbling, what I presumed to be a few tons of wheat which came I don't know whence. Below, unattended endless conveyors carried unbroken rows of bags full of flour, carried them into specially constructed box-cars, all painted white, inside and out; when these were filled, they were noiselessly shunted away by electric motors.
>
> "You may say, of course, it is much the same here; but it is different, too. For one thing, there is the town; the mill is not surrounded by an interstellar vacancy; for another, there are men in this mill, at least in spots. At Arbala, everything proceeded as in a void; no vestiges of the past were to be seen or inferred. It was uncanny. Though it was much smaller than the mill here, it was the pure essence of the thing.
>
> "One trifle interested me. On the lake behind the dam of which I had a glimpse through an upper window lay a fleet of perhaps a hundred giant sea-planes. What they were for, I couldn't guess. . . ." (p. 230)

The hundred giant sea-planes are more than an accident of Grove's imagination: they indicate again a fearful preoccupation with vastness, in this case a frenetic preoccupation with overcoming the vast emptiness of the Canadian landscape, in which the immensely powerful (yet in this context, tiny) mill has been set. Grove more than once imagines the Clark mills filling the whole of the earth, having displaced mankind altogether, and then he imagines the earth as a manless mill-planet dusting its way toward chaos through vast interstellar spaces. Man is dwarfed by his works; his works are dwarfed by the landscape; and then, man and his works are dwarfed or annihilated by space itself.

The mill, however, is not simply a creature of surrealist or science fiction, for again and again the mill is presented as a manifestation, not only of man's nature (man as *homo faber*), but of the earth itself. It is no accident that the mill as mechanism achieves a life-like growth expanding and diversifying in a unified way: Sam consciously designs the mill in accordance with the aesthetic principle of 'organic unity' whereby art simulates nature's efficient order. Moreover there are several suggestions that the mill possesses not a man-made but a primodial relation to nature:

> It had been placed where it is because of what the engineers said; they could not go further north because the river-bed consists of shale and quicksand, down to a depth to which no struts could be set. The mill had to stand on the *bed-rock with which it forms a monolith.* All growth had to be to the south where the so-called vaults which hold the turbines and the dynamos were blasted out of the *living rock.* (p. 65) [italics added]

The mill's growth begins to take on a plastic or malleable aspect like that of a living thing: 'The growth had been automatic and inevitable: as if from below, from out of the still plastic igneous bed-rock of the earth, new units had been pressed up like intrusive dykes, hardening on exposure to the air, and cooling' (p. 220). In Maud Dolittle's summary at the end of the book, the Clarks, in relation to this living thing, become little more than dwarfed midwives bring this creature to birth: 'It had grown as the product of its own logic: it had grown out of the earth. The Clarks had been mere pygmy helpers in bringing it to life' (p. 388). To claim such a natural origin for the mill is not to tame the awesome and frightening connotations of Grove's central image, for Grove suggests quite clearly that this 'natural' growth is a sinister growth. In Miss Charlebois' words:

> . . . whenever a vacancy occurred, through the death of an operator, or through somebody's throwing up his job, that

vacancy was never filled. A change was made in the line-up by the engineers, which made it possible to dispense with the services of that operator. That gave the process of unbroken if slow growth the weird appearance of a decay. (p. 213)

As the mill grows the town shrinks. Later Edmund, arguing from this inexorable development, declares that the unemployed will be sterilized and that the mass of superflous men will wither away. Captain Stevens sees in this strange growth, the image of a parasitic organism devouring its host: 'It was a queer thought, that of the mill which ran independently of human labour enclosing, as it were, that other, older mill which was still run by hand: a starfish enveloping an oyster to suck its substance was not more sinister. The men crouched under the threat; but they could not help themselves' (p. 304).

The mill, however, takes on a much larger dimension than this suggestion of a natural yet sinister growth. It development is associated throughout the book with large macrocosmic patterns working through time, natural cycles to which man contributes his small part, natural cycles to which the mill contributes its own large part, such a large part indeed that it becomes a partner of evolution exacting precise motions from man who becomes a dwarfed subordinate in the macro-processes. The mill as it is related to the image of cosmic wheels or cycles, and man as he is tied to that same image become together an even more frightening reality. When Sam attempts to recapture or enucleate his past, there seems little hope for his redemption: it becomes clear that the road he rides upon, the Loop, is little more than a circle or a wheel and that it is a correlative of his thought. The Loop was built by Sam in the empty wilderness so that his women would have somewhere to drive along in their automobiles; but where do they drive except, like the old musing man, in a pointless circle?

Even the small routines of Sam's life bespeak the same monotony and pointlessness of existence, and as the old man has ceased to be an agent of change, he becomes instead a still channel through which and around which things happen. Sam's dead routine is caught in the monotony of the following short sentences:

The senator was up again and had resumed his old routine. In the morning he rose around eight o'clock; at ten he listened to Captain Stevens's report; at eleven he went out for the drive with his daughter-in-law; after lunch he say down for a nap;

and in the evening he walked about in the house, often till
midnight; and when he went ot bed, there were days when he had
not spoken a word to anyone. (p. 286)

This indifferent man, barely existing in the present while he is
attempting to make sense of the past, is symbolic of what is
happening to mankind in the fictional world of *The Master of the
Mill:* man ceases to be a willing a resolute being as his powers are
completely displaced by the inexorable logic of technology and
evolution. Man becomes a creature disassociated from his own self-
asserted time:

> Those who watched him had a peculiar impression: as if time
> were accelerated in passing by him; as water flowing in a stream
> is accelerated when it approaches a narrows. His own functions
> had slowed down, while those surrounding him went on at
> their usual rate, so that they overtook him unawares. This fact
> he betrayed by occasional brief remarks of surprise. "What?
> Already?" (p. 286)

Sam's unreality, his displacement outside his own time, is of
course not simply the displacement of the senile mind; his plight is
repeated by the unfortunates who like their masters serve the mill.
Near the beginning of the book, Rodgers explains to Sam the
workers' strange nervous restlessness by arguing that the mill has
become so much their master that they are no longer promoted to
better jobs; the mill simply exacts precise, repetitious reactions at an
even, accelerating tempo. Part of Sam's early utopian purpose, then,
was to put an end to this unnatural mechanization of human labour
by replacing man with machines, but the unforeseen consequence is
unemployment and the new alienated reactions of the engineers and
technicians, these masters of the mill whose job it is to run the self-
operating whole. As the old Senator remembers entering the new mill
with his son, he recaptures this image of the frantic and endless
endeavours of the testers—a joyless combination of St. Vitus and
Sisyphus:

> A white-frocked figure was jumping from chute to chute,
> dipping into each, and preparing, in a test-tube, a mixture to
> which he finally added a few drops of acid. Shaking it up,
> thumb over the mouth of the tube, he looked at it briefly, and
> then discarded it, glass and all, into a hole gaping under a table,

pressing a few signal buttons by means of which he communicated with an engineer in a glass cage half-way to the roof. He had hardly done this when he started the whole process over again; and, like him, two dozen others were doing the same. (pp. 377-78)

The inhumanity of this 'activity' is underlined by a shorter description of tasters who 'reached alternately for a loaf, cut off a slice, bit off a corner, chewed it, and spat it out again into spittoons shaped like trumpets from which it was sucked away into the waters of the river swirling below the mill: no ice ever formed there except at the edges' (p. 378).

The unfrozen ice can be seen as a poetic image pointing to the unnaturalness of these alienated men. The most telling image regarding the Senator's betrayed dreams of a liberated mankind, however, is seen once again in the following nightmare image. Here the purposeless circle or wheel takes on the dimension of the round ball of earth, devoid of man, dusting its way through empty interstellar spaces: 'He silently laughed at the idea of the mill as a whole revolving around the sun or some other star, like a meteor through a final chaos, scattering flour-dust in its interstellar wake; but the laugh was bitter' (p. 377). This grotesque image of the manless-mill-planet is not unrelated to the winter setting of the novel's ending: the leave-taking from Arbala back to Langholm across the frost-locked vastness of Northern Ontario; the battles between the strikers and the company men which echo across the glazed ice in the silent night; and the final shooting almost by accident of Edmund who stands alone atop the soaring hill. Grove's descriptions of this vast, winter wasteland and Maud Dolittle's description of the absurd cycle of man's history transform *The Master of the Mill*, not into a tragic work, but into a nightmare prophecy. Indeed there is nothing left for man to do, no redemption or justification, except that of working blindly and collectively within man's illusory dreams and within an inscrutable macrocosmic order. Grove predicts the dilemma of *homo faber*, or technological man, as he shows Sam Clark captured by his means, and now in his partially conscious realization of his dilemma without any end or purpose or will.

The cold, vast and impersonal setting of Canada is entirely appropriate to this prophecy, especially as Grove is enabled to represent the swift development of the surreal science-fiction mill from virtual wilderness in three, even two generations. The foreshortening of the industrial revolution into such a short passage of time, and the isolation of technological development in the vast spaces of Canada, create a powerfully appropriate context which emphasizes the nightmare urgency of Grove's prophetic novel.

---

[1]Frederick Philip Grove, *Consider Her Ways* (Toronto: Macmillan, 1947), pp. 168-69. Subsequent references to this work (*CHW*) appear in the text.

[2]Frederick Philip Grove, *The Master of the Mill* (Toronto: Macmillan, 1944), p. 387. Subsequent references to this work (*MM*) appear in the text.

Paul Hjartarson

Of Greve, Grove, and Other Strangers: The Autobiography of the Baroness Elsa von Freytag-Loringhoven

In 1983 Lynn DeVore published an article on Djuna Barnes' *Nightwood* that is of considerable importance to the study of Frederick Philip Grove's writing. In the article, titled 'Backgrounds of *Nightwood*: Robin, Felix, and Nora,' DeVore argues that the novel developed out of and perhaps can best be understood in the context of Djuna Barnes' relationship with the titled Greenwich Village eccentric, Baroness Elsa von Freytag-Loringhoven, an artist's model, avant-garde poet, and painter, who was apparently a protégé and mistress of Marcel Duchamp and who so impressed William Carlos Williams that he devoted a chapter of his autobiography to her.[1] The Baroness wrote her own untitled and unpublished autobiography which, after Elsa's death in Paris in 1927, Barnes undertook to edit for publication. The autobiography never found its way into print but, according to DeVore, material from Barnes' various draft 'forewords,' and from the autobiography itself, entered into the composition of *Nightwood*, particularly into the characterization of Robin and Felix (79). Indeed, DeVore argues that the Baroness' autobiography 'serves as a reliable guide to Barnes' masterpiece, a voice that extends and amplifies the potential meanings of the novel' (89).

DeVore's conclusions are, I think, questionable. What cannot be questioned, however, and what makes the article of interest to Grove criticism, is that DeVore identifies Baroness Elsa von Freytag-Loringhoven as Elsa Ploetz, born in 1874 in the northern German town of Swinemünde—*the same Elsa Ploetz* who on August 22, 1901 married the Berlin architect, August Endell, and who one year later eloped with the translator and author, Felix Paul Greve. DeVore, in short, identifies Baroness Elsa von Freytag-Loringhoven as Frederick Philip Grove's German wife (81-83). What is more, DeVore reveals that in the unpublished autobiography the Baroness left her own account of their unusual relationship. That fascinating account offers another perspective on the European life of the enigmatic Felix

Paul Greve; moreover, it sheds light on his 'missing years,' that is, on the three years between Felix Paul Greve's 'suicide' in September 1909 and 'Fred Grove's' appearance in Winnipeg in December 1912. It does so, however, by introducing into the narrative of 'FPG's' life a figure no less fascinating and enigmatic than Greve himself, the woman known in New York's Greenwich Village as 'the Baroness.'

I

In *My Thirty Years' War: An Autobiography* Margaret Anderson, who with Jane Heap edited *The Little Review* (1914-29) first in Chicago, then in New York, and finally in Paris, describes Baroness Elsa von Freytag-Loringhoven as 'perhaps the only figure of our generation who deserves the epithet extraordinary'.[2] Certainly this Greenwich Village eccentric dressed and behaved in extraordinary ways, and it was her strange appearance and behaviour that caught and held most people's attention. She enters into a great many memoirs of Greenwich Village in the years immediately following the first world war but, as Andrew Field points out in his biography of Djuna Barnes, she enters those narratives primarily as anecdote and legend:

> Margaret Anderson did mention that the Baronin had hair the colour of a bay horse, but everyone else mentions only the times that she shaved and shellacked her head. That she wore postage stamps on her cheeks. . . . That she wore battered and worn metal tea immersion balls on her breasts as jewelry. That her hat collection at different times included a coal skuttle, a peach basket, a velvet tam-o'-shanter with feathers and spoons hanging from it, and once a cake, replete with lit candles. That she wore stuffed birds. That her lipstick was black, her face powder bright yellow, and [that] when her head was shaven, she sometimes painted her skull purple. She had a patchy old fur coat and a Mexican blanket and would regularly walk the streets of the Village from five to six with nothing else on, which occasioned a few wild forays with the police. It is said that she could throw a rather good punch and run well. Yet, in spite of such regular self-exposure, there is considerable confusion on the part of memoirs even about the basic contours of her body. One source has it that she had a lean masculine figure, while another claims that she possessed a perfect torso. Apart from her paraphernalia, scarcely anyone except those in

the close circle of *The Little Review* seems to have seen her at all.[3]

Most accounts of the Baroness focus on the paraphernalia, and on the 'good stories' her eccentric behaviour occasioned—whether she was attempting to seduce William Carlos Williams or simply to create a scene. Some of her contemporaries, such as William Carlos Williams, Hart Crane, and Wallace Stevens, feared her. (In his autobiography Williams reports that he bought a punching bag and trained to protect himself from her advances [169].) Others, however, showed grudging respect for the Baroness' genius, and some, like Margaret Anderson and Jane Heap at *The Little Review*, and later Djuna Barnes herself, championed her avant-garde work.

When Djuna Barnes and the Baroness first met is unknown. According to DeVore, 'their relationship began in approximately 1918 in America when Barnes was solidly entrenched in New York Art circles.'

> At that time Barnes was a freelance reporter for all the major New York newspapers; she was closely associated with the Alfred Stieglitz "291" group then moving beyond Imagism and greatly affecting her poetry and that of William Carlos Williams and Mina Loy; she acted in and wrote for Eugene O'Neill's Provincetown Theatre; and she was directly affiliated with Margaret Anderson and Jane Heap's *The Little Review*. She met Elsa at this time through the *Review*. Elsa, then forty-four, had come from Germany with Baron Loringhoven, who at the outbreak of war had returned home and soon committed suicide. Left alone, Elsa drifted among Greenwich Village groups. (74-75)

Anderson and Heap apparently became aware of Djuna Barnes' work shortly after they moved *The Little Review* to New York in the early months of 1917; Barnes first contribution to the *Review* was the short prose piece, 'Finale,' published in the June 1918 issue.

According to Anderson, the Baroness' first contribution, the poem 'Mefk Maru Mustir Daas' which appeared—along with a story and a poem by Barnes—in the December 1918 issue,[4] was one of only two unsolicited manuscripts *The Little Review* ever published (177). Anderson recounts that the Baroness submitted the poem under the name 'Tara Osrik' but later visited the *Review*'s office and wrote out her 'real name,' for Jane Heap. The first poem Elsa submitted, however, was not 'Mustir' but 'Love—Chemical Relationship,' which appeared in the June 1918 issue, the same number in which Djuna Barnes was first published. Anderson states that 'Mustir' was dedicated to Marcel Duchamps but no dedication appears in the review; it is possible, however, that she has confused that poem with 'Love-Chemical Relations,' which is in fact addressed to Duchamp.

In walking into *The Little Review* office, 'Baroness Elsa von Freytag von Loringhoven' entered the New York literary arts scene; little is know of her prior to that time. In *My Thirty Years' War* Anderson summarizes in a paragraph what she knows, and what was known in Greenwich Village circles, of the Baroness' past life:

> She had come to New York to the Ritz with the late Baron von Loringhoven, who hurried back to Germany at the outbreak of the war and then, not liking war, shot himself—an act which his wife characterized as the bravest of his life. After the Ritz The Baroness drifted from one adventure to another. Tired of conventional living, she became an artist's model. Tired of conventional dress, she began creating costumes which resulted in her arrest whenever she appeared upon the streets. Tired of official restraint, she leaped from patrol wagons with such agility that policemen let her go in admiration. Finally, tired of not eating, she found work in a cigarette factory where she provoked such wrath that one of her co-workers in a rage reminiscent of Bizet knocked out two of her teeth. Oddly enough this did not detract from her distinction. (179)

When she submitted her first poem to the *Review*, she 'lived in a tenement of two rooms with three dogs' (179) and provided for herself by 'posing as a life model for artists such as Glackens, Henri, Bellows, and Genthe, many of whom rendered her in non-representational fashion' (Field, 82). In short, she seems to have gravitated toward the kind of artists' circle in which Greve's Fanny Essler moves as a young woman and to have made the transition from resident of the Ritz to a condition approaching that of a 'bag lady' in just four years. If the Baron left her any money when he returned to Germany in 1914, it could not have lasted her very long.

By all accounts, Djuna and Elsa did not get along very well when they first met. 'I cannot read your stories, Djuna Barnes,' Margaret Anderson reports the Baroness as saying, 'I don't know where your characters come from. You make them fly on magic carpets—what is worse, you try to make pigs fly' (182). Given such comments and the difference in their personalities—Barnes was as withdrawn and as taciturn as the Baroness was outspoken and given to creating scenes—it is a wonder they got along at all. According to Anderson, 'Barnes didn't appreciate the Baroness at first' but later gave her work 'grudging admiration' (182). The relationship may indeed have blossomed only later, in their correspondence, when after returning to Germany, Elsa wrote her Greenwich Village friends pleading for money and moral support.

DeVore states that 'Elsa, like Barnes, was in Europe after 1918 trying to establish herself as a literary artist by publishing in little magazines' (76). But that seems unlikely. By all accounts she was destitute when the Armistice ended the first world war and made travel in Europe feasible once more. When she returned to Europe in 1923, homesick for her native Pomerania, her passage was paid by friends and acquaintances, including Williams who states in his autobiography that he 'gave her two hundred dollars to get out of the country' (169). Elsa, however, was not only destitute but without citizenship papers. According to Barnes, when the Baroness boarded the *S.S. Yorck* in April 1923, she was without either money or papers—her only possession, her one remaining dog. Once in Germany, without either money or citizenship papers, she was trapped; she was, in her own words, 'captive in dead Germany' (DeVore, 78).

From Germany she wrote her friends—Djuna Barnes had herself moved to Paris—pleading for assistance; she needed money and she needed help in obtaining a permit to leave the country. 'I am in the hands of "charity," ' she writes to Djuna Barnes in a letter subsequently published in *transition* as part of a commemoration of her life, 'and must be "thankful" for it.'

> I cannot describe it. I am just out of the hospital. We must look the monster in the face that is my life [sic]. I am badgered about as if I had been a culprit, having been robbed, bearing the empty title of that poor dead, swindling miserable suicide, my last husband.[5]

Although others helped, Djuna herself became the mainstay of Elsa's life in Germany, and later, in her final days in Paris. Although Barnes was entering the formative stages of her own career, and was busy and frequently on the move, she kept up a steady correspondence with Elsa, providing her with money, and no less importantly, with moral support. According to Anderson, 'when everyone else,

worn out with her, felt resourceless before the havoc that her mere
existence caused, Djuna's maternity came to the rescue and sustained
the Baroness' (182).

At some point Djuna asked Elsa for details about her life—
apparently with the idea of making the Baroness' plight known and
thereby possibly securing her release. (The Baroness was finally
granted a permit to live in Paris in 1926.) In Germany Elsa herself had
found temporary refuge in, or had been consigned to, a Christian
home for the destitute in Potsdam that seems to have combined the
operations of a poor house with that of an insane asylum; and from
there she began recounting the story of her life to Djuna, whom she
regards as her one remaining friend. Thus began the autobiography
Lynn DeVore describes as 'perhaps the most stunning, unusual
record to have emerged from the 1920s' (78).

II

The Baroness' autobiography is part of the Elsa von Freytag-
Loringhoven Collection, itself part of the larger Djuna Barnes
Collection, held by the University of Maryland Archives at its College
Park campus. The Baroness' letters and manuscripts, both poems
and the autobiography, were among the many boxes of papers Djuna
Barnes deposited with the Archives in 1970. (Fields states in his biography of Barnes that she was the Baroness' literary executor [15].)
The autobiography itself survives in at least two different stages of
composition. It exists, first, as fragments in the many and volumi-
nous letters Elsa wrote Djuna Barnes from Germany. At some point,
however, Elsa stopped simply recounting events in her letters and
began writing the autobiography itself. This second stage is
represented by a holograph of the autobiography which Elsa
apparently wrote and mailed to Djuna in instalments.[6]

In the autobiography Elsa states that the doctors at the home for
the destitute in Potsdam permit her to write—and provide her with
the necessary supplies?—only because of her name and station (3.14).
(One wonders whether the doctors did not also view the writing as
therapy.) In a note to a 'Frau Doctor Simsa' at the end of one part,
Elsa complains that it is difficult to write in the 'home' because she
cannot escape either the idiotic or the pious talk, because she lacks
not only privacy but light, and because her room is freezing cold; she
also states that she has had to rewrite the whole section because she
has difficulty expressing herself (3.41). DeVore states that Djuna
Barnes typed a draft of the autobiography from Elsa's 'wildly

scribbled original version' (79) but the holograph, unlike many of the letters, is, for the most part, clearly legible. (What is more, it is for the most part beautifully written; her English is idiosyncratic but energetic, forceful and clear—a perfect vehicle for her unusual personality.) The autobiography, of course, also exists in the 205-page typescript Djuna Barnes made from the holograph when she began editing it for publication.

Although Elsa's autobiography covers the years from her birth in Swinemünde in 1874 until approximately 1904, it focuses on her adult life, particularly on her relationship with Felix Paul Greve. The autobiography is very much a narrative of adult sexual relations, of what now might be understood as 'sexual politics,' and Elsa describes her ten years with Greve as the most intense and the longest lasting of her many relationships. As DeVore observes, the Baroness reveals 'frankly and without any embarrassment' (78) the intimate details of her life. It is, at once, both a very shocking and a profoundly moving story—one that easily confirms Margaret Anderson's perception of the Baroness as an 'extraordinary' person.

Elsa centers her autobiography on the period between her first meeting with Greve in 1902 and her reunion with him following his release from prison in 1904, but in narrating the events of this two-year period she recounts incidents both from her childhood and from her later life with Greve in America. It is impossible, however, to understand the narrative of her *past* loves apart from her *present* life; the essence of Elsa's autobiography lies, as Roy Pascal argues it does in all autobiography, in the 'interplay'—he also terms it a 'collusion'—between the events of the autobiographer's previous life and the particular viewpoint from which he reviews and interpret them.[7] We are seldom permitted in Elsa's autobiography to forget the NOW of her narrative; we move repeatedly between the THEN and the NOW, between Elsa's passionate account of a past full of life and lovers and her tearful rebellion against her present condition, an existence bereft of lovers, friends, art, indeed, any of the pleasures she cherishes. At times, she rebels against the autobiographical act itself, proclaiming that she wants to *forget* the past she writes down, asserting that she should find lovers here and now. Aware at one point that she has strayed from her narrative of past events, she declares that her present self belongs in her autobiography, and that when she writes of past events her present self rebels against and becomes jealous of the '*other*.'

She dispenses with her childhood in Swinemünde in the opening pages, moving rapidly over her mother's mental illness and death, her father's decision to remarry, her hatred of her stepmother and her own decision, at age eighteen, to leave home. She characterizes her father, a mastermason, as alternately violent-tempered and tearfully sentimental; her mother, who wanted to be a musician and whom, Elsa says, married beneath herself, as cultured and sensitive. The narrative will be familiar to readers of *Fanny Essler* and *Maurer-meister Ihles Haus* and confirms Marcus Behmer's identification of Elsa as the model for Fanny Essler; indeed, in the autobiography Elsa herself asserts that her life provided the 'material' for both of Greve's novels (2.2).[8]

Some of the 'material,' however, Greve did not use. In the autobiography, we learn, for example, that Elsa's mother died from syphilis which she contracted from her husband on their wedding night and for which she was, Elsa states, too embarrassed to seek treatment. Elsa herself had secondary syphilis which manifested itself early in her adult life and for which she was repeatedly in need of treatment. (According to William Carlos Williams, the Baroness once advised him that what he needed to make himself great was 'to contract syphilis from her and thus free [his] mind for serious art' [165].)

Her early life in Berlin is very much like Fanny's. She lives with a maiden aunt who is scandalized by her conduct with men and who eventually kicks her out; she works for a time as a 'chorus girl' and sleeps with men but she is too shy to ask for money and never finds anyone willing to support her; and she eventually meets and has affairs with a number of artists. While in Italy with 'Richard'—called 'Stumpf' in *Fanny Essler*—she receives a small legacy from her mother's estate and moves to Munich to study art. There she renews her acquaintance with August Endell and, like Fanny, she is the one who proposes marriage. She meets Greve sometime after her marriage to Endell in August 1901. (She meets him, as she had earlier met August, at a gathering in Munich at the home of 'Dr. Phil,' whom she elsewhere identifies as the poet, Karl Wolfskehl.)

She does not marry Endell out of love or sexual attraction but, the older Elsa realizes in retrospect, out of a desire to try the 'famed state' of matrimony. August, however, proves impotent—parents, she remarks, have no conscience in naming their children—and his impotence almost immediately causes problems. She confesses to having a strong sexual drive—she describes herself at eighteen as 'mensick'—and refers to her 'sex psychology' and to the 'sex logic' implanted in her; marriage, unfortunately, stimulates that drive without ever satisfying it. In desperation, her husband sends her to a North Sea sanitorium to have her womb 'massaged.'

There at the dinner table Elsa finds herself talking incessantly about the splendid 'Mr. Felix,' whom she initially hates because of his stunning manner and his impeccable dress but with whom, she begins to realize, she is madly in love. Elsa describes him as over six feet tall and elegant, with misty blue eyes, blond hair, and a 'severe saucy nose' (2.9). Although she admits to herself that she loves 'Mr. Felix,' she declares that she has no intention of acting on that love. She is not about to leave her husband; the younger Elsa is, the older narrator declares, too conventional to contemplate that. What is more, she believes that the cultured 'Mr. Felix,' whom she thinks is a millionaire, is out of reach, and her husband, who on her return from the sanitorium is forced to agree that she can take lovers, reinforces her feeling that the situation is hopeless.

While she is in the sanitorium, Felix, who is keeping her husband company in Berlin, sends her a copy of his newly released translation of Oscar Wilde's *Bunbury*. (At this point in their relationship she believes that Felix translates more for pleasure than for money, and declares that he started the first Wilde craze in Germany.) Thus begin the series of events that result in Elsa's seduction of the younger and relatively inexperienced Greve. With him she first experiences sexual satisfaction; he becomes, for a time, her 'sexsun.'

Their relationship, however, ultimately repeats the pattern of virtually all Elsa's loves. She seems initially to idolize the men to whom she is attracted. In one instance, after reading Knut Hamsun's novel, *Mysteries* (1892) and being very much taken by the character of Nagel, she decides that a stranger she subsequently meets in a hotel lobby is the embodiment of Nagel, whom the older Elsa describes as the younger woman's 'idol of the present.' In this case, as in all the others, including that of 'Mr. Felix,' the story of the relationship is a narrative of growing disillusionment. Felix is initially her 'half-god'; in the end, however, she realizes that he has 'earthen' feet. What makes her affair with Greve different is that, looking back on the relationship twenty years later, she still loves as well as hates the man. (She declares at one point that he owes her 'repenting damages' for what he has done.)

When Felix and Elsa inform her husband of their love, he is devastated and cries. They make plans to travel in Italy together, and Felix, out of pity, Elsa says, agrees to let August accompany them. What is more, *he* lends Endell the money both for a new 'outfit'— August has apparently taken to imitating Felix's English dress—and for travel expenses. If Elsa's version of events is correct, then the newspaper account of Felix's trial, which D.O. Spettigue cites in

FPG: The European Years is wrong, for in that account Greve is alleged to have borrowed that money, 200 M, from Endell.[9] But, then, in that account, Endell does not accompany the lovers to Rome and Palermo.

According to Elsa, prior to Felix's imprisonment August had reluctantly agreed to be named as the 'guilty' part in a divorce on the understanding that Elsa would not press him for alimony. However, when Felix writes August from prison requesting early repayment of the money the architect owes him so that Elsa will have some money on which to live, Endell agreed to repay that money on the condition that *his wife* consent to be named as the guilty party. Elsa states that when the divorce documents arrive for her signature, she does not at first recognize that the case referred to is hers, so much has Endell altered events to disguise his role in the affair. Presumably, August's narrative has *Felix* borrowing money from him and not the reverse. The older woman states that her younger self signed the documents in disgust—and against Felix's advice—to obtain the money (3.40-41). Interestingly, the newspaper account cited in *FPG: The European Years* states that Greve's best friend and fellow student, Herman Kilian, feeling responsible for his friend's conduct, paid Endell the 200 M Felix has reportedly borrowed from him!

One of the questions Spettigue leaves unanswered in *FPG: The European Years*, and which remained unanswered at Felix's trial, was what he did with the 10,000 M he borrowed from his friend, Kilian (97). Elsa indirectly suggests an answer in her autobiography, though the answer she supplies is all but incredible. Very early in their relationship, she states, Felix told her that while he was in Munich he had fallen helplessly in love with a woman who begged him for money to repay 10,000 M her brother had embezzled. He obtains the money for her and then proposes to her. She agrees to travel with him in Italy and to think over his proposal but she finally decides against either marrying him or parting with her virginity. Felix is subsequently accused of ruining the woman's reputation by travelling with her and so leaves Munich for Berlin. (Elsa subsequently refers to this as Felix's story of the 'travelling virgin.') If this incredible story is to be believed—and over the ten years Elsa spent with Felix she learned to believe less and less—then Felix went to prison for money he borrowed for someone else!

The central event in Elsa's autobiography is undoubtedly Felix's sudden return from Palermo to Bonn where he is arrested as he steps from the train. When he leaves Palermo, Felix tells Elsa only that he has to return to Bonn for a week because he has a sizeable investment in a failing bank. (To the extent that Kilian *was* the source of Felix's money, his bank *was* failing.) She hears nothing from him for a week and, at last, wires 'Mr. Kilian.' He wires her, the older Elsa remarks, in the prose of a perfect gentleman, that Felix has been arrested for fraud. She then receives a letter from Felix in which he informs her that Kilian himself had laid the charge and that he had wired Felix about a failing investing to lure him back to Germany for the arrest.

For the first time in her relationship with Felix, Elsa seriously doubts him and thus she begins to unravel the series of lies he has told her. (She begins to question, among other things, the story of the travelling virgin.) Although she has in the past, she states, occasionally doubted Felix's wealth, she has not wanted to inquire for fear of embarrassing him. Now she feels justified in reading his correspondence. In Kilian's letters she finds evidence of what she regards as his latent homosexual love for Felix. (A physical love she feels is, on Felix's side at least, impossible.) Kilian, she conjectures, had his friend arrested not because of the money but because of her— because she has come between the two men. The older woman states that finally her younger self turned her face away from this 'mysterious' affair because she does not know what to make of it, though she considers the arrest grossly unfair to Felix. Kilian has not acted like a gentleman: he should, she insists, have first given his friend an opportunity to repay the money. His action in having Felix arrested, she declares, looks to her like the vengeance of a woman who feels herself wronged (3.10).

Although Elsa places much of the blame for the catastrophe on Kilian's shoulders, and although she is too much in love with Felix either to confront him or to give him up, she finds that she can no longer trust anything he has told her about himself. As one example of Felix's 'liecraft,' she tells the story about his broken kneecaps; she is forced to realize that it is a fabric of lies when she tells it to a young doctor in Palermo who is courting her. Felix apparently told her that he broke both kneecaps in a bicycle accident. Racing down a steep hill he lost control of the bicycle and landed on railway tracks, breaking not only his kneecaps but his collar bone. I've forgotten, the older woman states, whether or not he says he fainted; it would depend on whether he wanted me to sympathize with or to admire him while I was in agony with him over the oncoming train. Felix cannot remove himself from the tracks; the train comes ever nearer; the rumbling of it increases. Prostrate on the tracks, he thinks of nothing but the oncoming train, the older woman remembers him saying, as her younger self sits listening breathlessly, her heart pounding. At the last minute, by a desperate twist of his perfect muscles, he flips himself off the tracks and out of danger. The skeptical doctor, who is courting her, doubts the story and the muscle strength it supposedly demonstrates. As proof of the story's authenticity, Elsa informs the skeptic that Felix has shown her how his kneecaps move freely on his knee. The doctor, of course, proceeds to demonstrate that both his kneecaps and her's have the same ability to move; and she is forced to recognize Felix's 'liecraft.'

After Felix's arrest, August offers to take Elsa back. She scorns that offer. Sitting in the Potsdam home, the older Elsa laments the younger woman's inability to do the expedient and practical thing. As a result, the older woman complains, she sits in the poor house while August lives in comfort as a university professor in Breslau. 'I would not have been I,' she states, however, in words strangely reminiscent of the later Frederick Philip Grove, had I acted in any other way. Instead of returning to Berlin with her husband, she chooses to proceed with the divorce and to wait in Italy for Felix's release from prison. There, out of boredom and the desire to find someone who will support her while Felix is in prison, she has several affairs. (Flirting with men, she says, is the only occupation she ever learned.) The second half of the autobiography is taken up with her account of these affairs, an account she offers to explain her personality, particularly what she calls her 'sexpsychology.' She seems forever attracted to men who either take little interest in sex or who turn out to be homosexuals. (In Rome in the months immediately preceding Felix's release from prison, she is attracted to a man who turns out to be both a homosexual and a priest.)

The narrative ends or, rather, breaks off, when Elsa bids a tearful farewell to her Roman friend and returns to Bonn to wait for Felix in a taxi at the prison gate. However, in the older woman's frequent digressions and interjections throughout the autobiography, we learn something both of their reunion and of their subsequent life together. We learn much less than we want to know, but then, as Elsa herself observes at one point in her autobiography, this is *her* life story and not Felix's.

In Italy, Elsa resolves that when Felix is released from prison she will tell him of her affairs and 'take his decision.' She also recognizes the need to confront him about his lies. The confrontation comes on the day he is released after 'his first swell supper in freedom' with her. When she asks him why he lied, he declares simply that she was a 'tempting victim.' The older Elsa wonders why Felix responds in that way, why he did not simply continue to lie. She declares that she would have preferred it that way and would have believed him if he *had* lied. She did not, she declares, want to see his 'earthen' feet. But, of course, she has weapons of her own with which to fight back. She tells him of her affairs, and though he is hurt, he 'forgives' her. Sitting in the Potsdam home, the older woman, however, suspects that he never truly forgave her, and that he simply clung to her because after his term in jail he had no other friends (3.22). She affirms nevertheless that they were passionately tied at the time and that neither one really wanted to know the truth about the other.

The most important years in their relationship, as in Greve's career, are those following Felix's release from prison and about them we know very little. About their travels, about Felix's work as a translator, about his meetings with Gide, about the composition and publication of both *Fanny Essler* and *Maurermeister Ihles Haus* we learn next to nothing; we learn simply that Felix's career as a translator flourishes and that they both have high hopes for *Maurermeister Ihles Haus*, hopes that are not realized. We learn only what Elsa wants to tell us and she is concerned with the gradual deterioration of their relationship. The glimpses she gives us of their later life will not be entirely foreign to readers of *Fanny Essler* for that life resembles the working out of Fanny's relation with Reelen.

Felix, she says, gives her all the luxuries he can afford, and very often more. But he grows increasingly ashamed of what he calls her 'unladylike' conduct and instructs her in how she is to dress, wear her hair, etc. (The model for such conduct is apparently Felix's mother.) What is more, he frowns on any public display of emotion between them; that, according to Elsa, is the 'parole' of 'high class life.' And she wants none of it. He grows jealous of the sexual attractions she radiates and seeks increasingly to control her behaviour. What once attracted him, she declares, now has to be 'leashed for his service.' What bothers her most, however, is that, like Reelen in *Fanny Essler*, he grows increasingly colder toward her, never dropping his mask of rationality, never expressing his emotions if he can prevent it, and hence never giving her the love she so desperately needs.[10] She had sensed, the older woman states, a 'mechanistic,' distance quality to his lovemaking from the start, but it becomes in the years following his release from prison, she asserts, the dominant trait of his character. She rebels and they fight, she forcing him to admit his jealousy, he wanting her to make some concession to what others think. They fight until they both shake 'with raging lovehate—up to the killing point' (3.26) and then they become lovers again.

In the Baroness' eyes, Felix becomes what she despises— conventional. Because of what she describes as Felix's 'narrow jailor attitude,' they are increasingly thrown on each other's company. Felix acts as though he were her master but she increasingly recognizes that he is in reality her slave, and she wonders why he fails to recognize his own power over her. She describes their relationship as a 'glorious castle' built 'with so much blood, passion and honest will,' a castle built to last but which slowly begins to crumble until finally in America it collapses (3.27).

They make the decision to move to America, Elsa states, because of Felix's growing disgust at his inability to earn enough money as a translator, because of his unhappiness at his editors' failure to appreciate his work, and because of his dismay at the public's neglect of his original works in favour of his translations. The main reason, though, as Spettigue conjectured in *FPG: The European Years*, seems to have been money; it was never enough for Felix, Elsa remarks, and it never promised 'the big possibilities of "business" ' (2.1). So 'he broke off—or down—his career' and decides to become, of all things, a 'potatoking' in America. Elsa says nothing either about their preparations or their travel plans other than that Felix arrived in the States 'via Canada' (2.1); however, the implication is clearly that Elsa was a party to the 'suicide' and subsequently joined Felix in the States.

They settled, Elsa remarks in passing, 'in the midst of the county of Kentucky in the small farmcountry' (2.3) a comment that brings to mind Spettigue's attempts, reported both in *Frederick Philip Grove* (43-44) and in *FPG: The European Years* (174) to substantiate Catherine Grove's assertions that her husband had taught in Kentucky and had owned land there. Elsa's comments, however, are probably too vague to result in any new discoveries. She states simply that once in America Felix became absorbed in the 'primitive struggle for life' and ceased having sexual intercourse with her. Neither Felix nor Elsa would be, one suspects, well suited to farming life—assuming farming was what they were engaged in—but Elsa would clearly seem to be the less suited of the two. He complains that she fails to support him 'in the hardest struggle of his life'; she wants to know whether he thinks sexual intercourse is a luxury restricted to cultured people with leisure time (2.32). A year after their arrival, she asserts, he abandons her—and presumably the farm—leaving her 'helpless in this strange country.'

How she survived we do not know. Amongst the notes Djuna Barnes made while preparing the autobiography for publication is one in which she writes that the Baron was Elsa's third husband and that after she was abandoned, Elsa lived somewhere in Kentucky or Virginia in a tent with negros who were without shoes and that she made her way to Cincinnati where she began posing. Since the Baron left her in New York, the notes presumably refer to Elsa's abandonment by Felix. Whether the notes are based on Greenwich Village rumour or on Elsa's own statements, we cannot tell. Apparently she made her way from Cincinnati to New York and from there back to Germany. In Germany she met and married Baron Freiherr von Freytag von Loringhoven in 1913 with whom she returned to New York prior to the outbreak of war.

III

The account I have given here does not do justice either to Elsa herself or to the fascinating narrative she has left. Baroness Elsa von Freytag-Loringhoven is a literary figure in her own right and her autobiography would merit study even if she had never met Felix Paul Greve. (DeVore studies it solely in relation to *Nightwood* and argues—questionably, I think—that Felix in the novel is based on Felix Paul Greve, and Robin, on Elsa.) For readers of Grove's texts, the Baroness' autobiography is a source of new biographical information; however, it leaves a great many things unsaid and raises as many, if not more questions, than it answers. It offers glimpses into Greve's life in America but leaves us wanting more. Did Greve farm in the States? Where? In Kentucky? (There is no 'county of Kentucky' in the state of Kentucky.) Did he 'ride the rails' *after* he abandoned her or are the experiences recounted in *A Search for America* entirely imaginary? Who, we are forced to ask again, is the woman in Arkansas Frederick Philip Grove refers to in his February 10, 1914 letter to Issak Warkentin? In addition, the autobiography suggests possible new readings of Grove's novels. What are we, for example, to make of Reelen, 'the Prince—HE,'—not to mention his creator—in the light of Elsa's narrative? How might we now understand Clara Vogel and Ellen Amundsen in *Settlers of the Marsh*? Is *Settlers of the Marsh*, in part, a textualizing of Felix's life with Elsa in America? Such questions will continue to tease many of Grove's critics for years to come—and to infuriate those who want attention focused solely on the texts. Our attention, however, keeps being diverted by new discoveries—discoveries that change the context in which we read Grove's texts. For Felix Paul Greve life was a text he kept revising and we, his readers, keep encountering new versions of the stories he lived and wrote.

[1] DeVore's article appeared in the *Journal of Modern Literature*, 10 (1983), 71-90; Williams tells the story of his encounters with the Baroness in chapter 28 of *The Autobiography of William Carlos Williams* (New York: Random House, 1948), 163-69.

[2] *My Thirty Year's War: An Autobiography* (New York: Covici, 1930), 177.

[3] *Djuna: The Formidable Miss Barnes* (1983; rpt. Austin: Univ. of Texas Press, 1985), 80.

[4] *The Little Review*, 5 (December 1918), 41. 'Love—Chemical Relations' appeared in volume 5 (June 1918), 58-59.

[5] *transition*, 11 (February 1928), 21.

[6] All references to the autobiography are to the holograph contained in the Elsa von Freytag-Loringhoven Collection, Box 1. (The folders are unnumbered.) Because each part of the manuscript is paginated separately, I have identified passages by both part and page number: the first number within the parentheses indicates the part; the second (following the period), the page number. I should like to thank the staff in the Special Collections Division of the McKeldin Library at the University of Maryland, College Park—especially Blanche T. Ebeling-Koning, the Curator for Rare Books and Literary Manuscripts there—for assisting me in my research.

[7] *Design and Truth in Autobiography* (Cambridge: Harvard Univ. Press, 1960), 10-12.

[8] The letter is cited by D.O. Spettigue in his article, 'Fanny and the Master,' published in this volume.

[9] *FPG: The European Years* (Ottawa: Oberon, 1973), 95-96.

[10] D.O. Spettigue and A.W. Riley, Introduction, *Fanny Essler*, trans. Christine Helmers, D.O. Spettigue and A.W. Riley (Ottawa: Oberon Press, 1984), 10.

*In the summer of 1942, at the age of sixty-three, Grove accepted work
as a manual labourer in a canning factory near Simcoe. In* Frederick
Philip Grove *(1969) Douglas Spettigue records Catherine Grove's
view that her husband took the job 'out of bravado . . . to show what
he had been reduced to.' Spettigue himself conjectures that Grove
took the work 'to provide experience for "The Seasons" ' (76), a book
on which he had been working for several years and which he himself
described as a 'panoramic novel of Canadian life, with town, city, and
open countryside' (L, 386). Whatever Grove's motives, ten weeks into
the job he 'was disabled by an accident which,' according to his own
account, 'permanently injured his right elbow' (L, 438; cf. 421).
Grove never did complete 'The Seasons'; he did, however, complete
another text, 'Postscript to* A Search for America,' *a personal essay in
which, as in both 'In Search of Myself' and* In Search of Myself, *Grove
rewrites his life's story. In his postscript to the earlier text, the
narrator in effect ends his 'search for America' in the following
exchange, at the cannery, with another elderly worker, an Oxford
graduate. 'How did you get here,' the novelist asks his fellow worker.
The other man 'drew up his eyebrows and, after a momentary
hesitation, said a single word, "Drink!" Next he smiled and asked,
"And you?" "Literature," I replied.' Thus does Felix Paul Greve,
alias Frederick Philip Grove, dramatize his fate as a writer in this
country.*

Frederick Philip Grove
Postscript to A Search for America

A few years ago *A Search for America* was placed on the
curriculum in English of the University of Toronto. The examiner
who read the papers set on this course told me that the most frequent
criticism levelled against the book by candidates was the
'incredibility' of a man of the author's supposed knowledge and
culture not finding some position befitting his attainments. The
book records that this rather highly-educated young man became
successively a waiter in a cheap eating-house, a book-agent, a farmhand, a factory worker. It omitted a good many of the more gruelling
experiences the author went through in the twenty years during
which he never succeeded in raising himself above the status of a
labourer, in spite of the fact, or perhaps because of it, that in the
meantime he wrote a number of books which in later years proved

successful, *A Search for America* among them. It did not mention, either, that twenty years had gone by before he entered the teaching profession. Nor did it mention how he began to publish his books while still teaching; how an accident forced him to give up his teaching career till he was 'over-age' for that occupation; how he farmed till increasing years drove him into retirement; nor how his books failed to supply him with the necessities of life.

Another thirty years have since gone down the stream; and it may interest some of my young critics to hear that, after fifty years on this continent, during which he wrote and published the dozen books or so which have earned him what reputation he enjoys as a Canadian writer, he had, in order to make his daily bread, at last to return to the status of a labourer with which he began his life in America. When that happened he was seventy years old.

On the last day of June of the current year, having at long last secured a job, I entered a canning-factory in the southwest of Ontario. The opening of which I took advantage came with the beginning of the rush in the pea harvest. I was engaged to remove empty boxes as the truck-loads from the threshing-fields brought the full ones in—a humble job. Two or three, rarely four men were employed in unloading them from the trucks; one man, I, was employed to remove the 'empties.'

Just a word about the lay-out of the work.

At the end of a long, narrow platform running along the outside of the building and communicating with its inside through two open windows, there is a hopper capable of holding between 500 and 600 pounds of peas. At its bottom this hopper opens upon a revolving drum with large grooves so spaced that each deposits its small load into one of the 'pea-buckets' which follow one another at given intervals, slung to two roller-chains which run from the ground up to, and through, a window on the top floor of the factory. These pea-buckets swing freely, so that gravity holds them upright. The whole arrangement is, in the factory, called the 'boot'; since the endless chains, descending on the outside, and ascending next to the building, run straight up till they reach the top window, where they bend over, running on cog-wheels, and enter through it, the rough outline of the whole arrangement may, with some help from the imagination, be compared to that of an inverted boot. Upstairs, and inside, this conveyor system passes over a second hopper where each of the buckets—a poor name, since they have the form of half cylinders—is tilted to discharge its load.

It is the task of the men below who unload the trucks to keep the hopper at the end of the platform filled. The hopper discharges into

the 'pea-buckets' about one forty-pound boxful of peas every five
seconds, so that about every five seconds a box full of peas has to be
discharged into it. At this rate it takes forty minutes to unload a 500-
box truckload directly into the hopper. But when the work in the
threshing-fields, between eleven and twenty miles away, runs
smoothly, this rate of discharge is too slow. Consequently, if there are
more than two men available for unloading—two are all that are
needed to keep the hopper filled—the extra man or men simultaneously unload on the platform, stacking the full boxes, to be
discharged into the hopper during a slack period, for it happens
sometimes that no new truck has arrived from the threshing-fields
when the old one is despatched. This involves double handling; and
when the platform is filled to the height of about seven feet, the
remainder of the load—if there is hurry; and there usually is—must
be unloaded on the ground. This requires triple handling, for the
boxes have to be handed down, handed up again, and then dumped.
Generally speaking, this process of unloading the trucks is, on that
account, extraordinarily inefficient.

There are other factors which contribute to that result. Thus the
floor inside the building, where the 'empties' have to be handled, is at
a different level from that of the platform. If the man removing the
empties does not happen to be on the spot—under certain
circumstances he has to take fifty or more steps to get rid of them and
to come back—the empty boxes have simply to be dropped through
the window, with much damage to the boxes. This is against orders,
but it cannot be helped, for the hopper has to be kept filled, and the
men have no time to be careful.

It will be seen that, inevitably, the machine sets the pace. In that, it
comes into conflict with human nature. Most of the men employed
are lusty young fellows who, at least before noon, have plenty of
energy to spare for fooling and horseplay. It usually begins with the
throwing of handfuls of peas into each other's faces, or stuffing them
into open shirt-fronts. The next moment there is a tangle of wrestling
and writhing bodies, while the yard resounds with shouts and
laughter. A few seconds later a warning call rings out, coming from
myself, 'Peas, boys, peas!' For the hopper is rapidly running down;
and, should it run empty, the break in the work would be discovered
upstairs by foreman or superintendent. Now the boxes begin to fly
through the air; nobody carries them over; everybody throws them; to
the distress of the man who handles the empties, for he cannot keep
up with the deluge. Yet he does not resent it, for the mere sight of
young human flesh in play has something refreshing in this
atmosphere of unremitting toil; and if, for the moment, his work

becomes frantic, he laughs with the rest. Yet, when the boxes come flying there is a great deal of waste, for the peas spill in all directions like water splashing.

The work is both seasonal and intermittent. The summer's pea-rush lasted, this year, for three weeks and a day; and then there follows a lay-off of several weeks till tomatoes begin to come in. What made this particularly annoying was the fact that even within the rush there were breaks; one day it rained, and threshing stopped; another day the harvest in a given field was finished in the middle of the afternoon, and the machines had to be moved. At once the superintendent appeared and sang out, 'That's all for to-day; report tomorrow morning at seven.' And all those who were not engaged as steady hands working all year—and the latter were a mere handful—'punched out.' In my own case this happened once, on a Saturday afternoon, within half-an-hour of my arrival. It had cost me about thirty-cents to come in; my wages for that half-hour amounted to seventeen-and-a-half cents.

A few words about the regulations governing payment. Most hands arrived several minutes ahead of time. If they are a quarter-minute late, the penalty is a quarter-hour's pay. I, having to go three-and-a-half miles to get to the factory, usually arrived at least ten minutes ahead; I had to consider the possibility of unexpected delays. Now the rule is that nobody is paid for work done before the bell rings. On the other hand, there might be a load in when quitting-time came, at twelve noon, or at six p.m. In that case we were required to go on with the work that had been begun till it was finished. It is true that, if a truck arrived a few minutes before the bell, we usually managed not to start the work, under some pretext or other; the reason being that again there was no pay unless overtime amounted to at least a quarter-hour; twenty or twenty-five, even twenty-nine, minutes counted as fifteen; and consequently there was at such times an inhuman rush. There was no time-and-a-half pay for over-time; only straight time counted. It was not uncommon for the work to go on till midnight; once it went on till just after three, and once till a quarter-past-four in the morning. The next day one of the lustiest young fellows who, by the way, had to go six miles to reach his bed was much subdued. 'Not feeling well Frank?' I asked. 'Tough,' he said; 'tough!' Yet this man, who is paying for a small farm, arrived next morning at eight o'clock, or slightly ahead of the hour. Like myself, he was one of the boys who cannot loaf away the few extra minutes when work was waiting that had to be done in a hurry.

That is one of the surprising things. Nearly everybody worked as if he were attending to his own personal tasks which did not admit of his shirking. On the other hand, everybody, of course, was willing to take advantage of a lull, such as arose between loads. Or an extra man momentarily out of a job appeared and took the place of one of the men working with me, and even my own place.

Another remarkable thing was that the vast majority of the men showed themselves not only decent but kind and considerate—a thing I had not expected. This showed itself in such trifles as their way of speaking to me. All but one man invariably called me 'Mr. Grove'—or 'Professor Grove'—whereas everybody else was called by his first name. Nobody except the superintendent, who is constitutionally unable to look on when anyone is not working at top speed, ever asked me to do a job beyond my powers or one which involved a disagreeable task. The men invariably tried—not always succeeding—to place the empty boxes in such a way that they were easy to pick up. One box was placed on the edge of the hopper, in a precarious equilibrium; a second box was upended into it; and a third box was inverted over the second. By that time I was usually back to receive this nest and to dispose of it. When there was room to stack these empties in the immediate neighbourhood of the window through which I had to reach for them, this gave me a welcome succession of moments of leisure which lasted perhaps from fifteen to twenty seconds. But that was rare except immediately after a truck reloaded with empties had left. Naturally, when it came to loading empties—which had to be done past the man or men who dumped the 'fulls'—one took those nearest to hand at the window. This was the hardest part of the work because it was always done in a great hurry; the driver of the truck was anxious to get back to the threshing-field. As a rule a chain of two, three or four men formed to handle the empties till the truck was filled to capacity. On one occasion, no spare hands being available, two of the bosses jumped in, the superintendent and the assistant manager. Things hummed. One of the men who usually worked next to myself, said afterwards, 'They come here for a few minutes and act as if they wanted to show us what work is; and then they go to their offices to rest.'

It occurred to me that it would not be a bad thing if once in a while, if only for a single day, all managers had to do the work of the men—not for a few minutes, but for ten or fourteen hours. They would learn how the men feel. The trouble with such an arrangement would be that it could not be reversed; the men could not take the places of the managers in order to receive similar enlightenment; they would lack the knowledge required.

Mostly, when a truck arrived to be unloaded, a foreman appeared, with the obvious intention of seeing to it that no time was wasted.

This was entirely unnecessary; but from my point of view, that of the observer, it was instructive. It served to differentiate between the attitudes of the men. Some, a very few, ostentatiously speeded up under the eye of authority; by far the majority paid no attention whatever and went on in their even, efficient way; a few defiantly relaxed their efforts rather, even going so far as to do the forbidden thing, such as lighting a cigarette, right under the eyes of the boss. Invariably, the first to do so was the driver of the truck, who felt secure because men available for that work were scarce. Having connived at one infraction of the rules, the foreman could hardly object to others breaking them as well; it was sometimes comical to see him try not to notice what was going on.

This leads me to another point which, in my opinion, is of great importance. Throughout the premises, inside and out, 'No Smoking' notices are posted, even in the enormous yard enclosed by a board fence. The first night, about ten or eleven o'clock, I, not knowing this, climbed during a lull out of my window on to the platform, and thence jumped to the ground to have a quick smoke. I was at once seen from a window; and a watchman promptly appeared to call my attention to the prohibition. I could see no reason why a person craving a smoke should not indulge in it where I was. Yet such is the rule. The watchman told me that there was only one place where smoking was allowed—the lavatory. I soon found out that this lavatory was, in addition, the social centre of the establishment; for that reason I must speak of it at some length.

No matter what else, in this whole experience, may remain a vivid memory, I am sure I shall never forget the lavatory. Among the permanent employees there were certain apparently unattached individuals whose function it seemed to be to jump in where an extra hand was needed. In our department, the receiving department, Dan, an elderly man, was thus employed, a kindly, unobtrusive fellow who most of the time flitted about like a shadow. But whenever the work became frantic, he was on the spot to lend a hand. On occasion, when matters went their even if heavy course he would appear and watch for a moment; and, deciding that this or that man looked fagged, he would step or climb up to him and nod backward. Whoever was thus favoured promptly disappeared on his way to the lavatory, rolling a cigarette; for with one or two exceptions all the men were smokers. So far as I observed, nobody ever took advantage of Dan, but reappeared, refreshed by a drink of water and by a brief indulgence of the craving for tobacco, within ten minutes. The same thing happened in every department; for there were invariably from two to fifteen men in the lavatory, all of them talking or laughing, in groups and smoking.

Since Dan extended his help, by taking over a job, with great impartiality, I soon came to know the place and the men who frequented it. No boss ever entered; it seemed that a tacit understanding between men and management marked this retreat as a sanctuary.

This, then, was the social centre of the factory where the talk was always confidential and sometimes violent; there was something furtive about its atmosphere. If it was used by the men during a lull, they arranged that one of each particular group remained outside and called the rest when they were needed. Dozens of times, when a truck arrived in the yard, I ran and called, 'Frank'—or 'Jimmie,' as the case might be—'Peas!' And everybody from my department would rush out, throwing away the cigarette or, more commonly, pressing its burning end out and slipping the remainder into a pocket. Everybody resented the fact that no other place was provided for the brief rest.

It was here that I had one of my most memorable meetings. Repeatedly, in passing to and fro, I had met a slender, aristocratic-looking, elderly man. He had passed me without a sign of recognition, quiet and reserved. Yet I knew that already he had singled me out, perhaps recognizing me from having passed my place in the country and having seen me on the lawn, perhaps from having heard the men call me by my name. Twice, during my stay at the factory, it happened that we met alone in the lavatory. The first time as I entered he shot me a sharp glance from under grey eyebrows, standing otherwise motionless. Suddenly, as I lighted my cigarette, he threw his away and, straightening his stoop, looked me briefly in the eye, at the same time extending his hand and sweeping it with a circular turn around the place, not even the slightest motion of his facial muscles betraying his distaste. But I understood and nodded. He gave a brief laugh and left. The second time I spoke to him, asking 'How did you get here?' He drew up his eyebrows and, after a momentary hesitation, said a single word, 'Drink!' Next he smiled and asked, 'And you?' 'Literature,' I replied. He laughed. 'They say you are a linguist,' he said next. 'What languages?' 'The usual ones,' I said; 'French, German, Italian, Spanish.' 'Latin and Greek go without saying?' he asked, preparing to finish his smoke. I laughed. 'Of course.' 'I thought so,' he said, throwing his stub away and turning to the door. 'They do, with us.' This time I drew up my eyebrows. 'Oxford,' he said, and shrugged. It was the first gesture I had seen him make, apart from that circular sweep of the hand. And, in Greek, he muttered the line from Euripides' Heracles which means 'May I not live without the muses!' Then he was gone.

A week or so later I met him a last time, on the occasion when I, having been laid off, made a round of the whole factory. He was working, 'kicking buckets' as they call it in factory jargon, that is, moving huge steel baskets filled with hot cans along the overhead monorail towards the enormous cooling-vat filled with water through which the cans travel on their way to the warehouse.

It was the third time in my life on this continent that I met an Oxford man under strange circumstances. The first was in the middle of the nineties of the last century, in the wheat-threshing fields of the Dakotas; the second in 1928 when I was making a lecture-tour through Canada: a farmer in the northern Peace River Valley shame-facedly confessed to me his educational antecedents.

As for the lavatory, the management could not easily make a better investment than by installing a small room with a few comfortable chairs—inexpensive camp-chairs—and smoke-stands where the men could meet as they do now, but under conditions which would raise their feeling of their own dignity. A small investment would pay enormous interest in contentment, loyalty, and raised morale; it would make the men feel that the management recognized them as human. The management knows that the men meet where they do; they know that they cannot eliminate the small waste entailed by the men's taking matters into their own hands by slipping away from their work for minutes at a time. If this were openly acknowledged, I feel sure that the men would see the necessity of cutting this waste to a minimum. As it is, they compare in their own minds the ease and even luxury which manager, assistant manager and superintendent enjoy in their private offices.

I witnessed one incident which was revealing. The man who happened to be 'kicking the buckets,' that is, removing the huge circular steel baskets when they were filled with hot cans, and starting them on their way to the cooling-vat between factory and warehouse, left his post after having pushed an empty basket into the place of the full one removed. No doubt he judged he was perfectly safe in slipping away for a smoke. But he was delayed. For the machines to vary in the rate of delivery is practically impossible, so that the fault must have lain with the man. This is what happened. To the left of the man filling the basket the full cans come travelling along, boiling hot. A girl adds sterilized water to make them brimful as they travel past in an intricate pattern. A plunger dipping into them removes just enough of this water to make room for the slight convexity of the lid. Thus they enter the stamping-machine, which puts the lids on with a steady rhythm, perhaps one a second. As this machine ejects them they are pushed or push one another on to a short inclined plane of polished steel, whence gravity moves them forward to a level steel table where they bunch together in a certain way. The man who removes them into the steel basket slips a leather strap around a bunch of anywhere from two to eight cans—according to their size— and swings them into the basket which hangs from the monorail at a level lower than that on the table. When the basket is full, the man who 'kicks the buckets' removes it along a branch of the monorail and pushes an empty basket into place. It was at this stage that the mishap occurred, for the man had not returned. The one next in line, who slips the cans down from the table, had to remove the full basket and reach for the empty one. This took more time than he could spare from the work which was properly his; and the full cans began to clatter to the floor. The noise instantly brought the superintendent upon the scene, at the precise moment when the 'bucket-kicker' returned. The superintendent received him with a volley of abuse, swearing at him. The man did not say a word as he resumed his work; but his face held a dark frown. Later on I had an opportunity to speak to the man, who had had to repair his omission. He said that, no matter what might have been the consequence, if the superintendent had spoken to him as he did to the other man, he would have laid him flat on the floor with a single swing of his powerful fist. 'It is true,' he added, 'the man was at fault; and it is hard to tell what I'd have done had I been at fault.' Perhaps I should add that it was a hot summer day; and even in winter this spot is a nasty place to work in, on account of the damp head which comes from the sterilizing vats hissing with superheated steam. The men work in clouds of this steam, and the sweat streams from their bodies. Nobody liked the superintendent, as compared with the assistant general manager, a slim, always-smiling young man. The manager himself, though seemingly omnipresent, was too far removed to be either liked or disliked. He went through the factory like a divinity to be gazed at, not to be spoken to.

A word regarding the canning process as a whole. Three such processes were going on, of which I was concerned with only one, the canning of peas. In addition, sour cherries were put up, and chicken soup was made. Of the latter I heard stories which made my skin creep. Generally, it seems to be a fact that nobody employed in the factory to whom I had a chance to speak would have eaten any product made there. Personally I can speak of peas only. Now green peas are a crop which spoils very readily. A few hours are sufficient to sour them; and now and then it happened that a load spoiled on the way from the threshing-field; some of these fields are over twenty miles away, and the roads are rough. When such a load came up to the receiving platform, it emitted a stench which proved almost too strong even for the men used to it. In such a case, the superintendent promptly appeared in the yard, to reach into a few of the boxes, and, according to the degree of heat he found in the peas, to give his verdict. As a rule that verdict was, 'Shoot them up, boys!' In only one case, when a load had come in about five o'clock in the morning, having been threshed during the night, the order was to empty all the boxes into vats of cold water which stood ready and then to 'shoot them up,' thus cooled. The smell of that load remains an abiding memory with me; but the men, though they would not have bought a can of peas for their own households, assured me that, in the finished product, no housewife would have found anything to object to.

The human element entered the process again at the pea-grader on the top floor. Washed and sterilized, the peas entered a huge revolving drum with perforations of various sizes in its cylindrical shell. Through these perforations the peas were discarded on to tables over which moved endless belts of celluloid. On both sides of these tables stood a dozen men and women, each picking out impurities with bare hands: thistle-heads, lumps of soil, coal, and so on. Thistle-heads were extraordinarily numerous. At this work, according to the foreman in charge, women were vastly more efficient than men. But, since a good many men have steady jobs, they were assigned to this task whenever there was no other urgent work for them to do. The women displaced were promptly asked to 'punch out.' The foreman, who knew me, said contemptuously, 'You can't expect men to pick clean.' Whether this was a slur on the men or the women, I could not decide.

There are occasional gaps in the mechanical process where the human element enters. Apart from them, one can almost say that the human hand does not touch the product. The machines which, successively, advance the canning process from stage to stage are ingenious to a degree. On occasion they seem to show almost human characteristics. Thus, when the open but filled can moves under the piston of the stamping machine, a hot and sterilized lid descends between the rods and there hovers for the minutest fraction of a second; the can moves up and comes to a momentary stop; it looks for all the world as if the lid hesitated in order to take aim; then, with great but accurately-calculated force, the piston comes down on the lid and stamps it on; you look, and already the can is no longer there; the next one moves up; and the process is repeated. The cans come in a steady stream; in a steady stream they move on.

It was at this point that, in watching, I was first struck by another peculiarity. Whenever the plunger comes down to remove surplus water and thus make room for the convexity of the lid, a few peas are carried away over the edge of the can. These peas accumulate till there is a pile of them on the floor. From time to time they are swept up, to be discarded into a waste tank the contents of which are once a day hauled away for pig-feed. If you don't get it in the cans, you get it in the pork. While it waits for the truck which takes this waste away, it spoils and ferments.

I walked through the rest of the factory which was operating in the service of the peas; and almost everywhere such piles of waste accumulated. On the top floor as well as below, at the receiving end, the floors and the platform outside, and also the ground over which the trucks drove up, were covered with a pea-slush which made it exceedingly hard to keep your footing. Very shortly my shins were raw with sores and bruises caused by my slipping against the edges of boxes. The trucks that bring the peas have their floors similarly covered; for it is comparatively rare for a box to be picked up without a little of its contents being spilled; occasionally such a box would slip from the hands of the operator; more frequently a steady stream of peas ran out from breaks or holes in the wood of which it was made. Add to that the peas wasted by the human element where it entered into the process: the peas thrown at passing girls, inside or outside the factory; the peas pilfered by the girls as they passed in order to be thrown back, from a distance, at the boys, and so on.

I tried to estimate that waste. Suppose that, within a given time, the total process covers the yearly demand of one thousand house-wives; if the peas wasted could have been saved, at least fifty additional housewives, preserving them in the old-fashioned way, could have covered their needs. I was vividly reminded of a western farmer who having threshed his wheat, hand-threshed, during the winter by means of a fanning-mill, the strawstack left by the machine. At a time when wheat still sold at $2.00 a bushel, he recovered 204 bushels, or two-thirds of what he would need next spring for seed.

That is the price we pay for machine operation: an enormous waste of production. Seeing that, in a money sense, labour is the largest item in the cost of production, this is perhaps unavoidable; we have no choice except between wasteful production and reduced production. Still, must the waste be so appalling?

My work at the factory, the pea-harvest being over, ceased on July 21. In the three weeks I had earned $48.75 and then was laid off indefinitely till tomatoes should come in. This was unavoidable. The thing that infuriated me was the shorter lay-offs during the three weeks. The first time that such a break occurred, on Saturday, July

4th, I was told to check out after half an hour's frantic work, as I have mentioned.

Yet when, having gone home, I was sitting in the shade of my trees, I said to my wife, waving my arms at my surroundings, 'This is more nearly Paradise than I have ever realized. The other thing is undiluted hell.'

The experience and its sequel were extraordinarily illuminating to me. When I was laid off for the long July-August lull, being pressed by my necessities, I promptly applied, personally or by letter, for work at various other factories, mostly on war-production; entirely without success. Which reminded me of the years summarized in *A Search for America*. Wherever I went in person, I was met with the greatest courtesy till the purpose of my call was mentioned, when the courtesy promptly changed into suspicion. The American and Canadian employer distrusts the educated man, unless he has worked up through the regular channels or enters through them. It often looks, to-day as well as in the nineties of the last century, as if he resented his very existence.

Personally, I can see no ground for such prejudice. Anything that needs to be done forms part of the work of the world as I know it. Provided it does not require what is beyond my powers, I am willing to do it, whether the work is manual, clerical, or instructional. I cannot lift heavy weights; and I cannot teach Russian because I don't know it. These two things are, to me, entirely on a level; there is no difference in the prestige involved.

But such a difference exists in the minds of employers. They look me up and down, they listen to my speech, and they laugh; already they have decided that they don't want me; they are even inclined to resent my application. If others—husky, dark-skinned applicants— are waiting, they turn to them and engage them in a few words for work which I could do just as well and perhaps better.

In the early years of *A Search for America* I never dreamt of this interpretation—namely, that here as well as in Europe it is practically impossible to step out of your 'class' except by the slow degree of degeneration or of the struggle for advancement. Just what it is that makes employers unwilling to use me—and others—I don't know; I have the impression that they don't know themselves. But instinctively they turn to the man who looks the part to be played and whose language is adequate to that part.

Perhaps there is a fear of criticism or subversive influence. As a professional friend of mine expressed it to me, they fear 'ideas.' It is true, of course, that when inefficiency or injustice comes to my notice, I register the fact mentally; and if any executive thought it worth the while to ask me, I should tell him of my observations. Otherwise I take the world as I find it. But I speak to a 'boss' as to my equal; if he resents it, the fact is revealing.

As for my experience, the conclusion I have drawn from it is that the greater part of what I had to say about the relation of capital and labour, in *A Search for America,* was right; at certain stages of my life as lived in the intervening years I had begun to doubt it. Employment adequate to my preparations for it I cannot secure because I did not come to it along the prescribed channels; employment inadequate and wasteful, in a national sense, I cannot secure because I habitually live on a level beyond it. I am back where I was in 1892 or 1893. My life has run full cycle.

IV

The Figure of Posterity

In the opening entry Grove describes the genesis of Thoughts and Reflections, 'a sort of intermittent diary' he kept between March 14, 1933 and June 3, 1940. It is clear in the opening entries that Grove's intention in the diary is not to set down his innermost feelings but to record for posterity his occasional 'thoughts and reflections.' In short, Grove is clearly writing for a public, however remote, writing to persuade that public; the diary is, in many ways, another apologia for his life and work, a defence against the lack of understanding he finds about him. It is of interest to Grove scholarship for at least two reasons. First, it provides a valuable record for a decade in the writer's life which is not otherwise well-documented, the decade in which he completed Fruits of the Earth (begun in Manitoba), the 'Ant-Book', subsequently published under the title, Consider Hey Ways, Two Generations, The Master of the Mill, and In Search of Myself (not to mention numerous unpublished manuscripts, including 'Felix Paul's Career' and 'The Seasons'). Thoughts and Reflections contains, among other things, valuable information about the composition of these books, Grove's reading during this period, and the thoughts that occupy him. The diary is, however, important for another reason. Grove may have begun Thoughts and Reflections as a record of his best thoughts for posterity, but time transforms it; as each year passes, it becomes more and more a reflection of his inner life. In it he records his delight in the recognition of a line of poetry, his satisfaction in an abundant corn crop, his joy at skating again for the first time in decades, his mixed feelings when, having purchased a radio, he hears again the classical music he associates with his youth. It becomes, too, an outcry against the poverty, isolation and neglect he feels as a writer in this country; and, as such, it gives us glimpses into Grove's state of mind during what were undoubtedly the bleakest years of his writing career in Canada.

Thoughts and Reflections, which survives on loose leaves apparently cut from the diary, is held in the Grove Collection. The handwriting is often cramped and difficult to read, and that difficulty is frequently compounded by cancellations and interlinear emendations. In transcribing the diary I have sought to provide a reading text; I have thus not indicated either cancellations or emendations. I have, however, resisted the temptation to standardize both the entry headings and punctuation, preferring to leave these irregularities as signs of the original text. Notes, including translations of the Greek and Latin, follow the text.

Frederick Philip Grove
Thoughts and Reflections

1933.

March 14. Every now and then a third or fourth-rate journalist—mostly it is a female—calls on me and tries to extract my opinion on such things as I may have formed an opinion about. I am not very communicative with them, my reason being that, since my books would not be read by the paper-reading public, even if they were read at all, I fail to see how my view can possibly interest them. But since I am equally convinced that my books—which take a long view of things—will one day be read, though perhaps never by a wide public, it strikes me that there may at some future date, be a public which will be interested in the stand I take with regard to this or that question of the day or to any other thing. If I had had a suitable book to write in handy, I might long ago have started a sort of intermittent diary. Since I did not have such a book, the occasion for that thought has remained unrecorded till now.

As I stop and think, it seems that the present moment is altogether dominated—for me—by the fact that my book *Fruits of the Earth* has recently appeared in print, without making the slightest impression, either in the press or among the public. Reviewers fail to see the essential points: to one of them the most striking thing about it is its simplicity: apparently she—it is a 'she'—has read the words without seeing anything behind them.

Among my few acquaintances, the only thing said that struck me at all as worth recording was the question why I did not set down any idea of the ideal man. As though it were within my choice and volition to write what I want to write! Besides, would not my idea of the perfect man be an absolute and utter irrelevancy? I replied that figures in fiction conform as little to formulas as figures in life.

I wish I could, with perfect simplicity and lucidity, set down the process by which a figure arises in my mind. But it is too complex a thing. A few points may be worth recording. Thus there is always, at the first beginning, a sudden thrill, liberated perhaps by a word overheard or by some thing read (of the latter, the thrill more commonly is one of contradiction than of agreement); this thrill may pass away; or it may, in rare cases, persist and pursue me. It may be the initial impulse for much imaginative work in mentally otherwise unoccupied hours; if it is, there will come a time when that figure and a destiny stand out conjointly in my mind; in other words when a story—which, on the total, is entirely imaginative, though, in minor points, it may owe much to personal experience—is formed. Again, as in the case of the initial thrill, the story may simply rest, it may lapse in my memory and ultimately be forgotten. If I were a professional writer, I believe, I should never allow that to happen. But if it is not forgotten, it is because it has proved sufficiently vital to hold me till it becomes a torment to leave it unborn. Which, of course, means nothing whatever with regard to my own identity with that figure; nor even with the mind that records its doing.

Then, very unwillingly, I get ready for writing: and now comes the essential point: the characters whose story it is have by that time assumed a being and a life of their own. In my first draft I have to explore them as though they were persons actually living. Mostly I put them through many experiences which I ultimately omit from the record. But, as a preliminary, I cannot help that: in order to make them live for myself, I must know how they will behave even under such circumstances as may have no bearing on the book as it will be when finished. In other words, I have to live with them and to observe them under the conditions of actual life. The few who appreciate my books have always commented on the power with which I set the central characters before them. I believe, if there is truth in that comment, it is due to the fact that my whole later work, I mean the architectural work of building up a final form and the work of condensation and filing, consists in elimination instead of expansion. A thousand reactions to a thousand different situations go to change a single reaction to a single situation. As an example I will mention the very brief scene, on page 111 of *Fruits of the Earth*, between Abe Spalding & Blaine. That this should remain entirely unnoticed by the average reviewer, is perhaps natural; but it is rather discouraging.

March 15   In glancing over what I wrote yesterday, I am struck with an important omission which, I believe, might prove illuminating to young authors.

When, as often happens, the central figure in a story is suggested to me by some actual person seen or by some thing overheard that was actually spoken, I have for decades now (ever since I learned my early lessons) strictly avoided meeting that person again, seeing him in other circumstances or hearing more of his talk. If the thrill of which I spoke was genuine and vital, it has done its work; and any further acquaintance with the originator of that thrill can only interfere with the imaginative creation of which he was the occasion. It may destroy it; it is certain to confuse it. From that moment on the character, as he lives in my imagination, is a thing alive; a thing that has its own rights and must not be warped. This is essential for imaginative creation.

This has, of course, nothing whatever to do with that accuracy of descriptive and historical detail that may enter into the story and which is required for the vitality of the total picture of life if description and history are of real though perhaps transfused things. If both are of imaginary things, as in my 'ant-book,' it is essential that they should at least carry conviction; and, in that respect, nobody has ever excelled Swift.

There is, further, this to be said, that a work of narrative art must, in its total import, conform to the general verdict passed on life by the best minds of the time which produced it: which implies that it may, even in this respect, run counter to the verdict or the taste of what is called the general public: perhaps it even *must* do so; for the taste of the public is necessarily fifty years behind the finer taste of those best minds: this is a tragic thing, because it means that, within the present system, the truly creative mind is doomed to a sordid sort of poverty, to much suffering, often to mental starvation not to mention physical starvation which does not matter. For, except in the case of the strongest minds, it is very hard to go on with an imposed and heavy task without feeling that one meets with the approval of those who surround one. However, what, in the long run, does the suffering of an individual matter?

Yet, even in jotting down these notes, I feel, perhaps from some such reason, the same sort of reluctance to commit myself to writing which I always feel when it comes to writing a new book.

No adverse criticism of that new book of mine has hit me quite as hard as a well-wishing English reviewer's bland statement that this is a 'thrilling romance' of Canadian life. Romance!!!

March 22 Romanticism! They talk of the romance of business: what they mean is the apparent marvel of the contrast between humble beginnings and the seeming splendour of ultimate success; and they overlook the far from romantic, slow climb that connects the two by an infinite number of sordid and often questionable steps.

They talk of the romantic career of Napoleon, or Caesar, or Alexander: and what they mean is exactly the same thing which they mean when they talk of the romance of business.

Romanticism in literature, at least in the English and Latin sense (leaving out the purely Teutonic mysticism of nature and the soul) has been essentially the cult of the distant, the mediaeval, and the marvellous: in other words, the cult of that which we do not understand. *Omni ignotum pro magnifico.* The true heir of the romanticism of Scott and Hugo, f.i., is the modern detective story: it shows romanticism in its last stages of decay.

In politics, romanticism has, for the last fifty or a hundred years, been called Imperialism. Romanticism is essentially the desire of mankind for splendid and almost miraculous results—a desire so fundamental and so strong that it is willing to shut its eyes to crime, cruelty, waste, blundering, etc., provided these lead, by ever so devious ways, to an ultimate success.

Nothing has done more harm than romanticism in literature, for romanticism in politics has been its direct result. The holy Roman Empire of the middle ages was romanticism; German and even English imperialism were the outcome of the German 'Sturm und Drang' and of Scott's romantic fiction respectively. In England, Kipling has been the last of the romantics: in him it has become jingoism. It sometimes seems to me as though boys of 12 and girls of 16 determine, not only our taste in literature, but through it, ultimately, our policies as well. Clear-headed, sober realism has been submerged in a flood of silly emotionalism. *Vide* Flaubert, *L'Education sentimentale.* This pervades even the craze and confusion which has invaded the titles of our books.

March 23. In completion of the note I set down on March 14, regarding the genesis of a leading character or figure, I might perhaps say that the whole web of *Fruits of the Earth* arose out of a single fact. Some time around the turn of the century I came, in south central Saskatchewan, across a man who had that very day arrived by train. He was alone in a field; nowhere could I see any buildings. The field in question was virgin prairie, miles from the nearest town or settlement. I was driving a load of wheat. And when I first saw this man—he was enormously tall and strong; and his figure, at first sight, was outlined against the sky, for he was topping a hill—it struck me that never before had I seen a human being in these parts. I stopped and waited till he approached the trail. Then I hailed him and asked him about himself. He had arrived shortly after noon, had come out to his claim, with his horses and his wagon, and had intended to go back to town once more to fetch the remainder of his chattels. But, having a plough along, he had, when he saw the smooth expanse of his claim, been unable to tear himself away and had started breaking. It so happened that, being involved in a sort of rebellion of the 'hands' on the company farm where I was working, I was, that night, chosen as the scape-goat by the manager and summarily dismissed. I never saw the lone settler again. But the memory of his figure remained with me; and years, yes decades later, when I was riding along with E.S. Gardiner, 'realtor' of Rapid City in Manitoba, and heard something of the so-called 'Rugby' Farm which we were passing, things suddenly jumped in my brain, as in a kaleidoscope: mysteriously that man had received a name, and his whole history stood outlined in my mind. When I got home, that day, I began to write the book in its first form.

April 6   A few more reviews of my books have come. These attack me because they find me 'gloomy.' One of them talks of my 'congenial task of showing the vanity of human life' etc. Suppose this were so. Suppose, even, the view of human life disengaging itself from my pages were that of Shakespeare's *Measure for Measure, Troilus & Cressida*, or *Timon of Athens*—it seems to me that, in such a fact, no critic has a right to find the basis for condemnation. The only question that concerns him is how it is done, badly or well, successfully or unsuccessfully. I am by no means sure of the value of my book, though I do believe that its characters live. If Shakespeare had left us no other work but the three plays mentioned, or even one of them, he would still be a very considerable figure in the history of English, yes, universal literature, outtopping Chapman, Jonson, Beaumont, and Fletcher. The question is not, does he flatter us and our prejudices? Or does he thunder? If he thunders with a voice that dominates other voices, he has greatness. It is true that he could never have been a popular playwright. But what does popularity or unpopularity matter? A great but unpopular writer is simply one whose influence on succeeding literature is indirect rather than direct—but, for that matter, that influence may be just as great if not greater than the influence of very popular successes. Ex. Goethe as compared with Schiller. Even Shakespeare found *Hamlet*—one of his most popular works—insufficiently successful and followed it by *All's Well That Ends Well*, for the sake of that popular success which he could not dispense with and which was threatened by the competition of younger men—actors as well as playwrights (Kemp going over to Henslowe's). But if there had been no such popular success at all, the only thing we could say would be, 'So much the worse for Shakespeare!' Yet, the critic, if he were a critic—i.e. the man who *directs*, instead of voicing, the popular verdict—would still have to point to the author of *Timon* as the author of a play which contains very great things. Not, of course, that I mean to compare myself with Shakespeare. But it is the principle involved; and I do believe there is some little merit to be acknowledged in my book.

In something I read yesterday, I found this question: Which was the real Beatrice: the very ordinary young woman who was the wife of her husband and whom her husband saw from day to day? Or the one about whom Dante wrote his *Vita Nuova?* This is indeed a problem of metaphysics: perhaps, considering our human limitations, it is the fundamental problem of metaphysics or at least contains it. I have an idea as though someone of greater powers than myself had discussed this in detail; but it happens so often that I do not know whether a thought is mine or someone else's. And perhaps it does not matter.

But this is the point: Have 'I'—perhaps I should say, Has the 'I'— any objective existence? It certainly has for others. I hardly know who the F.P.G. is who is compact of contradictions. But my friend who loves me and my enemy who hates me is very sure that he knows me. I am the one who affects friend or enemy in a certain way. They carry about with them a picture of me; and every action and speech of theirs, whether they are conscious of it or not, somehow takes this picture of me into account; just as I take into account the picture I carry about with me of them. Thus, whether I am an individuality or not, there lives in others an individuality which may not be I but which is occasioned by myself. If, among friends and enemies, there were something like an aggregate or collective consciousness, the picture of me mirrored in it would contain as many contradictions and variations as I am conscious of in myself, though they would not necessarily be the same.

I had a peculiar experience the other day. A man came to my door and, I, happening to be near it, answered his knock myself: he at once plunged into fluent sales-talk. Now anyone who goes about the country, trying to sell people what they do not need and what they often do not want, antagonises me. I answered very briefly, declining to listen to him and closing the door. Then I at once returned to my seat at a window overlooking the driveway and resumed a book in which I had been absorbed. Now I had barely looked at the man when he stood at the door. But, in returning to my seat, I unconsciously focused my mind's eyes on his appearance which was no longer before my bodily eyes: I saw a man who seemed to have suffered from want, clad in very shabby clothes, his cheeks hollow; and I had already, still half unconsciously, wondered whether this man's real desire had not been for a meal rather than for selling me whatever he may have had to sell. Just as I sat down and reached for my book, I saw him issuing from the porch, saw him from a corner of my eye merely; and he saw me. Although I did not face him, I saw him raising a fist at me and shaking it; and at the same time I heard him shouting something. I did not understand what his words were; and, as often happens with me, since I am nearly deaf, I was, for a second, mentally occupied with fitting the disconnected sounds which I had heard into some intelligible context. The result of this mental reconstruction was this: 'I have as much right to live as you have.' At once, remorse at my curtness filled me like a flood; consternation broke the thread of my thought—which was that of the book I had been reading—and I rose again, to return quickly to the door and to ask him in. I even remember the trend of my thought as I did so. 'I have no more money than you have, my dear; but I have food in the house; and if you are in need of food, you may share it while I have any myself.' But it so happened that the stranger had seen me rise again; my motion, I suspect, was sudden and abrupt; and he read into it a threatening meaning; for he started to run. He was outside my frontyard—having come to a side door; and he reached its corner, at the highway, before I reached the door. My impulse, therefore, remained unavailing. He was beyond reach of my voice.

The picture this man carried away of me was very far from resembling myself—if, for the moment, I may talk of myself as though I were something. Yet it was occasioned by actions and sayings done and uttered by those outward appendices which form my body and which stand, to the world at large, as controlled by myself and, therefore, indicating a hidden entity, namely my 'I.' That picture has now assumed an independent existence and is travelling through the world. It may be very potent in the so-called actual world: the stranger may be profoundly influenced by it in his attitude towards capitalism: for, he must necessarily assume that, since he saw me in a large house surrounded by plantations of flowers, with fat meadows stretching away to the west and large farm buildings enclosing the barn-yard, I must be, as compared with him, a wealthy man. He cannot know that, conditions being as they are, and I owing considerable sums on the property, the property rather owns me than I the property. He cannot know that I and mine must work more hours every day and more strenuously than he would care to work for a living, in order not to lose the savings of many decades invested in the land and the buildings; nor that, if I did so lose them, I should at once lose the very possibility of rendering such services to people rather than myself as at present induce these people to pay me out of their superfluity; and that, then, I should be in precisely his own position. He misinterpreted motions of mine; and that misinterpretation has assumed a very real power to produce results. Perhaps he will address a crowd of starving men on the point of an emotional outburst: and when he tells them of the incident, that outburst will take place and they will be swept off their feet with anger and indignation: perhaps it will precipitate a rebellion and an ultimate revolution: a revolution which may, if successful, benefit me infinitely more than them: that is the irony of it.

Similarly, Aeschylus, Homer, Shakespeare, Goethe are to us what influences us and continues to do so. *Cogito ergo sum* is a fallacious argument; it begs the question: but *cogitas ergo sum* might well be defended. It postulates that I live as long as others do: there is a real immortality in this. For, whether a person stands out among the multitude by virtue of some great achievement or remains obscure throughout life, his influence will live; in the latter case perhaps at first in a very small circle; but unless that small circle ceases to exist altogether, it will slowly and by imperceptible degrees spread through ever-widening circles—being diluted it is true, as it does so— till it pervades all mankind. This may be looked upon as a sort of determinism; but it may also prove the basis of a new ethics vastly more powerful and binding in its imperative than the doctrine of retribution is in a personal future life. And the great ones—like those mentioned above—are living today in a sense vastly more real than they could have been said to live in when they were alive in the flesh.

April 10 D.H. Lawrence, Aldous Huxley: bleeding souls. The former because he came from the working classes and, not having become really free, as, in a sense, the much inferior Arnold Bennett became free, never got over the fact: he goes on, throughout life, seeing society as consisting of classes (as it does, of course) instead of seeing the common humanity throughout the classes. Gerhart Hauptmann did the same in his early work; but, like Bennett, he became free. Huxley tries to write out of a fund of disgust: great art cannot thus be written. This was clear in *Point Counter Point.* But one might still have had hopes as to the final issue. *Brave New World* is an admirable piece of work in many ways: but it is done with the head, not with the soul: it is an end, not a beginning. I doubt whether, in further work we can look for a new departure. And Lawrence, alas, is dead. His *The Virgin and the Gypsy* has the same theme as my own *Maid of all Work.*

April 13 What does this vaunted material civilisation amount to when 90% of the people never enjoy any of its 'blessings' except the privilege of paying for them? And worse, still, these 90% have to pay for them—what the 10% enjoy—in labour. They haven't any other currency.

Is there no remedy? No, none that does not involve the thing which everybody is afraid of, namely the application of ideas to life. If it were not for that fear, we could experiment. Small experiments have been made, it is true; but they need to be made on a larger scale. For one cannot expect success when a handful of people are pitched defenceless, against packs of wolves. Russia has won undying glory by having dared. It may well be that it will fail; the world is against it; but even if it does, its example must surely inspire others, sooner or later.

April 26   I have been re-reading a few of Conrad's books. There are two groups. To one belong such things as *The Nigger of the Narcissus, The Shadow Line, Typhoon,* and others. To the second group, *Almayer's Folly, An Outcast of the Islands, The Rescue* etc. I do not care for these latter. Somehow it seems to me that Conrad falls down when he goes ashore. I am not interested in these Lingards, Almayers, and Willemses; and his Malay or half-caste women remain incomprehensible to me; sometimes even incredible. They seem 'posed.' Whereas I thrill to his sailors' world: the men in conflict with the sea. I consider *Typhoon* his crowning achievement. Even those books which, like *Lord Jim* or *Nostromo,* mix land and sea are, to me, only half admirable and half exasperating. Nevertheless, he remains a phenomenon, the more so since he is essentially Slavic. The Slav genius for minute psychology is, in him, transferred to the minute observation and description of nautical phenomena. The sea, the wind, the sun are unmistakably alive. More so than in any other writer I know.

September 5.   For the first time since early in the spring I sit at my desk; and as I look over the fragmentary papers which have accumulated on a corner of its top during the last winter, I run across this book which was to contain some sort of diary and which has not been opened or even touched for over 4 months.

These four months have been filled by manual work. On April 28 seeding started on my farm; and the peculiar season with its drought, which has now lasted more than 3 months, made seeding operations merge into haying, haying into harvesting, and harvesting into the fall preparations for next year's crops. There have been days, and there have been weeks when I worked harder than any hired man or casual labourer. There have been nights, and many of them, when I have felt so tired and exhausted that I should much rather have allowed myself to drop in my tracks than summon a last remnant of available energy in order to go to bed. My hands are hardened with calluses; my hair is bleached by the sun and the wind; my very bones retain their weariness and will do so for weeks to come.

I have asked myself and still ask myself: what gain have I to show for it? Materially, in one sense, the gain is nil. The good and the bad the season has brought seem to balance each other so evenly that it looks as though I were back exactly where I was when I started. We have lived through the summer, that is all; and perhaps we have lived at a disproportionate expenditure of human energy: we have lived as work-horses live, from one satisfaction of natural wants to the other. Perhaps I might say, we have existed.

Yet that is not the whole story. While we have not gained materially, we have ensured the continuity of life: we have reaped enough to carry us through the winter; we have fought weeds (a desperate fight in a year like this), in a manner which will enable us to start next year's crop without an undue handicap. When, day after day, the sun burned down on us, relentlessly; when parching winds persisted in withering up our garden-crops till the leaves and vines lay daily flat on the ground; where sun and wind combined in a fierce onslaught on all plant-life, seemingly determined to grant us no respite till life was either exterminated or so enfeebled as to succumb to the coming winter's cold, we have patiently stirred the top-soil in the hoe-crops, so as to give the wind only dry dust to carry away instead of precious moisture; we have carried water where we could, so as to ensure life in the teeth of adversity; we have pastured cattle along road-sides when the regular pastures would no longer yield them that satisfaction of a full belly without which cattle cannot live. I myself have sometimes—in fact, quite often—taken the latter task upon myself for portions even of the night. And we have come through. Others have no feed for their stock and must sell; some are forced off their land, some live on capital or borrowed funds: we have held our own.

I take pride in the fact that this was done by dint of mere labour: such labour as does not involve the impoverishment of others as any method involves which is based on trade. It has been a clean way of holding our own.

Other factors enter into a certain contentment which the summer leaves behind: memories of short rests in the intervals of frantic work, taken in the shade of a basswood tree which stands in the margin between my corn field and a new seeding of alfalfa hay, on a knoll of my slightly rolling land where every ambling breeze seems amplified to the senses, because it becomes perceptible to eye and ear as well as to the steaming pores of the skin; there at regular intervals, once every two hours or so, I used to strip my shirt off before I threw myself down in the grass; occasionally, though rarely, my wife would come with the little boy, carrying a fresh, cold drink of water in a little covered pail; memories also of clear moonlit evenings when, after dark, I was watching the cattle along the road-side; memories of low, snow-white, creeping mists that formed, on such occasions, first over the creek running through the meadow and the field adjoining to the west; and finally engulfing everything except the large domes of the few trees which form the landmarks of my farm; as I moved about from place to place, following the cattle, in a sort of furtive, surreptitious way (for all was hidden by the mist) I noticed the cold and warm streaks in the air; and finally, when I drove the cows back into the enclosure where they spent the night, the return to the yard, where the large buildings retained the heat of the day, and where, therefore the air was clear, held an impression of home-coming and welcome which was never dulled in its appeal.

I have thought a little, too; not much. My mind has been a blank more often than not. But a few fundamentals have made themselves clearer to me. If I were to say in a few words what they are, I might be at a loss. But perhaps I have never been more deeply impressed with the fact that after all man and his life are, in spite of all his antics, as much part of the cosmic process as they ever were. Nothing that he can do amounts to a great deal. In the last resort, we are playthings of nature. When the sky clouded up, three or four times during the season, and the clouds divided to go by, north or south of us, neighbours, in casual conversation, expressed hope or anxiety. I looked up and decided to wait. What did it matter? I had done my share. If nature refused to do hers, no rebellion, no worry on my part would change things. Right now, when the ground is dry to a depth of several feet; dry as dust,—when the soil is dust—they wait for a rain before doing their fall seeding: I do my share and seed. If rain does come, I shall be ahead of them: if it does not come, they will be ahead of me: they will have saved their seed; what does it matter? More than ever I am determined to do my share, let the event take care of itself. Some distant observer, equipped with powerful aids to television might record events as I record them: over this part of the earth's surface no vapour masses seemed to form, for one reason or other. That underneath, in the mats of greenery, there were little beings that thought themselves great, as the special objects of an imaginary power's care, moved by intense emotions of fear, anxiety, hope, despair, or triumph, escapes that observer.

And so, with this day, when I have sat down again at my desk, I am moved also by the realisation of the incongruity contained in the fact that I am sitting here precisely for the purpose of recording some of those emotions of fear, anxiety, hope, despair, or triumph that are disturbing those little human beings whose motions are hidden from the distant observer's eye by the seasonally self-renewing greenery of this earth.

I did emphatically not sit down in order to inscribe these lines or any lines in this book: I sat down in order to prepare 5 lectures on the appreciation of literature: what a jest!

September 13.   I am in the midst of the preparation of my lecture on Poetry; and I wish to record a singular thrill. For many years the cadence of a line from the mass of poetry handed down to us under the name of Ovid has haunted my memory. I have never been able to hunt it up: I have no money to buy books with. Since it is now more than 40 years ago that I read it, it was difficult for me to say exactly where it occurred. Yet, having retained, at least so I thought, and so it has proved to be the case, two words from the line accurately, I have, in the course of decades, asked half a dozen people who professed themselves to be classical scholars to locate or to complete it for me. Not one was ever able to do so. Yesterday, in reading Mackail's *Lectures on Greek Poetry,* I ran, quite by chance, across the full line,

Somnia formoso candidiora die;

and I had a thrill of such power as I do not recall having had for years. Ever since, I have repeated the line to myself with a feeling of positive happiness; and I am glad to say it seems as lovely to me as it ever did in the dim past when I first met with it. Fortunately, its provenance is also mentioned by Professor Mackail, so that at last I shall be able to restore it, in my memory, to its proper setting.

Sept 22   Reread the following.

Housman, *A Shropshire Lad*—very fine; true poetry; few notes, but those of exquisite beauty.

Housman, *The Name & Nature of Poetry* (this, new reading)—what I should have expected. He sees one side of poetry, not the other, higher one—where clear vision and accurate and profound thought become poetical. Besides, poetry is or arises in the reader or listener: what is or goes on in the poet when he writes it is irrelevant—he himself, against his will, admits as much when he speaks of the genesis of 'I hoed and trenched and weeded.' Still, a valuable booklet.

Franklin—*Journal of a Journey to the Polar Seas:* an elemental book of very high rank—an old favourite of mine. It has all the earmarks of great art and is yet an almost literal transcript of actual experience.

Fielding—*Tom Jones*. A silly book, half of it intrinsically false, yet full of actual life. I cannot swallow Saintsbury's apology.

September 29

Last night I attended a huge semi-public social function in town where I met several hundred of the so-called 'best' people. A number of them sought me out. What amazed me was the utter inanity of the conversations these men and women attempted with me. I tried— very unsuccessfully, I am afraid, to let myself down to their intellectual level. I was distinctly dull. As the evening progressed, games were organised; and there was a great deal of noise and laughter. Much of it was very funny, indeed: as, f.i., the game of 'musical chairs'; I could not help laughing myself. But the laughter left a bad taste in my mouth; and the fun was of a low order. It was decidedly not because I am averse to fun or laughter that I felt badly about it; for I am fond of a laugh; and I have the reputation of having, on occasion, a ready wit. But this disgusted me as a distinct waste of my time and energy. I felt that I should be in bed, sleeping. I have had the same feeling on the occasion of a reception given in my honour in Toronto; and against that memory stands another, of an evening spent in the house of Dr. W.J. Alexander, with Barker Fairley, Professor Davies and a few others as my fellow-guests. There, too, we laughed a great deal; and individually not one of us perhaps was intellectually superior to a good many of those present on the previous occasion. But as a group we were not afraid to speak of the things that interested us; and neither were we afraid of ideas. Had I, last night, dared to speak of any of the things that have lately passed through my mind, I am sure I should have shocked even those who could have apprehended them. Ideas are distinctly 'suspect' in most Canadian gatherings. In order to be popular, you have to create and uphold the fiction that you are fundamentally a happy and innocent little child that wishes for nothing so much as for a happy and innocent entertainment fitted to your own age and innocence.

But this is not at all what I wanted to say. When I came away, it was raining—the 3rd rainy night we have had since Sept 26 when the long summer drought of 115 days came to an end at last. It continued raining till after one o'clock: a warm, mild summery rain delicious to the senses. It sounded so welcome on the roof of the house and in its rain-pipes—almost like the purling of milk in the pail—that I lay awake till it stopped, enjoying the primitive feeling of being out of it, of being sheltered; and indulging in memories of nights when, in the dim past, this feeling was intensified rather than frustrated by the imperfection of the shelter which I enjoyed: as, f.i., under a culvert where one's main preoccupation was with keeping out of the drip that came through imperfectly fitted planks. But at last I went to sleep.

At about four o'clock I awoke; and the sky, visible through my west window, was brilliantly clear, with a moon in its second quarter shedding a snow white light from the west in which the roof of the west wing of the house looked like pearl-grey velvet, still glistening, though, with wetness. I rose and went to the window to look out over my meadows and fields. There was a dense mist, lying about 25 to 40 ft thick over the landscape, according to the conformation of the ground, for the upper limit of the mist was a perfect plane, flat as a table top; and no breath was stirring. The moon was about to set in this mist, its rays coming about parallel to the plane of the surface. Here and there, being just above the level of this atmospheric lake, the tops of the trees rose above it like dark, wooded islands casting long moon-shadows towards the east on the white sheets. I felt transferred back in time to my early youth when I used to enjoy the sight of such mists in the valleys of the Alps. Mere size is nothing in such enchantments. These tree-tops stood as much like sentinels above a world sleeping under the mist as the Matterhorn and Schreckhorn had done then: and any thing may be imagined underneath. This morning there was, underneath nothing but the light valley of the creek crossing my farm; and on its banks, no doubt, the cows were reposing, with their legs doubled up under their bodies and their jaws moving sideways over each other as they chewed the cud.

I went back to bed when I began to shiver; and I did not get up again till after six when the sun had just risen and was slowly lifting himself, as with an effort, above the vapour which, in the east, was already beginning to rise. But in the west it still lay smooth and level; and as I dressed, I could watch the disintegration of its perfect surface: wherever I knew a knoll to be hidden by it, it began to heave; and then a flat surface established itself once more at a lower level, especially in the slight valley of the meadow traversed by the meandering creek leaving the knolls as islands in the white sea.

Suddenly I heard a commotion in the yard, near the barn. No doubt George had finished the morning's milking and a moment later I heard him as, with raucous cries he drove the cows down, through the gate, into the meadow. And as the animals began to move about in the mist which was still hiding them, the smooth surface above began to break, in huge waves, resembling the waves of water, but with this difference, that the motion of these waves seemed enormously retarded: a space they would, in water, have moved through in seconds, they took, in air, minutes to traverse. It was an hour before I could see the animals.

I wondered how many of last night's guests had seen this marvel of nature this morning: or how many had experienced any thing as fine and pure since they separated in the rainy night.

October 10.   For some time, two weeks or so, mists have been the rule in the morning; and for the last three days we have had heavy nightly rains which have brought the greater part of the leaves down to the ground where they form a dense, thick, and sodden carpet.

This is the time of year when I am homesick for the wilderness. If I surrender to my dreams, I see myself camping in the bush, in an open shed, with a sound roof on which the streaky rain patters down, driven by the wind. In front of the open shed there is a huge fire which dies down at night, but not to the point where there is no light or heat radiating from it. In fact, since in the dream-landscape, with my shed near the edge of a steep and deep ravine through which a clear, black-watered brook purls down to the lake, I am always awake. I rise from my pinebough couch before the wetness overpowers the dark-red glow of the embers and replenish the fire, with fuel which I have provided in day-time. In this dream, in which I indulge every year when autumn comes, that is—this, apart from dreaming and thinking (dreaming within the dream), is my only occupation. I do not even provide for meals.

I wonder whether this dream is a survival from the times of my early days on this continent when, suddenly transplanted from surroundings of the most advanced European 'culture,' I was confronted with a civilisation which, at least in those aspects which it presented to me, was purely material; so that I fled it in disgust and revelled in the satisfactions of dream and thought, providing the body with primitive comforts barely sufficient to release the mind for its proper functions.

I have since spent an inordinate amount of time and endeavour in trying to conform: i.e. in trying to provide for myself a material setting not too much at variance with the ideas prevalent on this continent; and perhaps, in doing so, I have lost my soul. I can aver, for my justification, or at least in extenuation of this sin against the holy ghost of my destiny (which I am afraid I have missed) that I have done what I have done, not for my self but in order not too grievously to disappoint those who have hitched their destinies to my own.

Nevertheless, I am often overcome with a sense of the tremendous waste the process has of necessity involved.

Nov 6. I have now been at work again for two weeks or so on the ant-book which was first sketched in 1919 and first written in 1920 and rewritten more than once in the interval that has since elapsed. All my work on it has been carried on under peculiar difficulties; and I intend putting down what these difficulties consist in at present.

In the first place, as to health: My ears have never given me so much pain; and that pain induces an excruciating headache; my abdomen, too, does not leave me an hour of rest; and I seem to be unable to throw off a racking cough which I contracted months ago.

In the second place, as to money: there have been weeks, this fall, when there was not a cent in the house and when we were put to the most amazing shifts to provide for the daily food, in spite of the fact that we were all working our heads off.

In the third place, as to time: I go to bed early, because only when I get sleep aplenty, can I concentrate; I get up, in the morning, at 7; It takes me till 8:30 or 9 o'clock to get ready for there is always something to be looked after in farm, barn, or house. At 12 o'clock I must cease writing; for dinner must be on time for my wife's sake. Till then, two classes of youngsters are being taught in the house; and what with singing, recess, and physical exercises, there is not a minute's quiet to be had while I am trying to concentrate my imaginative powers on a world so different from our own as that of these ants. From 1 o'clock on it is my turn to teach: 1st, 4 elementary classes; 2nd a grown-up class in French literature; 3rd a subnormal boy of 19 years whom I am trying to teach 4 yrs. Latin and French in a single year. In addition to that, I have, on an average, one or two addresses and lectures to prepare and to deliver every week, so that there is not a breathing space during the week-end.

In the fourth place: there is constant worry; and when the worry is slightly relieved, by an occasional gift of $50 or $100 (I have had one each of these two amounts since summer), coming from a millionaire interested in Canadian letters, it is replaced by resentment at the fact that I should be unable to do any writing at all if it were not for these. This resentment is, of course, not directed against the person of that millionaire to whom, on the contrary, I feel profoundly obliged. But the face remains that I resent my fate which forces me to pursue my writing in the face of what seem almost insurmountable difficulties.—My last book, *Fruits of the Earth*, has, during the first year (and that, according to my experience, means altogether) brought me the sum of $151.22; to which I must add $14.35 brought by *A Search for America*. It is true, on these two books I had, last year, a total advance of $300.00. But the year's sales leave me in debt to the publishers to the amount of $134.43—another worry.

Nevertheless, I have not, since 1923, lived so completely in a world of my own making; and never before in my life, I believe, have I written with any thing that could be called 'gusto' to the same degree to which I do now—a fact that, when I reflect upon it, rather amazes me.

Nov 11   But, as I think over what I have set down under date of Nov. 6, another difficulty seems to eclipse all those I have mentioned, namely that I have absolutely no one to whom I can talk, to whom I can read what I have written. When I was young and lived in constant touch with the young literati of Europe, especially in Paris and Munich (Andre Gide in the former, Stephen George and his satellites in the latter métropolis), often some amazing conception of mine, immature as all of them must have been since I have lived to discard them all, exploded into its iridescent and fullblown form at the spark which was struck in conversation with this or that one of my fellow-enthusiasts. Out of the clash of ideas arose an ever new and more striking train of ideas. My whole conception of the artist's duties, as, f.i., laid down in *It Needs to be Said*, sprang up fully armed, in a conversation with H.G. Wells as we were walking on the cliffs of Sandgate, overlooking the channel. My whole individualistic leanings which, politically, demand communism or socialism (an extreme socialism) or even anarchy as their setting, sprang up within me in a conversation with Gide, over an excellent dinner at Paris, when we were talking of Wilde who had recently been released from prison. Those ideas of poetry which I am going to expound to an audience here on the 28th of this month, owe their origin to another similar conversation (or shall I call it an argument) with Gide over another excellent dinner (I believe it was at the Tour d'Argent) where I condemned the work of a man who was then a very young German, Vollmoeller, as being derivative, a side-shoot of that Viennese poetry that grouped itself around Hofmannsthal.

All that is a thing of the past; and now I appear to myself like a solitary sailor on a derelict ship which has sprung a leak and collected in its hold enormous quantities of water which he painstakingly pumps up to pour into his books.

More than ever am I convinced, had the conditions of my life been favourable, that I could have done things to amaze the world.

Thus, in my present task, I am working entirely in the dark: I must strike laughter out of my fellow-men if I am to succeed: but laughter that frees thought: and I don't know whether or to what extent I succeed. If I could test the effects of what I am writing, I might adjust the ingredients that go into my work. As it is, it all remains guess-work.

But—I have been told that the Royal Society of Canada has awarded me the gold medal for literature! What is the Royal Society of Canada? Who are its members?

Nov 24 I am, from day to day, hopelessly floundering about, up to my neck, in a dismal swamp. That swamp is my ant-book which, after 14 years of work on it and thought on it and worry about it, I am trying to put into a final form. The thing is there, as a whole, on paper, and in my mind. Every detail is there, on paper and in my mind. Yet, essentially, the book is unwritten even today; and whenever I am through with a day's (i.e. 3 hrs) work, I am profoundly happy in looking back and at the same time profoundly unhappy in looking forward. I live only in those 3 hrs of the morning; but I dread the coming of the morning. Yet nothing, when that morning *has* come, could keep me away from my desk. I cannot even persuade myself to take matters stoically and to trust myself from day to day. When the idea for this book arose in me, around Christmas 1919, it came like a flash prostrating me. The first draft—containing practically everything that has ever gone into it or will ever go into it—was written down in an amazing rush; and while writing it, I felt I wanted to publish it at once. Strange to say, had I published it at once, it would have been valueless as a piece of imaginative literature; but it might have gone down in the history of literature as an amazing series of prophecies. It was at once too anthropomorphic and not enough so. I saw that when, in spring 1920, I made a typescript.

I am now firmly convinced that I have the final form. But have I? Or will the new Ms. again lie for 14 yrs, being worked at, changed, despaired of and loved at the same time?

As I said, I cannot get to the point where I trust myself or the book; for it has a logic of its own and a life of its own. I am always doubtful whether I do not simply waste my time. Then I read some essay or some exposition by a contemporary writer; and I take heart of courage [sic]: for I find that I am not all along; that, after all, we are, by our own separate paths, travelling in the same direction; shall we arrive at the same goal?

Dec 9   By chance I opened this book at my entry of April 26; and, in pondering over it, I have forgotten what I meant to say today. That note seems unfair to Conrad though, who, after all, must remain one of the greatest writers of my time. I am doubtful whether I was right in calling *Typhoon* his crowning achievement: there is so much, so much. Perhaps that crowning achievement is *Youth*. But in *Nostromo* there is a break: the book paints a canvas too vast for the ending: for Captain Fidanza's little amours and his tragedy if such it can be called. I think it would have been better to let the book close with Captain Mitchell's reminiscent ramblings to the casual tourist, leaving old Viola, Mrs. Gould, Nostromo, etc. suspended, as it were, in mid air among the larger destinies of a nation. Even Dr. Monygham jars on me: not in the beginning when he forms part of the canvas; but towards the end where he become sentimentalised. Conrad wants us to understand too much. He can tie a knot; he cannot resolve it. He is too much the 'artist'—not enough the critic.

His technique is admirably adapted to the short story; less so for the novel. One is apt to become impatient. It is also admirably adapted for the sea-yarns in which those continual digressions and side-steps are justified, technically, as a means of showing the ramifications of those little worlds represented by his ship's crews. When he stands on land, the minuteness of the descriptions often has the very opposite effect from the one intended: instead of enhancing life or the feeling of life, they bestow something of the nature of marionettes on living human beings 'The Return'; 'Tomorrow.'

Nevertheless, taking his work by-and-large, these are small blemishes. Literature would be the poorer if *Nostromo* were to disappear. For Conrad is great, perhaps, apart from Hardy, the greatest writer that lived around the turn of the century: the most capacious mind; and he is unique: there can be no Conrad-school, for it would presuppose a group of men all having his peculiar racial antecedents. As I said, he is a phenomenon.

Jan 12, 1934   I have finished what I consider the final draft of my ant-book. It has been a desperate pull. On the average, I believe, I have been once a week on the point of giving up. From 3 to 4 hours teaching a day; managing a farm; preparing lectures. What time was left, was given to the book. No doubt it has suffered. The final Ms. is not quite finished. But the work left to do is *manual* labour. For I simply have no energy for the *labor lunae* which requires a free mind.

In order to counterbalance the intensity of my work, my reading (at night, in bed) has been very desultory: Bates, Belt, Darwin,

Whymper, Captain Cook—exploration, adventure. That sort of thing relieves me; it is a soporific.

Feb 20 The state of the world has been troubling me much of late. I sometimes think that there can be nothing ahead of us but a revival of barbarism. Yet I try to face things. Much could be done if some single nation had the courage to let reason rule.

What is the function of the state? Not the actual, empiric function, but its function as seen *sub specie aeternitatis*. It is clearly one of integration. It is clearly this: to provide a social framework within which all can flourish. Taking human nature for what it is, it can best fulfill that function by protecting its minorities. The majority can take care of itself: it needs no protection; but every minority, every heterodoxy, every heresy does; and it does not get it. But the heterodoxy of today is the orthodoxy of tomorrow; and without the freedom to grow and to develop according to the natural law inherent in it, it is bound to be an abortion, and when it displaces, when it dislodges the majority from the seat of power, in the realm of politics or the realm of the spirit, it will do so convulsively; it will do so by violence, thereby setting itself up as merely a new tyranny in lieu of the old one. This happened even in Russia for which I have much sympathy otherwise.

As it is—well, read Thucydides, opening of Book I . . .

I have heard nothing so far as to my ant-book.

April 22 Seeing the last sentence above, I can now add that the publishers, when they read the Ms. of that ant-book, dropped it like a hot potato. Oh, well . . .

By this time my winter's lectures also have gone down the stream of time; a late spring is on its halting way; I am a year older than I was when I began to jot down these notes; and I am trying desperately to hew another book into shape.

Jan 30, 1935 Nearly a year has gone by since my last entry; and it has been the hardest year I have lived through, my 63rd. I have thought hard and worked hard, with never a let-up for a day. As for my work, I have written 2 books, and I consider both of them a failure: both were 'aus dem Kopf gemacht' as Merck wrote to Goethe 160 years ago: so their result has been precisely nothing. But I am at it again; and this time I am in hope; for, as far as my thought during the year goes, I have learned, or rather I have arrived at one singular conclusion, namely that if I want to pour life into an imaginative figure, that life has to come out of unspent energy saved from dispersal in physical expenditure, chiefly sexual. Just as the sun only can build up by the slow process of photosynthesis: what sex can do, is, merely to break the synthesis down in dispersal: the great thermodynamic law of the degradation of the forms of energy. Thus also, imaginative 'creation' is a slow photosynthesis. In other words, and to put it crudely but accurately: imaginative creation is a sort of spiritual man's sex: a thing that makes me shudder and from which yet I cannot, and I feel must not, rid myself if ever I want to say what, at the moment, only I can say and which needs to be said. As far as life goes, the artist, whenever artist, is sterile; that is his curse.

Jan 31. And yet . . . Successfully to shadow forth a single utterance of an imaginative figure is a triumph greater than any bugle-sound can express; with that triumph I am very familiar: or, perhaps, I merely think I am. Since my own time has denied me recognition, it is for posterity to decide. All would be well if one had the certainty of a Milton.

In order to satisfy and lull my conscience, my economic conscience, I teach 3 short lessons now before dinner, from 11 to 12. That has cut the time for my own work down to 2 hours a day, from 9 to 11, and during even those two hours I look after the heating of the place and often after the little boy, my youngster, when he clamours for attention.

Feb. 5. 1935 Last Sunday morning W.L. Grant died at Toronto. It was a great shock to me when, over the telephone, I was briefly given the news, read from a daily paper. He was the only man I had met in 40 years, in Canada, with whom I felt absolutely at home no matter what the topic under discussion might be. He was the most modest of men, in spite of very solid achievements. He had been ill for a number of years, yet he always spoke lightly of his illness. We had only rare and few contacts. We never corresponded; I don't think there is a letter of mine to him in existence, though, somewhere, I have a letter from him—a letter that was the beginning of our friendship. Yet, when we met, mostly at his house—the principal's residence of Upper Canada College—there was never any transitional interval of strangeness during which we readjusted ourselves to each other or in which we had to try to reknit our relationship. We smiled at each other and were off, taking up as it were our conversation of yesteryear as though it had been broken off a minute ago. He does not seem to have been popular; neither am I. Perhaps our perfect understanding of each other was partly due to the fact that we were almost exactly of the same age and had had a similar background. But there was much more. Canadian as he was, he was at the same time, at least within the circle of my friends, the last of the good Europeans, understanding, f.i., the emotional entanglements of the Central European situation just I did or thought I did. I remember particularly well how, a few years ago, when he had been in Switzerland and the Bavarian Alps, he mentioned a trifling incident illustrating the commitment of a whole generation of the peasant population of Carinthia to hatred of the French; he had said a few words only when I raised my hand in a gesture of understanding anticipating all that was to follow. 'Well *you* know,' he said and did not go on. If the men sitting at Geneva were such as he, matters would straighten themselves out in no time—for good-will calls forth good-will. But, of course, Geneva is the politicians' paradise. What a farce! And what a loss to me that such a man should be gone!

Jan 5 1936 Again nearly a year has gone by; and I have struggled along with a book. Heaven knows how humbly. I should like to put down many things; but I mistrust myself . . .

Franz Werfel, *The Forty Days*—a magnificent conception, often magnificently done; yet, as a whole, a failure. Why? The mass struggle should have crystallised in the struggle of a single figure in order to become tragic. Gabriel Bagradian fails to come off.

Robert Briffault, *Europa*—another magnificent conception: the corruption of European high society, pointillistically, almost atomistically done: a book of utter, absolute despair. I cannot convince myself that this is Europe: if Europe were given with entire truth, this would be a great book. What makes it fall short of greatness is what is missing: it may be that corruption is our ultimate goal: that is what we are drifting into: but there is the revolt against it: and nowhere is that revolt as intensely alive as in Europe as witness Fascism and Communism: what is missing is the cry of defiance against destiny: if that cry were in the book, it would be tragic instead of being gloomy. Many, of course, will put it down as mere pornography; and they will be profoundly mistaken: the book is an indictment; but there is no defence, much less a verdict.

As I see it, only a new war can liberate Europe; the old war having enslaved it (to Americanism?).

Jan 12 The turn of a year seems actually to favour meditation, retrospection, criticism. I have been reviewing the last two years and tried to extract the essence of their import to me. They were filled, of course, with my almost incessant endeavour to construct an architec-

tonic whole out of the ideas and conceptions that, since 1929 when I
first conceived the book, have crystallised around *The Master of the
Mill,* and that task is not finished yet. I sometimes wish I could leave
it standing as a fragment: but a fragment of Goethe's, Shelley's,
Wordsworth's—yes; a fragment of mine: no, emphatically.

Then I have asked myself why this has been such a titanic task. The
answer is that I do not live alone; that others share my life; that I must
think of them; that I must make their lives bearable at least. So, in
1934, I rebuilt the outside of my house; last summer, the inside,
installing a water-supply, etc. This task, done under my personal
supervision, required the constant facing of concrete things and
problems: it has externalized me: I have had to turn myself inside out:
wrestling with often unwilling, sometimes dishonest workmen who
tried to get the money I did not have but had to borrow without
giving an adequate return; wrestling also with details of
arrangements which required the nicest planning to make the best of
the available space. And the worst of it is that the work has left me in
debt, so that for another two or three years and maybe longer every
effort must be put forth to cover the cost: I am right now, from day to
day, supervising the feeding of the cows, so as to squeeze, from day to
day, a little more milk out of them, at 2¢ a pound, than they would
normally give. Every penny counts. Is it worthwhile? Perhaps it is.

But I cannot but think with longing of an existence demanding a
mere minimum of externalisation in a one-roomed shack, which I
could heat with brush-wood gathered by way of exercise, where I
could feed myself with the plainest and least expensive foods, so that
my mind would be undisturbed by worry, left free to wrestle with
what I cannot but consider my real task, whether the result amounts
to anything in the long-run or not: so long as in the end, I could say, I
have done what I wanted to do, to my own satisfaction: I wonder
whether at any time, anyone can say that? Except, maybe, such as
Arthur Wesley who became the Duke of Wellington. But if I admit
that, I must admit that external success is a worth-while aim; and also
that, in that sense, I have failed in the most dismal way. However . . .
slowly, *The Master of the Mill* is creeping towards completion.

Feb 18   I had to go out last night and heard that a former pupil of
mine J.J. who, a few years ago, entered the University of Toronto to
study science is going to work in a local jam factory beginning with
next summer. Smug women gushed over the fact that a brave young
spirit had been broken by the all-around pressure of stupid uncles, all
sitting on money bags. In their, and in his mother's, view his soul had

been saved for commerce. I listened in silent scorn and at last left in a towering anger. *Sic perit gloria animae.* A few years ago, when the revolt against aunts and uncles was on, I might have said, *Parturiunt montes*; now I can add, *Nactus est ridiculus mus*; for there is not future tense about it any longer. It's all cut and dried.

Feb. 21 I have just finished writing the first draft of the end of *The Master of the Mill.* Since I am under at least a moral if not a legal obligation to finish that book in time for the international competition—which I am entering much against my wish, urged by Button and others, I have been working, for over a year, against time. But, quite apart from that, it has been a terrific pull. I have, of late, read a great deal of Antarctic exploration; and for some time I have felt pretty much as Scott—whom I dislike—must have felt in 1911/12 when he pulled south to reach the pole. It's a race against everything—the weather, the surface, the food-supply, the oil, etc. It has always been one of my desires to go on one of those expeditions, as a naturalist, as a photographer, a recorder, as what not, as cook if need be. It was one of the tragedies of my forties that I was pronounced physically unfit; of my fifties that I saw old age creeping upon me, which excluded me from the list of eligibles. I half believe that I went into the wilderness in Manitoba, teaching in little rural schools, partly at least, to satisfy that craving for arctic endeavour by a substitute, however mild. Now, that I have reached that old age (64 a week ago today) I still have my regrets; but I see that the whole of my life has been the striving after things which were denied me; my lot has been resignation, not always easily accepted; but it's all the same.

March 21. This is the commencement of spring; but another heavy snowfall cloaks the world in white; and the browns and greens are once more relegated into the realm of dreams. I read Ford Madox Ford's 'Personal Remembrance' of Joseph Conrad's, feeling profoundly stirred by the tragedy of that life. But, surely, at least he had the inner certainty of an ultimate success to bear him up—success, I mean, of course, of no material nature. He must have known that he was constantly 'doing' things, doing them once for all, finally—a knowledge which I do not have. The despair which knows no relief is almost more than I can stand. I often wonder whether anyone else has ever stood it without drawing the final conclusion.

April 2. The great luminaries of science, the Eddingtons, Jeans's, Thomsons, etc., are at bottom despondent: they try to head back into some sort of deism, if not theism, yes, even Christianity. Superstitions are never refuted by facts that contradict them: they merely require elaboration to embrace new facts. That is the reason why a superstition becomes more complex as it grows older. Science behaves in exactly the same way; and it might well be that it does so for the same reasons, namely because no ultimate reality corresponds to it. Of course, there are two kinds of sciences: one which while posing as pure science, has, nevertheless all the time one eye on the practical conclusions that may perhaps be drawn from its findings: f.i. when the structure of the atom is investigated with the view of releasing the energy latent in its differentiation into protons and electrons. This, to me, is rather a shabby thing. The other boldly faces its own problems: why should there be sciences? Einstein's answer, as opposed to that of the English scientists, who at bottom remain evangelists, is almost refreshing: it arises out of man's urge to construct for himself a model of the universe which he can grasp with his imagination: never mind whether it corresponds to its original or not. That is courage.

April 6   The appeal to intuition and instinct (Bergson) is at bottom a detour back to revelation.
History: A rationalism of what led up to (or, with the popular fallacy, produced) the present. Like democracy, it necessarily neglects the minorities. He who, by divination or stupidity (chance) helps to bring about what is remains the great man: how could he who helped to bring about *me* fail to be great? He who perhaps had the vision of a better world to come but failed to hit the path of least resistance which development was to go is a mere rebel.
Science: Whatever we are must have been contained, not merely potentially, but germinally—in the sense in which the child is as old as the parent—in the youngest nebula. Pantheism in this sense is the only cosmogonic system which seems compatible with reason: if we decline it, there is only a *credo quia absurdum* left. The question is, of course, to what extent *our* reason is reason.
Civilisation: Just as the strength of a chain is determined by its weakest link, thus the state of a nation should be measured not by its highest but by its lowest member. Only if even the poorest member of a community lives in a state of plenty should we speak of prosperity. Only if the least educated stands on the level of, let me say, a Hamlet, should we speak of an educated nation. So long as education (by which I do not mean the 'induction' of the schools) is purely sporadic or atomistic, the state is in danger, no matter what its form. But if that ideal were realised, forms of government would be

irrelevant: anarchism in its highest sense would become possible; yes, as it is desirable, it would be inevitable.

April 7. 'Humanism,' so-called, vs. 'Superhumanism' (Aldous Huxley). Is not this just playing with words? Whether we call it Perfectionism or Superhumanism, what does it matter? Between these hectic modern formulations and the older ethics, whether formulated by Pascal or Spinoza (Christian, Jewish), there is at bottom only one difference, namely that 'we'—for on that point I can include myself—are inclined to restore to the bodily functions their innocence—which is all to the good. In other words, 'our' eschatology is different. We have abolished hell and thereby eliminated one more fear. But then, generally speaking, our interest in ethics has waned. Perhaps because we are too narrowly beset by its problems: they have become problems of immediate, practical policy: it was a choice between 'the dole' and a new 'Bauernaufstand.' And we should feel ashamed of taking credit for doling out the dole. Are we going to deny that, if we want to get back to an ordinary feeling of decency about our attitudes, we need unattainable ideals? I've had my say about them somewhere else. The point is, perhaps, that we have merely shifted our point of view. Our eschatological shivers are concerned, not so much with our personal, immediate fate after death—we are inclined to take that lightly—as with the fate of the race and its abode. Our outlook has lengthened; we are, therefore, farther from any solution than mankind ever was, consciously. If we despair, our lack of faith is more rational; if we don't, there may be two reasons: we may be more callous or we may be braver than was the past. When I ponder Pascal's 'fameux morceau' dealing with the Deux Infinis I doubt the latter. At any rate, if I were to choose between Aldous Huxley and Blaise Pascal, I should not hesitate. It befits the frog to approach the mountain with reverence.

Ultimately, there is only one problem; and it is epistemological. Can we or can we not escape from our senses? But it is a fundamental characteristic of man to desire that escape. In that desire alone lies his dignity; it alone marks him off from the rest of animate creation. Surely no Huxley is going to persuade us to a shallow optimism.

That shallow optimism is shown up in his essay on Revolution. I sometimes wonder whether, in thinking of it today (this is 1936) its writer has the saving grace of feeling ashamed of himself. If he does there may be hope for him, 'well-born and well-bred'—he calls himself.

August 10, '36.   I treated myself yesterday, on the gramophone, to
the Ninth Symphony (Beethoven's—is it necessary to name him?);
and it made me homesick for Europe—the landscape of lower
Austria, Upper Bavaria—and for my youth. If it is true for the new
generation that 'it will not do to play Beethoven after Debussy,' as
one of its members recently said to me, then I pity the new generation.
No need for me to say anything about the music, to analyse it or
interpret it; others have done so better than I could do it though I have
never read anything that seemed adequate. My personal preference—
if such there is, for any part—goes to the slow movement: the Presto
overwhelms me, but it does not touch me to tears; and the first
movement is too intimately personal to me for me to detach myself
and admire Beethoven: it is not he, but I that am speaking. The
Scherzo is the voice of rollicking universes, enormous, but too god-
like for a mere human like me: if Hardy, in *The Dynasts*, had been
able to laugh at it all, he might have created something corresponding to it in literature.

I had intended to follow it up by the 9th Sonata; but I couldn't. It
would have been like descending from something cosmic to . . . what?
Perhaps in a week or so. I'll follow it up by the Eroica, the fifth,
which is something like a human translation and which I have not
heard for over forty years. I do not possess [it]. If I ever get it, I wonder
whether it still can exist by the side of the Ninth. Perhaps it can, it
also being Beethoven. Wagner, without the operatic staging, cannot.

Aug. 11.   Another summer is on the wane: the driest summer on
record in these parts: economically the hardest I have ever lived
through, not including those of my direst poverty. Yet cows
somehow live; calves are born; and the farm survives. I am writing a
novel dealing with the actualities of the situation.

Aug. 17.   If only one knew. There is in me, these days, a restless
disquietude: have I done what I could do? Have I not perhaps failed
in putting forth that last effort needed to make this or that work of
mine one which would *stand?* Perhaps, if today, or yesterday, or the
day before, I had stuck to my task for one hour longer . . . perhaps. I
say, I might have imparted to the written word that last incandes-
cence which would have enabled it to throw the spark of life . . .

When nobody else has a corn-crop around here in Norfolk
County, I have the best and most abundant crop I have ever had. I am
afraid I was boasting about it the other night when a neighbour of
mine remarked upon it. 'No,' I said, 'it isn't the soil. It's cultivation.

As for corn, anybody can have a good crop if he goes to quite the necessary trouble. I've plowed that field twice,' I said, 'and I've manured it twice. And then I've harrowed it 32 times: once east-west; then north-south, then twice diagonally at right angles, and that I've done eight times.' The neighbour laughed. 'Yes,' he said, 'if that's your secret, it's easy enough to be a good farmer, provided you have someone else's sweat to use.' Miss——said the other day, 'you must be in league with the devil to have a crop when everybody else is burned out.' And was she not right? Have I not been in league with the devil of capitalism? But there is another side to it, too; when there was no work for anyone, I have kept two men employed, working for them myself, going without many things in order to pay them their wages; working harder than ever, borrowing money which will have to be repaid when the teaching season starts again. And perhaps I have worked too fast, trying to force matters instead of letting them come; working till I felt exhausted, and, perhaps, not harrowing my book thirty-two times as I had vicariously harrowed the cornfield.

If only . . .

Aug 23   History is an immense simplification. If all the factors that make up a given historical situation, let me say like the present, were known, everything would, for any such situation, look dubious as it does today. Only the event clarifies; and concerning the past, events are known; they are unknown concerning the present. No occurrence, no personality is of any paramount importance; they become important if the event lies in the line which they mark. If the event had lain in a different line, their opponents or their opposites would have become important; they themselves would have sunk into oblivion. That is the pragmatism of history: he is a great man whom the event aligns with itself. We say he foresaw the event and aligns himself with it. This is very rarely, if ever, the case. That is also the reason why history kills the past: the past was a present: the present is conflict; when the present becomes the past, the conflicts have been resolved. Who knows whether the defeated sides did not represent reason and truth? (Cicero—Catilina)

Aug 30.   This has been the most disastrous summer on record in this district. Instead of increasing my herd, I have diminished it by sacrificing several head; both to provide money for paying wages and to save feed. Everything was parched; there was no pasture; apart from the corn nothing grew. Grass did not grow; I seeded some ten acres of it; it came up and died, that was all. It will take a year's hard work to make up for it. Yet, does it matter? One lives and defends life. . . . Success is not the measure; the measure is in the intensity of the effort. But health has been bad; well, even the sensation of pain remains a manifestation of life.

There was a woman here yesterday, wife of a would-be writer, trying to sell me her husband's book. I told her at last that I could spend $20,000 on a single order for books which I covet; but her husband's would not be among them. That settled the matter; but not before she had whined for half an hour about the predicament of the Canadian writer, lowering, in my eyes, the whole level of the profession. If the man threw his book on the market and left it to find its way, I'd respect him as a man if not as a writer. Is it not enough to have had one's say? I have rarely been so profoundly stirred to anger.

Oct. 23.   For my own education I have read half through a book by Edgar Wallace: *The Frightened Lady*. When I consider the cheapness of its effects, the amazingly bad writing, and the vulgarity of it all, I am despondent. If that is what the public buys, no wonder that good books go begging. Yet the man had talent: there are occasional phrases which are good. 'The dough of his pomposity' comes to mind.

Nov. 15. I have read two cathedral stories in succession: Walpole's *Inquisitor*, and Trollope's *Barchester Towers*. Of the two I prefer the latter. There are all sorts of things that shock me: the names, f.i., Mrs. Brundie, the Lookalofts, Drs. Fillgrave and Rerechild, Farmer Subsoil, the Rev. Mr. Inoverful, etc. Passages like 'And where would be my novel?' The disquisitions about the technique and the characters. In my first indignation I ask myself, whether this author really means to pay me so poor a compliment as to think it necessary to expound his text to me. On second thought I laugh; but not with, rather at, the author. On third thought I come to the conclusion that I can well afford to overlook such childishness, in return for what I am getting. How four-square Dr. Grantly stands to the wind, or, perhaps, to the light in his dining-room! What a courage in delineation a man like Slope attests! It's amazing. Nothing like that in Walpole: his figures are blurred, down to Penny Marlowe. It is as though, in making a photograph portrait, the lens were, perhaps intentionally, adjusted slightly out of focus, in order to avoid sharp lines. Both writers are verbose, of course. But I don't lose my temper about Trollope's verbosity. And how much clearer, sharper his cathedral stands against the sky! And the close; and the rectories, etc.

Of course, I will not defend Mrs. Proudie against Henry James. She borders on caricature; and there is little blood-warmth. Proudie himself, of course, is not supposed to have blood in his veins.

Nov 22. I ran across a saying of Schopenhauer's: no matter what course of action we pursue, there is always some urge in our nature (probably 'Drang'; for I ran across it in translation and have since been trying to reconstruct the German text) which could only find satisfaction in a contrary course.

This is one of the profoundest things I've read in a long while; and I could not defend myself against the desire to draw the application for myself.

I have chosen, deliberately, poverty and the arduous life. Deliberately; for I had some experience of the opposite. I have similarly chosen a life in which the concomitant of poverty rules: a strict, scrupulous honesty which, f.i. forbids me to buy what I cannot immediately pay for. This, in my case, the case of the productive artist, should, logically, lead me to a life of absolute self-denial: I have led such a life; but it has been vitiated by the fact that I am married and have a child. Even marriage and procreation I should have denied myself. I have done this for the purpose of writing my books, writing them without a view to the market.

But there is in me—and I have, for a short period of my youth and early manhood, given in to that element—the exactly contrary desire of a reckless spender: I have always considered, especially when in contact with my wealthy friends, that nobody knows quite as well as I do how to spend money. I have dreamt of what I would and could do if I were a millionaire; and when I look at my millionaire friends, I always say to myself, 'What a mess they are making of their lives!' In fact, I am a born spender.

Probably that is the reason why, in spite of my intellectual assent to the doctrines of socialism or communism, my inner nature has always stood aloof. Very likely, if I were a millionaire, I should be a better socialist than I am as a poor man. 'Christ's Alternative to Socialism'? Why, it is socialism; but socialism from above, not from below. 'Give to the poor that thou hast and follow me!' Christ had a sense of humour; the rich man, not a socialist, turned away. 'for he had many possessions.' What a satire hidden away in the gospel! But that is exactly what the other element in my own nature could cause me to do.

Jan 27 1937 During the last three or four days I have gone through what may appear to many as a trivial, but what seems to me a very peculiar experience. About 2 weeks ago my little boy received a pair of skates; and they made him superlatively happy. Naturally, it fell to my task to take him to the ice; and as, from the shore of the ponds, I watched and instructed him, I found certain muscles of mine executing involuntary movements; it was these muscles which urged me on. Last Saturday I borrowed a pair of skates for myself and, after 45 years went on the ice for the first time. I at once flew away, as sure on my feet as I ever was, in spite of my 65 years. That, perhaps, was nothing to wonder at; it was the same thing as happened to me some 5 yrs. ago when, after 40 years, I plunged for the first time into deep water and swam as well as I had swum in my youth.

The peculiar thing happened on Sunday. Without being conscious of what I was doing, I surrendered myself to my muscular impulses; and soon I found myself describing certain figures on the ice which I did not consciously remember. Thus, describing, on my right foot, an awkward arc, I brought my left foot slowly forward, swinging it around my centre of gravity as a pivot. Then, having reached the point where the initial impulse of that arc was nearly exhausted, I brought the left foot sharply forward, meanwhile assuming a perpendicular position. This threw my right foot, on the ice, sharply back, in a straight line; and a moment later, I found myself describing a second forward arc on the outward edge of my skate. I could not tell how I had done it. Then, without being aware of my intention, I repeated the same movement on my left foot, thereby closing the figure: like this:

 ; and, repeating and repeating the alternation from foot to foot, I soon marked out, on the ice, a distinctly visible figure which, *only now*, brought back to me the mental memory of a favourite display of skill on the ice which I had practised 50 years ago. This was, to me, a very striking example of purely muscular memory.

Surrendering myself to these awakened muscular memories, I soon found myself describing other figures as well; especially one which I could not possibly have *thought* up out of the past; but which my muscles remembered, like this:

with a double reversal of the arc in each of the four limbs of the figure and one reversal of direction in each half, at the point: from a to b being run backward; then, from d to e, forward again, on the other foot; and from e to f. backward.

To my surprise I found myself performing feats of balance which I could not but admire; and which, above all, brought back, to my mental memory, the happy days of my youth when, for many hours together, I revelled in the mere display of my physical powers and skill. The thrill I got out of this—and am getting out of it—is far greater than the thrill I got out of my first flight in an aeroplane, 11 years ago, over the Pacific near the Oregon coast. I sometimes wonder, now, whether we were meant for mental feats when the performance of physical feats can fill us with such exultant happiness. I made up my mind not to let a day pass by without skating while there is ice and while I have these borrowed skates; and also, to do a good deal of swimming next summer. I only regret that the state of my ears debars me from diving. Incidentally, I resolved to supervise my little boy's apprenticeship on the ice, day after day; so that he will not miss one of the purest sensations which I have known in life. He must learn to swim, too, next summer; and I hope he will be made as happy as I have been, in the mere practise of physical skill.

What made me write down this note, however, is that, to me, very strange phenomenon of a muscular memory across the gulf of nearly half a century. I mean to make up for what I have lost in life by being—I, essentially am amphibian—marooned, for 40 years and longer, in the centre of a great continent.

Note added to this on Feb 14.: Had a crash: one foot got caught in a crack in the ice and brought me down, injuring hip and elbow: a serious point at my age; and willy-nilly the skating had to end.

I have read Hardy's *A Pair of Blue Eyes* which I don't think I had ever read before. As far as Hardy's work is concerned, taking it as a whole, it seems a mere trifle; but, having recently read a number of ultra-moderns, Aldous Huxley, Irene Rathbone, etc; and semi-moderns, like Somerset Maugham (*Cakes & Ale*) and George Moore (*Esther Waters*), I am tremendously impressed by his power of laying bare the slightest, sometimes almost imperceptible movements of a soul, often without expressly analysing them (esp. between Knight and Elfride). As usual, there is also the magnificence of the landscape, Cornish, I suppose. How he instinctively goes to the remote, concentrating all his powers on the innder *peripeteia*. No wonder, he gains in influence while others decline. He is *the* great late Victorian;

more modern than many of the Edwardians or Georgians. I don't
know just how much my skating has to do with it. There is the
expanse of the ice, filling the hollows of my fields; and I describe on it
little inconsequential figures. The ice is nature, or life, or what you
will; and the tragedies of Stephen Smith, Harry Knight, and Elfride
Swancourt are such little inconsequential figures: what do they
matter? Set them into their proper perspective; and they matter no
more than the death of a mosquito that has alighted on my ear. This
proper perspective, in a tremendous, wide urge towards life, on
Egdon Heath, in the Fjords of the Cornish coast, and so on, which
Hardy achieves, almost instinctively, that is what, over and above his
psychological subtlety, gives him his greatness, his 'envergure' as,
some dozen years ago, I called it; the Germans, I believe, call it
'Schwungweite.' He sails like an eagle over the landscape, noting the
details, but seeing the curvature of the earth from horizon to horizon.

Jan 29.   From skating to the unconscious: it seems a leap but is not.
For it may be said that, during the 45 yrs, while I never went on the
ice, I knew unconsciously how to skate. The muscular memory of
which I spoke had, as far as my mind went, lapsed into the
unconscious; it had been 'repressed'—in the Freudian sense.

But right there seems, to me, to lie the weakness of Freudianism: in
addition to this lapsed memory there is something else in the
unconscious, namely that which, so far, in the human mind and
consciousness, is merely potential. It is true that, not having any
access to books, I cannot be sure that this conception is really missing
in Freud; I am merely judging from such echoes as I have read and
such discussions as I have heard. But, if there is any meaning at all,
apart from the accumulation of discoveries and inventions, in the
idea of progress, it can be only this that, potentially, there were
nascent, or germinally contained in primitive man, the beginnings of
all such things as, in the course of time, have, so far, found this
development. Thus, f.i., the potentialities of Christianity must have
lain dormant, or not yet awakened, in the Graeco-Roman world; that
is, in its subconsciousness. The unfolding of this subconsciousness,
the gradual making, of it, conscious, constitutes human progress or
evolution; and for this it is quite irrelevant whether we assume that
evolution to have proceeded by slow variation or sudden mutation.
That '*natura non facit saltus*' seems a maxim definitely abandoned
by biology. But though every *saltus* seems to be a jump into the
unknown which—like the tusk of the narwhale—may lead to
ultimate disaster, it is certain that no *saltus* can be undertaken
without its possibility—its date—as it were, being given in what

preceded it; in other words, without its being contained in the preceding stage of evolution; and this applies necessarily to the mental as well as to the physical. Thus the idea of sin in Greek tragedy (ὕβρις) is contained in the idea of gentlemanly fighting with which the *Iliad* is informed. Similarly, the Aeschylean idea of atonement, is contained in the pre-Aeschylean idea of sin. The idea of civilisation (in my opinion arising out of the idea of the desire for security, at first probably purely economic security) sprang out of the herd-idea (hunting in tribes or clans, with primitive communism). Etc. etc.

But why stop with man? If man developed or evolved out of an animal ancestry, then, one day, we should be able to go farther back, behind man; and we should be able to assert that the whole modern civilisation, material and mechanical as well as cultural and spiritual lay subconsciously dormant in those animal ancestors of man who are still so problematical. If it is true that, somewhere in man's ancestry, in tracing it backward, we come upon marine creatures, fishes perhaps, though not necessarily, we must assert that in these marine animals all the potentialities of our present-day civilisation, such as it is, were subconsciously given; and that all evolution consists in one or two things: a working, from the unconscious, from the potentialities latent in any given phase, into the conscious; or a budding out and developing of physical characteristics not yet apparent to such apparency (as f.i., the wing of the imago of the common grasshopper are potentially present in the wingless larva that comes from the egg).

Then, why stop with the animal creation, short of postulating the miracle? Of course, if we assume every *saltu* or mutation to be a creative miracle performed by some superhuman miracle-man or miracle-god, there is the end of that. But, if such a *saltus* is merely the sudden drawing of a sum, or the summing up of addenda already given, then it resembles rather a revelation or unveiling of that which was already there than a miracle. I being a novelist (though one who has not succeeded in putting forth his innermost ideas) the conception of a miracle is profoundly repulsive to me—in spite of the fact that (according to Dostoievski) the cry for the miracle is a cry fundamental to human nature. If organic life, at some stage of the evolution of this earth (and we know nothing of other worlds), arose spontaneously, by some chance encounter of the chemical constituents of the perhaps ever so humble first living being, then we cannot stop there: we must say that, subconsciously, the whole modern human world was contained in the prime elements of this planet when it was torn from the vitals of the sun, whether by tidal action or not matter how; for this is an a-priori conclusion, arrived at by a process of deduction which is the crown and end of antecedent induction. When I watch—as I have done—the slow but unfailing accretion of crystals, I cannot defend myself against the conclusion that there, in the orderly assembling of molecules we have the first beginnings of organism; and would it be wrong to say that the amorphous aspect of inorganic nature is due rather to the breaking up of crystalline structure than to any state antecedent to such crystalline organisation? Crystallisation would be re-crystallisation, rather.

I would, then, say that all evolution, from the inorganic, so-called—or the crystalline—to the organic—or living—up to and including man is, not so much a creation, as a revelation of the unconscious or subconscious potentialities combined even in the atom.

Sometimes I go so far—especially when I ponder the conclusions at which physics has arrived with regard to the structure (or the life?) of the atom—as to conceive the whole visible universe as an organism in which suns may be protons and planets electrons or what not. And then an idea of God arises: as the not yet entirely conscious, but gradually becoming conscious universe: a new sort of pantheism or Judaism.

Feb. 2.   At any rate, there is no escaping from this dilemma that mind, soul or whatever you care to call it (and perhaps one should be satisfied with some such appellation as consciousness or sentience) is either a separate creation (in the Darwinian sense) arising out of a separate originator, personal or impersonal, or inherent in matter. from a lifelong observation of 'matter,' in the accepted sense, whether inorganic or organic, in crystals or in trees, f.i., I should be inclined to believe that, just as according to latter-day physics, matter=energy, thus energy=sentience; and that, therefore matter=sentience—which sounds startling and may or may not be so.

April 13.   I have been reading a good deal of antarctic and arctic exploration again; and, since I now know the main outline of what has been done in either field, it is perhaps natural that I should concentrate my attention upon the human faces behind the narratives. To my surprise—for I thought I did not like him—Scott comes out first. The chief reason, I believe, is that he keeps his eye constantly on the object and never attempts to improve his presentation of it by the graces of wit, humour, or fine language.

Nansen, equally to my surprise, came off least well, with his everlasting zwei-Seelen philosophy. It is strange how little of his narrative is concerned with the object, how much with himself: did he not realize that an explorer who is worth his salt (i.e. a man of action) should be, if he isn't, an explorer to the point where his exploration makes it impossible to be a philosopher besides? That, at best, he might be— what he is—a second-hand and second-rate philosopher? Sometimes he makes the impression as if he were himself impressed with the fact that he can quote Goethe: but he never does so to illustrate or illumine his immediate object; when he does it, it is invariably in order to remind the reader of how interesting is his own soul—which, consequently, loses all interest; whereas Scott who rarely speaks of himself and never with a view to posing as a personality for that very reason grows upon one as the truly heroic figure he was.

Ponting and Priestley are dwarfs compared with Scott. Ponting deals largely in comic phrases; and his attempts at humour are painful. Priestley would gain tremendously in impressiveness if he were not so intent on showing up as a hero. Campbell is better; but, then, one everlastingly asks himself, Why did these people go through the hardships at Evans Coves: what for? Where are the results to justify the sufferings they underwent? Priestley's volume, therefore, impresses me like a novel written on a theme which, at best, would justify a short story. I am doubtful about Shackleton. He was nearly always insufficiently equipped: as though he rushed in for the sake of its being he who does the thing: if he had waited, someone might have forestalled him. The story of the Quest is one of simple, utter incompetence. Yet the man did one or two magnificent things.

Remains Scott: and I wish I had his 4 vols (of the *Discovery* and the *Terra Nova* days) on my shelves. They are a classic. Perry cannot compare with him: he was of too coarse a fibre.

Sverdrup, by the way, in the fourth quarter of Nansen's *Farthest North*, is considerably better than the sentimental doctor himself: *he*, though he does not see a great deal, sees what he sees with his eye on the object, instead of on himself. Similarly Ponting is much better than in his narrative where he simply describes: his penguin chapters are almost good (apart from the writing which is largely second-hand: stencils or clichés).

Have, by the way, just finished first draft of *Felix Powell's Career*. Believe I shall rather like it—have been busy on it since Nov. 15.

May 16. Darwin's biography, by his son. The man emerges, for me, with a tremendously enhanced stature. I had always considered his stumbling on the idea of evolution as a chance happening, as Roentgen stumbled on the rays which have revolutionised modern physics. I know, of course, from my reading of ½ doz of Darwin's books (among which I have always loved the Beagle vol., reading it on an average once every two years or so, for the last 30 years) with what exceeding care he documented every step in his argument. But I took him for a much more plodding pedestrian than he really is. The story of the preparation for and the ultimate writing of the *Origin* has become one of the great poignant stories for me: the struggle of genius reaching beyond its grasp and thereby stretching, by slow degrees, its own stature till it stands over-life-size, tragic in its greatness: f.i. his concern about what might happen if he died, in 1845, 14 years before the completion of the work: his sole concern being about the idea not himself: science must prosper even though he perish, setting aside from £400 to 500 for someone else to finish and organise his work. The constant struggle with ill health, though not, in his case, with poverty. Etc. etc. Also the straightforward honesty or honorableness with which Wallace's work was acknowledged. For the first time he stands, to me, in the forefront of the very considerable men whom the 19th century produced. His life, like that of R.F. Scott, becoming an inspiration. I might reach higher myself, stretch my gifts, though, if I had friends like Henslow, Hooker, Lyell. Yet it is touching to hear this man say (in a letter to Jenyns, if I remember right). 'I am a bold man to lay myself open to being thought a complete fool, and a deliberate one,' or words to that effect, especially when one considers that his argument forms today the corner-stone in the building of all modern biology. As I said, like most biographies of really great men, it makes an amazing, often appalling story.

May 17. I have just played a game of patience and successfully cheated chance. Why a man should play patience without pitting his brain against the stupidity of chance is beyond my grasp. It goes without saying that any interferences with chance in a game *à deux* or *à trois* is quite out of the question and not to be thought of. But I resent the phrase used by lookers-on, 'you are cheating yourself.' I am not cheating anyone. I am merely engineering my shuffling in such a way that I come out once in two games, proving to myself that brain can beat chance.

January 3, 1938   For the first time in my life on this continent (in 46 years), I have had music every week (mostly over the radio). Within 3 weeks I have heard Beethoven's 2nd, 3rd, 6th, and 9th symphonies; Schubert's 7th, Tchaikowski's 5th & 6th, Sibelius' *Finlandia* and one unnamed symphony; besides numerous concertos, among them Bach, Beethoven (the lovely opus 125), Tchaikowski, etc. etc. Of operas, Wagner's *Walküre*, Mozart's *Don Giovanni*, Gounod's *Romeo and Juliet*, and Verdi's *Trovatore*.

It is demoralising, and it has completely crippled me for the moment. The thing has a curious effect hearing, in addition, because they are forced on me, Weber (*Euryanthe*), Puccini (*La Bohème*), Offenbach, etc, I feel as if I had moved and lived on, whereas the world has stood still: as if I had, 40 years ago, left a great city with its multifarious distractions, travelled over a world, leaving all that behind, outgrowing it, and had, at last, come to another great city (a composite city, this time) and found the same divertissements going on there; in fact, as if I had, at the end of my journey, returned to the same city and found it much changed. This does not apply to Wagner for whom I used to share a high enthusiasm. That it should also apply to Verdi is not surprising. Beethoven and, to a less extent (because less familiar to me, with a few notable exceptions), Bach have always been with me; whereas Wagner had become a mere memory of an outgrown phase. Even in Wagner, though, there are exceptions: 'Am stillen Herd,' f.i. from *Die Meistersinger*. With 'Im fernen Land' the case is different. It also was with me throughout: but not as a living part of me (as, f.i., the third, slow movement of the 9th of Beethoven); rather as a fossil which had power to stir me chiefly by reason of having once stirred me when I was a young man. Whenever I thought of it—as of the Walküren-Ritt—what came to life in me, was not the music, but my own younger self, my own youth—a vanished world.

I cannot entirely welcome all this. It disturbs me too profoundly. It saps my own creative power, and even my desire to create. It has all been said: Beethoven has said it: he has said most of what I might say in the first movement of the 9th. He has posed the questions; and there are no answers.

A story that has moved me deeply during the recent holiday season is Herman Melville's *Billy Budd*—in spite of its romantic implications.

Now it is over I hope; and I shall have to find my slow way back to my *Peasant Revolt* ('Democracy?')

[Just happened to read the note of Nov. 24, 1933 on my ant-book: 'I am now firmly convinced that I have the final form. But have I?' Well—I had not; I know that the book will still have to be written.]

April 6.   Again over three months have gone by since my last entry; and I am running across this book by the mere chance of my cleaning my desk. What have these 3 months brought me?

A sort of Peasant Revolt inside of me. They have been three months of the profoundest economic depression through which I have lived; and, therefore, of the most frantic endeavours to break it. Everything seemed to have gone wrong. There was practically no income: $4.75 a week or within a few pennies. I had to have paper: I had to have many trifles. But, in order to be able to spend 23¢ on a box of matches, I had to plan for weeks ahead and to gather the sum together by pennies. The strange thing is that, within this great, relatively prosperous country, it would be entirely within the possibilities for a man like myself who refuses to apply for help, to starve to death if he persists in doing what he was meant to do, namely in standing critically face to face with things, instead of immersing himself in them. Of course, I am too old now in any case. But, had I foreseen what has happened—that, as a writer, I should be forgotten in my retreat—would it have made any difference in the past when I was still young enough to do other things? As a matter of fact, I am just obstinate enough not to mind for myself; I could live in a hovel and go on, damning the world. But my wife? And my boy?

June 3, 1940   The problem of survival for the human race is one of production; at least if the mechanisation of life is to go on.

We are, at present, clearly living on capital. We are using up oil and minerals at an appalling rate. But, no matter what the rate, so long as the fact remains that, in addition to what is being produced by utilising the energy coming to us from the sun, we are using what, of that energy, has been stored on earth in by-gone aeons, we must face that other fact that, the earth being limited in time as well as space, that stored energy is limited and will be exhausted sooner or later. Now it is time that the energy coming to us from the outside is far from being completely utilised by production; and that that utilisation can be enormously increased; but it is equally true that it is limited and perhaps even that it is diminishing.

But, of course, man is improvident.

Notes

it is a 'she'

The only known review of *Fruits of the Earth* by a woman, Mary Davidson, appeared in *The Twentieth Century* (15 Mar. 1933); Davidson's review does not, however, stress the simplicity of the novel.

a 'thrilling romance' of Canadian life

This reference, like the reference in the preceding entry, is vague; consequently, conclusive identification of the review is difficult, if not impossible. I cannot find any reviewer who celebrates *Fruits of the Earth* as a 'thrilling romance,' though some come close: Robert Gernon, reviewing it in *Everyman* (4 Feb. 1933), describes *Fruits of the Earth* as a 'thrilling story'; while John C. Moore, reviewing it in *the Bookmark*, terms the novel 'as exciting as a thriller.'

omni ignotum pro magnifico

'unknown to everyone because of its grandeur'

'Rugby' Farm

Compare the 'Author's Note' to *Fruits of the Earth*. Included in the correspondence held in the University of Manitoba's Grove Collection is a letter to the novelist from J.M. Allan, the secretary-treasurer for the rural municipality of Elton, in response to Grove's request for information about the 'Rugby' farm; the letter is dated February 14, 1928.

cogito ergo sum/cogitas ergo sum

René Descartes' famous *cogito ergo sum*, 'I think; therefore, I am' which Grove counters with *cogitas ergo sum*, 'You think; therefore, I am.'

somnia formosa candidiora die

The line, *somnia formosa candidiora die* ['beautiful dreams more shining than the day],' is quoted in J.W. MacKail's *Lectures on Greek Poetry* (London: Longmans, Green and Co. Ltd., 1910) on p. 95; it is from the *Sappho Phaoni*.

gold medal for literature

The Royal Society awarded Grove the Lorne Pierce Medal, given for distinguished service to Canadian literature, in 1934.

labor lunae

'the labour of the moon'; that is, night labour

sub specie aeternitatis

'underneath the appearance of eternity'

sic perit gloria animae

'thus perishes the glory of the soul'

Parturiunt montes/Nactus est ridiculus mus

The reference here is to Horace: 'The mountains are in labour' and 'a ridiculous mouse is born.'

urged by Button

Henry Button (1884-1962), who in 1936 was editor of J.M. Dent and Sons in Toronto, publisher of *Fruits of the Earth*. Attempts to identify the 'international competition' have proved inconclusive. For a discussion of the evidence, see Paul Hjartarson, *Frederick Philip Grove at Work: A Study of the Drafts of* **The Master of the Mill** (Diss. Queen's University, 1981), pp. 91-93.

οἵη περ φύλλων γενεή, τοίη δὲ καὶ ἀνδρῶν.

From Book 6 of the *Iliad*: 'As is the generation of leaves, so is that of man.'

Ford Madox Ford's 'Personal Remembrance'

The reference is presumably to Ford's *Joseph Conrad: A Personal Remembrance* (1924).

credo quia absurdum

'I believe because it is absurd,' that is, there is only one conclusion left—that one must believe because it is absurd.

natura non facit saltus

'Nature does not make jumps.' υβρις is Greek for 'hubris,' overbearing pride or presumption.

Paul Hjartarson and Douglas O. Spettigue

SELECTED BIBLIOGRAPHY

(The following bibliography is based upon a more detailed and comprehensive bibliographical study of Frederick Philip Grove's writing, including his work as an author and translator in Germany, to be published by The Bibliographical Society of Canada.)

Books by Frederick Philip Grove

Wanderungen. Munchen: In Kommission I. Littauer, 1902.

Helena und Damon: Ein Spiel in Versen. München: In Kommission I. Littauer, 1902.

Oscar Wilde. Moderne Essays, No. 29. Berlin: Gosse und Tetzlaff, 1903; rpt. 1907; rpt. *Oscar Wilde.* Transl. and Introd. Barry Asker. Vancouver: William Hoffer, 1984.

Randarabesken zu Oscar Wilde. Minden: J.C.C. Bruns, 1903.

Fanny Essler: Ein Roman. Stuttgart: Axel Juncker, [1905]; rpt. [1907]; rpt. *Fanny Essler.* Transl. C. Helmer, A.W. Riley and D.O. Spettigue. Ed. and Introd. A.W. Riley and D.O. Spettigue. 2 vols. Ottawa: Oberon, 1984.

Maurermeister Ihles Haus: Roman. Berlin: Karl Schnabel, 1906; rpt. Dresden: Carl Reissner, 1909. transl. as *The Master Mason's House.* Transl. Paul Gubbins. Ed. and Introd. A.W. Riley and D.O. Spettigue. Ottawa: Oberon, 1976.

Over Prairie Trails. Toronto: McClelland and Stewart, 1922; rpt. Toronto: Macmillan, 1929; rpt. Introd. Malcolm Ross. New Canadian Library, No. 1. Toronto: McClelland and Stewart, 1957.

The Turn of the Year. Foreword Arthur L. Phelps. Toronto: McClelland and Stewart, 1923; rpt. Toronto: Macmillan, 1929.

Settlers of the Marsh. New York, George H. Doran; Toronto: Ryerson, 1925; rpt. New York: Grosset & Dunlap, [1927]; rpt. Introd. Thomas Saunders. New Canadian Library, No. 50. Toronto: McClelland and Stewart, 1966.

A Search For America. Ottawa: Graphic, 1927; rpt. 1928; rpt. Carillon Book Club of Canada. Ottawa: Graphic, [1928]; rpt. as *A Search for America: The Odyssey of an Immigrant*. New York: Louis Carrier, 1928; rpt. With Author's Notes to the Fourth Edition. Toronto: Ryerson, 1939; rpt. as *A Search for America: The Odyssey of an Immigrant*. With Author's Notes to the Fourth Edition. Introd. Stanley E. McMullin. New Canadian Library. No. 76. Toronto: McClelland and Stewart, 1971.

Our Daily Bread: A Novel. New York: Macmillan; Toronto: Macmillan, 1928; rpt. London: Jonathan Cape, 1929; rpt. as *Our Daily Bread*. Introd. D.O. Spettigue. New Canadian Library, No. 114. Toronto: McClelland and Stewart, 1975.

It Needs to be Said . . . . Toronto: Macmillan, 1929; rpt. Introd. W.J. Keith. Ottawa: Tecumseh, 1982.

The Yoke of Life. New York: Richard R. Smith; Toronto: Macmillan, 1930.

Fruits of the Earth. London, Toronto: J.M. Dent and Sons, 1933; rpt. Introd. M.G. Parks. New Canadian Library, No. 49. Toronto: McClelland and Stewart, 1965.

Two Generations: A Story of Present-Day Ontario. Author's Limited Edition. n.p. n.d. [1939]. Toronto: Ryerson; 1939.

The Master of the Mill. Toronto: Macmillan, 1944; rpt. Introd. R.E. Watters. New Canadian Library, No. 19. Toronto: McClelland and Stewart, 1961.

In Search of Myself. Toronto: Macmillan, 1946; rpt. Introd. D.O. Spettigue. New Canadian Library, No. 94. Toronto: McClelland and Stewart, 1977.

Consider Her Ways. Toronto: Macmillan, 1947; rpt. Introd. D.O. Spettigue. New Canadian Library, No. 132. Toronto: McClelland and Stewart, 1977.

Tales From the Margin: The Selected Short Stories of Frederick Philip Grove. Ed. and Introd. Desmond Pacey. Toronto: Ryerson-McGraw-Hill, 1971.

The Letters of Frederick Philip Grove. Ed. and Introd. Desmond Pacey. Toronto: Univ. of Toronto Press, 1976.

*The Genesis of Grove's **The Adventures of Leonard Broadus:** A Text and Commentary*. Ed. with commentary by Mary Rubio. Guelph: Canadian Children's Press, 1983.

CRITICISM

I BOOKS

Pacey, Desmond. *Frederick Philip Grove*. Canadian Men of Letters Series. Toronto: Ryerson, 1945.

Sutherland, Ronald. *Frederick Philip Grove*. New Canadian Library, Canadian Writers, No. 4. Toronto: McClelland and Stewart, 1969.

Spettigue, Douglas O. *Frederick Philip Grove*. Studies in Canadian Literature, No. 3. Toronto: Copp Clark, 1969.

Pacey, Desmond. Ed. and Introd. *Frederick Philip Grove*. Critical Views on Canadian Writers, No. 5. Toronto: Ryerson, 1970.

Stobie, Margaret R. *Frederick Philip Grove*. Foreword by Doris B. Saunders. Twayne World Authors, No. 246. New York: Twayne, 1973.

Spettigue, Douglas O. *FPG: The European Years*. Ottawa: Oberon, 1973.

Nause, John. Ed. and Introd. *The Frederick Philip Grove Symposium*. Reappraisals: Canadian Writers. Ottawa: Univ. of Ottawa Press, 1974.

Raths, Deborah. Comp. *Register of the Frederick Philip Grove Collection*. Winnipeg: Dept. of Archives, Manuscripts, and Rare Books, Univ. of Manitoba Libraries, 1979.

II SELECTED ESSAYS

(Many essays on the Canadian novel, or on Canadian literature generally, include discussions of Grove's writing. This bibliography is limited to articles in which Grove is the focus of study; it does not include review essays, newspaper articles, essays in reference works or chapters of book-length studies.)

Ayre, Robert. 'Canadian Writers of Today—Frederick Philip Grove.' *The Canadian Forum*, 12 (Apr. 1932), 255-57; rpt. in Pacey, *Frederick Philip Grove* (1970), pp. 17-24.

Bader, Rudolf. 'Frederick Philip Grove and Naturalism Reconsidered.' *Gaining Ground: European Critics on Canadian Literature*. Western Canadian Literary Documents Series VI. Ed. Robert Kroetsch and Reingard M. Nischik. Edmonton: NeWest Press, 1985, pp. 222-33.

Bailey, Nancy I. 'F.P.G. and the Empty House.' *Journal of Canadian Fiction*, 31-32 (1981), 177-93.

Birbalsingh, Frank. 'Grove and Existentialism.' *Canadian Literature*, 43 (Winter 1970), 67-76; rpt. in *Writers of the Prairies*. Ed. Donald G. Stephens. Vancouver: Univ. of British Columbia Press, 1973, pp. 57-66.

Boeschenstein, Herman. 'Frederick Philip Grove: Lehrer, Dichter und Pionier, 1871-1946 [sic].' *Festgabe fur Eduard Berend zum. 75. Geburstag*. Weimar: Herman Bohlan, 1959, pp. 257-71.

Cohn-Sfetcu, Ofelia. 'At the Mercy of Winds and Waves? *Over Prairie Trails* by F.P. Grove.' *University of Windsor Review*, 11 (Spring-Summer 1976), 49-56.

Collin, W.E. 'La tragique ironie de Frederick Philip Grove.' *Gants du Ciel*, 4 (Hiver 1946), 15-40; rpt. *White Savannahs*. Ed. Germaine Warkentin. Literature of Canada: Poetry and Prose in Reprint. Toronto: Univ. of Toronto Press, 1975, pp. 304-29.

Collins, Alexandra. 'An Audience In Mind When I Speak: Grove's *In Search of Myself*.' *Studies in Canadian Literature*, 8.2 (1983), 181-93.

Craig, Terrence L. Ed. and Introd. 'Frederick Philip Grove's "Poems." ' *Canadian Poetry*, 10 (Spring/Summer 1982), 58-90.

—'Frederick Philip Grove's Dirge.' *Canadian Poetry*, 16 (Spring/Summer 1985), 55-73.

—'F.P. Grove and the 'Alien' Immigrant in the West.' *Journal of Canadian Studies/Revue d'études canadiennes*, 20.2 (Summer 1985), 92-100.

Dewar, Kenneth C. 'Technology and the Pastoral Ideal in Frederick Philip Grove.' *Journal of Canadian Studies*, 8 (Feb. 1973), 19-28.

Gide, André. 'Conversation avec un Allemand quelques années avant la guerre.' *Nouvelle revue française*, 71 (1 Aug. 1919), 415-23; rpt. *Ouevres complets*. Ed. L. Martin Chauffer. Paris: Nouvelle revue francaise, 1935, pp. 133-43; transl. Blanche A. Price under the title 'Conversations with a German Several Years Before the War.' *Pretexts: Reflections on Literature and Morality by Andre Gide*. Ed. and Introd. Justin O'Brien. Greenwich Editions. New York: Meridian Books, 1959, pp. 234-42; rpt. Delta, 1964.

Giltrow, Janet. 'Grove in Serach of an Audience.' *Canadian Literature*, 90 (Autumn 1981), 92-107.

Healy, J.J. 'Grove and the Matter of Germany: The Warkentin Letters and the Art of Liminal Disengagement.' *Studies in Canadian Literature*, 6 No. 2 (1981), 170-87.

Heidenreich, Rosmarin. 'The Search for FPG.' *Canadian Literature*, 80 (Spring 1980), 63-70.

Hjartarson, Paul. 'Design and Truth in *In Search of Myself.*' *Canadian Literature*, 90 (Autumn 1981), 73-90.

Holiday, W.B. 'Frederick Philip Grove: An Impression.' *Canadian Literature*, 3 (Winter 1960), 17-22; rpt. *Writers of the Prairies*. Ed. Donald G. Stephens. Vancouver: Univ. of British Columbia Press, 1973, pp. 51-56.

Kaye, Frances W. 'Hamlin Garland and Frederick Philip Grove: Self-Conscious Chroniclers of the Pioneers.' *Canadian Review of American Studies*, 10 (1979), 121-36.

Keith, W.J. 'The Art of Frederick Philip Grove: *Settlers of the Marsh* as an Example.' *Journal of Canadian Studies*, 9 (Aug. 1974), 26-36.

—'F.P. Grove's "Difficult" Novel: *The Master of the Mill.*' *Ariel*, 4, No. 2 (1973), 34-48.

—'Grove's "Magnificent Failure": *The Yoke of Life* Reconsidered.' *Canadian Literature*, 89 (Summer 1981), 104-17.

—'Grove's *Over Prairie Trails*: A Re-examination." *Literary Half-Yearly*, 13 (July 1972), 76-85.

—'Grove's Search for America.' *Canadian Literature*, 59 (Winter 1974), 57-66.

Knister, Raymond. 'Frederick Philip Grove.' *Ontario Library Bulletin*, 13 (1928), 60-62; rpt. *Frederick Philip Grove* (1970), pp. 11-17; rpt. Raymond Knister, *The First Day of Spring: Stories and Other Prose*. Ed. and Introd. Peter Stevens. Literature of Canada: Poetry and Prose in Reprint. Toronto: Univ. of Toronto Press, 1976, pp. 435-39.

Kroetsch, Robert. 'The Grammar of Silence: Narrative Patterns in Ethnic Writing.' *Canadian Literature*, 106 (Fall 1985), 65-74.

La Bossiere, Camille R. 'Of Words and Understanding in Grove's *Settlers of the Marsh,*' *University of Toronto Quarterly*, 54 (1984/5), 148-62.

Makow, Henry. 'Frederick Philip Grove.' *Profiles in Canadian Literature*. Ed. Jeffrey M. Heath. Toronto: Dundern Press, 1980, pp. 49-56.

—'Grove's "The Canyon." ' *Canadian Literature*, 82 (Autumn 1979), 141-48.

—' "Ellen Lindstedt": The Unpublished Sequel to Grove's *Settlers of the Marsh*.' *Studies in Canadian Literature*, 8.2 (1983), 270-76.

—'Grove's "Garbled Extract": The Bibliographical Origins of *Settlers of the Marsh*. *Modern Times: A Critical Anthology*. Ed. and Introd. John Moss. The Canadian Novel, Vol. 3. Toronto: NC Press, 1982, pp. 38-54.

—'Grove's Treatment of Sex: Platonic Love in *The Yoke of Life*.' *Dalhousie Review*, 58 (Autumn 1978), 528-40.

—Ed. and Introd. 'Letters From Eden: Grove's Creative Rebirth.' *University of Toronto Quarterly*, 49 (Fall 1979), 48-64.

Mathews, Robin. 'F.P. Grove: An Important Version of *The Master of the Mill* Discovered.' *Studies in Canadian Literature*, 7.2 (1982), 241-57.

McDonald, R.D. 'The Power of F.P. Grove's *The Master of the Mill*. *Mosaic*, 7 (1974), 89-100.

McKenna, Isobel. 'As They Really Were: Women in the Novels of Grove.' *English Studies in Canada*, 2 (1976), 109-16.

McMullin, Stanley E. 'Grove and the Promised Land.' *Canadian Literature*, (Summer 1971), 10-19; rpt. *Writers of the Prairies*. Ed. Donald G. Stephens. Vancouver: Univ. of British Columbia Press, 1973), pp. 67-76.

Michael, Friedrich. 'Verschollene der frühen Insel.' *Börsenblatt für den deutschen Buchhandel*, 28, No. 17 (29 Feb. 1972), 79-82; rpt. in *Der Leser als Entdecker; Betrachtungen, Aufsätze und Erinnerunger eines Verläger*. Sigmaringen: Jan Thorbecke Verlag, 1983, pp. 236-40.

Middlebro', Tom. 'Animals, Darwin, and Science Fiction: Some Thoughts on Grove's *Consider Her Ways*.' *Canadian Fiction Magazine*, 7 (1972), 55-57.

Mitchell, Beverley, S.S.A. 'The "Message" and the "Inevitable Form" in *The Master of the Mill*.' *Journal of Canadian Fiction*, 3, No. 3 (1974), 74-79.

Nesbitt, Bruce. 'The Seasons: Grove's Unfinished Novel.' *Canadian Literature*, 18 (Autumn 1963), 47-51.

Pacey, Desmond. 'Frederick Philip Grove.' *Manitoba Arts Review*, 3, No. 3 (1943), 28-41; rpt. *Essays in Canadian Criticism 1938-1968*. Toronto: Ryerson, 1969, pp. 5-21.

—'Frederick Philip Grove: A Group of Letters.' *Canadian Literature*, 11 (Winter 1962), 28-38.

—'In Search of Grove in Sweden: A Progress Report.' *Journal of Canadian Fiction*, 1, No. 1 (1972), 69-73.

—'On Editing the Letters of Frederick Philip Grove.' *Editing Canadian Texts*. Papers Given at the Conference on Editorial Problems, University of Toronto, Nov. 1972. Ed. Frances G. Halpenny. Toronto: A.M. Hakkert, 1975, pp. 49-73.

Pacey, Desmond, and J.C. Mahanti. 'Frederick Philip Grove: An International Novelist.' *International Fiction Review*, 1, No. 1 (1974), 17-26.

Pache, Walter. 'Der Fall Grove: Vorleben und Nachleben des Schriftstellers Felix Paul Greve.' *Deutschkanadisches Jahrbuch/German Canadian Yearbook*, 5 (1979), 121-36.

—'Dilettante in Exile: Grove at the Centenary of His Birth.' *Canadian Literature*, 90 (Autumn 1981), 187-91.

—'Comparative Aspects of German Canadian Studies. The Case of Frederick Philip Grove.' *Annals/Annalen 4. German-Canadian Studies in the 1980s*. CAUTG Publications No. 9. (Vancouver: CAUTG, 1983), pp. 185-96.

Perry, Anna. 'Who's Who in Canadian Literature: Frederick Philip Grove.' *Canadian Bookman*, 12 (Mar. 1930), 51-53.

Pierce, Lorne. 'Frederick Philip Grove (1871-1948).' *Royal Society of Canada, Proceedings and Transactions*, Third Series, 48 (June 1949), 113-19; rpt. *Frederick Philip Grove* (1970), pp. 188-94.

Raudsepp, E. 'Grove and the Wellsprings of Fantasy.' *Canadian Literature*, 84 (Spring 1980), 131-37.

Riley, Anthony W. 'The Case of Greve/Grove: The European Roots of a Canadian Writer, '*The Old World and the New: Literary Perspectives of German-Speaking Canadians*. Ed. and Introd. Walter E. Reidel. Toronto: Univ. of Toronto Press, 1984, 37-58.

Sandwell, B.K. 'Frederick Philip Grove and the Culture of Contemporary Canada.' *Saturday Night*, 61 (24 Nov. 1945), 18; rpt. *Frederick Philip Grove* (1970), pp. 56-59.

Saunders, Doris B. 'The Grove Collection of Papers in the University of Manitoba: A Tentative Evaluation.' *Papers of The Bibliographical Society of Canada*. Toronto: The Society, 1963), pp. 7-20.

Saunders, Thomas. 'The Grove Papers.' *Queen's Quarterly*, 70 (1963), 22-29.

—'A Novelist as Poet: Frederick Philip Grove.' *Dalhousie Review*, 43 (1963), 235-41; rpt. *Frederick Philip Grove* (1970), pp. 88-96.

Sirois, Antoine. 'Grove et Ringuet: Temoins d'une époque.' *Canadian Literature*, 49 (Summer 1971), 20-27.

Spettigue, Douglas O. 'Frederick Philip Grove: A Report from Europe.' *Queen's Quarterly*, 78 (1971), 614-15.

—'Frederick Philip Grove in Manitoba.' *Mosaic*, 3 (1970), 19-33.

—'The Grove Enigma Resolved.' *Queen's Quarterly*, 79 (1972), 1-2.

Spettigue, Douglas O., and A.W. Riley. 'Felix Paul Greve redivivus: zum fruheren Leben des kanadischen Schriftstellers Frederick Philip Grove.' *Seminar. Journal of Germanic Studies*, 9, No. 2 (1973), 148-55.

Stensberg, Peter A. 'Translating the Translatable: A Note on the Practical Problems with F.P. Grove's *Wanderungen*.' *Canadian Review of Comparative Literature/Revue canadienne de literature comparée*, 7 (Spring 1980), 206-12.

Stich, K.P. 'Extravagant Expression of Travel and Growth: Grove's Quest for America.' *Studies in Canadian Literature*, 6 (1981), 155-69.

—'F.P.G.: Over German Trails.' *Essays on Canadian Writing*, 6 (1977), 148-51.

—'F.P. Grove's Language of Choice.' *Commonwealth Literature*, 14 (Aug. 1979), 9-17.

—'Grove's New World Bluff.' *Canadian Literature*, 90 (Autumn 1981), 111-23.

—'The Memory of Masters in Grove's Self-Portraits.' *Études Canadienne/Canadian Studies*, 12 (1982), 153-64.

Stobie, Margaret R. ' "Frederick Philip Grove" and the Canadianism Movement.' *Studies in the Novel*, 4 (1972), 173-85.

—'Grove and the Ants.' *Dalhousie Review*, 58 (1978), 418-33.

—Ed. and Introd. 'Grove's Letters From the Mennonite Reserve.' *Canadian Literature*,' 59 (Winter 1974), 67-80.

Thomas, Clara and John Lennox. 'Grove's Maps.' *Essays on Canadian Writing*, 26 (Summer 1983), 75-79.

Thompson, Eric. 'Grove's Vision of Prairie Man.' *Ariel*, 10, No. 4 (Oct. 1979), 15-33.

Thompson, J. Lee. *Settlers of the Marsh.' Journal of Canadian Fiction*, 3, No. 3 (1974), 63-73; rpt. *Modern Times: A Critical Anthology*. Ed. and Introd. John Moss. The Canadian Novel, Vol. 3. Toronto: NC Press, 1982, pp. 19-37.

Webber, B. 'Grove in Politics.' *Canadian Literature*, 63 (Winter 1975), 126-27.

Wiebe, Rudy. 'A Novelist's Personal Notes on Frederick Philip Grove.' *University of Toronto Quarterly*, 47 (1978), 188-99; rpt. *A Voice in the Land: Essays By and About Rudy Wiebe*. Ed. W.J. Keith. Edmonton: NeWest Press, 1981, pp. 212-25.

INDEX